THE SOCIAL FABRIC

American Life from the Civil War to the Present

Volume II

EIGHTH EDITION

JOHN H. CARY
Late, Cleveland State University

JULIUS WEINBERG
Late, Cleveland State University

THOMAS L. HARTSHORNE
Cleveland State University

ROBERT A. WHEELER
Cleveland State University

LONGMAN

An imprint of Addison Wesley Longman, Inc.

New York • Reading, Massachusetts • Menlo Park, California • Harlow, England
Don Mills, Ontario • Sydney • Mexico City • Madrid • Amsterdam

Acquisitions Editor: Jay O'Callaghan
Development Manager: Betty Slack
Executive Marketing Manager: Sue Westmoreland
Project Coordination and Text Design: Ruttle, Shaw & Wetherill, Inc.
Cover Design Manager: Nancy Danahy
Cover Designer: Kay Petronio
Cover Illustration: "Landing the Plane," © 1995 PhotoDisc, Inc.
Full Service Production Manager: Joseph Vella
Senior Print Buyer: Hugh Crawford
Photo Researcher: Photosearch, Inc.
Electronic Page Makeup: Ruttle, Shaw & Wetherill, Inc.
Printer and Binder: The Maple-Vail Book Manufacturing Group, Inc.
Cover Printer: Phoenix Color Corp

Library of Congress Cataloging-in-Publication Data
The social fabric / [edited by] John H. Cary, [. . . et al.]. — 8th
   ed.
        p.   cm.
     Includes bibliographic references.
     Contents: v. 1. American life from 1607 to 1877 — v. 2. American
life from the Civil War to the present.
     ISBN 0-321-00303-9 (v. 1). — ISBN 0-321-00305-5 (v. 2)
     1. United States—Social conditions.   I. Cary, John H. (John
Henry), 1926–   .
HN57.S623   1998
306'.0973—DC21   98–18492
                                                                       CIP

Copyright © 1999 by The John H. Cary Estate

Please visit our website at http://longman.awl.com

ISBN   0-321-00305-5

12345678910—MA—01009998

To the Memory of
Harry W. Langworthy III
Colleague and Friend
T.L.H.

Contents

Preface

I know histhry isn't thrue Hinnessy, because it ain't like what I see ivry day in Halsted Sthreet. If any wan comes along with a histhry iv Greece or Rome that'll show me th' people fightin', gettin' dhrunk, makin' love, gettin' married, owin' the grocery man an' bein' without hard-coal, I'll believe they was a Greece or Rome, but not befure.

Mr. Dooley, Finley Peter Dunne's comic Irish philosopher, expressed those sentiments in the early twentieth century, and at the time he spoke it is certainly true that "history"—that is, what the people who called themselves "historians" wrote—dealt only with politics, diplomacy, government, and famous leaders and that it ignored the daily lives of ordinary men and women. In the last few decades, however, a large section of the historical profession has staged a conscious and determined reaction against this tendency. For some time now, increasing numbers of historians have been mining a wide variety of materials to discover what there is to be known about the mass of men and women who tilled our fields, built our cities, and fought our wars. While it may be true, as one historian has said, that "the past is another country," reading this new sort of history can help to remind us that we have a great deal in common with the people who lived there. Furthermore, understanding what they did and why they did it can help us gain an understanding of our own lives.

This anthology of readings for college history courses was created out of the belief that adding the kind of history described by Mr. Dooley to conventional political, diplomatic, and constitutional history would make the mixture more meaningful to college students. This and Volume I of *The Social Fabric,* which covers the period from the earliest settlement of the English colonies in North America to Reconstruction, attempt to incorporate fighting and getting drunk, making love and marrying, and being in debt and desperate into the story of the American past. Covering the time from the end of the Civil War to the present, this volume includes descriptions of the segregation of African Americans during Reconstruction, labor conditions and labor violence in the late 1800s, the impact of the Great Depression of the 1930s, and the social protest movements of the 1960s and 1970s.

In addition to offering pictures of the lives and attitudes of ordinary Americans, we have made a conscious effort to portray the diversity of American life. Thus, there are essays dealing with women as well as men, Native Americans and African Americans as well as whites, immigrants as well as the native-born, and the poor and oppressed as well as the rich and powerful. We also focus on the way in which sectional, class, racial, ethnic, and religious differences have often divided the nation and even, on occasion, threatened to tear it apart. In the end, however, for all their diversity, the American people have also shown an abiding respect for values and traditions they hold in common and that bind them together.

We have prefaced each of the readings with an introductory note that explains the relation of the particular subject to broader developments in the history of the period. Each selection is also accompanied by an illustration that provides a visual commentary on the topic. At the end of each selection there are a series of questions that students may use to review what they have just read and that also suggest subjects for further reflection or class discussion. Finally, we add some suggestions for further reading for those who want to go more deeply into particular subjects.

THE EIGHTH EDITION

This edition of Volume II of *The Social Fabric* retains many of the readings from the previous edition. Three new selections have been added. One concerns the role and impact of women on the program and activities of the Ku Klux Klan in the 1920s. The second deals with the educational benefits extended to the veterans of World War II under the GI Bill of Rights and the effects of that program on the veterans and the nation as a whole. The third focuses on the rise of the religious right in the 1970s and 1980s by looking closely at one campaign in which religious belief and political action came together.

We are extremely gratified by the response of both teachers and students to this anthology. Their comments and suggestions for improvement have been important and valuable aids to us in our continuing effort to make these volumes as useful and interesting as possible. We are grateful for their help.

We hope that these volumes live up to the high standards established and maintained for so long by our late colleagues John H. Cary and Julius Weinberg. The original idea for these volumes was theirs, and we hope that we have succeeded in being true to their intention and that our efforts would meet with their approval.

T.L.H.
R.A.W.

THE SOCIAL FABRIC

Volume II

PART I

EXPANSION AND CHANGE

The quarter-century after the end of the Civil War was a period of tremendous growth in the United States. Perhaps no period in American history has seen so much profound change packed into so short a time. It was then, for example, that the United States leapfrogged from fourth to first place among the nations of the world in terms of total industrial output, with its mills and factories turning out more goods than its three closest competitors combined. In the meantime, the nation had to face the problems, physical and emotional, stemming from the Civil War. Repairing the war's devastation was an enormous challenge. So was inventing a new status for the four million people who had been freed from slavery as one of the war's by-products.

Another challenge, and opportunity, was opening up the trans-Mississippi West, most of which was still "unoccupied" at the end of the Civil War, but had been filled with white settlers by 1890. And while Americans were moving west, they were moving from the countryside into the cities in even greater numbers, creating a whole new set of problems for America's urban areas.

Growing industries demanded better transportation systems, more workers, new marketing techniques, and so forth, and in meeting these demands, Americans confronted a whole new series of problems. These included the proper relationship between business and government and between employers and employees, and how, if at all, to attempt to control the ruthless scramble for wealth that marked the time.

Since many of these problems were new, or at least existed on an unprecedented scale, there were no effective guidelines on how to address them. Americans had to make up their responses as they went along, and frequently their ideas and institutions trailed behind the need for readjustment to rapidly changing conditions. Violence was a not infrequent result of these challenges. Racial violence, violence directed against Native Americans, the characteristic violence of the frontier, and labor violence are some examples. It is no wonder that many historians see the period as one not only of enormous growth but also of disorganization and suffering.

The essays in this section discuss some of these trends. The first details the ways in which white southerners tried to minimize the effects of the Civil War by establishing a system of racial laws and customs that would preserve white supremacy. The second shows how Native Americans were pushed out of the way by advancing white settlement and had their cultures altered and nearly destroyed in the process. The subject of the third is the lives of the farmers who settled the Great Plains during this period, while the fourth and fifth cover labor conditions in the growing industries of the time, showing the exploitation and violence that became so rampant as to be almost "normal."

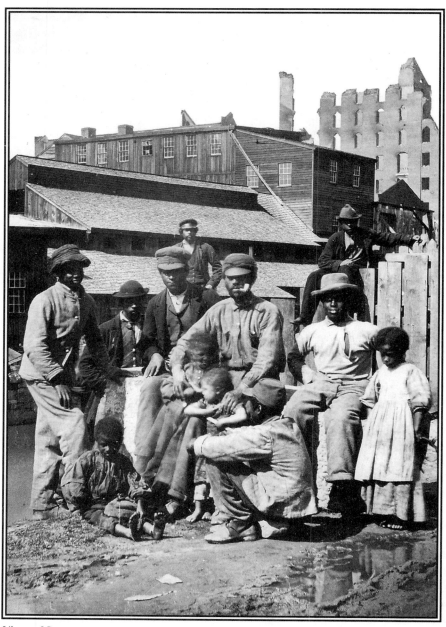

Southern blacks in the post-Civil War South soon learned that emancipation did not bring social equality.

1

After Slavery

JOEL WILLIAMSON

Few dreams in the history of the United States have been so cruelly unrealized as the hope that with the end of the Civil War and the destruction of the institution of slavery, black Americans would be accorded some measure of equality and opportunity in American life. With the end of the war in 1865, reform-minded Republicans, known as Radical Republicans, sought to make this dream a reality. Through their control of Congress they initiated Reconstruction, a program designed to restructure the social and political relations between whites and blacks in the defeated South. In 1865 and 1866, Congress funded the Freedmen's Bureau to feed, clothe, and protect the ex-slaves; civil rights legislation was passed in 1866 and reinforced by the Civil Rights Act of 1875, intended to outlaw varied forms of segregation; and three amendments were added to the Constitution. The Thirteenth Amendment (1865) outlawed slavery, the Fourteenth Amendment (1868) extended federal citizenship to blacks and made illegal many parts of the black codes, and the Fifteenth Amendment (1870) protected the black man's right to vote.

Despite this and other legislation, and despite the ascension to power of Reconstruction governments in the southern states—state governments in which political power was shared by a combination of southern scalawags, northern carpetbaggers, and emancipated blacks—the Radical Republican effort to reconstruct the relations between the races in the South ended in failure. The first stage of that failure, what one historian has so aptly called "darkness at noon," came with the end of Reconstruction. Reconstruction was ended by the disputed election of Republican Rutherford B. Hayes over Democrat Samuel J. Tilden in 1876 and by the Compromise of 1877, in which the rights of black Americans were made secondary to the economic opportunities and social privileges of white Americans, both Democrats and Republicans. The second stage in the disfranchisement and segregation of American blacks came between the end of Reconstruction and the American entry into World War I in 1914. Often referred to as "second-class citizenship," this system of racial subordination had much in common with the system of *apartheid* recently dismantled in South Africa.

The selection that follows tells us about the origins of the southern caste system. In his book *After Slavery: The Negro in South Carolina during Reconstruction, 1861–1877,* Joel Williamson finds that patterns of segregation came to South Carolina in the Reconstruction period. Williamson thus refutes a cardinal assumption made by C. Vann Woodward, the dean of southern historians. Woodward contends that until the 1890s, southern whites still held open options in their treatment of southern blacks and that "Jim Crow," the disfranchisement and the segregation of blacks, was a product of decisions made by southern whites *after* Reconstruction, closer to the turn of the century. Williamson's essay, taken from his study of the Reconstruction in South Carolina, demonstrates that in South Carolina this was not so.

The physical separation of the races was the most revolutionary change in relations between whites and Negroes in South Carolina during Reconstruction.

Separation had, of course, marked the Negro in slavery; yet the very nature of slavery necessitated a constant, physical intimacy between the races. In the peculiar institution, the white man had to constantly and closely oversee the labor of the Negro, preserve order in domestic arrangements within the slave quarters, and minister to the physical, medical, and moral needs of his laborers. In brief, slavery enforced its own special brand of interracial associations; in a sense, it married the interests of white to black at birth and the union followed both to the grave. Slavery watched the great mass of Negroes in South

---

Carolina, but those Negroes who lived outside of the slave system were not exempt from the scrutiny of the whites. Even in Charleston, the free Negro community was never large enough to establish its economic and racial independence. In the mid-nineteenth century, as the bonds of slavery tightened, the whites were forced to bring free Negroes under ever more stringent controls and to subject their lives to the closest surveillance.

During the spring and summer of 1865, as the centripetal force of slavery melted rapidly away, each race clearly tended to disassociate itself from the other. The trend was evident in every phase of human endeavor: agriculture, business, occupations, schools and churches, in every aspect of social intercourse and politics. As early as July of 1865, a Bostonian in Charleston reported that "the worst sign here . . . is the growth of a bitter and hostile spirit between blacks and whites—a gap opening between the races which, it would seem may at some time result seriously." Well before the end of Reconstruction, separation had crystallized into a comprehensive pattern which, in its essence, remained unaltered until the middle of the twentieth century.

There is no clear, concise answer to the question of why separation occurred. Certainly, it was not simply a response of Negroes to the prejudiced fiat of dominant whites; nor was it a totally rationalized reaction on the part of either race. Actually, articulate whites and Negroes seldom attempted to explain their behavior. Yet, the philosophies and attitudes each race adopted toward the other lend a certain rationality to separation, and, if we are always mindful that this analysis presumes a unity which they never expressed, can be applied to promote an understanding of the phenomenon.

For the native white community, separation was a means of avoiding or minimizing problems which, they felt, would inevitably arise from the inherent inferiority of the Negro, problems which the North, in eradicating slavery and disallowing the Black Code, would not allow them to control by overt political means. In this limited sense, segregation was a substitute for slavery.

Thus, first, total separation was essential to racial purity, and racial purity was necessary to the preservation of a superior civilization which the whites had labored so arduously to construct, and suffered a long and bloody war to defend. After the war, that civilization was embattled, but not necessarily lost. Unguarded association with an inferior caste would obviously endanger white culture. In this view, children were peculiarly susceptible to damage. "Don't imagine that I allow my children to be with negroes out of my presence," wrote the mistress of a low-country plantation in 1868, "on one occasion only have they been so with my knowledge." Even the Negro wet nurse, that quintessence of maternalism upon which the slave period paternalist so often turned his case, emerged as the incubus of Southern infancy. "We gave our infants to the black wenches to suckle," lamented an elderly white, "and thus poisoned the blood of our children, and made them *cowards* . . . the Character of the people of the state was ruined by slavery and it will take 500 years, if not longer, by the infusion of new blood to eradicate the hereditary vices imbibed with the blood (milk is blood) of black wet nurses.". . .

Separation also facilitated the subordination of the inferior race by constantly reminding the Negro that he lived in a world in which the white man was dominant, and in which the non-white was steadfastly denied access to the higher caste. Further, the impression of Negro inferiority would be constantly re-enforced by relegating the baser element, whenever possible, to the use of inferior facilities. The sheer totality of the display alone might well serve to convince members of the lower caste that such, indeed, was in the natural order of things.

Many whites had envisioned the early elimination of the freedman from the southern scene, and many had eagerly anticipated this event. In time, however, it became evident to all that the Negro would be neither dissolved nor transported to Africa. In a sense, separation was a means of securing the quasi elimination of Negroes at home. It was, perhaps, a more satisfactory solution than their demise or emigration, since it might produce many of the benefits of their disappearance without losing an advantageous, indeed, a necessary supply of labor.

Finally, separation was a logical solution to the problem posed by the widespread conviction that the races were inherently incompatible outside of the master–slave relationship. If the white man could not exist in contentment in the proximity of Negroes, then partial satisfaction might be achieved by withdrawal from associations with members of the inferior caste. This spirit was evident among some of the wealthier whites who voluntarily dispensed entirely with the services of Negro domestics. Elderly William Heyward, in 1868 still second to none in the ranks of the rice aristocracy, stopped taking his meals at the Charleston Hotel because, as he said, he found "the negro waiters so defiant and so familiar in their attentions." "A part of the satisfaction is," he explained to a friend, "that I am perfectly independent of having negroes about me; if I cannot have them as they used to be, I have no desire to see them except in the field." Planters were often manifesting precisely the same sentiment when they deserted their land and turned to grain culture, or to the use of immigrant labor. Separation was also a way of avoiding interacial violence. B. O. Duncan and James L. Orr, both native white Republicans, argued against mixing in the public schools because they were convinced that minor irritations between children would generate major altercations between parents of different races. Conceived as a means of avoiding violence, separation, ironically, was subsequently enforced by the use of violence. . . .

Contrary to common belief, the separation of the races was not entirely the work of the whites. Suspicious, resentful, and sometimes hateful toward the whites, chafed by white attitudes of superiority, and irritated by individual contacts with supercilious whites, Negroes, too, sought relief in withdrawal from association with the other race. In many instances, the disassociation was complete—that is, many Negroes left the state. During the war, Corporal Simon Crum of the First South Carolina declared his intention of leaving South Carolina after the capitulation because, as he phrased it, "dese yer Secesh [secessionists] will neber be cibilized in my time." For those who could not or would not leave, alternative forms of withdrawal were possible. A major facet in the new pattern of agriculture was the removal of Negro labor from the immediate supervision of white men. As the Negro agriculturalist moved his labor away from the eye of the white man, so also did he move his family and his home. Plantation villages became increasingly rare as Negro landowners and renters either built new houses on their plots or, in a rather graphic symbolic display, laboriously dragged their cabins away from the "Negro street." Negroes in the trades and in domestic service followed similar trends. Furthermore, Negroes chose to withdraw from white-dominated churches, though they were often urged to stay, and they attended racially separated schools in spite of the legal fact that all schools were open to all races. Negroes also tended to withdraw from political association with members of the white community.

Finally, on those few occasions when Negroes entered into polite social situations with whites, northern as well as southern, they were often ill at ease. For instance, while driving along a road near Columbia, a planter and his wife met William, "a fine looking light mulatto" who had been their stableboy as a slave. William was driving a buggy and seated beside him was a young white woman, elegantly attired. The woman was a "Yankee school marm," probably one of the new teachers in Columbia's Negro school. As he passed his late master and mistress, the Negro averted his gaze and did not speak. The following day, he approached the planter and apologized for having been escort to a "white woman." He had met the teacher at a celebration, he explained, and she had insisted on his taking her to see the countryside.

During Reconstruction, the Negro's withdrawal was never a categorical rejection of the white man and his society. In the early days of freedom, it was primarily a reaction against slavery, an attempt to escape the unpleasant associations of his previous condition and the derogatory implications of human bondage. However, as the memory of slavery faded, a more persistent reason for withdrawal emerged. Essentially, it was the Negro's answer to discrimination. Almost invariably, attempts by individual Negroes to establish satisfactory relations across the race line were unsuccessful, and, all too often, the pain of the experience was greater than the reward for having stood for principle. During Reconstruction and afterward, only a few were willing to undergo such pain without the certainty of success. It was much easier, after all, simply to withdraw.

Withdrawal as a solution to the race problem was by no means satisfactory to the Negro leadership. Implicit in the behavior of Negro leaders during Reconstruction was a yearning for complete and unreserved acceptance for members of their race by the white community. However, overtly, and rather politically, they carefully distinguished between "social equality" and what might be appropriately termed "public equality." For themselves, they claimed only the latter. "Our race do not demand social equality," declared W. J. Whipper, a member from Beaufort, on the floor of the house of representatives in Columbia. . . .

What the Negro leadership did insist upon was public equality, that is, absolute civil and political parity with whites and full and free access to most public facilities. These latter included restaurants, bars, saloons, railway and street cars, shipboard accomodations, the theater, and other such places of public amusement. Once they gained political power, Negro leaders hastened to embody this attitude in legislation. Within a week after the first sitting of the Constitutional Convention of 1868, a Negro delegate introduced a resolution which was eventually included in the state's bill of rights: "Distinction on account of race or color, in any case whatever, shall be prohibited, and all classes of citizens shall enjoy equally all common, public, legal and political privileges." Similarly, one of the first bills passed by the Republican legislature prohibited licensed businesses from discriminating "between persons, on account of race, color, or previous condition, who shall make lawful application for the benefit of such business, calling or pursuit." Convicted violators were liable to a fine of not less than $1,000 or imprisonment for not less than a year. During the debate on the measure in the house, not a single Negro member spoke against the bill, and only five of the twenty-four votes registered against it were cast by Negroes, while fifty-three of the sixty-one votes which secured its passage were those of Negro legislators.

Negro Congressmen were no less ardent in championing the same cause in Washington, particularly in 1874, when a federal civil rights bill was up for consideration. ". . . Is it pretended anywhere," asked Congressman R. B. Elliott, who had only recently been denied service in the restaurant of a railway station in North Carolina on his journey to the capital, "that the evils of which we complain, our exclusion from the public inn, from the saloon and the table of the steamboat, from the sleeping-coach on the railway, from the right of sepulture in the public burial-ground, are an exercise of the police power of the State? . . . Are the colored people to be assimilated to an unwholesome trade or to combustible materials, to be interdicted, to be shut up within prescribed limits?" Several days later, in the same place, Congressman R. H. Cain declared, "We do not want any discrimination to be made. I do not ask any legislation for the colored people of this country that is not applied to the white people of this country. All that we seek is equal laws, equal legislation, and equal rights throughout the length and breadth of this land."

It was upon this emotional, uneven ground that an essentially new color line was drawn. It was established in a kind of racial warfare, of assaults and withdrawals, of attacks and counterattacks. Nevertheless, well before the end of Reconstruction, both forces had been fully engaged and the line was unmistakably formed.

Even before the Radicals came into power in South Carolina in 1868, native whites had already defined a color line in government-supported institutions, on common carriers, in places of public accommodation and amusement, and, of course, in private social organizations. The degree of separation in each of these areas varied. In many instances, obviously, some compromise between expense and the desire for complete separation had to be made. Usually, the compromise involved the division of available facilities in some manner. If this was thought to be inconvenient, Negroes were totally excluded.

Typical was the treatment of Negro and white prisoners in the state penitentiary under the James L. Orr regime [1865–1868; South Carolina]. Criminals of both races were confined in the same institution but were quartered in separate cells. Ironically, the racial concepts of white prison officials sometimes redounded to the benefit of Negro inmates. Minor violations of prison rules were punished every Sunday by the offenders being tied closely together, blindfolded, and forced to work their way over a series of obstacles in the prison yard. The chief guard explained that the white offenders were placed in the most difficult middle positions of the "blind gang" because "they have more intelligence than the colored ones and are better able to understand the rules of the institution."

It is paradoxical that the Negro leadership, once in office, pressed vigorously for an end to separation in privately owned facilities open to the public but they allowed a very distinct separation to prevail in every major governmental facility. The most obvious instance was the schools, but the distinction also stretched into the furthermost reaches of gubernatorial activity. For example, a visitor to the state insane asylum in Columbia in 1874 found that "The Negro female inmates occupy a separate part of the same building" in which the white women were housed.

On the other side, within a month after they had gained the vote, Negroes in South Carolina opened a frontal attack against racial discrimination on common carriers. Typical was their assault on the Charleston Street Car Company. At the time of its inauguration, the facilities of the company consisted of double tracks running the length of the peninsula with a spur branching off near the mid-point. Horse-drawn cars, each manned by a driver and a conductor, ran along the tracks at regular intervals. The cars contained seats in a compartment, and front and rear platforms. Before the cars began to run in December, 1866, the question of the accommodation of Negro passengers was thoroughly canvassed. "Proper arrangements will in due time be made to allow persons of color to avail themselves of the benefits of the railway," the management assured the Negro community, but it had not then decided between providing "special cars" for the Negroes as was done in New Orleans, "or assigning to them a portion of the ordinary cars as is more usual in other cities." Negro leaders rejected both alternatives. As a Northerner wrote from Charleston in January, 1867, "Every scheme that could be devised that did not contemplate the promiscuous use of the cars by whites and negroes alike, was scouted by the Negro paper here; and the result is that negroes are now debarred the use of the cars altogether, unless they choose to ride upon the platform.". . .

After the Negro gained political power, the battle against discrimination became more intense and assumed a wider front. The so-called antidiscrimination bill, passed in the summer of 1868, on paper was a most formidable weapon. In essence, it imposed severe penalties upon the owners of public accommodations who were convicted of discrimination. Burden of proof of innocence lay on the accused, and state solicitors (public prosecutors) who failed to prosecute suspected violators were themselves threatened with heavy punishments.

The effect of the new legislation on common carriers was immediate. A Northern teacher returning to Beaufort in the fall of 1868, after a few months' absence in the North, observed a portion of the results:

> We took a small steamer from Charleston for Beaufort. Here we found a decided change since we went North. Then no colored person was allowed on the upper deck, now there were no restrictions—there could be none, for a law had been passed in favor of the negroes. They were everywhere, choosing the best staterooms and best seats at the table. Two prominent colored members of the State Legislature were on board with their families. There were also several well-known Southerners, still uncompromising rebels. It was a curious scene and full of significance. An interesting study to watch the exultant faces of the negroes, and the scowling faces of the rebels. . . .

The same legislation applied to railway facilities; and, apparently, it was applied without a great amount of dissent. Adjustment was made easier, perhaps, by the acquisition of some of the railroad companies by Radical politicians within the state, or by Northern capitalists, and by the close understanding which usually prevailed between Republican officeholders and those Conservatives who managed to retain control of their railroads. While formal discrimination was not practiced by railway operators, unofficial racial separation did occur on a large scale. On all of the major lines first- and second-class cars were available. Most Negroes apparently deliberately chose to ride in the more economical second-class accommodations, and virtually all of the whites—particularly white women—took passage on the first-class cars. The separation thus achieved was so nearly complete that the first-class car was often referred to as the "ladies' car." It is highly relevant that the first Jim Crow legislation affecting railroads in South Carolina provided for the separation of the races only in the first-class cars, because, of course, this was the only place on the railroads where there was any possibility of a significant degree of mixing. . . .

In the winter of 1869–1870 and through the summer which followed, a concerted attempt was made by the Negro leadership to win the full acceptance of Negroes into all places of public amusement, eating, drinking, and sleeping. Special provisions for the accommodation of Negroes at public entertainments had been made in ante-bellum times, but physical separation of the races was invariably the rule. In December, 1868, Charles Minort, a mulatto restaurateur and lesser political figure, nearly provoked a riot in a Columbia theater by presuming to seat his wife and himself in the front row, a section traditionally reserved for tardy white ladies. Presumably, he should have chosen seats among the other Negroes present who "had taken their seats, as has always been the custom, in the rear." Minort yielded to the clamor of the whites in the audience, but, a year later, the Negroes of Charleston instituted judicial proceedings against the manager of the Academy of Music for refusing to mix the races in the boxes of the theater. The management barely succeeded in winning a postponement but was able to complete the season before the case came to trial.

In the spring of 1870, Negro leaders in Charleston launched an attack against discrimination in restaurants, bars, and saloons. On March 25, for instance, Louis Kenake, accused of violating the antidiscrimination act, was brought before Magistrate T. J. Mackey and put on a bond of one thousand dollars while awaiting trial. Other white restaurant keepers of Charleston united to oppose and test the validity of the act, but, in the week which followed, at least six additional charges were lodged against operators of such businesses. The assault was not confined to Charleston and demonstrations by Radical politicians were frequent during the campaign of 1870. In April, a Laurens woman wrote to her son in Missouri that "On Monday the yankees & some negroes went to Hayne Williams' and asked for drink, which 'Ward' refused them, that is, to drink at the gentlemans bar. They quietly marched him off to jail, & locked the doors, putting the keys in their pockets. The family are all at Spartanburg, we look for H. Williams to night, and I am afraid of a fuss, for he is a great bully." In the same month, during a Radical meeting in Lancaster, a Negro was refused service in a local bar with the comment that no "nigger" could buy a drink there. Lucius Wimbush, a Negro senator, hearing of the incident, went to the bar, ordered a drink, and was refused. He immediately had the barkeeper arrested and placed under bail. . . .

Negroes were also ambitious to open sleeping accommodations to their race. In the summer of 1868, as the first Negro legislators gathered in Columbia, native whites had been extremely apprehensive that they would attempt to occupy rooms in the city's hotels. Even *The Nation*, which had applauded the opening of common carriers to both races, declared that hotels were another and "delicate" matter, where separation was everywhere observed. The white community was vastly relieved to find that no such invasion was attempted, one upcountry newspaper having sent a special correspondent to Columbia to ascertain the fact. Nevertheless, when Negro legislators debated the antidiscrimination bill early in the session, they made it very clear that hotels were included. William E. Johnson, the African Methodist Minister then representing Sumter County in the statehouse, noting that the management of Nickerson's Hotel was concerned lest Negroes apply for rooms, declared that if he found private accommodations filled he would want to know that this resort was open to him. George Lee, a Negro member from Berkeley, observed that a group of junketing legislators had recently failed to find lodging in Greenville and that this law was desired to prevent that sort of occurrence. "Equal and exact justice to all," he demanded, ". . . it is what we must have." Negroes were subsequently allowed to attend meetings in Columbia hotels, but it is apparent that none were ever given lodging.

Negroes also decried the fact that places of permanent rest occupied by whites, as well as those of a more temporary variety, were denied to their race. For instance, S. G. W. Dill, the native white Radical who was assassinated in Kershaw in the summer of 1868, and Nestor Peavy, his Negro guard who was killed in the same assault, were buried in racially separated cemeteries.

Thus, from 1868 until 1889, when the antidiscrimination law was repealed, Negroes in South Carolina could legally use all public facilities which were open to whites. However, in actual practice, they seldom chose to do so. "The naturally docile negro makes no effort at unnecessary self-assertion," a Northern visitor in Charleston explained in 1870, "unless under the immediate instigation of some dangerous *friends* belonging to the other race, who undertake to manage his destiny." This particular reporter was certainly prejudiced against the race; but four years later another Northern observer congratulated the Negroes of South Carolina on the "moderation and good sense" which they exhibited in their "intercourse with the whites." He concluded, "They seldom intrude themselves into places frequented by the whites, and considering that in South Carolina they have a voting majority of some thirty thousand and control the entire State Government, it is somewhat remarkable that they conduct themselves with so much propriety." Indeed, after 1870, even the Negro leadership hardly seemed inclined to press further their political and legal advantage to end separation. Of the numerous charges lodged under the antidiscrimination law, not a single conviction was ever recorded.

Even when Negroes pressed themselves in upon the prejudice of whites, the latter adjusted by total or partial withdrawal, so that a high degree of separation was always and everywhere maintained.

Some whites responded to the pressure by total withdrawal, that is, by leaving the state entirely. Of course, many of those who left South Carolina did so primarily for economic reasons, but many also departed from purely racial motives. A Winnsboro lawyer and pre-war fire-eater revealed the thinking of many emigrants when he asked William Porcher Miles, in April, 1867, how he could live in a land where "Every 'mulatto' is your Equal & every 'Nigger' is your Superior." Pronouncing the Negro majority "revolting," he advised Miles to go to England. ". . . I have no doubt you could succeed & at any rate w[oul]d not have as many Negro Clients & negro witnesses to offend y[ou]r nostrils as in the USA. I can't conceive of any ones remaining here who can possibly get away—Suppose, it were certain, wh[ich] it is not, that no U S Congress will ever pass a Law requiring that your Daughter & mine shall either marry Negroes or die unmarried. Still the Negro is already superior to them politically & to their Fathers also, & must ever be so henceforth.". . .

After Negroes were firmly entrenched in official positions in government, native whites evinced a distinct tendency to refrain from associations which recognized the authority of Negro officers over white citizens. For instance, in the heavily Negro county of Abbeville, in 1870, a distressed guardian asked one of the magistrates, who happened to be a Democrat, to dispatch a constable to return an orphan girl stolen away from his house. "When you send for Laura," he begged, "please send a white man, as she is a white girl under my charge, and I would not like to subject her to the mortification of being brought back by a colored man. Besides that I would be censured by the community as they would know nothing of the circumstances of the case.". . .

Withdrawal was also the means by which native whites combatted attempts by Republican officials to end separation in institutions supported by the government. The withdrawal of native whites from the University and the State School for the Deaf and Blind at the prospect of Negro admissions are illustrations of white determination either to maintain separation or to dispense with the services afforded by related state institutions. If the Radicals had attempted to end separation in the common schools, it is virtually certain that the whites would have removed their children from these schools too. As one post-Redemption [post-Reconstruction] proponent of universal education argued, separation was essential to academic progress. Only by this means, he explained to Governor [Wade] Hampton, could it be achieved "without any danger of social equality—*and this is the great bug bear.*" Doubtless, it was the threat of withdrawal by the whites which dissuaded the Radical leadership from further attempts to end separation in institutions over which they had, by political means, absolute control.

Whites also refused to engage in normal civic activities in which the color line was not distinctly drawn. Thus, native whites chose not to join militia companies in which Negroes participated and were reported to be extremely apprehensive of being forced to undergo the "humiliation" of joining a mixed company. Too, whites were reluctant to sit with Negroes in the jury box. An elderly Spartanburg farmer verbalized his feelings on this point in the summer of 1869: "When I go to court & see negroes on the jury & on the stand for witnesses it makes me glad that I am so near the end of my race to sit on a jury with them I dont intend to do it we have a law that exempt a man at 65 & I take the advantage of it." This kind of withdrawal often reached odd extremes. In the spring of 1870, at the peak of the Negro leadership's drive for admission to privately owned public accommodations, the white Democrats of the Charleston Fire Department refused to decorate their engines and join in the annual parade because Negro fire companies were being allowed to march in the procession. . . .

Native whites also tended to withdraw from public places where the color line could not be firmly fixed and the Negro could easily assert his equality. "The whites have, to a great extent—greater than ever before—yielded the streets to the negroes," wrote a Columbian on Christmas Day, 1868. Similarly, in Charleston, in the late spring of 1866, a young aristocrat noted that the battery with its music and strollers had been yielded to the ladies and gentlemen of non-noble lineage on Saturdays, and by all whites to the Negroes on Sundays. On Saturdays, he declared, "the battery is quite full of gentlemen and ladies but it is not much patronized by the elite. . . . On Sunday afternoon the ethiops spread themselves on the Battery."

The same reaction was manifested by the whites wherever the Negro leadership succeeded by legal means in ending separation. For instance, when Negroes won admission to the street cars of Charleston, the whites simply withdrew. "On Sunday I counted five Cars successively near the Battery crowded [with] negroes, with but one white man, the Conductor," wrote a native white in May, 1867. "The ladies are practically excluded." When the Academy of Music was threatened with a discrimination suit in 1870, the white community replied with a counterthreat to withdraw its patronage and thus close the theater. Adjustment which fell short of complete separation remained unsatisfactory to whites. "Even the Theatre is an uncertain pleasure," complained a Charleston lady in 1873, "no matter how attractive the program, for you know that you may have a negro next to you." Probably many of her contemporaries found the exposure too damaging and stayed home.

The social lives of native whites were, of course, absolutely closed to Negroes. Access to the homes of the whites was gained by Negroes only when they clearly acquiesced in the superior-inferior relationship dictated by the owners, and even then entrance was often denied. "I told him I would never allow negroes to go in it while I owned it," wrote a Laurenville woman, incensed that a man who had bought her former home had rented it to Negroes. In spite of the fact that some Negro domestics lived in quarters behind the houses of their employers, whites were already rejecting Negroes as neighbors. A real estate agent in Aiken in 1871 responded to this sentiment when he refused offers from Negroes for city lots at triple prices because, as he explained to the owner, "purchasers among the whites will not settle among the Negroes, and I am afraid to sell to only a few of the latter." Negroes were also not permitted to join any of the numerous social organizations in which native whites participated. The Patrons of Husbandry (the Grange), waxing strong in the state in the early 1870s, was not only exclusively white in membership, but was accused of widening the racial gap by its attitudes and actions toward Negroes. Of course, such separation had been practiced before, but the exclusion of the Negro in freedom from the social organizations of the whites was not so much tradition as it was deliberate decision. . . .

Separation is, of course, a relative term. It was obviously not possible for Negroes and whites to withdraw entirely from association with each other. If intimate contact led to irritation and violence, it also led to warm personal friendships—often with the superior–inferior, paternal bias, but no less real for all of that. Cordiality could and did breach the barrier of race. Yet the fact remained that it was difficult to establish a human bond across the color chasm and, once established, the tie had to be assiduously maintained against the constant erosion induced by a thousand and one external forces of social pressure.

That there was sometimes tenderness between individuals of different races is abundantly evident. On the Elmore plantation near Columbia, in the fall of 1865, the young white master was nightly importuned by the Negro children to get out his fiddle and play. Frequently he did so, the dozen or so Negro boys and girls dancing around the fire, begging for more after the fiddler had exhausted himself in a two-hour concert. The concern of many late masters for their ex-slaves was matched by the interest of individual Negroes in the welfare of their recent owners. A freedman seeking relief for a white family from a Bureau officer explained his motivation: "I used to belong to one branch of that family, and so I takes an interest in 'em." Occasionally, ex-slaveowners retained the friendship and assistance of their erstwhile bondsmen when all others had deserted them. . . .

Sometimes, intimacy became miscegenation. The census reports are uncertain witnesses and contemporaries are typically mute on the point; but scattered references suggest that racial interbreeding was markedly less common after emancipation than before. "Miscegenation between white men and negro women diminished under the new order of things," a Bureau officer later wrote. "Emancipation broke up the close family contact in which slavery held the two races, and, moreover young gentlemen did not want mulatto children sworn to them at a cost of three hundred dollars apiece. In short, the new relations of the two stocks tended to separation rather than to fusion." A

Northern traveler visiting the state in 1870 concurred: "From all I could see and learn, there are far fewer half-breed children born now than before the Rebellion. There seems, indeed, a chance that the production of original half-breeds may be almost done away with. . . ."

Legal, moral, and social pressures exercised by the white community upon its members, as well as the physical separation of the races suggest that these were valid observations. The Black Code pointedly declared that "Marriage between a white person and a person of color shall be illegal and void," and when the code was revised in 1866 this portion emphatically remained in force. Children born of Negro mothers and white fathers, so recently especially prized for their pecuniary value, became simply illegitimate issue and a liability to the community. In addition, the laws of bastardy came to be applied against the fathers of mulatto children. Perhaps most important was the fact that, in the minds of the native whites, children of mixed blood personified the adulteration of the superior race and embodied in living form the failure of Southern civilization. Many whites, turned to soul-searching by their defeat, fixed upon miscegenation as their great sin. "It does seem strange that so lovely a climate, and country, with a people in every way superior to the Yankees, should be overrun and destroyed by them," wrote a rice aristocrat in 1868. "But I believe that God has ordered it all, and I am firmly of opinion with Ariel that it is the judgment of the Almighty because the human and brute blood have mingled to the degree it has in the slave states. Was it not so in the French and British Islands and see what has become of them."

Just as complete separation of the races was physically impossible, there was little possibility that miscegenation might entirely cease. One does not have to travel far into contemporary sources to discover instances in which white men had children by Negro women. In 1867, a lowcountry planter, accused of fathering the mulatto child of his Negro house servant, wrote plaintively to his mother: "This child was begotten during my absence in Charlotte & Charleston, from the middle of December until nearly the middle of January, & the Father of it was seen night after night in Emma's house, this I heard on my return, but as it was no concern of mine I did not give it a thought. She was *free*, the Mother of 5 Children & could have a dozen lovers if she liked. I had no control over her virtue." In 1874, a planter on the Cooper River in St. John's noted the existence of circumstances on his plantation which might have led to similar results. "Found a white man staying with one of the colored people on the place," ran the laconic note in his journal. "He being engaged in rebuilding Mayrents Bridge." Some of these liaisons were of prolonged duration. In 1870, Maria Middleton, a Negro woman, brought suit against a Pineville physician for failure to support her three children which he had allegedly fathered. Strangely, the defendant's lawyer did not deny the paternity, but sought dismissal on the plea that the plaintiff had no legal grounds for suit.

Once in power, the Radicals hastened to repeal the prohibition against interracial marriage. Thereafter, informal arrangements were sometimes legalized. In the spring of 1869, a reporter stated that three such marriages had occurred within the state—a Massachusetts man had married a Beaufort mulatto woman, and two white women had married Negro men. In 1872, the legislature explicitly recognized interracial unions by declaring that the "children of white fathers and negro mothers may inherit from the father if he did not marry another woman but continued to live with their mother."

There were a surprisingly large number of cases in which white women gave birth to children by Negro fathers. During his stay in Greenville, Bureau officer John De Forest heard of two such births and noted other instances in which white women were supported by Negro men. Such situations, he believed, were largely the result of the loss of husbands and fathers in the war and the destitution of the country generally. In 1866, in neighboring Pickens District, a case came into the courts in which Sally Calhoun, "a white woman of low birth," and a Negro man were brought to trial for the murder of their child. Ironically, the Negro was freed, though obviously implicated, and the woman was convicted and imprisoned. Apparently, some of these liaisons were far from casual as a Spartanburg farmer rather painfully suggested to his brother in Alabama: "My dear Brother as you have made several Enquiries of me and desiring me to answer them I will attempt and endeavor to do So to the best information that I have on the Various Subjects alluded to by you the first Interrogatory is Relative to John H. Lipscomb's daughter having Negro Children, I am forced to answer in the affirmative no doubt but she has had two; and no hopes of her Stopping. . . ."

By the end of Reconstruction, Negroes had won the legal right to enjoy, along with whites, accommodations in all public places. In reality, however, they seldom did so. On the opposite side of the racial frontier, the pattern of separation was fixed in the minds of the whites almost simultaneously with the emancipation of the Negro. By 1868, the physical color line had, for the most part, already crystallized. During the Republican regime, it was breached only in minor ways. Once the whites regained political power, there was little need to establish legally a separation which already existed in fact. Moreover, to have done so would have been contrary to federal civil rights legislation and would have given needless offense to influential elements in the North. Finally, retention of the act had a certain propaganda value for use against liberals in the North and against Republican politicians at home. Again and again, the dead letter of the law was held up as exhibit "A" in South Carolina's case that she was being fair to the Negro in the Hampton tradition [a reference to the relatively mild and paternalistic forms of racism practiced by upper-class whites, who, for many years, were led by Governor, and later senator, Wade Hampton]. After the federal statute was vitiated in the courts, after racial liberalism had become all but extinct in the North and as the Negro was totally disfranchised in South Carolina, the white community was ready and able to close the few gaps which did exist in the color line, and to codify a social order which custom had already decreed.

Ultimately, the physical separation of the races is the least important portion of the story. The real separation was not that duo-chromatic order that prevailed on streetcars and trains, or in restaurants, saloons, and cemeteries. The real color line lived in the minds of individuals of each race, and it had achieved full growth even before freedom for the Negro was born. Physical separation merely symbolized and reinforced mental separation. It is true that vigorous assaults by one side or the other forced the enemy to yield his forward trenches and to alter slightly the precise line of the color front. It is also true that material changes in post-Reconstruction Southern society pushed the trenches into areas which had not existed before. This often gave the illusion of basic change, of a breakthrough by the dominant whites in the war of races, whereas, actually, it merely represented the extension of the old attitudinal conflict onto new ground, only to bring with it the stalemate that marked the struggle elsewhere. Viewed in relation to the total geography of race relations, the frontier hardly changed; and the rigidity of the physical situation, set as it was like a mosaic in black and white, itself suggested the intransigence of spirit which lay behind it. Well before the end of Reconstruction, this mental pattern was fixed; the heartland of racial exclusiveness remained inviolate; and South Carolina had become, in reality, two communities—one white and the other Negro.

REVIEW QUESTIONS

1. What motives, according to the author, led Southern whites to seek segregation from their ex-slaves? Does Williamson consider these motives to be entirely rational?

2. What were the basic demands of the black leadership?

3. List the various institutions of the South in which segregation took place, and explain how.

4. Williamson draws a distinction between separation by segregation and separation by withdrawal. When did Southern whites tend to practice one and when the other?

5. Intimacy between the races does not appear to have ceased after emancipation. What evidence does the author have for this, and how does he account for it?

6. Would you, on the basis of this selection, agree that segregation began in the immediate postwar years? If so, why; if not, why not?

FOR FURTHER READING

James G. Randall and David Donald, *The Civil War and Reconstruction* (1960); Kenneth M. Stampp, *The Era of Reconstruction* (1965); Eric Foner, *Reconstruction: America's Unfinished Revolution, 1863–1877* (1988), are general histories of the process of pasting the Union back together after the Civil War. The issue of race relations is central in Vernon C. Wharton, *The Negro in Mississippi* (1965); Herman Belz, *Emancipation and Equal Rights* (1978); and Howard Rabinowitz, *Race Relations in the Urban South* (1978). Racial violence is the primary focus of Allen W. Trelease, *White Terror: The Ku Klux Klan Conspiracy and Southern Reconstruction* (1971), and George C. Rable, *But There Was No Peace: The Role of Violence in the Politics of Reconstruction* (1984). C. Vann Woodward's *The Strange Career of Jim Crow* (1974) takes the story of white southerners' attempts to preserve white supremacy from the end of Reconstruction through the 1960s. Another of his books, *Origins of the New South* (1951) is a classic treatment of the history of the South in the post-Reconstruction era. Edward L. Ayers, *The Promise of the New South* (1992), is a recent worthy successor to Woodward's book.

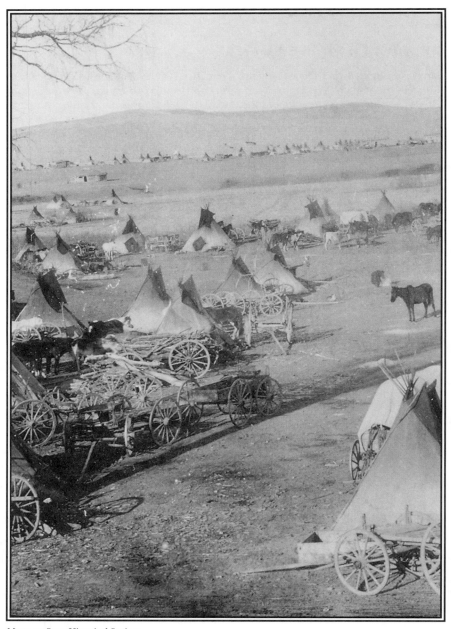

Montana State Historical Society

Native American camp, Pine Ridge, South Dakota.

2

The Reservation and the Destruction of Indian Culture

ROBERT M. UTLEY

Westward expansion has been a feature of American history from its very beginnings. Never was that expansion more rapid—one might almost say frenzied—than in the quarter-century after the Civil War. It encountered many obstacles, some natural, some human. One of the human obstacles was the presence of Native Americans, defending their lands and ways of life against the inroads of whites.

Whites dealt with the problem with the same basic strategy they had used from the early 1600s on: get the Native Americans out of the way, peacefully if possible, with violence if necessary, but in any case do not allow them to block the path of "progress." In the late 1800s this strategy resulted in a series of confrontations, often violent, ending in the confinement of the remaining populations of Native Americans to reservations in those areas that whites had no interest in. While not all whites agreed with General Philip Sheridan when he reportedly said, "The only good Indian is a dead Indian," and while some contemporaries protested against what they saw as the injustices being done to Native Americans, resistance to the policy of removing them from the path of white advance was never effective.

The following selection deals with only one of the many tribes of the trans-Mississippi West, the Sioux. Their culture and history differ in some ways from those of other tribes, but their experiences on reservations are broadly similar. For one thing, they all had to deal with the Indian agents who served as the link between them and the United States government. Some of them, like James McLaughlin and Valentine McGillycuddy (referred to in the following selection), were sincerely devoted to doing the best job they could, but others were political hacks who were often corrupt or incompetent, or both. A more important shared feature of the reservation experience is that it altered or even destroyed traditional Native American ways of life.

Sioux Falls, South Dakota, sported a festive air as the United States District Court opened on April 23, 1891. The streets teemed with townspeople, farmers, rough-hewn frontiersmen, and reporters from eastern newspapers come to cover the trial of a bewildered Sioux youth of twenty-two named Plenty Horses. He stood charged with the murder of an army officer during the recent Ghost Dance troubles on the Pine Ridge Reservation. His acquittal on the grounds that he acted as a combatant during a state of war made legal history. . . . But the trial also set the stage for a scene somberly symbolic of what had happened to the Indians of the American West in the short span of a decade.

On the edge of town an imaginative entrepreneur had built a corral and succeeded in assembling a herd of seventeen buffalo. The eastern visitors and, for that matter, the local residents themselves came to gawk at the shaggy, lumbering animals. Most had never seen one in the flesh. Among the viewers was a delegation of Sioux brought from Pine Ridge Agency to testify in the trial. The sight of the buffalo gave such joy to the Indians that they cavorted about like excited children. Broken Arm and He Dog even climbed into the pen and tried to hug the animals, only to be thrown roughly aside by a surly shake of the head. They then, as a reporter described it, "scampered about, although at the risk of their lives, and in general made so free with the animals that the latter looked around as though dazed at the proceedings."

Scarcely twenty-five years earlier, perhaps thirteen million buffalo darkened the Great Plains. They provided the Plains Indians with food and almost every other material want and contributed vitally to the shape of their political and social institutions and spiritual beliefs. They made possible the nomadic way of life that had endured for more than a century. In 1867–68 the Union Pacific Railroad divided the buffalo into two great herds, northern and southern. In 1871 an eastern tannery hit upon buffalo hides as a source of

---

commercial leather. By the hundreds "hide hunters" spread over the Plains, slaughtering the buffalo at the rate of three million a year. By 1878 the southern herd had been obliterated. By 1883 a scientific expedition could find only two hundred buffalo in all the West.

For the Plains Indians, the disappearance of the buffalo was a shattering cultural catastrophe, and it had another portentous consequence: it left no alternative to the reservation. Now a breakout from the reservation no longer held the hope of old that food could be found and pursuing bluecoats eluded or fought off. For the first time the reservation actually offered a testing ground for the government's civilization program. In other parts of the West, too, outside the buffalo ranges, Indians confronted a similar reality. Game and other resources that supported a roving life of freedom—not least of these resources open land itself—shrank as swiftly as the country filled up with white settlers.

"All our people now were settling down in square gray houses, scattered here and there across this hungry land," recalled the holy man Black Elk of the Teton Sioux Reservation in the 1880s, "and around them the Wasichus had drawn a line to keep them in. . . . The people were in despair. . . . Hunger was among us often now, for much of what the Great Father in Washington sent us must have been stolen by Wasichus who were crazy to get money. There were many lies, but we could not eat them. The forked tongue made many promises."

Life was every bit as bleak as Black Elk remembered, and it grew bleaker as nostalgia burnished yet more brightly the memory of the old free life that had been lost. It could never be recaptured, for now the line that so disturbed Black Elk truly locked the people in, forcing them to cope with rather than run from the efforts of government agents to destroy all vestiges of the old life. On most of the reservations the story was basically the same, varied only by personality, plot, and tempo. Black Elk's people, the Sioux, offer graphic personification of a process repeated among Indians all over the West. . . .

No matter what the reaction of individuals or factions, the government programs relentlessly chewed up the old ways. . . . The tribal identity, the tribal character, began to change, abruptly and swiftly, as soon as the Sioux faced the reality of reservation confinement. Almost overnight, a whole way of life had vanished, and thus whole clusters of habits and customs, activities, attitudes, values, and institutions lost relevance and meaning and likewise began to vanish.

Once warfare had consumed much of the men's time and thought and energy. With fidelity to prescribed ritual, they had fashioned and decorated weapons, planned and carried out raids on enemy tribes and invading whites, celebrated success, and mourned failure. War societies united men in common purpose, triumph, tragedy, and loyalty. Warfare opened the way to prestige, honor, wealth, and high rank. Now warfare no longer provided a foundation for this elaborate cultural edifice, and it crumbled.

Once the hunt had given order and organization to the yearly life cycle of band and tribe. The tribal circle, the police societies (Akicitas) that regulated its movement and configuration and saw that the hunt proceeded according to approved custom, the deeply embedded beliefs that formed a spiritual connection between Sioux and buffalo, and the constant preoccupation of women with the preparation of meat and hides and the crafting of clothing, tipis, utensils, and artwork—all ended as the buffalo and the life it supported vanished.

Pathetically, the Sioux tried to preserve a faint taste of the hunt. Like the buffalo of old, steers issued as rations were gunned down by breech-clouted horsemen, after which the women moved in to butcher the carcasses. But a visiting government commission saw this as "a disgrace to our civilization" that could only "perpetuate in a savage breast all the cruel and wicked propensities of his nature," and the Indian Bureau moved to stamp out the practice.

To take the place of the buffalo and the hunt, the agents constantly demanded that the Sioux turn to farming. For the time being, there would be the beef, coffee, sugar, and other rations promised in the treaties. But these would not last forever, and the Indians must learn to till the soil. These Indians had not tilled the soil since drifting out onto the Plains generations before. Labor of this sort demeaned Sioux manhood. As Red Cloud informed [Valentine] McGillycuddy, "the Great Spirit did not make us to work. He made us to hunt and fish." And, he added, not illogically, "the white man owes us a living for the lands he has taken from us." Besides, it required little foresight to see that growing crops would put an end to free rations. And so the Sioux resisted. But as the years passed, more and more moved out from the agencies and scattered over the land, built rude cabins, broke a patch of sod, and planted just enough seed to keep the agent from hounding them. . . .

The Sioux political system did not collapse as quickly as the economic, but it endured severe stresses that contributed greatly to the cultural breakdown. Some political institutions simply disappeared because the context in which they had existed, the tribal circle, had disappeared. Others persisted but came under vigorous government attack—none more so than the chieftainship.

The war on the chiefs bewildered the Sioux. On the one hand, the agents tore down the chiefs. On the other hand, they did things that built them up. McGillycuddy, for example, "deposed" Red Cloud and declared every man his own chief. Instead of chiefs drawing rations and redistributing them among their people, now every man might draw rations for his family. Yet when McGillycuddy needed Indian cooperation or acquiescence in some especially unpopular measure, the Oglalas [a branch of the Sioux] observed that he dealt through Red Cloud. In fact, the government provided Red Cloud with a shiny black carriage, built him a frame house more imposing than the agent's own, and periodically brought him to Washington for a state visit replete with all the ceremony accorded a foreign potentate. As if this were not confusing enough, the government still could not resist manufacturing chiefs. . . . There were so many chiefs, real and counterfeit, strong and weak, that one never knew where authority actually resided—if indeed anywhere.

Theoretically, supreme authority resided in the agent, and with strong agents like [James] McLaughlin and McGillycuddy this was largely true. But agents came and went, and more were weak than strong. During the tenure of weak agents, the established chiefs usually asserted themselves, only to be suppressed when a strong agent inherited the post. Agents enjoyed a number of advantages in the contest for supremacy. For example, rations could be withheld to enforce conformity in a wide range of official demands, such as requiring that children be placed in school or that crops be planted. Another advantage lay in the Indian police force. Police service involved enough attributes of the old life to be popular and to inculcate in the policeman a sense of duty and loyalty to the agent. In the hands of a forceful agent, the police proved highly effective. Finally, the slow but steady dispersal of the people in family groups across the reservation weakened the chieftainship simply because a chief's hold depended in part on the proximity of families in band groups. By the close of the 1880s the chieftainship still existed, but it had been badly weakened and subjected to such mishandling by whites and Indians alike that a chaos of authority plagued the Sioux.

In the reservation environment the spiritual life of the Sioux also eroded. Here, too, the passing of the old ways undermined established beliefs and practices. The vision quest, for example, once marked a boy's passage to manhood and determined intensely personal and intensely sacred meanings and habits that guided his course through life. Their relevance, however, depended in large part on war and the hunt, and these no longer occupied the Sioux.

The more visible expressions of the Indian spiritual world drew direct government fire when the Indian Bureau issued its "List of Indian Offenses" in 1883. Now a medicine man could be hauled before the Court of Indian Offenses for providing his people with spiritual counsel or for practicing the rituals and incantations of his calling. One by one the old-time shamans died without passing their lore to apprentices.

But the hardest blow came with the ban on the Sun Dance. Once the centerpiece of the social and religious fabric of the Sioux, the Sun Dance provided an annual forum for spiritual communication and comfort. No other institution afforded so pervading a sense of religious security. No other event so strengthened the values and institutions of society. Of all the voids that settled into Sioux life in the early reservation years, this emotional void was the worst.

Missionaries hastened to fill the void. Except at Standing Rock, with its Catholic agent, Episcopalians led the field, followed closely by Congregationalists and Presbyterians. They contradicted one another in their teachings and forever ridiculed the old Indian ways, but they made progress. They were kind, they conducted rituals that the Sioux liked, and their churches were about the only place where Indians actually experienced the Christian precept that all people, even Indians, stood equal in the eyes of God. But the main explanation for the spread of Christianity lay in the nature of the Indian spiritual belief, which did not bar the new from living comfortable next to the old—so long as the Christian holy men did not demand too insistently that the old be cast aside. The Indian spiritual life centered on a quest for personal power. The white man quite visibly possessed power. Therefore, his God might also be petitioned for power along with all the traditional Sioux deities.

Explaining his own religious experience, one of Pine Ridge's staunchest progressives, George Sword, also explained what had happened to many of his people under the influence of missionary teachings:

> When I believed the Oglala Wakan Tanka was right I served him with all my powers. . . . In war with the white people I found their Wakan Tanka the Superior. I then took the name of Sword and have served Wakan Tanka according to the white people's manner with all my power. I became the chief of the United States Indian police and held the office until there was no trouble between the Oglala and the white people. I joined the church and am a deacon in it and shall be until I die. I have done all I was able to do to persuade my people to live according to the teachings of the Christian ministers.
>
> I still have my Wasicun [ceremonial pouch containing personal sacred objects] and I am afraid to offend it, because the spirit of an Oglala may go to the spirit land of the Lakota.

Like Christianity, education elicited ambivalent reactions from the Sioux. On the one hand, they sensed its importance in helping them to cope with the white people in the new world forced upon them. On the other hand, they feared what it would do to the hearts and minds, indeed the Sioux identity, of their children. On both counts, of course, they were right.

The Oglalas and Brules [another branch of the Sioux] had hardly settled at their new agencies in 1879 when Captain Richard H. Pratt descended on them to recruit pupils for his new school at Carlisle, Pennsylvania. He left with sixty boys and twenty-four girls—and left behind parents anguished over the parting and fearful for their children's fate in a far-off place peopled only by whites. Spotted Tail visited Carlisle a few months later and had his worst fears confirmed: his own children, locks shorn, Indian garb discarded in favor of tightly buttoned military dress, engaged in chores no Indian had ever done before. After an angry scene with Pratt, he stormed out with his children and thereafter set his influence against Carlisle. Even so, Sioux continued to enroll and receive a rudimentary classroom and industrial education. But then they came home to find themselves almost aliens among their own people and with no place to apply their newly acquired skills and learning. One such Carlisle graduate was Plenty Horses, the youth arraigned for murder but acquitted in the federal court at Sioux Falls in 1891. To the jurors he explained his motive:

I am an Indian. Five years I attended Carlisle and was educated in the ways of the white man. . . . I was lonely. I shot the lieutenant so I might make a place for myself among my people. Now I am one of them. I shall be hung and the Indians will bury me as a warrior. They will be proud of me. I am satisfied.

Day schools and boarding schools proved less repugnant than Carlisle and its sister institutions because the children stayed closer to home. Even so, parents found many of the rules and routines deeply offensive, and they resisted. Agents frequently had to resort to suspension of rations to fill the classrooms. At Standing Rock in 1884, for example, McLaughlin assigned quotas to the various bands and stopped issues until they were met. "But I afterward learned," he later confessed, "that there was not an *orphan child* over five years of age left in the camps after this 'conscription.' " And so, like the churches, the schools had their effect whether the Sioux resisted or not. By the close of the 1880s, the adults were confused and resentful, and the children, exposed to both white and Indian environments, were torn by conflicting values. . . .

And so the Teton Sioux ended the decade of the 1880s depressed, despairing, and drained of hope for improvement. The old values, the old verities, the old ways, and the old institutions fell irrevocably away. Nothing solid or satisfying took their place. That the people could not help giving up the old, that they could not help sampling or even embracing some of the new, only deepened the malaise. The long and exhausting battle over land, ending in defeat accompanied by a dramatic show of government bad faith—or so it appeared to the Indians—made matters even worse. The winter of 1889–90 brought hunger and perhaps even some starvation, which was in part a consequence of the ration cut. Epidemics of measles, influenza, and whooping cough swept the reservation with fatal effect. Summer drought in 1890 blasted into total ruin such crops as had been planted. Never had the fortunes of the Sioux reached lower ebb. Never had their sense of who they were been more blurred.

Other Indian tribes endured similar though usually less demoralizing stresses during the 1880s. The reservation program tore down the traditional culture without substituting the new at which it aimed. The Dawes Act set in motion a concerted drive for allotment in severalty and the cession of surplus lands. All over the West, Indians closed the decade beset by more or less cultural disintegration and by feelings of helplessness and hopelessness. Symptomatic of their condition was the fervor with which most greeted the stirring message that came out of the west in 1890, bringing with it the promise of a way out of the morass into which the white people had forced them.

A prophet had appeared among the Paiutes of Nevada. He preached a new religion. It was a religion that offered hope for the Indian race—hope not dependent upon promises of the white men. He held forth a vision of paradise in which all Indians would at last be free of the white burden and reside for eternity in a blissful land, a land without white people, a land inhabited by all the generations of Indians that had gone before, a land bounteous in game and all the other riches of the natural world, a land free of sickness and want, a land where all peoples dwelt in peace with one another. It was a religion that combined many of the old spiritual beliefs with the new teachings of the Christian missionaries. The injunction to live in peace, for example, drew on Christian dogma. Indeed, the prophet [Wovoka] came to be known as the Messiah, and when pilgrims from reservations all over the West gathered at his brush lodge he showed them scars on his hands where centuries before the whites had nailed him to a cross. But his promise was of an exclusively Indian world, and it could be simply attained by practicing the tenets of his faith and dancing a prescribed "Ghost Dance.". . . .

No Indian agency exhibited a more conspicuous personification of the evils of the spoils system than Pine Ridge. . . . Pine Ridge was recognized as "Pettigrew's Place." Richard F. Pettigrew, senator from the new state of South Dakota, pledged the post to Daniel F. Royer, physician, pharmacist, and local politician of Alpena, South Dakota. Middle-aged, with thinning hair, stringy mustache, and cherubic face, Royer had fallen on bad times and now needed a chance to recoup his finances. Although he wanted to be registrar of the Huron land office, Pettigrew could offer only an Indian agency. But another candidate with good Republican credentials and equal need appeared in the person of Bishop J. Gleason. Not until the middle of 1890 did Pettigrew work out a solution: Royer would get the agency and would at once appoint Gleason his chief clerk. With understandable though not necessarily inaccurate bias, the man fired as chief clerk recalled of Royer and Gleason: They were "broken down small politicians . . . overwhelmingly in debt. They came to the reservation as political adventurers in search of fortunes."

Royer installed himself at Pine Ridge Agency on October 1, 1890, just in time to confront the Ghost Dance. The Sioux pilgrims to Nevada had returned with word of the new Messiah during the previous March, but not until after a summer of cascading afflictions did the Sioux turn seriously to the hope he held forth. Cannily, old Red Cloud steered his usual ambiguous course. If the story were true, he said, "it would spread all over the world." If false, "it would melt like the snow under the hot sun." Little Wound agreed, but he spoke for most of the chiefs in urging the people not to take a chance. "You better learn this dance," he warned, "so if the Messiah does come he will not pass us by."

And they did learn the dance. All over Pine Ridge Reservation, and on the others as well, the people abandoned their cabins and pitched their tipis in the cottonwood groves. Hypnotically, in slow shuffling cadence, they danced around sacred prayer trees. As the intensity and excitement mounted, some fell to the ground, to die and go to heaven and there talk with the Indian Messiah and see the beautiful new world foretold. They came back to describe their experiences and to urge others to dance with a passion that would reveal to them, too, a vision of the promised land.

Unhappily for Royer and the other Sioux agents, the apostles who preached the new religion among the Sioux, chief among them Short Bull and Kicking Bear, added a feature that formed no part of Wovoka's message. The prophet taught nonviolence, even in thought. The millennium would occur through divine instrumentality; Indians need only follow the rituals and precepts of the new religion. But among the Sioux the travail and resentment of recent events allowed the priests to twist Wovoka's pacifistic doctrine. Now they suggested that the time of deliverance might be advanced by direct action, and that the people should not fear such a drastic course because the special "Ghost Shirt" worn by the dancers would turn the white man's bullets. With this assurance, the Sioux, in contrast to the faithful on other reservations throughout the West, grew increasingly turbulent and defiant.

Whether a steadier agent could have contained the trouble at Pine Ridge can never be known. Suggestively, McLaughlin succeeded at Standing Rock, and McGillycuddy had weathered crises as bad. But Royer, one of the worst specimens ever produced by the spoils system, was weak, excitable, and easily panicked, so much so that the Sioux named him "Young-Man-Afraid-of-Indians." He quickly made himself a target of contempt and ridicule, and he proved utterly wanting in any ability to stem the drift to anarchy. Repeatedly he ordered the dancers to stop dancing and return to their cabins, but they simply laughed at him. Repeatedly he bombarded his superiors with frantic appeals for soldiers. At last, in late November 1890, he could no longer be denied, for the Pine Ridge Sioux and a sizable infusion from Rosebud had got so far out of hand as to threaten the lives of agency personnel and spread fear of massacre among settlers outside the reservation. . . .

Big Foot and his Miniconjou band lived on the south side of the Cheyenne River about ten miles below its forks. They belonged to the Cheyenne River Reservation, but the land agreement of 1889 had left them outside its boundaries. A leading nonprogressive, Big Foot had warmly embraced the Ghost Dance and thus had got his name on the list of troublemakers who should be arrested. Actually, his ardor for the new religion had cooled considerably, and his reputation as a peacemaker had elicited an invitation from Red Cloud and other "friendlies" at Pine Ridge to come down and help end the troubles there. When Big Foot and his people started south, . . . [Major] General [Nelson] Miles and everyone else assumed they were headed for the Stronghold to cast their lot with the dancers.

Goaded by a furious Miles, military units combed the frozen plains looking for Big Foot. They failed chiefly because Big Foot was not aiming for the Stronghold but for Pine Ridge. At last, on December 28, a squadron of the Seventh Cavalry found the fugitives. Big Foot, prostrated in a wagon with pneumonia, agreed with the officer in charge to accompany the soldiers to their camp. It lay in the valley of Wounded Knee Creek about twenty miles east of Pine Ridge Agency. That night the rest of the Seventh Cavalry rode out to Wounded Knee, and Colonel James W. Forsyth took command. Daybreak of December 29, gray with threatening storm, revealed Big Foot's tipis, sheltering some 350 people, closely surrounded by five hundred cavalrymen and commanded from a nearby hilltop by four small-caliber Hotchkiss cannon. It was not a reassuring sight.

No one on either side that morning had any thought of a fight. Certainly not the Indians, as the army later charged; they were outnumbered, surrounded, poorly armed, and had their women and children present. Certainly not the soldiers; they clearly saw their advantages, and so unconcerned was Colonel Forsyth that he failed to dispose his units so that their fire would not endanger one another. But Forsyth had orders to disarm Big Foot's people, and taking an Indian's gun from him always unleashed emotions that could override logic. That, not an outbreak of treacherous Indians or a massacre plotted by brutal soldiers, is what happened at Wounded Knee.

As the search progressed, powerful tensions rose on both sides. A medicine man pranced about inciting the men to fight; their Ghost Shirts would protect them, he said. Nervous troopers fingered their carbine triggers. One seized a deaf man and grasped his rifle. It went off. The chanting priest threw a handful of dirt into the air. A knot of Indians dropped their blankets and leveled Winchester repeaters at a rank of soldiers. Both sides fired at once, and the fight that neither side intended or expected burst upon them.

In a murderous melee at close range, soldiers and Indians shot, stabbed, and clubbed one another. Weakly, Big Foot rose from his pallet to watch. A volley killed him and most of the headmen lined up behind him. Abruptly the two sides separated, and from the hill the artillery went into action. Exploding shells flattened the Sioux tipis and filled the air with deadly shrapnel. In less than an hour most of the fighting had ended, leaving the battlefield a horror of carnage. Nearly two-thirds of Big Foot's band had been cut down, at least 150 dead and 50 wounded, and perhaps more who were never reported. The army lost 25 dead and 39 wounded. . . .

Wounded Knee was the last major armed encounter between Indians and whites in North America. A few scattered clashes occurred later, but Wounded Knee was the last of great consequence. Even so, neither Wounded Knee nor the Ghost Dance "outbreak" that formed its backdrop deserves to be viewed as an episode in the Indian Wars of the United States. More fittingly, warfare ended in 1886 at Skeleton Canyon, Arizona, with the collapse of the last armed resistance to the reservation system. Instead of armed challenge to the reservation, the Ghost Dance was a desperate bid for divine salvation where all else had failed. Among the Sioux it assumed a militant form, but still it need not have ended in violence save for an incompetent Indian agent and a tragic accident born of mutual distrust, misunderstanding, and fear.

Rather, both in fact and in symbol, Wounded Knee assumes a larger significance, for it marks the passing of the Indian frontier. A little more than two years after Wounded Knee, the young historian Frederick Jackson Turner appeared before a convention of the American Historical Association in

Chicago. Pointing out that the census of 1890 had failed for the first time to trace a frontier of white settlement in the West, he expounded his provocative interpretation of "The Significance of the Frontier in American History." For generations to come the Turner thesis would profoundly influence American historical thought and spark heated controversy among historians. For more than four hundred years, Indian conflicts had flashed across the successive frontiers that Turner postulated. Coincidentally, the last serious conflict occurred in the very year, 1890, that he chose as the end of America's frontier era. . . .

More plausibly than as a single line that disappeared when whites conquered the wilderness, the Indian frontier may be viewed as zones of ethnic interaction that faded when whites established political domination over the Indians. In this formulation as well as in Turner's, the Ghost Dance and Wounded Knee signal the end of the frontier period. For the Sioux, despite a decade of reservation experience, the loss of their freedom and traditional way of life seemed unthinkable until the bullets of the Seventh Cavalry penetrated their Ghost Shirts and shattered the dream held out by the Indian Messiah. After Wounded Knee, the Sioux resignedly submitted to the reservation system and thus implicitly surrendered the last vestiges of sovereignty to the invader. In varying degree, although no other Wounded Knees dramatized the surrender, the same thing happened on reservations all over the West. Indians embraced the Ghost Dance and the last hope of salvation it offered. When the miracles failed to occur, the reality of their political subordination could no longer be denied or ignored. Thus on December 29, 1890, the Indian frontier of the American West vanished in the smoke of Hotchkiss shells bursting over the valley of Wounded Knee Creek.

REVIEW QUESTIONS

1. The selection mentions the Dawes Act (1887). Refer to your textbook or some other source to find what this law provided and what its consequences were. How was it linked to the policy of confining Native Americans to reservations?

2. Detail the specific ways in which Sioux life and culture changed on the reservation. Consider such areas as politics, economics, and religion.

3. Native Americans did not always agree on the proper response to whites' efforts to dominate and control them. What specific evidence of such disagreements can you find in this selection?

4. Explain the appeal of the "Ghost Dance." What did it promise its followers? What was it about their current circumstances that would incline them toward it?

5. How does the "Ghost Dance" resemble and differ from Christianity?

6. Utley's account of the Battle of Wounded Knee in 1890 implies that it was a fight no one wanted and no one really started, but rather erupted out of mutual misunderstanding and suspicion. Assuming he is correct, do you think Wounded Knee was a representative example of Indian-white violence in the West? Why or why not?

FOR FURTHER READING

Robert V. Hine, *The American West* (1984), and Patricia Limerick, *The Legacy of Conquest: The Unbroken Past of the American West* (1987), are general histories that provide background for understanding the context of relations between whites and Native Americans. Books dealing specifically with Native Americans include Ralph K. Andrist, *The Long Death: The Last Days of the Plains Indians* (1964); Leonard A. Carlson, *Indians, Bureaucrats, and Land: The Dawes Act and the Decline of Indian Farming* (1981); Frederick E. Hoxie, *A Final Promise: The Campaign to Assimilate the Indians (1880–1920)* (1984); and Philip Weeks, *Farewell, My Nation: The American Indian and the United States* (1990). David Hurst Thomas, et al., *The Native Americans: An Illustrated History* (1993) provides a wealth of pictures to accompany a general account of Native American culture and history from the prehistoric past to the present. Robert M. Utley, *Lance and Shield: The Life and Times of Sitting Bull* (1993), is a biography of the Sioux leader that also says a great deal about the history and fate of his people. Helen Hunt Jackson, *A Century of Dishonor* (1885), is a vivid expression of the late nineteenth-century view that official government policy toward Native Americans was misguided and unjust. Books expressing a similar view about more recent times include Vine Deloria, Jr., *Custer Died for Your Sins* (1969), and Dee Brown, *Bury My Heart at Wounded Knee* (1971).

Farmers on the Great Plains often resorted to cooperation to cope with the harsh environment, but creating settled conditions was also the result of individual drive and determination and a source of personal pride.

3

The Farmers' Frontier

ROBERT V. HINE

The quarter-century after the Civil War was a period of very rapid growth for the United States. A significant part of that growth was geographical. At the end of the war, the area west of the Mississippi River was sparsely populated except for the first tier of states on the west bank, Texas, and a line of settlement on the Pacific Coast. But by 1890, according to the official census of that year, this hitherto largely empty territory had been settled. It was no longer possible to draw a line on a map of the United States marking the boundary between settled and unsettled areas. The frontier, which according to Frederick Jackson Turner's theory of 1893 had been the chief determining element in forming the United States, had come to an end.

The process of settlement was filled with danger and excitement and has continued to exercise a firm hold on Americans' imaginations. We still entertain ourselves with stories of battles with Indians, of prospectors searching for the elusive big strike that would make them wealthy overnight, of cattle barons and cowboys in conflict with the elements or each other in their efforts to raise beef to feed the growing cities of the East. But while fur trappers before the Civil War, and miners and cattlemen afterwards, played vital roles in opening up the trans-Mississippi West and awakening people to its enormous possibilities, its actual settlement was accomplished by less glamorous figures in less exciting ways. It was farmers who were primarily responsible for establishing a settled society in the area from the Mississippi to the Pacific, and their story, while not having the same aura of glamour as surrounds the mountain man or the prospector or the Indian fighter or the cowboy, has its own share of human drama.

In the first place, farmers on the Great Plains had to learn to adapt to an unfamiliar and harsh environment. Bitter cold in winter, burning hot in summer, lacking timber and stone for building materials, and subject to periodic droughts, windstorms, and insect plagues, the Plains were a mighty challenge to those who chose to try their fortunes there. Further, as they learned the techniques enabling them to deal with nature, they found themselves confronted with other problems, particularly steadily falling prices for the crops they grew and large fixed debts for the land, tools, and machines they needed to grow them. Caught in this economic squeeze, farmers began to band together to seek solutions to their problems, first through the Patrons of Husbandry, or Grange, in the 1870s and then through the Populist Movement in the 1880s and 1890s. These attempts at political action enjoyed only partial success, but did pave the way for some of the reforms of the Progressive Movement of the twentieth century.

In the meantime, however, farmers on the Plains still had to learn to deal with the everyday problems created by the stringent conditions under which they had to live. The following selection from Robert V. Hine's *Community on the American Frontier: Separate But Not Alone* talks about some of the problems, including the psychological ones, they endured and the methods they devised for trying to cope with them.

"I was alone all the daylight hours with the cattle, and all around me the prairie was dying. The sound of death was in the wind that never stopped blowing across the whitening grass, or rustling the dead weeds at the edges of the fields. There was a forlorn, lonely note in the bawl of a calf for its mother and in the honking of wild geese down the pale sky." Grace Snyder's thoughts were the aftermath of death, the obliteration of a distant neighbor boy who had died while hurrying through his noon dinner. She and her family had walked the half mile to the funeral, where the glass-topped coffin exposed the bloated face of John, as lonely in death as the prairies were in life. Grace had known solitude playing among the bleached bones in the buffalo wallow, she and her sister alone because the Snyder farm was so far from neighbors. Grace's father had migrated with his proud wife and three daughters from Missouri to the Platte River Valley in Custer County, Nebraska. That was 1885, and Grace was three. Their father had preceded them and prepared housing, but Grace later remembered her first sight of "two naked little soddies" on a

---

bare, wind-swept ridge. Nothing else. The flatness of the prairies threatened her with a child's unconscious fear of abandonment, perhaps of lost identity, perhaps even of oblivion beneath that unbroken sky. . . .

Seth Humphrey became a mortgage collector, traveling across the Great Plains in the early 1890s. Everywhere he found abandoned claims, shacks pulled apart and used by others, the winds and the horizon taking their toll. Guy Divet, an Irishman who had come to Dakota with his family in the 1870s and prospered, told the story of another couple who had not. Ned and his young, pregnant wife moved into the neighborhood, and in their first winter Margie was "sick and out of her mind with loneliness and fear." So the warm, caring Divets took them in for the winter, putting up a bed in their living room.

That spring Mrs. Divet helped with the birth, but the young mother remained half-crazed, and the young father grew more and more depressed. So they left with Margie still ill. The neighbors raised thirty-six dollars to help them. The baby died on the journey, and the mother shortly after. Ned sold the wagon and team to pay for the burials. "Grist for the prairie mill," the Divets said. Ned's claim was jumped, but before that the Divets rode over to see his cabin. There were unwashed dishes and a homemade crib. The Divets piled dry weeds, lit them, and watched reverently as the cabin burned to the ground. It did not take long.

But the fire could not erase the memory, and the prairie continued to stare. Mrs. Divet herself developed a goiter, and when her husband offered a visit to her family in Wisconsin, she refused, sadly pointing to her straggly hair and sagging body and "this hideous bag that hangs at my throat." "No," she cried, "its too late now. I don't want to go." The Divet manuscripts are memorials to "the frayed ends" of these lives, "the heartstrings broken in the process of uprooting never to be brought together again."

The lives of the Snyders, the Humphreys, and the Divets were in many respects full and rewarding. Nevertheless, as with all settlers on the Great Plains between the Civil War and the close of the century, the fact of isolation underlay all other facts, social, economic, and political. Isolation was the environment in which the structure of the community must grow. Shortly after the turn of the century, when the President's Commission on Country Life asked over 100,000 rural inhabitants what could improve their lives, an overwhelming response was better roads, or, in other words, a way of overcoming isolation.

Eugene Virgil Smalley spelled out the central problem in similar terms. A newsman, he had lived and worked from Ohio to Minnesota, served in the government, and traveled abroad. "In no civilized country," he wrote, "have the cultivators of the soil adapted their homelife so badly to the conditions of nature." He saw only one solution: to draw farmers together into village communities. He knew that it would be difficult because of land laws and, even more important, American ways of thinking. There is an old western saying, he quoted, that the prairies would not produce until the Indian was beaten out of them, something savage wrested from the land by individual struggle.

Smalley told of four farm families who, like many others, had decided to work more closely by building their houses and barns on the adjacent corners of their claims. But in a few years they had all moved to the far corners because, they explained lamely, when they were together their chickens had gotten mixed up. Such was the "crusty individuality" that Smalley felt had produced the inheritance of isolated lives. . . .

Some cultural identities, however, did stem from the use of, if not love of, the land. Sometimes one part of the ecology, one feature of the natural environment, can become the center of the culture, the heart of the community, like corn for the Latin-American natives or the buffalo for the Sioux. Thus on the plains cultural differences arose between wheat and corn farming. Corn cultivation spread into the plains following the water-courses, and carrying a certain life-style. The cornhusker reflected his "corn-belt mentality" when he spoke of huskings, cribs, and fodder, topics irrelevant to the wheat grower. And, more basically, he and the wheat farmer would argue over proper use of the upland plains. Each wave of newcomers to Nebraska between the 1850s and 1880s brought new and conflicting concepts of land use. In time attitudes would change, but before the late 1870s two potential cultural communities existed.

Separate crop cultures, however, did not really develop on the plains, partly because the environment was a common hazard, a common hardship, and it dictated fast, cooperative action from cornhusker, wheat grower, or cattle grazer alike. Prairie fires, for example, were a threat to all. And wolves, jackrabbits, and rattlesnakes, like fires, were more effectively controlled by cooperative drives. Cooperative coyote hunting in pioneer Nebraska was probably the only occasion when farmers, cattlemen, and sheepmen worked in concert—although afterward, eating cold pies with their wives in the nearest barn mow, in their conversations they dwelled on only safe topics like past hunts. Natural disasters such as floods could be better withstood by groups. The common threat of the environment is suggested in the tall tales and weather jokes. Why did the western farmer so love to tell of the drought when the fish in the river kicked up such a dust that the volunteer fire department had to sprinkle them down? Or why did he like to repeat the details of the well that ran so dry that a tornado lifted it from one county to another? Perhaps because the common experience welded them in a psychic community. That same drought of the tall tales, for example, brought the farmers of Roten Valley, Nebraska, to act in concert regarding their suffering livestock. Thus the environment bred cooperative action.

Prairie farmers followed a long tradition of frontier cooperation. In colonial New England all nonfarming artisans and laborers were required by law to help with the mowing and reaping. In western Pennsylvania in the eighteenth century neighbors would donate three days to build a newcomer's house, including furniture. In Kentucky about 1810 an observer described a cooperative "bond of amity." "In no other part of the world," he wrote, "is good neighborship found in greater perfection." Everywhere the tradition was built on the problem of getting big jobs done, tasks too large for the individual—clearing acres of land, house and barn raising, road building, threshing before the rains. These were situations in which men were grappling most desperately with the environment.

On the plains cooperative house raising retained its full vigor. Howard Ruede, a thin young Pennsylvania Moravian who went to Kansas in 1877, explained that neighbors would gather from miles around to construct a settler's house, and they would finish in a day. Eleven men had helped a neighbor shortly before, though Ruede was sure six could have done the job. Houses were raised frequently enough that men fell in accustomed roles based on their skills. Such raisings were not always signs of stability, for many a house soon needed moving, sometimes for long distances, as to a new homestead. More often, though, the move for which the neighbors would gather would be short, like putting Percy Ebbutt's cabin on rollers to relocate on a hilltop or dragging Faye Lewis's house on skids to a site nearer the well.

Hospitality itself was largely an exchange of goods and services. A farmer, for example, would sometimes have to ride for days to round up stray cattle, but he would never want for lodging or provender. Some distant, lonely neighbor could be found for roof, a meal, and hay. "You'll do the same for me," he would hear, "when I'm in your parts." It was an outright exchange, the neighbor expecting reciprocity. When the farmer moved on main-traveled roads, he would more likely pay for his lodging. In such a situation the Snyders were once amazed to be charged a whopping eight dollars.

The height of cooperative work came at harvest time. In those autumn days of thronging threshers and aching backs, the traditions of cooperation prospered. Crews made the rounds from farm to farm, and men sweated together over one another's fields. The men talked at dinner, cooked by women whose backs also ached. Later there was talk in the barn as the men waited for a squall to pass. One Iowa farmer described these moments as "inner neighborhood." Such was the conversational stuff of community, and it grew from simple but universal topics like the weather—the breeze from the east, the nervousness of the horses, the "sun dogs" in the west that portended storm. Or it could be the state of the crops or the advantages of this country over another region or another land.

The threshing crew was a mixed lot. In addition to the local neighbors exchanging work, there could be a few leftover hired hands, some unemployed seasonal workers like timbermen in Minnesota, perhaps a hobo, and a schoolboy or two. The nonneighbors were paid. A band cutter got $1.50 a day in Minnesota in the early 1880s. These men slept in haymows and were fed plenty of chicken and pumpkin pie. Ebbutt thought they "lived off the fat of the land."

The cooperative element in threshing should be placed in the context of a rather large, extensive operation that was partly local cooperation and barter, partly capitalistic investment, and partly involvement in wider economic markets. The threshing machine itself, for example, was usually owned by one or two of the neighbors, who would assemble the crew, arrange the schedule, and bring the rig around for a cash fee or a portion of the crop. If the machine was owned by a Swede and you were the only non-Swede in the area, your turn might well come last. But you probably had little choice, for the cost of a thresher in 1851 was $175. Few farmers could afford that, since most had already invested a minimum of $400 just to begin farming. . . .

. . . Threshing was typical of other mixes of cooperation, barter, and cash. If you exchanged work and brought along a team for a day, you got three days' work from a man without a team. In exchange for sporadic labor over many months as a hired hand, Howard Ruede received help in breaking three acres of his own land, 11½ bushels of wheat, a few bushels of rye, and five dollars.

Reciprocal labor resulted far more often from an absence of capital than from a desire to cooperate. Anyone could offer labor, but few could offer cash. . . .

. . . Howard Ruede's Kansas neighborhood in the 1870s circulated a paper seeking help in building the school, either work or money. Eighty-one hours were pledged, but only eighteen dollars in cash. Pockets then were empty because of hard times following 1873; but in depression or not, reciprocal work expanded the cash supply. The neighbors were a reservoir of cooperative labor that assumed the nature of capital. . . .

So the plains environment and an immature economy spawned cooperative activities that could become community. Irrespective of economic forces, however, the isolation of farms called up a strong psychic yearning for companionship. Starved emotions cried for nourishment. Certainly the community was small enough in numbers, but the distances reduced practical contacts to the level of acquaintances in a large city. Neighborhoods in Kansas are measured in miles, not blocks, wrote Charley O'Kieffe, adding sadly if not typically that there was little social intermingling, and only two dances a year.

Edgar Watson Howe had an explanation for the kind of gloomy picture O'Kieffe drew. Howe thought his neighbors in Missouri in the 1850s were so habituated to isolation that they could socialize for only a short time, as in church, and then they would immediately head for their farms to resume their lives of misery. It was an immature or arrested social life. Richard Weston had earlier described a frontier party in which forty couples engaged in "puerile and frivolous sport," like kissing games, and usually in silence because the art of conversation was so little known. Of course, the preponderance of accounts of social life on the plains frontier is of vital, engaging, lively times, but the more grim commentators would say that the happier descriptions were reflections of the infrequency of the contacts, etching them in memory and exaggerating them in reminiscence.

Still there is abundant evidence of pleasurable social life among prairie farmers. In North Dakota in the 1870s a ring of eight families rotated their dances every Friday night. Even Grace Fairchild, a big woman whose strong face reflected her hard life, recalled that the dances were so popular around her house that in rapid succession they outgrew the parlor, the machine shed, and the barn. These parties were usually open, nonselective affairs. At least Percy Ebbutt always assumed that if anyone had a party everyone else was invited.

There were quilting bees, husking bees, apple bees, and "fulling bees" (for the fulling or thickening of cloth). To be sure, all these had practical ends, but they skillfully blended play with cooperative work, "a means of enlivening the spirits of old and young." As in any other true community, these occasions sparked tension. Hamlin Garland remembered Mrs. Whitwell's ostracism from the quiltings because she was too loud and told vulgar stories. There were limits to which loneliness would compel acceptance, but Garland understood as well as anyone else the gratifying cohesive force in this cooperative socialization—the vigor, the laughter, the rejoicing. Imagine what it meant even to children playing together under the frame with adults chattering and stitching on the quilt above.

At least two holidays embraced the whole community. Decoration Day combined spring with a communal memorial. Everyone picked flowers, decorated the graves, and remained for the picnic. But no community event pulled together the straggling farms as did the Fourth of July. At some nearby fort or crossroad there were flags and speeches and cold chicken, and the day was full of horse races, foot races, sack races, and baseball. There were greased pigs, greased poles, and gallons of cold drinks. At Fort Scott, Kansas, in 1859 it took four horsedrawn wagons to draw ice for the lemonade alone. Faye Lewis, a shy adolescent in South Dakota, was taken to the celebration her first year on the plains. She feared that, for families like hers, farmers who could not afford the expense or time, it would be an "irresponsible and reckless binge," but she later understood the "immeasurable benefits" from the three days, from the four-hour wagon ride, the parade, the singing, the merry-go-round, the popcorn, the fireworks. For similar reasons Friday night "literaries," often sedate enough, occasionally reverted to nonsense: Resolved that pigs are smarter than sheep; or, Resolved that it is better to be kicked by a mule than bitten by a rattler.

Between special occasions and formal gatherings, there was always visiting. In Oklahoma in the 1890s, Allie Wallace thought that her house enjoyed so many visitors because her mother owned a sewing machine; but the need being met was deeper than practicality. Grace Snyder observed an increase in visiting during a period of extended drought. The relief of tensions through social intercourse was well expressed by Grace's father, who, even when weary, wished to go visiting. He took his family, weather permitting, as often as once a week, jolting over the miles, bearing a few gifts of flowers or fresh eggs, hoping for a sip of wine and a face. For a time isolation would thaw in the warmth of human contact.

Worship services, prayer meetings, evening sings, and especially camp meetings were social events too. Small groups of neighbors could always pray together in farmhouses, but the outdoor revivals, lasting from three days to a week, provided the most highly charged release of emotion. Families came from dozens or hundreds of miles. Religion in wagons, Charles Reed called it, and like most other farmers he happily welcomed any preacher who stopped at his sod-house door. The word flew. Soon there would be "tenting tonight" in the old grove at the forks of Clear Creek. Preachings and bonfires and a few true conversions there were, but the serious reclamation of souls was overlaid with the spirit of the Fourth of July. Everyone came—Baptists, Mennonites, Catholics. The circuit rider preached to a heterogeneous congregation. Most people went, even when they had to sit under clumps of hay on poles for shade. At least, Allie Wallace said, it "broke the monotony." Whatever their backgrounds, they joined or witnessed members of their community publicly confessing sin or publicly accepting the Lord. . . .

The place as an ecological system demanded economic cooperation, and the size of the group, small but scattered, shaped the need for social gatherings; but neither would bring community without the values of sharing and caring. Such values were once held aloft by Fred Shannon as a distinctive culture revolving around cooperative rural life. Such a cooperative culture based on values might indeed be a community, but, on the other hand, group cooperation does not necessarily mean community. Was it evidence of cooperative culture when, during a measles epidemic, neighbors fed stricken families and took in their healthy children to stem the spread of the disease? Or when neighbors banded together to help the surviving families of two murdered men? Or when settlers shared the cost of a school teacher by rotating her residence among them? Or when, after a disastrous fire, the farmers near Torkel Fugelstad threshed his crop while he was away?

Was, for example, Mrs. Lockhart living the cooperative life when, unpaid, she brought her "little kit and some tools" either to deliver babies or to prepare bodies for burial? Or the "angel of mercy," who came to the smallpox house to nurse the sick while others whipped their horses to get by faster? Or Mollie Sanford, who was always feeding wanderers? Or the bachelor nursing a neighbor through a long illness? Or the neighbors in North Dakota who walked to one another's farms after severe storms to make sure everyone could get out? Or the boy in Iowa who hunted daily to feed an entire area stricken by a grasshopper plague? Or Mrs. King, who, after caring for her own twelve children, nursed the neighborhood sick, carrying their chamber pots and wet-nursing their babies?

Like exchange work, altruistic acts embodied the techniques of survival. Mollie Sanford once said that she took care of others but also expected others to care for her when she needed help. In this sense charity is individualistic, and its arena may more realistically be called the neighborhood than the community. A neighborhood is a loose collection of people, informal, unofficial, with no binding force over its members. It is reflected in many simple acts like the willingness to stop and talk over the fence. The altruism of the plains farmer, the aesthetics of the cooperative life, may have stopped at the level of neighborhood.

Of course, if there was a community on the plains, individual tensions would rise within it. There is no paucity of evidence for individualism. When John McConnell, for example, distilled from his lifetime on the Illinois prairie a composite pioneer settler, his figure was not cooperative but proud and solitary. This farmer might welcome a stranger, but he would not want him to stay long. "It was but little assistance that he ever required from his neighbors, though no man was ever more willing to render it to others in the hour of need." These were types like Jules Sandoz in Nebraska, egotistical and even antisocial. They were not likely to keep memoirs. But their figures emerge in the accounts of others. They were smudges on the record of community building. When the Wares, dirty but proud, were kindly offered some potatoes to help them over a hard time, they went to the cellar and took a bushel of the biggest and best. The Cogills, when offered chicken feed, took fine seed corn. The Fairchilds once failed to tell a neighbor that he had eaten carbolic acid in their house because they were afraid they would be blamed if he died.

A strong competitive spirit was a boon to individualism and a bane to the furthering of community. "They were always racing in those days," Garland said. Holiday rivalries were perpetuated in the shooting matches and tugs-of-war. At log rollings men struggled to build the largest piles. Harvest crews raced to the ends of the rows. And those who did not win could still tell a tall tale, for the language was peculiarly braced with competitive exaggeration. Behind the bragging was often severe privatization. Some subjects were retained for the individual or family alone, topics into which the community had no entry. Curiously, for example, bedbugs, known to be legion and battled by all, could not be discussed.

The vigorous individualism of the plains farmer has been overemphasized in the annals of the West. But it should not be dismissed. . . . Among pioneers there was a common bond, so ingrained that conformity to it was assumed, and nonconformists were instinctively ostracized. The essence of the bond was endurance, the triumph over a hostile wilderness. Although the end might be a common tie, the beginning was not in the ethics of the group but in the supreme value of the individual.

Walter Prescott Webb claimed that the 100th meridian, symbol of the passage to the Great Plains, shook to the foundation the culture of those who crossed it. In one respect Webb was wrong—the plains did not change the institution of the family. . . . The pattern of frontier family life was remarkably nuclear and similar to patterns elsewhere in the nation. James Davis, for example, in a study of ten thousand pioneer households between 1800 and 1840, found practically no one living alone. Even the few hired hands resided in the households. On the northern plains families were small—at any given time the largest number of children was only one or two, owing to birth control (abstinence), the young age of the couples, and the absence of economic incentives for large families. The pioneer farm family was nuclear in the sense that it was isolated from the community, a separate unit not subject to community controls. Of course, there were exceptions where the family appeared to be intimately linked with the community. In the Dakotas in the earliest days baptisms, weddings, shivarees, and funerals were often community affairs. Weddings in Kansas dugouts often brought so many neighbors that they had to move outside for the feasting and dancing. At Bell's Lake, Iowa, worship was held in homes before the public services, reminiscent of Puritan family prayers, but Bell's Lake was an unusual community with a religious base.

Elsewhere most cases of community-oriented families came from the earliest dugout times. In the great thrust of the plains experience "the hearth of the lonely farm" was the center, with otherwise only kin and a few neighborly connections binding people together.

In fact, the family persisted through desperate circumstances. Children sometimes retained the family unit long after parents had died. A seventeen-year-old girl in early Texas, for example, maintained a house of seven brothers and sisters. A sixteen-year-old boy alone supervised two siblings. The community did not intervene in these situations unless the arrangement proved absolutely impossible.

Although often enough denied, social and economic class lines were always evident on the frontier. Some people lived in dugouts, and some in houses of pine boards. There was never any doubt in the mind of Allie Wallace that the Stewarts, who had built the biggest house in the area, were in a "different" category from the Germans and Russians in the neighborhood. She drew her "class" lines by means of the shawls of the immigrant women, their unshapely bodies from bearing babies, and the strict discipline their children received. These were hardly satisfactory guides to class distinctions, but they existed. Class consciousness was blurred, of course, by the proud equality stemming from shared hardships.

Still the community of endurance could not last indefinitely. For one thing, it was subject to invasions from outside. Think of land agents, "the wool hat people" as Grace Fairchild called them, filtering into a community's space. Mrs. Fairchild would give them a bed, meat, potatoes, and "spud varnish" for twenty-five cents, but the presence of these speculators did not please her, as if they embodied a vaguely threatening force. Seth Humphrey was playing a similarly invasive role when he came into Nebraska as a mortgage agent. He lodged with farm families but always left fifty cents on the table, symbol of the gulf between them. He noted too that as soon as a house was identified as a foreclosure the settlers quickly stole the movables. The same property was safe for months if the owner was only temporarily away. Humphrey told of a man named George who had combined with a fellow homesteader to build one house squarely across their common section line. Inside the house they dutifully slept and lived each over his own land. But the friend gave up and let the mortgage company foreclose. When Humphrey arrived, George was hitching a team to the house to pull it entirely on his own land. Humphrey protested. The man firmly explained, "I'm not touching yours; I'm pulling mine and yours is following." Knowing the climate of opinion, the mortgage man did not interfere. . . .

The environment, the place, inspired a community of hardship, but it also injected a constant dilution of community caused by separation. Even the cooperation of exchanging work and the emotionally warming social events and revivals seemed to be measures of separation rather than cornerstones in community. Altruism, heroic and soul-stirring as it was, remained individualistic, not group-oriented. The family, dominant, vital, clung to itself. Growing class distinctions, especially after the community of hardship was suspended and national economic forces pushed in, worked against unity. Thus the total experience was of limited associations, not genuine community. Grace Snyder's brooding thoughts of death as a child on the Nebraska prairie had foreshadowed the usual difficulties faced by community on the plains.

REVIEW QUESTIONS

1. According to Frederick Jackson Turner's influential essay, "The Significance of the Frontier in American History," frontier conditions created a strong sense of individualism in the people who lived there. Does Hine's account of the lives of the settlers on the Plains tend to confirm or deny that judgment?

2. What forces bred a spirit of cooperation among settlers on the Plains? Would city-dwellers of the time have more or less reason than these farmers to enter into cooperative arrangements with their neighbors?

3. Hine makes a distinction between cooperation and a true sense of community. What seems to be the essence of the distinction?

4. What did the settlers do for amusement? Which of their amusements were distinctively rural in nature and which would they have shared with people who lived in cities or small towns?

5. According to Hine, there was a conflict between the values of individualism and community on the Plains. Which predominated? Why? How, if at all, would such a conflict have been manifested in an urban setting at the time? How, if at all, is it manifested in American society today?

FOR FURTHER READING

Walter Prescott Webb's *The Great Plains* (1931) remains an instructive account of how geography and climate shaped the experience of settlers, while Everett Dick's *The Sod House Frontier, 1845–1890* (1947) provides vivid portraits of their everyday lives. Fred Shannon's *The Farmers' Last Frontier: Agriculture, 1860–1897* (1945) deals with the problems of all American farmers during the period, not just those on the Plains, and provides a good introduction to the farmers' turn to political action, a subject Lawrence Goodwyn takes further in *Democratic Promise: The Populist Movement in America* (1976). Gilbert C. Fite, *The Farmers' Frontier, 1865–1900* (1966), is a more recent treatment of the subject Shannon covers. Craig Miner, *West of Wichita: Settling the High Plains of Kansas, 1865–1890* (1986), and Joanna L. Stratton, *Pioneer Women: Voices from the Kansas Frontier* (1981), explore many of the same themes as the present selection. John C. Hudson, *Plains Country Towns* (1985), discusses urban life on the Great Plains. Finally, Hamlin Garland's stories in *Main-Travelled Roads* (1891) give insights into the inner lives of Plains settlers that cannot usually be found in conventional history books.

Women and children were a large part of the labor force in southern textile mills.

4

Labor in the Gilded Age

JACQUELYN DOWD HALL,
JAMES LELOUDIS, ROBERT KORSTAD,
MARY MURPHY, LU ANN JONES,
AND CHRISTOPHER B. DALY

There can be no doubt that the industrialization of the United States established the foundations for economic expansion, prosperity, and a standard of living higher than Americans had enjoyed in the past and higher, too, than the inhabitants of practically any other country in the world. But there was a price to be paid for these advances. Many of the fruits of industrialization took some time to become fully ripe and could only be enjoyed in the long run. In the short run, the process often led to social dislocation, confusion, conflict, and a great deal of misery.

The growing industrial labor force, or substantial portions of it, was one group that paid the price of industrialization. Largely without the protection that unions and labor legislation would later provide, industrial workers in the late nineteenth century were overworked, underpaid, routinely subjected to dangerous or unhealthy working conditions, frequently laid off without warning, and compensated little or not at all for such layoffs or for any accidents they suffered or diseases they contracted as a result of the conditions under which they worked. All of this helped to keep labor costs low and profits high. It can reasonably be suggested that America's industrial might was built not only upon the labor of its workers, but also upon their suffering.

Despite this, America's industries continued to attract workers. Beginning in the late nineteenth century, many of them came from Europe. An even larger reservoir of industrial labor, however, was made up of native-born Americans pushed off farms by the declining economic rewards to be found in agriculture and attracted by the prospect of the more or less steady pay to be had in industry. This was particularly true in the South, where the textile industry began to grow in the late nineteenth century. There were almost no immigrants to draw on to supply the mills' needs for workers, but there was a ready supply of rural folk willing to give up farming for "public work," as the early mill workers termed it. As the following selection by Jacquelyn Dowd Hall, et al. indicates, after a while, many began to doubt the wisdom of their choice, but by that time, it was too late to return to the agricultural way of life they had left. More important, it may well have been that they had had no real choice in the first place, having been driven into the mills by sheer economic necessity.

First-generation workers in southern mills had more to learn than just the mechanics of a new job. On the farm they had chosen and ordered their tasks according to their needs and the demands of their crops. Now they drove themselves to the continuous pace of a machine. Whereas most men, women, and children had once worked together and enjoyed the fruits of their own labor, now they were "hands," working under a boss's orders and for someone else's profit. Farm work, to be sure, had been hard, but mill work took a different toll. Millhands rose early in the morning, still tired from the day before. For ten, eleven, or twelve hours they walked, stretched, leaned, and pulled at their machines. Noise, heat, and humidity engulfed them. The lint that settled on their hair and skin marked them as mill workers, and the cotton dust that silently entered their lungs could eventually cripple or kill them. At best, mill work was a wrenching change.

Chester Copeland came from a long line of farmers and carpenters in rural Orange County, North Carolina, and he remained a devoted farmer except for brief, and unhappy, sojourns in the mills. To him, mill work was "nothing but a robot life. Robot-ing is my word for it—in the mill you do the same thing over and over again—just like on a treadmill. There's no challenge to it—just drudgery. The more you do, the more they want done. But in farming you do work real close to nature. There's always something exciting and changing in nature. It's never a boring job. There's some dirty jobs in

---

From *Like a Family: The Making of a Southern Cotton Mill World,* by Jacquelyn Dowd Hall, James Leloudis, Robert Korstad, Mary Murphy, Lu Ann Jones, and Christopher B. Daly. Copyright © 1987 by the University of North Carolina Press. Reprinted by permission. Used by permission of the publisher.

farming, but there's nothing you get more pleasure out of than planting, growing, and then harvesting. In other words, you get the four seasons just like there are in a person's life—the fall and winter and spring and summer."

Despite this loss of control, most workers stayed with the factory because it provided a steady income and the work seemed easier than farming, at least to some. Forrest Lacock found farming "a very satisfactory job—you've got no boss man." "But," he continued, "the trouble with what we call one-horse farming, you can't have an income sufficient to take care of all your bills. A public job is more interesting because you can meet your bills." Dewey Helms's father had another reason for coming to the mill. "He wasn't worried about the income he made on the farm; he made as much as he cared about. He wanted to get rid of the harder work. Working in the cotton mill was not as hard work as running one of them mountain farms." Mill work was not for everybody, but the majority of those who came to the factories "never did want to live on the farm no more. They learned how to work in the mill."

Reliance on the family labor system meant that the southern textile industry's growth was based to a large extent on the labor of children. Between 1880 and 1910 manufacturers reported that about one-quarter of their work force was under sixteen years of age, and many more child workers went unreported. Indeed, in the industry's early years, youngsters of seven or eight commonly doffed, spun, and did all sorts of casual labor. Originally the official definition of "children" applied to youngsters up to age eight but later rose to age twelve, then fourteen, and finally sixteen; nevertheless, young people remained crucial, both to the industry's profit margins and to their own families' survival.

Child labor was by no means unique to the South. The textile industry, wherever established, tended to rely on the labor of women and children. But the technical breakthroughs that enabled the South to enter and eventually capture the market in cotton goods also encouraged a particularly intense exploitation of the young. Women and children led the first wave of migrants to the region's mills, and manufacturers matched them with the low-skill jobs created by the advent of ring spinning. A study of women and children laborers conducted by the U.S. Bureau of Labor in 1907–8 found that half the spinners were under fourteen and 90 percent were under twenty-one. As Naomi Trammel put it, "That's where they put the children. You could run a frame where you couldn't run anything else."

Technology made child labor practical, but not necessary. The practice spread primarily as a solution to problems of labor recruitment and as a system of socializing and controlling a prospective labor force. South Carolina industrialist William Gregg, founder of Graniteville, the Old South's premier cotton mill, had hoped to attract the daughters of impoverished farmers. Young single women failed to show up in large numbers, but Gregg continued to believe that the "large class of miserable poor white people among us . . . might be induced to place their children in a situation in which they would be educated and reared in industrious habits." His words captured the industry rationale: children made up a large portion of the surplus labor in the country; the lure of wages for everyone in the family could induce hard-pressed farmers to cast their lot with the mills; and children who went to work at an early age would eventually grow into efficient, tractable, long-term workers.

Critics of child labor were not hard to find. In the 1880s and 1890s the opposition was led by the Knights of Labor and the National Union of Textile Workers (NUTW), who complained that the low wages paid to children held down the earnings of adults. But after the turn of the century a new group of middle-class social reformers took up the banner of the child labor crusade. Educational and religious leaders such as Alabama's Edgar Gardner Murphy and North Carolina's Alexander J. McKelway organized opposition at the state level and then helped form the National Child Labor Committee (NCLC). These reformers worried that the mills' unlettered children would one day become a blight on the body politic. "In a democracy," McKelway argued, "the people all rule. Also, the people are ruled. And when it comes to the people's ruling us by their votes, electing our governors and presidents, initiating and vetoing legislation, taxing our incomes, we grow mightily concerned over the intelligence and independence of the electorate. We do not like to trust our interests now and the lives and fortunes of our children to a mass of voters who have been deprived of all opportunity for an education . . . who have been embittered by the robbery of their childhood, who are the material for the agitator, and the prey of the demagogue."

Mill men themselves were divided on the issue of child labor. Some firmly believed that hard work, commencing at a young age, was the best education available. Others championed the practice as a necessary evil in the natural progress of society. Daniel Augustus Tompkins traced the problem to the poverty caused by the Civil War, particularly to the resultant lack of educational opportunities. "In the absence of schools, the discipline of the mill and its training down to twelve years of age is much better for children than idleness and no discipline or training. . . . It would be far better to have ample school facilities and compel all children to go to school ten months in the year, and give them the other two months for vacations and recreation. But in the absence of such facilities, the discipline and training of the mill is best for the children of working people." Whatever the personal feelings of mill men, their duties to their stockholders demanded that they oppose restrictions on the employment of children. The fact of the matter, as the president of the American Cotton Manufacturers Association admitted to McKelway, was that without the labor of boys and girls under the age of fourteen, Piedmont mills simply could not operate.

Bit by bit, reformers chipped away at the opposition. By 1913 North Carolina, South Carolina, Alabama, and Georgia had laws that prohibited the employment of children under twelve and restricted the hours of labor for those below fourteen. Exemptions and lack of enforcement, however, enfeebled state regulations. The 1907–8 Bureau of Labor study found that an astounding 92 percent of the mills in South Carolina and 75 percent of those in North Carolina ignored child labor regulations. Flora McKinney's boss was one of those who paid little attention to the law. Her family moved to Lando, South Carolina, when she was nine or ten, and she soon followed her father into the mill. "When I got old enough, well, I really weren't old enough, but they'd take children to work then. We were supposed to be twelve years old before we could go to work, but I've hid from inspectors a lots of times. They'd come through and the section in front of us would send word to hide the kids, and we'd run to the water house. Then we'd all cram in there 'til they left."

Given the inadequacy of state legislation, members of the NCLC felt the need for federal action. To mobilize public opinion against child labor, the NCLC devised a highly effective propaganda campaign. Key to this effort were the photographs of Lewis Hine, which poignantly revealed the youthfulness of southern workers. Hine's images—of little girls dressed in long skirts and aprons and little boys wearing their workingmen's caps and suspenders, all swallowed up in rows of towering machines—became the crusade's symbols of the worst evils of industrialization. The NCLC convinced the public and members of Congress that the employment of children had to be stopped. In 1916 President Woodrow Wilson signed the Keating-Owen Child Labor bill to achieve that end.

Adamantly opposed to federal intervention, which might open the way to other protective laws and undermine their competitive advantage over the North, southern industrialists fought back. When federal child labor legislation was first suggested, David Clark, editor of the *Southern Textile Bulletin,* organized mill owner opposition. The son of Walter Clark, who was chief justice of the North Carolina Supreme Court and one of the South's most liberal jurists, David Clark seemed an unlikely opponent of progressive reform. But as a young man, Clark embarked on a course quite different from his father's. After earning degrees in civil and mechanical engineering from the North Carolina College of Agriculture and Mechanic Arts and Cornell University in the late 1890s, David entered the textile business, first as a mill designer and later as an investor. When his own mill failed in 1907, he turned to textile journalism. As founder and editor of the *Southern Textile Bulletin,* Clark gained a reputation as "a volunteer spokesman for an ultra-conservative philosophy in business and education matters" and "a stirrer-upper of no mean proportions." Shortly after passage of the Keating-Owen bill, he arranged to test the constitutionality of the law. At Clark's behest, a Charlotte mill worker—perhaps fearful of losing his job, his children's earnings, or a combination of the two—petitioned the courts to restrain a local mill from discharging his two underage sons. A federal judge agreed that the law violated the rights of the worker, and a year later the Supreme Court concurred. The child labor law was dead.

Despite this setback, child labor gradually did decline, largely in response to changes in the industry and the growing supply of adult workers. The trend toward finer yarns, the integration of yarn spinning with cloth-weaving operations that required more strength and skill, and the technological advances of the 1920s all worked against the practice. By World War I the number of children under sixteen employed in the Carolinas had decreased to 6 percent of the total work force, almost the level in the leading New England textile states. Yet until 1938, when the federal Fair Labor Standards Act outlawed employment of children under sixteen, many southern industrialists skirted the law so as to make use of the mill village's young, and captive, work force.

Child labor involved more, however, than the exploitation of youth. There were stories behind the expressions captured on film by Lewis Hine, stories that fit neither the rationalizations of mill owners nor the fears of reformers. Mill work was a source of pride as well as pain, of fun as much as suffering; and children made choices, however hedged about by their parents' authority and their bosses' power.

For mill children, life was paced from the outset by the ringing of the factory bell. Working women, who often had to return to their jobs within a few weeks of childbirth, adapted their nursing schedule to breaks in the workday. "People used to go out," recalled Ada Mae Wilson. "They didn't have bottle babies like they do now. They nursed the breast. A lot healthier children. You'd come out at nine o'clock, and then at twelve you'd come home for lunch. And then at three they'd let you come back, and then you'd be off at six." If labor was scarce, a woman who had neither relatives nor older children at home might take her baby to the mill. Jessie Lee Carter had a neighbor with a nursing baby who would "take a quilt and lay that baby in her roping box while she worked. And she'd bring her baby down and keep it in the mill all day long."

As children got older, the mill was like a magnet, attracting their youthful curiosity and, all too soon, their labor. Until the 1920s no barbed wire fences, locked gates, or bricked-in windows separated the factory from the village. Children could easily wander in and out of the mill, and their first "work" might be indistinguishable from play. After school and in the summers, Emma Williams accompanied her mother to the mill. "I'm sure I didn't work for the money. I just wanted to work, I reckon. Oodles of kids. All of us used to do it together. [We] didn't do much, and it was real fun. I guess maybe one reason that it was fun was because that was the only time we got with other children. When we stayed home, well, we stayed home."

Most children first learned about factory labor when they tagged along with a parent or sibling, carried hot meals to the mill at dinnertime, or stopped by after school. But this casual contact had serious consequences, for on such visits relatives began teaching children the skills they would need when they were old enough for jobs of their own. Ethel Faucette carried lunch to her sister. "While she was eating," Faucette explained, "I learned how to work her job. I was already learned when I went to work." Geddes Dodson's father gave him specific chores during his daily visits. "When I was a little fellow, my daddy was a-working in the Poinsett Mill. He was a loom fixer. He'd run the weavers' looms through the dinner hour so they could go eat their dinner. We lived about a mile and a quarter from the mill, and I'd carry his lunch every day. He'd tell me to come on in the mill, and he made me fill his batteries while he run the weavers' looms—and I was just a little fellow. See, I knew a whole lot about the mill before I ever went in one."

"Helping," then, was a family affair, a form of apprenticeship by which basic skills and habits were transmitted to each new generation. But helping was also a vital part of the family economy and the mill labor system. A child's help could increase a parent's or older sibling's piecework earnings or simply relieve the strain of keeping up production. An Englishman who reported on the American textile industry visited a mill in South Carolina where weavers who had their sons or little brothers helping could take on two additional looms. Besides, with parents working twelve-hour days in the mills, children often had no place else to go. Owners profited from such family needs. Early child labor legislation in the Carolinas only prohibited "employing" children under certain ages, so owners could stay within the letter of the law by "permitting" or "suffering" underage children to "help." A story related by a federal investigator in Georgia illustrated the system's coercive potential. "A woman reported that her little daughter ten years old worked every day helping her sisters. The child quit for a while, but the overseer said to the mother, 'Bring her in; the two girls cannot tend those machines without her.' The mother asked that the child be given work by herself, but the overseer replied that the law would not permit it."

Given the laxity of enforcement, mill owners could essentially set their own policies according to individual conscience or the bottom line of profit and loss. Allie Smith provided a child's-eye view of the confusion that often resulted. Shortly after Allie's birth, her family moved to Saxapahaw, a community in Alamance County on the Haw River. By the time they left for Carrboro, in neighboring Orange County, when Allie was eleven, she knew how to spin from having helped an older sister. But Julian Shakespeare Carr, owner of the Carrboro mill, believed that mill men should voluntarily avoid child labor in order to stave off government interference. "When we moved to Carrboro," Allie recalled, "I thought I could go in and help her, and I did. But Mr. Carr owned this cotton mill, and I hadn't been over here long when he came over and said I couldn't come in and help. I would have to be on the payroll, so they put me on the payroll. And I worked there, I don't know how long—several months—and they said I couldn't work unless my father signed me up for being twelve years old. Well, he wouldn't do it. He said he didn't want me to work. They put me out and wouldn't let me work. And then when I got to be twelve, I went in and went to work."

Playing and helping could thus shade into full-time work. But getting that first official, full-time job was a major turning point. Managers, parents, and children themselves influenced the decision. Occasionally, mills openly dictated the age at which a child had to begin work. In 1904 the owners of a South Carolina mill mandated that "all children, members of a family about twelve years of age, shall work in the mill and shall not be excused from service therein without the consent of the superintendent for good cause." More often, pressure came from supervisors, who were personally responsible for keeping a quota of workers on hand. Jessie Lee Carter was four in 1905 when her family left their Tennessee farm for the Brandon Mill in Greenville. Six of her older brothers and sisters went to work right away; eight years later Jessie joined them. "When I got twelve years old, my uncle [who was a second hand in the spinning room] come to my daddy, and daddy let me quit school and go to work." During slack times children like Jessie Lee could be sent back to school, then called in again when the need arose.

For a large family with many mouths to feed, outside pressure was often unnecessary. Lela Ranier's parents took her out of school when she was twelve and sent her to the mill. "Ma thought it was time. They thought maybe it would help 'em out, you know. They was making such a little bit. And they thought the little bit I made would help." Lacy Wright's father asked him to quit school when he reached twelve because his two oldest sisters had married and Lacy's father could not support the family on $1.25 a day. Other children realized the importance of their labor to the family's well-being and took it upon themselves to get a job. This was particularly true in families where the father was dead or disabled. Grover Hardin, for example, dropped out of school after the second grade. "I started out in the mill—the main reason—to help my mother. She wanted me to go to school until I got in the fifth grade. I told her, 'You need the help worse than I need the education, because I can get it later on, or I can do without it.' And so I went to work as quick as I possibly could. I started in as a sweeper."

Many parents wanted their children to stay in school, but youngsters often had their own plans. Ila Dodson insisted on quitting school when she was fourteen. "I wanted to make my own money. I done had two sisters go to work, and I seen how they was having money, and so I couldn't stand it no longer. My parents wanted me to go on to school, but I couldn't see that. Back then, didn't too many children go on to high school. It was just a common thing that when they'd get old enough, let them go to work. I like to worried them to death." Finally, Ila's parents relented and agreed to sign her worker's permit, required at that time in South Carolina for children under sixteen. But, she recalled, "Mama wouldn't even take me to town to get it, and my daddy wouldn't go with me. I said, 'Well, give me the Bible and give me a dime and I'll go get it.' A nickel streetcar fare up there and a nickel back, and I [took] the Bible because I had to prove my age."

Alice Evitt and Curtis Enlow also preferred mill work to schoolwork. "They'd let you go in there seven, eight years old," Alice recalled. "I'd go in there and mess around with my sisters; they'd be spinning. I liked to put up the ends and spin a little bit, so when I got twelve years old, I wanted to quit school. So I just quit and went to work, and I was twelve years old!" Both of Curtis's parents and two of his sisters worked in the card room at a Greenville mill. During summer vacation Curtis joined them there. "I was about thirteen years old, and I decided I would go to work. Well, I went to work, and my dad says if I quit when school started, he'd let me work. I went back to school, but I wasn't learning nothing—I didn't think I was. So I went and told him, and he says, 'All right, you ain't learning nothing. Well, you can go back to the mill.'"

Mamie Shue's parents had better luck keeping her in school. Although North Carolina's compulsory education law at the time required attendance only until age fourteen, Mamie's folks used it to frighten her into staying in school until she was sixteen. "I hated school all my life. But my parents told me if I didn't go to school, they'd put my daddy in jail. And I loved my daddy to death. So I went to school 'til I was sixteen." She did, however, start working after school in the spooling room. "I was fifteen when I started doing that. So when I was sixteen years old, they just give me a job, 'cause I could spool as good as the rest of them."

Learning to "spool as good as the rest of them" was often a by-product of helping in the mills, but for those who had not started out as helpers—and even for some who had—learning constituted a memorable initiation into shop floor life. Few mills had a formal training program. Instead, "they would put you with someone to train you," or "your parents would take you in and train you theirself." Parents and surrogate parents took time out from their own work, which sometimes cost money out of their pockets, to help the young learn a trade. "That's the way the whole generation in Lando learned what they knowed," remembered John Guinn, "by the older generation." From the evidence of our interviews, adults did so willingly and well.

Mill managers expected children to master their jobs within a set length of time, usually about six weeks. During that period children worked for free or for a token wage. "I don't think they paid us anything to learn. But after we learnt, we got a job, a machine of our own." Some mills used this probationary period to take advantage of young people who were eager to work in the mill. Mary Thompson saw this happen in Greenville. "When I first went to work at Slater, they had boys to put up the warps on the back of the frames because they was heavy. They'd go out there in the country and get them boys and hire them and tell them they'd have to work six weeks without money. Well, that just tickled them to death, that they'd get a chance to work in a mill. And they'd work them six weeks, and they'd find something wrong with them and lay them off, and get other boys. And they run it a long time like that."

Almost all workers recalled proudly their ability to learn their jobs despite their youth. Naomi Trammell was an orphan when she went to work in the Victor Mill at Greer, South Carolina. "Well, I didn't know hardly about mill work, but I just went in and had to learn it. Really, I had to crawl up on the frame, because I wasn't tall enough. I was a little old spindly thing. I wasn't the only one, there's a whole place like that. And they had mothers and daddies [but they] wasn't no better off than I was. They had to learn us, but it didn't take me long to learn. They'd put us with one of the spinners and they'd show us how. It was easy to learn—all we had to do was just put that bobbin in there and put it up." Children learned quickly because most entry-level jobs required more dexterity than the technical know-how. It took a while to be proficient, but most children could learn the rudiments of spinning, spooling, or doffing in a few weeks. . . .

Workers' health was another casualty of the drive for profits in a region that placed no restrictions on capital and offered workers no protection.

Without unions, and without the legal and administrative apparatus that now provides a basic level of industrial health and safety, millhands were at the mercy of dangerous machinery. The threat to a worker's health could be as sudden and violent as the snapping of a bone or as insidious as the relentless clouding of a lung.

Cotton dust was a killer in the card room. "Some of that dust was terrible," Carl Durham remembered. "Whew! That dust would accumulate and you had to strip them cards out every three hours, get all that stuff out. It would get to where it wouldn't do its work, it would be so full of particles and dust. When I was coming along, and for a long time, that was all in the air. It's a wonder I can breathe, but somehow or another it didn't affect me like it did some folks. It just killed some folks." Durham's observations echoed the findings of medical researchers on both sides of the Atlantic. Cotton dust caused a number of health problems, sometimes resulting in death, but it did not affect everyone in the same way. It is now well understood that byssinosis, or brown lung, is a disease that results from prolonged exposure to cotton dust. Although the British government recognized the existence of byssinosis and began compensating victims in 1940, lack of research and resistance by the textile industry delayed any action on the disease in the United States until the 1970s.

Anyone who worked in the card room knew that the dust caused problems, but, like Grover Hardin, they "didn't pay much attention to it. See, there was a continuous fog of dust in the carding department at all times. When you hit the mill on Monday morning, you'd have a tough time. You'd cough and sneeze and fill your mouth full of tobacco and anything else to keep this dust from strangling you." This "Monday morning sickness" was the first stage of byssinosis, caused by irritation of the air passages. There would be little recurrence of the problem during the rest of the week as workers adjusted to the dust. But the coughing returned every Monday because a day or two away from the mill increased "susceptibility." After a period of ten years or more, the coughing became more persistent. Grover Hardin "got to noticing it bothering me. I took these coughs and I couldn't get over them, and I'd go home and cough and cough and cough." Rather than pay doctor's fees, he asked the advice of other workers who had the same problem—"the ones that was able to go to the doctor, I'll put it like that." Most told him they had "a little touch of asthma," so Grover took "home remedies" for asthma. "As time passed on, it'd get worse. On Mondays, I'd go in and it'd sure enough be worse by the night. Tuesday, Wednesday, it'd get a little better. I guess I'd get my lungs plugged up good. Over the weekend you'd clear your lungs up pretty good, then Monday morning, it'd be the same thing."

Like many workers with byssinosis, Hardin gradually began having difficulty running his job and started missing work. "Nothing I could take for asthma would do this breathing any good. I couldn't get no air in my lungs, and I slowed up. It got to where I had to push on the job to stay up in the mill. And when I'd get a spare minute I'd go over and lay in the windows and get all the air I could." Finally, he had to quit.

Dust was only one hazard in the card room. Accidents around the machinery mangled hands and arms; one worker called carding the "dangerousest job in the mill." In the early days, belts connected the machines to drive shafts high above, and carders had to pay careful attention as they cleaned and adjusted their equipment. "It was pretty dangerous," explained Carl Thompson. "You'd have to watch yourself. There were so many things that you could do. Even cleaning up, if maybe your brush would get caught in a belt or a pulley, it's going to jerk your hand. I've seen them jerked in the cards thataway and maybe get their whole arm and all broke and the skin pulled off, maybe slam through the bone."

One incident in particular accounted for Thompson's fears. "I'd seen so many get hurt on them, get their arms broke. That was when they had overhead pulleys, had the pulleys at the top of the mill. There was one man, his shirt or something or other got caught in the belt, and that belt throwed him to the top of the mill and busted his brains out. He just hit the ceiling of the mill. They had big beams up there, and he hit them, right at the back of his head. It killed him."

Working conditions were even more disagreeable in the weave room. The environment was dominated by the constant noise of banging looms and the eerie mist that descended from overhead sprinklers. "It was a loud, noisy place, and awful dusty and linty," remembered Edna Hargett. The moisture was particularly troublesome. "The weave room was always wet," explained Mack Duncan. "Back then, you had to have a lot of water in the weave room. The air wasn't conditioned like it is now, scientifically; there was just water being sprayed out. It was atomized and sprayed out to make the weaving run. It was wet in the back alley. There was a loom fixer taking a loom down one time, and he slipped and grabbed at the beam on the rail, and the beam probably weighed two hundred and fifty pounds, maybe more. It was above him, and it fell on him and killed him."

Less dramatic than occasional accidents, but no less threatening, were the complications that resulted from breathing warm, moist air filled with lint. Naomi Trammell was one of the fortunate ones; she had a doctor who recognized the problem. "I went to the weave room one time, and I like to took galloping TB. It'd be just wet all over, so hot, you know. And that just give 'em TB. That doctor told me when he doctored me about two weeks, 'Now, young lady, you can go back to the cloth room and live, or you can go back to the weave room and die, whichever you want to do.' So I went back to the cloth room."

Spinning had its own peculiar hazards. "Oh, it was awful hot," Alice Evitt remembered. "All that machinery a-runnin' makin' heat. It was bad. Terrible hot out here. You'd come out of there, your clothes was plumb wet." Mozelle Riddle described conditions in the Bynum mill. "It used to be so hot before they put air-conditioning in there. You could walk into the frames and burn your legs, that's how hot the heat was. Them motors'd burn you, when you'd walk around them. But we just got used to it. Didn't think nothing about it. It'd be eighty, oh shoot, it'd be ninety degrees in there in that spinning room.

Work and sweat, yes sir." Eva Hopkins recalled the heat, too. "They didn't have air-conditioning in the mills and it was terribly hot. They wouldn't let you raise the windows very high: air would come in; it would make the ends come down. Sometimes they'd let you prop a bobbin under them. I'd put the window up at the end of my frame, then here'd come the section man along and take it down. When he'd leave and go off, I'd raise it again. I couldn't stand the heat."

The threat of serious injuries was all around. Most of the fast-moving machine parts were exposed, and any slip-up could have disastrous consequences. Alice Evitt remembered getting her "apron tore off two or three times a week" while running speeder frames. "Back then, they didn't wear pants. Them big flyers flyin' around, they'd grab you and just wind your apron plumb up. I was just lucky I managed to stop 'em and didn't get my arms in them. Them flyers would break your bones. I know one lady—I didn't see her get it done—but she said she wore wigs [because] she'd got her hair caught and it pulled her whole scalp out—every bit of her hair. Them speeders was bad to catch you." Evitt and her co-workers often joked about such things. "Sometimes they'd get under the frames and reach and get a-hold of somebody's dress and jerk 'em. Make 'em think the machine had 'em. Try to scare them."

When accidents did occur, there was little relief for those who suffered. "Back before now," Mack Duncan recalled, "if you got hurt on the job, you just was hurt. If you couldn't work, you had to go home; you lost your pay. Back before World War II you didn't get much help." James Pharis remained bitter about the way he was treated when he had an accident in the mill. "I was about nine or ten years old when I got that hand hurt. I was riding on an elevator rope in the mill. My hand got caught under the wheel. That thing was mashed into jelly; all of it was just smashed to pieces. They took me down to the company store—the drug store was in the front end of the company store—never even notified my people or nothing. There were only two doctors in town at that time, and both of them was out of town on country calls. I sat there until about four o'clock. Nobody done nothing in the world for me. My people was never notified. Nothing said about it. You tear yourself all to pieces then, nothing said about getting anything out of it. Poor people like us, no use in suing. Poor people didn't stand a chance. If you done anything the company didn't like, they'd just fire you and tell the rest of [the owners] not to hire you. So there'd you be. People who lived under them circumstances, back in them days, was nothing they could do. So they didn't try to do nothing."

Lloyd Davidson summed up the situation. "The only insurance back then they had was to protect the company. They looked out for the company interest, but you didn't have any benefit. There was no retirement, no hospitalization, no benefits whatsoever, as far as for helping you. They carried insurance to protect the company. [People] probably have [sued], but it's a losing cause when you do. They have their own lawyers and they always have the upper hand, you might say. Kind of like David and Goliath. I reckon you could put it that way." . . .

REVIEW QUESTIONS

1. From this account, what would you conclude to be the most important reasons for people to be attracted to work in the mills? Were the reasons the same for children as they were for adult workers?

2. Detail the pros and cons of child labor from the point of view of mill workers, mill owners, and outsiders.

3. What specific conditions in the mills were dangerous or unhealthy for workers? To what extent do you suppose such conditions were duplicated or approximated in other industries, such as mining, steel making, or railroading?

4. How do you explain the apparent callousness of mill owners concerning the dangers their workers faced on the job? Why were the workers able to do so little to improve conditions?

5. To what extent have safety conditions in industrial work improved? Are workers in any industries today exposed to dangers comparable to those in the early textile mills?

FOR FURTHER READING

C. Vann Woodward, *The Origins of the New South, 1877–1913* (1951), is a general history of the South with particular emphasis on its economic development. Edward L. Ayers, *The Promise of the New South* (1992), is a more recent treatment of the same subject. Melton A. McLaurin, *Paternalism and Protest: Southern Cotton Mill Workers and Organized Labor* (1971), and David Carlton, *Mill and Town in South Carolina, 1880–1920* (1982), deal with the same subject as the present selection. Ronald D. Eller, *Miners, Millhands, and Mountaineers: Industrialization of the Appalachian South, 1880–1930* (1982), tells another part of the story of southern factory labor. Stanley Buder, *Pullman: An Experiment in Industrial Order and Community Planning, 1880–1930* (1967), and Crandall A. Shifflett, *Coal Towns: Life, Work, and Culture in Company Towns of Southern Appalachia, 1880–1960* (1991), both deal with company towns similar to those described in the selection. Melvin Dubofsky, *Industrialism and the American Worker, 1865–1920* (1975), has a more general focus. The essays in Herbert Gutman's *Work, Culture, and Society in Industrializing America* (1976), also discuss the working and living conditions American workers confronted in the late 1800s. Edward C. Kirkland, *Dream and Thought in the Business Community, 1860–1900* (1956), describes the ideas and values held by most American businessmen of the time, while Daniel T. Rodgers, *The Work Ethic in Industrial America, 1850–1920* (1978), analyzes a widely held and fundamentally important set of beliefs.

Pennsylvania State Archives, Charles H. Burg Collection

Strikers on their way to the Lattimer mines.

5

Labor Violence in Industrial America

MICHAEL NOVAK

Today state and federal laws protect the rights of workers to form unions and engage in collective bargaining for higher wages and better working conditions, but this was not the case in the late 1800s. Then, when workers tried to organize and act together to protect themselves against wage cuts, job insecurity, and long hours of labor, often under dangerous and unhealthy conditions, employers and others responded with fear and anger, especially when workers went on strike in the attempt to enforce their demands. This clash of interests and feelings resulted in many outbreaks of labor violence, such as the railroad strike of 1877, the strike by steel workers at Homestead, Pennsylvania in 1892, the Pullman strike in 1894, and dozens of others.

The present selection focuses on the massacre of nineteen Slavic miners in an eastern Pennsylvania coal town in 1897. The tragedy reveals elements common to many other instances of labor violence during the period. For example, when workers went out on strike, it was a fairly common practice for employers to hire armed private police. The stated reasons for this were "to preserve order" and "to protect private property," but usually the purpose was to guarantee that employers would have enough force on their side to break the strike by whatever means they thought necessary. In addition, employers usually had the support of local law enforcement officials and were often able to call on state and even the national government for help.

Finally, whenever the strikers were mostly foreign-born, as they were at Lattimer, ethnic and religious prejudices intensified the hatred directed toward them.

The outcome of the story of what happened at Lattimer is also important in understanding the labor situation at the time. Although the account makes clear that the sheriff and the deputies who killed the strikers could well be considered guilty of multiple counts of outright murder, they were never convicted; the jury at their trial chose to overlook much of the evidence. Some of the nation's newspapers criticized the verdict, but most applauded it, sharing the sentiments of the New York *Sun,* which said that the outcome showed that "American civilization is safe under the protection of the law."

On Friday morning, the sun rose brilliant. A gang of the breaker boys from Harwood planned to go swimming. By the time the men began to assemble for the march to Lattimer Mines, some had already been out over the hills in Butler Valley to pick berries. At nine o'clock, John Hlavaty, a Slovak from Lattimer, came to the home of Thomas Racek in Harwood and said again that the men at Lattimer planned to walk out that afternoon if the men from Harwood would come to call them out. Racek took Hlavaty to Jacob Sivar's house, and they called the men together. There was still discussion as to whether a large crowd should go to Lattimer or whether they should just send a committee. Some said everyone should go, or else the company might blacklist the men on the committee. This idea was generally approved.

The men recalled John Fahy's instructions of the night before about the sheriff and his armed men. Fahy had warned them not even to take marching sticks, like the garden fence poles that walkers in these parts usually carried. He instructed them about the rights of free assembly, but also about the sheriff's use of the riot act. Yesterday, he told them, the sheriff's men had fired warning shots and were reported to be more and more hostile; great caution was necessary. Fahy did not plan to accompany the marchers to Lattimer. He said he would be posting signs in nearby Milnesville; he would come over to Lattimer later. He never took part in marches.

John Eagler, who was to lead the march, was excited. He had sent a message to Alex McMullen inviting the McAdoo men to come along. McMullen said no. Echoing Fahy, he warned Eagler again not to march without an American flag. So Eagler told the men to hold off until he could find a flag to

---

From *The Guns of Lattimer,* by Michael Novak. Copyright © 1978 by Michael Novak.

carry. With three companions, Andro Sivar, Joseph Michalko, and August Kosko, he hiked over to Humboldt.

Those who waited behind decided that the youngest boys would not be permitted to march. It would be twelve miles or more, round trip, under a broiling sun. Only boys over fifteen would be allowed to accompany the men; these were sent inside to put on shoes and decent dress. Some of the men may have fortified themselves with a little whiskey; in any case, the sheriff was later to allege so. Meanwhile, unknown to the marchers, someone from Harwood—possibly an employee at the company store—telephoned Sheriff Martin about the plan to march, its route, and destination.

In the days just before the march, visible signs of conflict frightened some of the American women of Harwood, who nervously embroidered on them at the trial. Thus, for example, Mrs. Catherine Weisenborn heard one foreigner threaten another: "If you don't come, we'll kill you." She also testified she heard some strikers threaten people like her: "We'll show the *white people* what we'll do when we come back!" . . .

By the time John Eagler got back, the men had had time for an early lunch. A cheer went up when they saw Eagler and Sivar return with not one, but two flags. Stragglers poured out of the houses. Steve Jurich kissed his pretty bride, and the others teased them both. The older men waved good-bye to their families. At almost every doorway and out in the street women and children waved and shouted as the men moved into position. Eagler and Joseph Michalko walked down the line, telling individuals to discard their walking sticks and suggesting that they start out four abreast. There were between 250 and 300 men. They started from two separate locations and met at the picnic grounds. Joseph Michalko and Steve Jurich walked out in front with the American flags snapping in the breeze. A crowd of breaker boys fell in behind the flags, but their elders sent them unhappily away. As this unarmed band got themselves organized to answer the request of their Italian brothers at the Lattimer Mines, many were taking part in the first civic act of their lives. Most had not been in the previous marches; Eagler hadn't; Cheslak hadn't. Most had never laid eyes on Sheriff Martin; none, perhaps, had seen the guns of the deputies. It was just after one when the command "Forward march!" was shouted by Michalko.

As they walked along, they picked up new recruits. They did not aim to create a big crowd, and they did not plan to have a large rally. Frequently, they called out to friends lined up to watch them on their route. . . . The men were relaxed and festive. For the past year, most had worked only one day out of every two, and the activities of the strike—giving promise of some small but basic changes in their lives—seemed far preferable to being out of work.

The night before, the strikers had formulated three grievances and taken them to the superintendent at Harwood. They demanded a pay raise of 10¢ a day, a reduction in the price of powder from $2.75 a keg to $1.50, and an end to the company store and the company doctor. They particularly resented the prices at the company store: a dozen eggs that cost 13¢ at an independent store cost 23¢ from the company; butter at 8¢ a pound elsewhere cost 26¢; and the powder they needed for their work came from the manufacturer at 90¢ to $1.00 a keg. On the average, excess charges to miners in the Hazleton region worked out to $217.50 per capita per annum.

Their ranks swollen by recruits from Crystal Ridge and Cranberry, four hundred men were now raising a cloud of dust on their way toward Hazleton, jackets over their arms, their handkerchiefs often in use to wipe their necks and brows. No effort was made on this day, as there had been on others, to close down other breakers as they passed. They passed the Cranberry breaker, calling to their friends, shouting threats to scab workers. The marchers were unarmed and determined to be peaceful, in order to avoid trouble with the sheriff.

The strikers felt patriotic under the flag. They also felt protected. Marching down into the valley and up the opposite hill, the thin yellow dust rising in the still air behind them, many felt a surge of purpose and accomplishment. John Eagler, at nineteen, although walking at their head, was not really in charge; neither was Michalko. Older leaders like Anthony Novotny, Mike Cheslak, Andrej Sivar, and others quite naturally talked things through and decisions emerged among them by common consent. Each had been carefully reared not to be boastful, assertive, or proud. No one should be in the position of attracting criticism. The traditions of serfdom and peasant life operated like censors upon anyone who might stand out too far above the group. Oppression from above had been internalized. The community cut would-be leaders down to size.

Harwood lay two miles southwest of Hazleton. The plan was to proceed by the road at the bottom of Buck Mountain and on up through the city of Hazleton. This would be the shortest route to Lattimer Mines on the far northeast side of town. Even so, the march would be about six miles.

It was almost two when the marchers in the front line caught sight of armed men hurrying toward them in West Hazleton. . . .

Deputy Ario Pardee Platt boasted of ancestors who had fought in the Revolutionary War, in the War of 1812, and in the Civil War. (During 1861–65, little Hazleton had supplied almost two thousand men to the Union cause.) Platt was the chief bookkeeper of the Pardee company, and the general manager of its company stores in Hazleton, Harwood, and Lattimer Mines. It made his blood boil to see all these foreigners carrying the flag his ancestors had championed. Platt was looking for action, he had wanted action all along and was not happy with the overcareful way the sheriff had been handling things.

Thomas Hall, another deputy, was a leader in the Coal and Iron Police. He was a man who had organized the posse for the sheriff and who directed it in the sheriff's absence. Before the strike had even begun, as far back as August 12, the owners of the mine companies had called a meeting in Hazleton to discuss their dissatisfaction with the performance of the Coal and Iron Police. Even without a strike looming up before them, they were complaining that they were paying for one hundred policemen, paying well, too, and not getting the protection they needed. The police were spending too much time at Hungarian weddings, they said, and not enough time protecting property. They were paying for protection and they intended to have it. The tenor of the meeting was then leaked to the newspapers. So now, only one month later, Thomas Hall was not of a mind to occasion any further dissatisfaction from his employers. It would be his task to teach Sheriff Martin the way things were done in the lower end of the county and to keep the pressure on him to do them. His own neck was at stake.

Deputy Alonzo Dodson was a miner who lived in Hazleton. He was heard to say, "We ought to get so much a head for shooting down these strikers. I would do it for a cent a head to make money at it."

Deputies George and James Ferry—the latter known to everyone as Pinky—were also heard to say at Mckenna's Corner that they would blow the strikers' brains out. Perhaps it was the power of suggestion that was working on the consciousness of the deputies, for one of them, Harry Diehl, even threatened to blow out the brains of Herman Pottunger, if he did not get off the road. Pottunger himself heard Deputy Wesley Hall say of the marchers: "I'd like to get a pop at them." . . .

Also among the deputies were Robert Tinner, the superintendent of the Central Pennsylvania Telephone and Supply Company, Willard Young, a lumber merchant and contractor, and Samuel B. Price, who held the contract to build a new breaker in Harwood, work on which was being held up by the strike. All in all about forty deputies had accompanied Sheriff Martin to West Hazleton. Nearly all these men owed their livelihood, or a portion of it, to the mining companies. Other deputies were waiting for the marchers at Lattimer.

Sheriff Martin's fondest hope seems clearly to have been to put an end to the march right at West Hazleton. But he was in something of a spot. He knew he didn't have jurisdiction inside the city, at least not without consultation, and the marchers had already reached McKenna's Corner. He was being pressured to "teach the strikers a lesson" that would get them off the roads. His own inclination still seemed to be to keep matters peaceable and under his control.

The sheriff walked directly toward the two men carrying flags, Andro Sivar and Joseph Michalko. He had his pistol in one hand. He took the nearest man, John Yurchekowicz, by the coat, brandishing the revolver in his face, and announced vigorously: "I'm the sheriff of Luzerne County, and you cannot go to Lattimer."

Steve Juszko pushed past Yurchekowicz, saying defiantly, "Me no stop. Me go to Lattimer."

The sheriff again said: "If you go to Lattimer, you must kill me first."

John Eagler, who had been fifty paces back in the line when it stopped, walked forward and now spoke up in a reedy voice. "We ain't goin' to. We are going to Lattimer. We harm no one. We are within the law."

Before the words were fully out of Eagler's mouth, Anthony Kislewicz [variants: Kascavage, etc.] bent over for a flat rock (he later said) to strike a match for his pipe during the halt. One of the deputies brought the butt of his rifle down viciously on Kislewicz's arm. Then Deputy Hall moved toward Steve Juszko, who had stepped forward, and swung through the air twice with his rifle butt, crunching across the two arms the boy raised to protect himself and hitting his head. Blood flowed. Both arms hung limp.

The sheriff pointed his pistol right and left as though holding off a legion.

Ario Pardee Platt, fired up by the bloodshed, ripped the flag from Joseph Michalko's hands, broke the stick across his knee, and stood there shredding the flag with contempt. He dropped the torn rags in the dust.

John Eagler, watching Deputy Cook raise his gun, stopped to pick up a stone. The sheriff waved his pistol and Eagler dropped the stone. Other deputies mixed it up briskly with the marchers.

Deputy Cook fired a shot into the air and the hillside reverberated. The marchers did not move. They were baffled.

John Eagler stepped forward to obtain the name of the deputy he had seen hit Juszko. Sheriff Martin held Eagler with a gesture and pulled a paper from his pocket. The sheriff had seen disorder and now had his opportunity. "This is my proclamation and you can't go any farther. It's against the law."

Then Chief of Police Jones walked forward shouting to John Eagler and the sheriff, and Sheriff Martin put his paper back in his pocket. Jones told the sheriff the strikers had a right to march peacefully, and he, the sheriff, knew it. To Novotny the chief said he had confidence in the way the marchers were conducting themselves; he would let them march around the edges of West Hazleton but not go through the city. He was willing to show them how they could go, so as to continue on to Lattimer in peace. . . .

Murderous joking, meanwhile, seems to have gripped the deputies. They had talked all morning about shooting and killing. Herman Pottunger heard a deputy say quietly to a friend: "I bet I drop six of them when I get over there." August Katski and Martin Lochar stood near the trolley car as the departing deputies were boarding. Two deputies went after them and hit them, but one said: "Let them go until we get to Lattimer and then we'll shoot them." It may have been a form of macabre humor, intended only to frighten.

William A. Evans, the reporter, arrived just after the confrontation, while the men were still standing on opposite sides of the road. He saw one of the strikers picking up a stone as Ario Pardee Platt tore the flag. No stone was actually thrown.

Doctor John Koons of Hazleton was called by the chief of police to treat the two wounded men in the jail. One of the men—Juszko—had to be examined by force. His scalp wounds required nine stitches. Juszko appears to have been listed the next day as among the wounded in the hospital. Six months later, he was still unable to use his arms.

Chief Jones did, as he offered, point the way for the marchers to cut through West Hazleton, adding another mile or so to the trip. It was after 2:30 when the marchers returned to their original plan. Now only one American flag waved in the sun, but the men were feeling vindicated and safe under the law. Mike Krupa from Crystal Ridge had joined them in West Hazleton with several of his friends, and the marchers made Krupa and his friends throw away their walking sticks. George Yamshak also joined them and was told to throw away the small stick he was carrying. The marchers had learned that their best protection was lack of arms. . . .

Later, the editorialists were not to overlook the symbolism of the day and the hour. It was almost three o'clock and the detachment of deputies assigned to wait at Lattimer was restless. A mile away, at Harleigh, Sheriff Martin and the deputies who had seen action at West Hazleton sat in the trolley and waited. Some removed plug hats to wipe away the sweat under their hatbands. Others fingered their Winchesters. A few of them were later to claim that they believed then that the miners had guns in their pockets; some even may have believed it. . . .

For the deputies sitting on that trolley in front of Farley's Hotel in Harleigh, the waiting was almost over. In a cloud of dust, the marchers were beginning to appear around the bend, the lone American flag still at their head. The deputies watched the strikers pause while eight men or so from the first two lines huddled. The other marchers broke ranks to drink water from a pump. The question for the huddled leaders, posed by John Eagler, was whether to march first to breaker Number One in Lattimer Mines or to breaker Number Three. Finally the strikers started walking again. John Laudmesser, the hotel-keeper, counted the marchers as they passed, there were 424. . . .

In the past, strikers had often changed plans in unexpected ways, and the sheriff was taking no chances. He ordered the trolley to stay right alongside the marchers. For almost a mile, deputies and strikers went along eyeing one another. A few insults may have been exchanged. At the last fork in the road, when it was plain that the strikers could be taking no other road except into Lattimer, the sheriff ordered the trolley to speed up and race ahead to the village.

In Lattimer there was by now considerable commotion. The colliery whistle sounded a warning. Those deputies and private police who had already been waiting in Lattimer had made their preparations. One of them told Mrs. Craig, "Go inside, as there may be some shooting today." Trolley cars shuttled in from Milnesville, Drifton, and points north. Doors slammed. Some mothers hurried to the school to bring their children home. Fear of the foreigners had been intense ever since the Tuesday before, when a band of noisy strikers had marched through the village.

On his arrival by trolley, Sheriff Martin took command of the assembling deputies. His force, bolstered by some of the new deputies from Drifton, now numbered almost one hundred and fifty. Some of them stood guard at the breakers and the superintendent's office. He divided the others into three companies, under Samuel Price, A. E. Hess, and Thomas Hall. He called the men down off the trolley bank and stationed them across the single road leading into Lattimer, just before it forked into Main Street and Quality Row, with the schoolhouse lane above. Dissatisfied, he then ordered all of them off the road to take up positions in an enfilading crescent on the lower, north side of the road. In this way, they would be able to cover the entire length of the march as it filed in front of them. The Craig house on the end of Main Street was surrounded by a white picket fence. Inside, Mrs. Craig fretted nervously. Outside, across the street, stood a tall gumberry tree, later to become known as "the massacre tree." Almost in its shade, Sheriff Martin stood near the house with the white fence and looked up the empty road toward Harleigh. As he did so, A. E. Hess was showing his men one last time how to fire their guns.

From where the sheriff stood, the road swept gently upward over the brow of a distant hill. Not far from where it came over the hill, the trolley track crossed over it and continued to parallel it on the south but on a raised embankment. The marchers would come over the hill and then be caught between the embankment and the line of Winchesters. In addition, the road then gradually curved closer and closer to the deputies down toward the house where the sheriff was now standing. Thus, if the marchers kept coming, their first rank would be no farther than fifteen yards from the line of deputies, and those in the last ranks would be no farther than thirty or forty yards. The sheriff was satisfied and strode up the line a little, nearer to the center of his deputies. . . .

At last the marchers came over the hill. Next door to the Craig house, John Airy watched from his home as the unarmed marchers walked in rank toward him. As at West Hazleton, so at Lattimer the marchers felt secure under the law. In the first two rows were Steve Jurich, carrying the flag, John Eagler, John Pustag, Michael Malody, Mike Cheslak, wearing an odd pointed cap, Andro Novotny, and George Jancso. All were from the two counties of Šariš and Zemplin in Slovakia.

After dismissing their students when anxious mothers came to gather their youngsters, Charles Guscott and Grace Coyle, the teachers, stood at the doorway of the schoolhouse, and watched the slow-motion drama unfold. They stood about one hundred yards from the gumberry tree. About sixty of the ninety men in the deputies' line, they later recalled, had their rifles raised in firing position as the strikers, led by the flag, began to file past them.

Sheriff Martin told Hess and Price to keep an eye on him. He said he would find out the marchers' intentions. "If they say they are not going to do anything I may let them go on and we will go along with them." When the flag had come about two-thirds of the way past the far flank, Sheriff Martin strode forward as he had now done on four previous occasions to see if he could handle the situation alone. He had his revolver drawn. He held up one hand. The men kept coming as he advanced and he had his hand almost in their faces when he announced in official manner: "You must stop marching and disperse." Those a few ranks back could not hear him at all, and the others behind them could not see him. "This is contrary to the law and you are creating a disturbance. You must go back. I won't let you go to the colliery."

The front ranks stumbled, trying to halt. Someone from behind called out in English, "Go ahead!" The marchers behind kept coming. The front row was pushed forward.

Angered, the sheriff reached first for the flag. But Steve Jurich pulled it erect. Then the sheriff reached into the second row and grabbed Michael Malody by the coat, thinking that he was the one who had said, "Go ahead!" The sheriff didn't know which man was the leader. Frightened, Malody insisted he hadn't said a word. Andro Novotny, who was next to Malody, intervened in his defense. The sheriff then grabbed Novotny with one hand and pulled his revolver up, aiming it at Novotny's chest. By now, the sheriff had pulled four or more men to the deputies' side of the road. The other marchers continued on. Eagler was among those pushed partially forward down the road. Those near the sheriff—including, now, men from the rear like John Terri and Martin Shefronik (Šefronik)—were afraid and puzzled.

"Where are you going?" the sheriff asked, pulling on Novotny and beginning to panic. The front of the column was getting farther and farther past him. Novotny said in English, "Let me alone!" He swept his arms up and pushed the barrel of the sheriff's revolver away from his own chest.

George Jancso reached in and pulled the sheriff's other hand free from Novotny. The sheriff then grabbed Jancso's coat and pointed his pistol at Jancso's forehead; Jancso and Eagler heard the pistol snap—Sheriff Martin also felt it snap—but it did not fire.

In that instant, the sheriff's second in command, Samuel Price, left the line of deputies and stepped forward to come to the surrounded sheriff's assistance. Other deputies frantically called him back, since he was now in the line of fire. He stepped back.

Mrs. Kate Case from her third-floor window heard someone shout "Fire." She thought the deputies were firing over the marchers' heads. Then she saw some marchers fall. She screamed.

Novotny heard the sheriff command, "Fire," and Jancso heard him shout "Give two or three shots!" Some witnesses thought that in the struggle the sheriff had fallen briefly to his knees; others said he remained standing. His body was directly between the deputies and Jancso when a shot rang out, then three or four in unison. The sheriff raised both arms as though to stop the action. But a full volley rang out again and again.

Watching from the schoolhouse, Charles Guscott saw the first puff of smoke come from the fourth or fifth man from the farthest end of the deputies' line, Hess's men. It seemed to those closer that the whole line erupted with fire.

Steve Jurich had held the flag and was the first to fall. "*O Joj! Joj! Joj!*" he cried in the ancient Slovak cry to God. "Enough! Enough!" Bullets shattered his head and he died as he bled.

John Eagler saw Cheslak drop, his peculiar peaked hat falling from his head, so he, too, dropped to the ground. Eagler saw trickles of blood flowing in the dust toward him from Cheslak's head. He realized then that the deputies were not using blanks.

John Terri threw himself on the ground. Another striker fell on him, dead. Terri saw Cheslak beside him and tried to speak to him. Cheslak's eyes were open but he did not speak. Then Terri got up and ran.

Andro Sivar, in the fourth row, turned his back at the first shot. When the man beside him caught a bullet in the back, Sivar fell with him. Michael Kuchar, nineteen, was about ten yards from the sheriff and could neither hear nor see what was happening in front; at the loud shouting, he threw himself down. George Jancso tore himself from the hands of the sheriff and ran to throw himself in a ditch as flat and close to mother earth as he could press himself.

Martin Shefronik stood close to Jurich, and saw blood spurt out the back of Jurich's head and also from his mouth. As he dropped, Jurich was completely drenched with blood. Shefronik ran toward the schoolhouse, until he was thrown forward by the impact of a bullet in his shoulder. John Putski of Harwood also ran toward the schoolhouse until a bullet in his right arm and another in his leg spun him to the ground. Andrew Jurechek ran toward the schoolhouse and almost reached safety before a bullet struck his back and exploded through his stomach.

Watching from the schoolhouse, teachers Charles Guscott and Grace Coyle had looked on in horror as dust and acrid gunsmoke filled the air. "They're firing blanks," Miss Coyle said. "No, see them dropping," Guscott said. The firing went on for two or three minutes. Some deputies turned, wheeled, and followed running men, shooting some down at a distance of 300 yards. Many men ran toward the schoolhouse; one was hit, spinning, just before he reached the terrified teachers. Other shots crashed into the schoolhouse sending showers of splinters. Running toward the teachers, Clement Platek clutched his side; he too was crying: "*O Joj! Joj! Joj!*" The teachers saw, in addition to those mentioned: the brains of one man splattered forward; still another hapless man shot through the neck so that his head was almost severed. Grace Coyle ran forward to help Andrew Jurechek, who was clutching at the entrails slipping from his stomach and who cried out to her: "No! Me want to see wife. Before die." He died before her eyes. His wife was heavy with child.

Mathias Czaja had been standing ten or twelve feet from the sheriff. He had seen the sheriff pull his revolver and point it at the man with the flag. He had heard him say, "If you go any farther, I will shoot you." He had been fright-ened. He did not hear the order to fire. His back was blown open by a bullet.

Michael Srokach (Srokač) saw eight deputies run forward thirty yards or so to gain better shots. From the public road, the miners fled backward toward the trolley line and up over its bank, either up the hill west toward Harleigh or east toward the schoolhouse.

One man fled as far as a telephone pole on the trolley line when he was hit. He pulled himself up, holding to the pole. As other shots poured into him, his body buckled two or three times. He slid to the earth.

William Raught and another deputy, according to several witnesses, broke from the line of deputies in order to pursue the fleeing strikers. In order to get a line of fire, Raught and the other man climbed up on the trolley tracks, still firing. Srokach heard some deputies answer pleas from the wounded with the shout: "We'll give you hell, not water, hunkies!" Others heard: "Shoot the sons of bitches!"

The smoke from the first volley was thick. Dust was raised by men running. For a while it was difficult to see. From his home, John Airy saw deputies take careful aim and pick men off as they were running to get in the shelter of the hillside. "They shot man after man in the back," he reported. "The slaughter was awful." He estimated that the deputies fired "at least 150" shots. "They kept firing for some time. Men fell on the ground and screamed in agony and tried to drag themselves from the murderous guns. At last it was all over."

Cries of pain, groans, and shrieks remained. Andro Sivar got up from a cir-cle of dead and wounded. Andrew Meyer—seventeen-year-old breaker boy—pleaded for help for his shattered knees. John Slobodnik, wounded in the back of the head just above the neck cried out for water. Slobodnik and John Banko, also shot in the head, were carried by friends to Farley's Hotel in Harleigh, looking for medical attention of some kind. John Eagler ran, bent over, for 150 yards before he turned. He saw one of the men from Crystal Ridge bleeding from his arm and back. The man asked him: "Butty, loosen me suspenders and collar, they hurt me much." Eagler pulled down the man's shirt and saw a big hole in the back of his neck spouting thick blood. He pushed a handkerchief in the hole. Then he bent to help Frank Tages. He pulled off his own coat, put it around his friend, led him to a trolley car for a ride to the hospital. Sick and afraid, Eagler saw some of the deputies begin to offer water to the wounded. Then he started on the long walk back to Har-wood. In shock, he could not comprehend what had just happened.

Cornelius Burke was eleven years old and lived in Lattimer II, the next set-tlement up from Lattimer. During recess from school, he was overcome by cu-riosity about the commotion in town and ran down to Lattimer to see the ex-citement. He was part way up Main Street when he heard the terrific crack of rifles. When he got up to the site, he recalls, ". . . Oh, my God, the poor fel-lows were lying across the trolley tracks on the hillside, some had died and some were dying. Some were crying out for water." Connie picked up a little can and carried water to one of the dying miners. "It was a terrible sight and so much confusion existed. Everyone was running in all directions. They searched the men who were shot and found they carried no weapons."

One of the deputies, George Treible, was wounded by a bullet that creased both his arms. The Wilkes-Barre *Times* reported that he believed he was shot by one of his own men, who had wheeled to fire after the dispersing strikers. Bullets flew, Treible said, in every direction. Some of the deputies at the right end of the crescent (farthest from Lattimer), who seem to have fired most of the shots, were shooting back toward Lattimer at the strikers fleeing toward the schoolhouse. "The deputies," said the paper, "were not under control. The odor of smoke inflamed them."

The fury of some was not yet spent. Some of the deputies walked among the fallen, kicking them and cursing them. A. E. Hess told one bystander who was crying shame, "Shut up or you will get the same dose." John Terri, who had fallen beside Cheslak, went through the smoke of battle to find water for his wounded uncle and cousin. Asked for water, a deputy named Clark said, "Give them hell," grabbed Terri, kicked him, and held him prisoner for an hour. Joseph Costello, a Hazleton butcher, saw Hess kick a prostrate victim (who was in fact Andrew Meyer) and denounced Hess for the butchery. Hess told him, too, to shut up. Grace Coyle, the schoolteacher, upbraided Hess for his manner among the fallen, with his cigar in his mouth. Hess did not defend himself.

John Welsh saw Sheriff Martin after the shooting and asked him how he was. "I am not well," Sheriff Martin said.

The sheriff was pale and shaken. He turned his revolver over to a detective. Many of his deputies had fled and some went into hiding. Some of the others were lifting the wounded into conveyances. But John Airy witnessed the most saddening scene of all: "The trolley car in which the sheriff and his deputies came was right in front of my house and the officers got in it. They were laughing and telling each other how many men they killed." Another bystander also heard them: "Yes, and one of them said he took down a dozen 'Hunks,' and knew what he was shooting at every time. He was boasting of what a fine shooter he was. They sat there for some time, joking and laughing about it, and then they rode back to the city."

REVIEW QUESTIONS

1. What impression do you get of the relationships in this mining town—between the workers and their employers, the workers and the law enforcement officers, and among the workers?

2. Is there any nativistic (anti-immigrant) sentiment in the community? If so, what evidence is there for it; if not, how do you account for its absence? Also, do the nativistic tendencies appear to be universal in the community?

3. What is the attitude of the workers toward their adopted country—the United States? Document your answer.

4. What impression do you get of the degree of professionalism of the deputies?

5. Do you feel, on the basis of the narrative, that the verdict of the jury (see the Introduction to the selection) was a fair one? If so, why; if not, why not?

6. Turn to the author of the narrative. (a) Is he dispassionate in his account, or do you sense that he has some strong feelings about what happened? Document your answer—either way. (b) Does it surprise you to learn that he is a spokesman for ethnicity in our country, the founder of a movement to promote ethnic pride among immigrant groups and their descendants? (c) What evidence is there in this essay of ethnic pride on Novak's part? Is it, in your opinion, justified, or to put the question another way: did the miners, in your opinion, act in a legal and patriotic manner? If so, on what evidence; if not, on what evidence?

FOR FURTHER READING

In addition to the book from which the preceding selection was taken, Michael Novak, *The Guns of Lattimer* (1978), the following provide information on labor, unions, strikes, and labor violence in the late 1800s: Paul Avrich, *The Haymarket Tragedy* (1984); Melvin Dubofsky, *Industrialism and the American Worker, 1865–1920* (1975), and *We Shall Be All: A History of the Industrial Workers of the World* (1969); Philip Foner, *The Great Labor Uprising of 1877* (1977). Harold Livesay, *Samuel Gompers and Organized Labor in America* (1978), is a brief biography of an important labor leader. Stuart Kaufman, *Samuel Gompers's and the Origins of the American Federation of Labor* (1973), is a fuller account of Gompers' contributions to the labor movement. Milton Meltzer, *Bread and Roses: The Struggle of American Labor, 1865–1915* (1967), is a brief but valuable general history. Leon J. Wolff, *Lockout: The Story of the Homestead Strike of 1892* (1965), focuses on one of the most important labor struggles of the time. Paul Kraus, *The Battle for Homestead, 1880–1892: Politics, Culture, and Steel* (1992), is a more recent account of the same strike that provides fuller background on the steel industry and the town of Homestead. Leon Fink, *Workingmen's Discovery: The Knights of Labor and American Politics* (1983), deals with one of the important labor organizations of that era.

PART II

REORGANIZATION AND REFORM

Many Americans were deeply disturbed by what they saw happening to their nation in the late 1800s. Greed and callousness seemed to rule. The fantastic economic growth the country was experiencing carried a heavy price in human terms. Workers were exploited, and many small businesses were crushed in the ruthless competition that often prevailed. A gulf was growing between the haves and have-nots, and periodic economic dislocations, such as the depression of the mid-1890s, produced a sense of insecurity and even fear. Such conditions sparked vigorous protests and demands for change, and in 1896 people on both sides of the election contest were convinced that its outcome would determine the entire future history of the United States.

The election of 1896 did not turn out to be as significant as many contemporaries expected, but the deep divisions it revealed in the American people helped to demonstrate the need to come to grips with the problems generated by the previous 30 years of change. As a result, during the first two decades of the twentieth century, the United States was swept by the Progressive Movement, a widespread and broadly based impulse toward reform, whose basic thrust is revealed in the titles two historians used in their books about it: one spoke of "the quest for social justice," and the other of "the search for order."

Progressives addressed issues relating to corruption in municipal government, child labor, regulation of hours for working women, standards of cleanliness in the production of food, the overweening power of large corporations, and many others. Their fundamental goal was to take steps toward solving the new problems that had emerged and were continuing to emerge as the United States went through the transition from a rural and agricultural to an urban and industrial nation. The instrument they relied on was the power of government, especially the federal government, to control and regulate behavior believed to be illegitimate or threatening to social harmony.

As they addressed these issues, however, new threats arose. The mighty wave of immigration from Europe that had begun in the mid-1880s crested in the early years of the twentieth century. While many Progressives were sympathetic to the immigrants and were involved in efforts to extend assistance to them, other Americans, including many Progressives, were inclined to view immigrants as detrimental to the nation's social health because they represented diversity and potential disorder. These problems, real or imagined, were intensified by the increasing presence of African Americans in northern cities as hundreds of thousands of them moved northward in search of jobs, education, and freedom from the racial oppression they faced in the South.

The following selections illustrate the new problems and opportunities of the Progressive Era. One describes both the positive and negative aspects of life in America's rapidly growing cities. Two concern the lives of the newly arrived immigrants from Europe and their adjustment to their new homeland. The last deals with the migration of African Americans to the North, and what they found when they got to "the promised land."

The Byron Collection, Museum of the City of New York

Street peddlers and their customers on New York City's Lower East Side.

6

The City at the Turn
of the Century

DAVID NASAW

One vivid example of the expansion and change that were occurring in the United States in the late 1800s was the phenomenal growth of America's cities. Americans had been moving from the country to the city ever since the mid-eighteenth century, but never before on such a scale. The mechanization of farming lowered demands for agricultural labor while growing industries created job opportunities in urban areas. In addition, the 1880s saw the beginnings of a huge wave of immigration from Europe, with most of the new arrivals settling in cities. The result was that between 1880 and 1890 New York City's population grew by 50 percent, Chicago's by more than 100 percent, and Minneapolis-St. Paul's by 300 percent; other cities showed comparable rates of growth.

This urban explosion created an urban emergency. American cities had always suffered from crime, disease, poverty, and overcrowding, but such problems now threatened to become overwhelming. Rapidly increasing numbers both magnified existing difficulties and ensured that more people would be affected by them. It was essential to do something before cities became unlivable.

In confronting these problems, American people of the late 1800s and early 1900s essentially invented the modern American city. The story was not always pretty, being attended with considerable amounts of graft, greed, corruption, inefficiency, and failure, but in the end the foundations for many of the basic features of modern city life were laid. Public mass transit, municipal water and sewage disposal systems, the grid for generating and distributing electricity, and the telephone network, among other things, became characteristic of American urban life during this period. In addition, the problems that resulted from having so many people of diverse ethnic, racial, religious, and class backgrounds living so close together created a demand for higher standards of public comfort and safety to be maintained by professional police and fire-fighting forces. And ethnic diversity and the cultural variety and interaction it generated contributed to an enhanced vitality and creativity in artistic and intellectual life.

In the following selection, David Nasaw focuses on New York City, but much of what he says about the attractions and drawbacks of urban life there can be applied to other American cities around the turn of the century.

The early twentieth-century city was among the wonders of the New World. Concentrated within it were the marvels of the age. Electric lights made night into day. Subways, streetcars, and the elevated sped commuters through the streets. Steel-girded skyscrapers and granite railroad stations expressed its solidity and its power. Lobster palaces, vaudeville palaces, movie palaces, and department store palaces of consumption recreated in the present the mythic splendors of the past.

American cities had expanded in all directions in the decades surrounding the turn of the century: up with the skyscrapers, down into the subway tunnels, outward across the bridges and tunnels to the new streetcar suburbs. The central business districts, once crowded with warehouses but not much else, had been enlarged and subdivided into financial, government, manufacturing, warehousing, shopping, and entertainment districts, each with its army of workers.

Every morning swarms of commuters boarded their trolleys, trains, cable cars, elevateds, and subways for the ride to town. Three quarters of a million people flowed daily off the elevated into the Chicago Loop. They arrived in downtown Boston from Roxbury, West Roxbury, Dorchester, and the surrounding "streetcar suburbs." In Cincinnati, Columbus, and Pittsburgh, they took electric streetcars from the heights into the "flats" of the central city. In Manhattan, they trooped to work across the bridges, on the ferries, and by

---

streetcar, elevated train, and subway. Theodore Dreiser described the procession from his vantage point at the Williamsburg Bridge. "Already at six and six-thirty in the morning they have begun to trickle small streams of human beings Manhattan or cityward, and by seven and seven-fifteen these streams have become sizable affairs. By seven-thirty and eight they have changed into heavy, turbulent rivers and by eight-fifteen and eight-thirty and nine they are raging torrents, no less. They overflow all the streets and avenues and every available means of conveyance. They are pouring into all available doorways, shops, factories, office-buildings—those huge affairs towering so significantly above them. Here they stay all day long, causing those great hives and their adjacent streets to flush with a softness of color not indigenous to them, and then at night, between five and six, they are going again, pouring forth over the bridges and through the subways and across the ferries and out on the trains, until the last drop of them appears to have been exuded."

Those who arrived in the central business districts came to work, but they stayed to be entertained and to shop. The city's palaces of consumption were as new, as exciting, and as spectacular as its skyscrapers and bridges. The downtown department stores, huge as factories, luxurious as the most opulent millionaire's mansions, and jammed full of goods were a relatively new phenomenon in the life of the city. Until the 1870s there had been no real downtown shopping streets. City folk did their shopping in neighborhood stores or from itinerant peddlers. Local shops were specialized: butcher, baker, and candlestick maker had their own establishments where they produced and sold their own goods.

The extension of the streetcar lines into the suburbs and the new concentration of white-collar workers downtown provided retailers with hundreds of thousands of customers. Old-fashioned dry goods stores were expanded into department stores and then relocated and rebuilt along the busiest streetcar and subway lines to make shopping as convenient as possible for suburban women, tourists, and downtown workers.

Visitors to the city joined the commuters and workers on the shopping streets where the department stores were located. In Manhattan, the first "Ladies' Mile" was situated along Broadway and Fifth and Sixth Avenues between Eighth and Twenty-third Streets. There was nothing like it anywhere in the world. Wanamaker's, a sixteen-story cast-iron giant, was at Eighth Street and Broadway, Hearn's was on Fourteenth Street, and Siegel-Cooper's on Sixth Avenue and Eighteenth Street with its main attraction, "The Fountain," a circular marble terrace surrounding a mammoth marble and brass statue of "The Republic" shooting jets of water, "illuminated by myriad colored lights." Across the street from the Big Store was B. Altman's, a short walk away were Stern Brothers, Lord and Taylor, Arnold Constable, Best and Company, Bonwit Teller's, W. and J. Sloane, and Macy's.

As the city moved northward so did the department stores. Macy's in 1901 broke ground on its new Herald Square store—with one million square feet of floor space. Within a decade all the other downtown stores had relocated on Fifth Avenue or close by.

In Chicago, State Street was as grand a tourist attraction as New York's Fifth Avenue. One could wander up and down the avenue for days without running out of stores to visit and windows to peer into. There was Marshall Field's with its forty acres of shopping and its forty-five plate glass windows; Carson, Pirie, Scott's in its new building designed by Louis Sullivan; Fair, Rothschild's, Siegel, Cooper and Company; the Boston Store; Mandel Brothers; and the Stevens Store—all within walking distance of one another.

Every city had its own special stores, stores which had grown up with the downtown areas and, in the beginning, helped lure customers from the outskirts: Jordan Marsh's and Filene's in Boston, the original Wanamaker's and Gimbel's in Philadelphia, Kaufmann's in Pittsburgh, Abraham and Straus in Brooklyn, Rich's in Atlanta, Neiman-Marcus in Dallas, Goldwater's in Prescott and then in Phoenix, Arizona, I. Magnin's in San Francisco, Hudson's in Detroit, and Lazarus in Columbus.

The department stores were more than containers of goods or huge indoor markets. They were living encyclopedias of abundance designed to overwhelm the consumer with the variety of items available for purchase. The department stores brought together under one roof an unimaginable collection of commodities, catalogued by department, arranged by floor. Furniture, rugs, and bedding were on the upper floors; ready-to-wear clothing and shoes for women and children on the middle floors; bargain goods and groceries in the basement. The street-level floors displayed clothing and accessories for men, who it was feared would not take the time to ride to the higher floors; and for the women, dozens and dozens of alluring, lower-priced items: cosmetics, notions, gloves, stationery, hosiery.

What overwhelmed was not simply the variety of goods, but the variety and abundance of luxury goods, "from silk dresses and chocolate-covered candies to bicycles, cigarettes, and pink popcorn, which consumers had not produced themselves and which they did not need."

The department stores, by so artfully juxtaposing the necessary and the frivolous, redefined and intertwined needs with desires. There was so much there, at such a range of prices, it was difficult to know what to buy. Sister Carrie, recently arrived in the city from the countryside and looking for work, was directed by a policeman to "The Fair," one of Chicago's more massive and imposing stores. "Carrie passed along the busy aisles, much affected by the remarkable displays of trinkets, dress goods, stationery, and jewelry. Each separate counter was a showplace of dazzling interest and attraction. She could not help feeling the claim of each trinket and valuable upon her personally, and yet she did not stop. There was nothing there which she could not have used—nothing which she did not long to own. The dainty slippers and stockings, the delicately frilled skirts and petticoats, the laces, ribbons, hair-combs, purses, all touched her with individual desire."

One did not have to go inside to be touched by the magic of the stores. Plate-glass windows with superbly crafted displays highlighted by "the planned adoption of electrical lighting and of a new color technology, of drapery and mechanical props, of reflectors and wax mannequins, and even, occasionally of living models . . . consciously converted what had once been dull places stuffed with goods into focused *show* windows, 'gorgeous' little theatrical stage-sets, sculpted scenes, where *single* commodities might be presented in the best possible light." The banks of show windows opened up the street, extending the interior opulence of the palaces onto the sidewalks and inviting the passers-by to pause and dream of the splendors inside. Window-shopping, in essence no more than a dignified form of loafing, became a new and acceptable pastime.

If shopping brought people downtown, entertainment establishments kept them there after dark or, to be more accurate, after the sun went down. There was, in reality, no more "dark" in the theater districts. Street lighting, first by kerosene and gas, then by electric arc and incandescent lights, extended day into night. Theater marquees, billboards, and restaurants with plate glass windows revealing and highlighting the gaiety within converted dark, deserted streets into well-lit thoroughfares of fun and fantasy. Broadway, the Great White Way, illuminated for two miles between Madison and Longacre Squares, was the prototype for the all-night entertainment district, but every city had its theaters, its restaurants, its hotels, its vaudeville palaces, and motion picture shows.

Night life, once the province of lower-class characters and men who acted as if they were, had moved out from the tenderloin and vice districts into the lights of the new and expanded "Broadways." Every city had its cheap public dance halls, saloons, and whorehouses, but for those who wanted to be entertained without shame and guilt and in the company of respectable women, there were new and proper places to do it.

The vaudeville theaters were the first establishments to, quite literally, clean up their acts. Once a men-only affair, with prostitutes cruising the aisles, profanity rampant, "girly shows" on stage, and the aroma of stale beer inescapable, vaudeville had, in the 1870s and 1880s, been transformed into acceptable, wholesome entertainment for the entire family. "Jeering, drinking, smoking, and soliciting were all but abolished by policing. Managers also clamped down on vulgar stage language and actions, creating a strict system of censorship that outlawed the uttered 'hell' and 'damn.'" Animal acts, magicians, pantomimists, and ladies who played the "concertina, banjo, and xylophone" were brought in to replace the "blue" acts that had once been standard.

Though vaudeville shows could be seen in every town, at country fairs, and at amusement parks, it was in the cities that the theaters attracted the largest number of customers. In New York City there were, by 1910, thirty-one different vaudeville houses. Chicago had twenty-two, Philadelphia thirty.

Vaudeville brought the middle classes—in the thousands—downtown for the show. It was not, however, the only attraction of the entertainment districts. There were also the variety theaters and the music halls, where on any given night one could see operettas, new musical comedies like *Little Johnny Jones* and *George Washington Junior,* melodramas, or Shakespeare. Arnold Bennett, on his trip to the United States in 1912, was astounded to find "nearly twice as many first-class theaters in New York as in London."

Within walking distance of the theaters were restaurants to wine, dine, and be seen in. Dining out, once the preserve of society people who could afford fancy hotel dining rooms and restaurants like Delmonico's and of working men who frequented taverns, chophouses, and rathskellers, had become an acceptable—and accessible—form of entertainment for middle-class men and women. In New York City, the dozens of new "Broadway" restaurants which opened their doors between 1899 and 1912 "helped make the life of conspicuous consumption available to a wider portion of the city and the nation."

Patrons were not only wined and dined but also treated like kings and queens on holiday. Restaurateurs created sumptuous new interior decors to bedazzle their customers with a taste of luxury. "In Murray's [on Broadway in New York City], patrons entered the main dining room through a black and gold mosaic-lined foyer. The main dining room was built to resemble the atrium of a Roman home, complete with an open court with colonnades on each side. Surrounded by trees and statues and gazing out on an ancient barge fronting a terraced fountain crowned by a classical temple rising clear to the ceiling, diners enjoyed the illusion of being in ancient Rome or at a villa in Pompeii. . . . The classical porticos and temples provided a sense of restful magnificence, while the enormous height of the room and open space suggested the lofty opulence and power of the diner."

Entering the room was only the beginning of the treat. Eating in a lobster palace, like shopping in a department store, was an adventure, an excitement, an event to be savored. The beginning to a proper meal in hotel dining room or lobster palace was oysters (when not in season, clams could be substituted), followed by soup, hors d'oeuvres, fish, the entrée, the main course (usually a roast), the game dish, and dessert and coffee.

For those who preferred to keep the good time rolling late into the night, there were cabarets and nightclubs, another early twentieth century addition to city night life. Fast dancing, once practiced only in the cheap dance halls and bawdy houses, was a major attraction in the new clubs. And when people danced, they danced—not waltzes or two-steps—but the turkey trot and the grizzly bear to the syncopated ragtime beat of black musicians who, had they not been playing in the band, would never have been allowed in such respectable downtown establishments.

As Lloyd Morris has noted, it was just three miles from Rector's on Broadway, where twenty dollars would buy a dinner for five with two bottles of champagne, to the lower end of Orchard Street, where another restaurant "served a dinner of soup, meat stew, bread, pickles, pie, and a 'schooner' of beer for thirteen cents."

In New York City, as in Chicago, Boston, Cincinnati, Columbus, and almost every other city in the nation, the "other half" lived close by and a world away from the downtown business, shopping, and entertainment districts. H. G. Wells noticed during his visit in 1905 that there were "moments when I could have imagined there were no immigrants at all" in American cities. "One goes about the wide streets of Boston, one meets all sorts of Boston people, one visits the State House; it's all the authentic English-speaking America. Fifth Avenue, too, is America without a touch of foreign-born." And yet, Wells recognized, the America of the immigrant and the working class, though out of sight, was just around the corner, just down the street, just over the hill, "a hundred yards south of the pretty Boston Common," "a block or so east of Fifth Avenue," an elevated stop from the Loop in Chicago.

The two urban worlds did not mingle or mix. Each recognized the presence of the other, but neither went out of its way to cross over into the other's workplace or neighborhood. As Robert Shackleton noted in Chicago, the sellers and customers in the department stores were almost all "Americans." "The great foreign population of the city lives and does its shopping mainly in its own districts."

Most residents of the working-class city had no reason to travel downtown. Why leave the neighborhood where goods were cheaper and shopkeepers spoke your own language? Why go elsewhere to be entertained when you had little free time and the local streets provided all you needed in friends, family, neighbors, social clubs, saloons, and coffee houses?

Working men and women stayed behind in their own neighborhood because they were comfortable there. While the neighborhoods were not ethnically homogeneous, there were always enough "landsmen" clustered to establish and sustain churches, lodges, patriotic groups, food shops, bakers, butchers, restaurants, theaters, banks, and newspapers.

Settlement-house workers at the turn of the century and historians, more recently, who portray the working-class immigrants as helpless, hopeless, uprooted victims misread the historical record. On the downtown business, shopping, and entertainment streets the Italian, Polish, and Russian Jewish immigrants wearing dirty overalls and speaking foreign tongues might have been out of place. But in their own communities, they were at home.

The two cities, though geographically distinct, shared the same congested, polluted urban space. There were many constants in city life. No matter where you lived or worked, you were assaulted daily by the smoke, soot, and dust in the air; the noise of clattering cobblestones, cable cars, trolleys, and the elevated; the smell of horse dung on the streets. In the working-class and immigrant residential districts, these annoyances were intensified a hundredfold. It was in the city of the "other half" that the sewers were always clogged and the streets and alleyways filled with garbage. It was here that dead horses lay for days, bloated and decaying, children poking at their eyes and pulling out their hair to weave into rings. It was here that cats roamed at will through the streets, alleyways, backyards, roofs, and interior hallways, alley cats with gaping wounds, flesh hung loosely on starving bodies, wide frightened eyes, and the look, smell, and howl of starvation. It was here that tuberculosis raged and babies died of exposure or cold or heat or spoiled milk, that pushcarts, streetcars, and horse-drawn wagons fought for space, and children were crushed to death in the duel.

The residents of the working-class districts lived in a variety of dwellings: multistory tenements, converted single-family row houses, double-deckers, triple-deckers, wooden shacks and shanties. Wherever they lived, they were likely to live piled together, several families in space designed for one, several persons to a room.

Families made the best possible use of their limited space, rearranging their flats every evening to provide maximum sleeping room for children, relatives, and boarders. On his first evening in the New World, Marcus Ravage, future historian and author of *An American in the Making,* looked on in amazement as his relatives transformed their apartment into a "camp." "The sofas opened up and revealed their true character. The bureau lengthened out shamelessly, careless of its daylight pretensions. Even the wash-tubs, it turned out, were a miserable sham. The carved dining-room chairs arranged themselves into two rows that faced each other like dancers in a cotillion. . . . The two young ladies' room was not, I learned, a young ladies' room at all; it was a female dormitory. The sofa in the parlor alone held four sleepers, of whom I was one. We were ranged broadside, with the rocking-chairs at the foot to insure the proper length. And the floor was by no means exempt. I counted no fewer than nine male inmates in that parlor alone one night. Mrs. Segal with one baby slept on the washtubs, while the rest of the youngsters held the kitchen floor. The pretended children's room was occupied by a man and his family of four."

As the population and land values in the central cities increased, working people and the poor were forced to live in spaces that should have remained uninhabited. In Washington, D.C., and Baltimore, Maryland, cities within the city were built in the alleyways. In Pittsburgh and Chicago, investigators discovered hundreds of families living below street level in cellars, basements, and dark, dreary, "cavelike" dwellings. In Chicago, where landlords had increased their profits—and the congestion—by building on every inch of land they owned, "rear tenements" and wooden shacks facing on alleyways were built in the back of long, slender lots.

Cities with massive, multistory tenements had the worst congestion. In New York City, where a higher percentage of residents lived in tenements than anywhere else in the country, the congestion inside and out was beyond belief. Theodore Dreiser, among those visitors to the Lower East Side overwhelmed by the sight, reported having seen "block after block of four-story and five-story buildings, "all painted a dull red, and nearly all . . . divided in the most unsanitary manner. Originally they were built five rooms deep, with two flats on a floor, but now the single flats have been subdivided and two or three, occasionally four or five, families live and toil in the space which was originally intended for one."

Light, air, and privacy were at a premium for the working-class and immigrant residents of the early twentieth-century cities. In the typical New York City tenement, with fourteen rooms on each floor, only four—two in front and two in back—"received direct light and air from the street or from the small yard at the back of the building." A housing inspector testified that the inner kitchens and bedrooms on the lower floors of the tenements he visited "were so dark that the lights are kept burning in the kitchen during the daytime. The bedrooms may be used for sleeping at any time within the twenty-four hours, as they exceed the Arctic Zone in having night 365 days in the year."

Lack of windows meant lack of ventilation. The front and rear windows let in a bit of air—along with the noise and stench of street and alleyway. The interior rooms had windows, but because they opened onto airshafts and courtyards stuffed with rotting garbage, most residents kept them permanently closed.

The flats were dark, the hallways darker. In most tenements, the only light in the halls came from the front door when that was opened. A tenement house inspector testified that, in his experience, "the most barbarous parts of [tenement] buildings are the halls. A person coming in from the sunlight outside, plunges into these halls just like a car filled with men plunges and disappears in the black mouth of a mine shaft. If he is fortunate in not running against anybody, he stumbles along, finding his way with his feet. . . . [H]e hurries forward as rapidly as possible and rushes out upon the roof or into some open room, because the air is so dense and stifling [in the hallway] that he wishes to escape quickly."

Privacy was as treasured and rare in the working-class districts as fresh air and light. High rents forced families to economize on space and sublet rooms and parts of rooms to boarders. City dwellers shared their flats, their rooms, even their beds and their toilets with virtual strangers. In many tenements, the water closet was located in the hall or the backyard, where it was used by several families and their boarders and relatives. In Chicago, for example, a turn-of-the-century study found that only 43 percent of families had toilets in their flats, 30 percent had to use the water closet in the yard, 10 percent had a toilet in the basement or cellar, and another 17 percent shared a hall toilet with their neighbors on the floor.

Unventilated, overused water closets and backyard privies were bound to and did overflow continually, seeping waste through the floorboards and into the yards. The odor of human excrement joined that of horse dung from the streets and stables and of garbage rotting in the airshafts, inner courtyards, streets, and alleyways.

If we were to be moved backward in time to the early twentieth-century city, we would probably be most repelled not by the lack of privacy, or toilets, or space, air, and light, but by this stench. Without proper ventilation, the interior halls and rooms of the tenements retained their odors indefinitely. Inside and out, the air was not just heavy and fetid but, at times, unbearable. Cities like Chicago, Cincinnati, and Kansas City, with their slaughterhouses, packing plants, and streets clogged with hogs, sheep, and cattle smelled the worst, but no city was free of what we today would consider an overpowering stench.

The residents of the central cities struggled as best they could to find a breath of air, cool, fresh, clean air. Men, women, and children herded themselves into streetcars and subways for interminable Sunday excursions to the parks and beaches, looking for grass to walk on and air to breathe. In the summertime, when the air was so heavy and hot "it was painful to draw one's breath," entire families—abandoning their last grasp at privacy—relocated on the docks, in the parks, at the stoops, the fire escapes or up on the roofs. As Mike Gold put it in *Jews Without Money,* "People went exploring for sleep as for a treasure." "Like rats scrambling on deck from the hold of a burning ship, that's how we poured on the roof at night to sleep. What a mélange in the starlight! Mothers, graybeards, lively young girls, exhausted sweatshop fathers, young consumptive coughers and spitters, all of us snored and groaned there side by side, on newspapers or mattresses. We slept in pants and undershirt, heaped like corpses. The city reared about us."

Light, air, and privacy were scarce commodities in the working-class districts of the cities. But to paint too grim a picture of life in the early twentieth century, to speak only of scarcity, to emphasize only poverty is to caricature the conditions of daily life for many. The city was no golden land, but it was also no desert. There was plenty mixed with the poverty, abundance interspersed with scarcity. The city was many things at the same time to the same people.

Marcus Ravage, who arrived in New York City from his native Vaslui, Rumania, at the turn of the century, tried hard to organize his perceptions of this new land. He could not resolve the contradictions. He was disappointed on his arrival, "bitterly disappointed" at the "littered streets, with the rows of pushcarts lining the sidewalks and the centers of the thoroughfares, the ill-smelling merchandise, and the deafening noise," at the congestion inside the homes, and the boarders crowded into too little space, stuffed into too few beds. (In Vaslui, he remembered, only the "very lowest of people kept roomers.") And yet, at the very same time, he was astonished at the material abundance displayed amidst the poverty. His landlady scrubbed the floor, not with sand, but with a "pretty white powder out of a metal can." "Moreover, she kept the light burning all the time we were in the kitchen, which was criminal wastefulness even if the room was a bit dark." There was "eggplant in midwinter, and tomatoes, and yellow fruit which had the shape of a cucumber and the taste of a muskmelon." There was meat in the middle of the day and "twists instead of plain rye bread, to say nothing of rice-and-raisins . . . and liver paste and black radish." And then, as if he had not seen enough such wonders in his first day in the country, the young men calling on his Cousin Rose arrived that evening "with beer in a pitcher from the corner saloon." Common people—with beer in a pitcher—at home.

The city—not just New York City, but every early twentieth-century city—overwhelmed with its abundance. There were enough goods to go around town and back again. The department stores and specialty shops got the best of the lot, but the working-class districts, according to Harry Roskolenko, a poet and journalist who grew up on the Lower East Side, were stocked with their own "massive supplies of shoddy goods . . . leftovers from other years and seasons; things that could not be sold" elsewhere; and goods produced especially for sale to "the peddlers and the peasants and the proletarians jamming the sidewalks and gutters."

The pushcarts overflowed, the shops were littered with items for sale: umbrellas, stockings, boys' sailor suits with whistles attached, suspenders, gabardine overcoats, handkerchiefs, laces and ribbons and shoes and long underwear. There were carts filled with oranges and others loaded with bananas, herring came in barrels, milk was ladled out of forty-quart cans, potatoes dug out of fifty-pound sacks. Food, drink, and sweets could be purchased from peddlers and pushcarts, from stands, butchers, bakers, and grocers who sold it in cans, in boxes, in jars, in bottles, in packages, in bags.

Newcomers might have assumed that city markets had always displayed such variety and abundance, but many of the items now prominently displayed were as new to the city as the electric streetcars and lobster palaces. The banana, for example, among the most proletarian of fruits, had until the 1880s been almost entirely absent from the working-class shops and shopping streets. On arrival in New Orleans, "each fruit was wrapped individually in tinfoil and like a rare and precious object rushed to New York or New England, where, if it survived the journey, a single banana was worth a dollar."

Oranges were also a luxury item until the 1890s when, with the completion of the Florida East Coast Railway, they could be shipped north by rail instead of being imported from the Mediterranean.

Grapefruits were entirely new to the city. The old pear-shaped fruit, distinguished by its lack of juice, coarse rind, and expensive price tag had been redesigned by Florida growers who shipped them north in refrigerated boxcars. Between 1909 and 1920, annual consumption of the new pink fruit jumped from under a pound to over five pounds per capita.

The immigrants who arrived in American cities in the early twentieth century were astounded by the number of foods for sale and the variety of ways in which they could be purchased. Fruits, vegetables, soups, meats, even baby food, were sold fresh *and* in cans and tins. Propelled into the marketplace by new food companies alert to the advantages of national distribution, advertising, and brand name promotions, Campbell's soups, Heinz's fifty-seven varieties, and Libby's canned goods became part of the city's daily diet. Between 1909 and 1920, annual per capita consumption of canned fruits increased from under three pounds to over nine, canned soups from less than a third of a pound to two, and baby food from less than a tenth of a pound to over two.

The addition of fresh and canned fruits and vegetables to a diet that had once consisted of little more than bread, potatoes, crackers, and various forms of salted and preserved meats was no doubt beneficial. From a social standpoint, the availability of food in cans meant even more. Here was yet another item once exclusively the preserve of the wealthy (and of military expeditions which could survive on no other form of food) that had become part of the common folks' daily diet. The family that could now for the first time eat peas for dinner was certainly more pleased by the new addition to its diet than it was distressed by the nutritional loss suffered in the canning process.

Of all the foods entering the diet of the working people, none were as enticing, as aristocratic, as luxurious, and as plentiful as the sweets. One by one, luxuries like refined white sugar and chocolate and homemade delights like fresh ice cream were mass-produced, distributed, and marketed in the cities. Candy consumption increased from 2.2 pounds per capita in 1880 to 5.6 in 1914 and 13.1 in 1919; ice cream from 1.5 pounds in 1909 to 7.5 in 1920. To wash it all down, there was Coca-Cola, invented as a "remedy for headaches and hangovers" by an Atlanta dentist in 1886.

The new sweets further broadened and "democratized" the urban diet. Luxuries became commonplaces available for pennies from neighborhood shops and pushcart peddlers. And yet, there remained significant differences between the diet of the downtown gentleman and the factory worker's family. Both ate sweets and vegetables and meat. But the sirloin and spring lamb served in the lobster palaces was a far cry from the meat soup "made up of left-overs and ends and bones which the butcher sold for six cents a pound instead of throwing it away." Bananas and oranges and grapefruits were, for the first time, available downtown and in the slums, but only for the few who had the money to pay for them. For the rest, they remained as inaccessible as they had been in the days before refrigerated boats and boxcars carried them north.

In the midst of plenty, poverty and hunger remained. Within sight of the carts and shops filled with enough food to feed armies, parents struggled to provide for their families. Children grew up with what actress Ruth Gordon has called "the dark brown taste of being poor." Hy Kraft, later a successful Broadway playwright, never forgot what it was like to grow up poor. "A boy stands in front of a candy store—in front, mind you. He sees a hundred varieties of sweets, but he doesn't have a penny, one cent. Or he's in the street; a vendor pushes his cart, calling 'Icacrim sendwich, pennyapiss.' Other kids holler up to their mamas, 'Mama, t'row me down a penny' and the mama wraps the penny in paper and 't'rows' it down. This kid doesn't have a penny—one cent. And there's no mama upstairs; she's in the back of the basement."

Poverty was not unique to the metropolis, but nowhere else did it coexist with such splendor and spectacle. As Charles Zueblin, an authority on American cities, noted in the preface to his widely read volume on *American Municipal Progress,* "There is poverty in the country, sordid and ugly. But city poverty is under the shadow of wealth. Luxury flaunts itself in the city."

The city was suffused with contrasts: between the electrically illuminated magnificence of the downtown shopping and entertainment districts and the grayish squalor of the slums, between the abundance of goods offered for sale on the streets and the paucity of resources available to pay for them. Poverty and plenty lived side by side, in the same city, on the same block, in the same tenement flat. The contradictions that assailed Marcus Ravage on his first day in the city were inescapable. Wise men peddled suspenders on the streets while fools lived like millionaires. People slept crowded one on top of another, but they ate meat several times a week. Families shared toilets with complete strangers, but they were able to purchase shoes, stockings, and underwear for everyone—even for the children. It made no sense and yet it was real. It was the city.

REVIEW QUESTIONS

1. Put yourself in the shoes of someone just arriving from a rural home and getting a first glimpse of New York City. From Nasaw's account, what would you find most striking about that experience? What features of the city would have had the greatest impact on you?

2. What does Nasaw's portrait indicate as the main attractions and drawbacks of city life at the turn of the century? From your textbook or some other source, try to discover what important elements of city life he may have omitted in his depiction.

3. At the turn of the century many Americans believed that the American city was one of the nation's greatest disgraces. What evidence do you find in this selection to support or contradict that belief?

4. One of the themes in this selection is the ways in which the experience of the city differed for those who had money from those who did not. What were some of the differences? To what extent is it true that those who had little money suffered from the disadvantages of city life while unable to enjoy its advantages?

FOR FURTHER READING

Arthur M. Schlesinger, Sr., *The Rise of the City, 1878–1898* (1933), is a classic account of urban growth that contains a wealth of still valuable information. Raymond Mohl, *The New City: Urban America in the Industrial Age* (1985); Sam Bass Warner, Jr., *The Urban Wilderness* (1982); Zane L. Miller, *The Urbanization of Modern America* (1973); and Howard P. Chudacoff and Judith E. Smith, *The Evolution of American Urban Society* (4th ed., 1993), are more recent and cover a broader time span. Oscar Handlin, *The Uprooted* (2nd ed., 1973), and Alan M. Kraut, *The Huddled Masses: The Immigrant in American Society, 1880–1921* (1982), are readable accounts of the interactions between immigrants and the city. On urban culture and recreation at the turn of the century, see Lewis A. Erenberg, *Steppin' Out: New York Nightlife and the Transformation of American Culture, 1890–1930* (1981); Gunther Barth, *City People: The Rise of Modern City Culture in Nineteenth-Century America* (1980); John F. Kasson, *Amusing the Million: Coney Island at the Turn of the Century* (1978); and Kathy Peiss, *Cheap Amusements: Working Women and Leisure in Turn-of-the-Century New York* (1986).

The Jacob A. Riis Collection, Museum of the City of New York

A typical tenement courtyard—a playground for the children who lived there.

7

Immigration and Cultural Conflict

ELIZABETH EWEN

The United States has always been a nation of immigrants, but the wave of immigration that began in the mid-1880s and lasted until the outbreak of World War I dwarfed anything that had happened before. It was also different in kind. Contemporaries distinguished between the "old immigration," which had come primarily from northern and western Europe, and the "new immigration," which was coming mostly from southern and eastern Europe. The cultural differences between the new immigrants and the existing population of the United States, along with concerns raised by the sheer number of the new arrivals, were sufficient to trigger anti-immigrant feelings among many native-born Americans and lead to demands that further immigration be restricted.

Immigrants faced a wide range of difficulties. In addition to unfamiliarity with their new country's customs, language, and laws, they had to deal with keen competition for the jobs available to them, which were usually unskilled and low-paying. And they were the victims of overt prejudice and discrimination in many areas of life, including housing and employment.

One of the immigrants' responses to such conditions was to form compact communities in the large eastern cities where most of them settled. To many native-born Americans this was evidence of the immigrants' "clannishness" and another reason for regarding them with

suspicion. This view is hardly fair, however. For one thing, such settlement patterns were partly forced upon immigrants by discriminatory
housing practices rooted in strong anti-immigrant prejudices. It also
ignores the fact that it was entirely reasonable for immigrants to clus-
ter together with others from their native lands, who would be best
able to help them deal with the difficulties they encountered in their
new homeland—including prejudice.

Not that all native-born Americans were hostile by any means.
Many welcomed immigrants as a source of cheap labor. Others, including pioneers in the new profession of social work, began the settlement house movement, intended to provide them with cultural, vocational, recreational, and other kinds of assistance. Even the
best-intentioned settlement house workers, however, were likely to
agree that it would be best for all concerned, including the immigrants, if they could be induced to shed their old-country ways as
quickly as possible and become assimilated and "Americanized."

At least some of the immigrants thought the same thing. Immigrants' children were especially likely to be attracted by American
ways of life. Their parents, on the other hand, were more inclined to
try to preserve the language, customs, and culture of their homeland.
It was not simply a generational conflict, however, but a wide-ranging
difference of opinion among immigrants of all ages. The following selection discusses the health problems and the health-care methods of
immigrant women, mostly Jews and Italians, living on the Lower East
Side of New York City. It illustrates the cultural conflict between new
and old, European and American, that divided immigrants.

In the old country medical knowledge was rudimentary, doctors rare, life ex-
pectancy short, and infant mortality high. Women, to the best of their ability,
delivered babies, nursed young children, ministered to the sick, and, through
the application of folk medicine, intervened against the ravages of nature. In
sickness and in health, women depended on each other: health and hygiene,
childbirth, and infant care were in their hands.

The urban environment challenged this culture in many, often contradictory, ways. On the one hand, women were plunged into neighborhoods that
were dirty, unsanitary, and disease ridden. For people of all ages, death was as
common here as back home. On the other hand, American doctors and social workers preached a scientific, medical "enlightenment" to women that

---

From *Immigrant Women in the Land of Dollars,* by Elizabeth Ewen. Copyright © 1985 by Elizabeth Ewen.
Reprinted by permission of Monthly Review Foundation.

may have been progressive but was also disruptive. These messengers brought useful information and genuine concern in ways that often denied traditional community practices.

In Jewish and Italian culture women relied on midwives. In addition to aiding in childbirth, midwives acted as surrogate doctors, taking care of the sick, administering herbal medicines, and sometimes performing abortions. Knowledge about pregnancy, infant care, health, and illness was passed down across the generations, but the midwife was consulted for special advice. Midwives were also neighbors and friends, living in the same community, speaking the same language, and living the same kind of life. As they went from house to house, midwives passed on information and news, helping to tie the community of women together.

The practice of midwifery on the Lower East Side was common. Social workers were surprised to find that "the large immigrant population in America clings through custom and deeply rooted tradition to the midwife." They also noticed that the "midwife was an economic necessity to those whom she attends for, from her, the patient is able to secure both medical attention and nursery care at a cost which does not exceed a doctor's fee for medical attention alone." The midwife not only charged less than the doctor, but performed services the doctor did not: "The midwife acts not only as a visiting nurse, but as a general adviser and women's friend, neither of which functions are usually expected of the doctor." Doctors were thought of as strangers and were treated with suspicion, but the midwife was known and familiar, a part of the past as well as the present. F. Elizabeth Croswell, who studied midwives for the Public Health Committee of the Association of Neighborhood Workers, concluded: "Midwifery was a custom which had been sanctioned by usage for thousands of years and was in complete accord with the deepest, most sensitive prejudices. . . . Through it, women of the masses in their hour of travail have demanded aid from their sister women and received it." One of these prejudices, which was observed by Elsa Herzfeld, a social worker at Greenwich House, was that only the female sex may be present at a birth; therefore, immigrant women also preferred midwives because it was culturally taboo for men to be present at the act of birth. This taboo was extended to doctors who were male—as most doctors were: by definition they had no place at a childbirth.

The reliance on midwifery was closely connected to attitudes about the home: the home was known, the hospital was feared. Even if a pregnant woman wanted to go to the hospital, her husband or women friends would say that it was only "for them that don't know better." Hospitals were thought of as places where people either died or were experimented on—the antithesis of birth. Adriana Valenti, an Italian garment worker, noted that her mother had all of her thirteen children at home with a midwife. She recalled bitterly that her mother would have been alive if she had gone to the hospital for her last child, but her father did not want her to go: "They feared it so much, that if you go to the hospital you die; many babies would die." And although hygienic conditions were hard to come by on New York's Lower East Side, midwives were generally clean, as were their houses. Users distinguished between good and bad midwives: each midwife had a reputation that was known to the community of women she served.

In 1905 Elizabeth Croswell went through birth certificates in Manhattan and found that "42 percent of the total number of births reported in Manhattan in 1905 were attended by midwives." Adriana Valenti suggested that the number may have been even greater: "There were so many children born that sometimes midwives forgot to register them. They forgot me, for example."

The cost of a midwife was far lower than that of a doctor. The regular charge of a "pay doctor" was $10, while the midwife received between $1 and $5 and she "washes the baby and cleans up besides." In addition, midwives would often stay in the house, or check up on the mother for a week or two after the birth, helping with the housework and attending to medical and emotional needs. Since new immigrant mothers were usually without the help of their own mothers, this aid was crucial. Adriana Valenti's mother was so conscious of the fact that when she delivered her children she had no help from her own mother that she was determined to make up for this loss with her own daughters: "When we would give birth, for one month she would make us do nothing. She would say, 'I didn't have anyone, you have me to help, now you will have your health when you get old.'" Even so, many new mothers lost their health through childbirth and the burden of the housework that followed.

It was common not only for the midwife but for the mother (if present), aunts, and mother-in-law to help the new mother during the act of childbirth and the first months afterward. The women of the family and the midwife acted as doctor and nurse, friend and housekeeper to the woman giving birth. Letitia Serpe, an Italian woman from Bari, described the birth of her first child:

> I got my midwife through my mother-in-law. The midwife and I got acquainted a month before I delivered. When it was time, my mother-in-law, the midwife, my aunt, and I were all together in the bedroom. The midwife was lovely—clean—she was like a she-doctor today—that's what she was. I had a beautiful nine-pound baby and the midwife wrapped her in swaddling so her legs would grow long and straight. My husband didn't sleep in the house for a week. My aunt slept with me and took care of everything.

About half of the midwives interviewed in the Croswell study were between the ages of thirty-five and fifty-five and most had become midwives to supplement the family economy. The husbands of midwives held the diverse jobs common to immigrant communities, as carpenters, day laborers, street cleaners, tailors, and peddlers. The occupation of midwife was an acceptable means for a married woman to contribute to her family economy.

The medical practice of midwives included abortion, and it was variously estimated that there were about 100,000 abortions performed every year in New York City alone, although it is impossible to gather reliable figures on this point. It was common knowledge that midwives performed abortions, but the price was high and many women asked to pay in weekly installments. This fact horrified Margaret Sanger, who worked for a while as a midwife on the Lower East Side, and propelled her to agitate for a more adequate and safe method of birth control.

Both Jewish and Italian culture stressed procreation. Adriana Valenti, for instance, recalled that large numbers of children were a point of pride with Italian men: "When my father's friends would come to visit us, you know, the *paisanos,* they would say, 'How many children you have?' And if one had six, my father would say I have eight. Another would say ten. The larger the family, the better; they were so proud of big families." For the women, however, an additional child was often less a blessing than a "curse of God." In a world in which there was no adequate means of birth control, and where procreation was hailed as a virtue, many immigrant women went to incredible lengths to secure an abortion. Even so, the average number of children for Italian and Jewish immigrant families was about five. Emma Goldman, who also worked for a while as a midwife on the Lower East Side, was impressed by what she called "the fierce struggle of the women of the poor against frequent pregnancies."

Many women asked her to perform abortions "for the sake of the little ones already here":

> Most women lived in continual dread of conception; the great mass of married women submitted helplessly and when they found themselves pregnant, their alarm and worry would result in the determination to get rid of their expected offspring; it was incredible what fantastic methods despair could invent; jumping off tables, rolling on the floor, massaging the stomach, drinking nauseating concoctions, and using blunt instruments.

In July 1916, Margaret Sanger organized a birth control clinic in the Brownsville section of Brooklyn, a poor community of Jews and Italians. With two other women, she rented an apartment in the neighborhood and distributed handbills describing the work of the clinic in Yiddish, Italian, and English—despite the fact that disseminating birth control information was illegal in the United States.

One Italian woman, when asked if she would tell her priest at confession that she had come to the clinic, exclaimed, "It's none of his business. . . . My husband has a weak heart and works only four days. He gets twelve dollars [a week] and we can barely live on it now. We have enough children." The eagerness of immigrant women to have access to birth control information was demonstrated by the fact that in the *first day* of operation the clinic had 464 visitors.

Unfortunately, these women's case histories were confiscated by the police when, several days later, they closed down the clinic, destroyed the files and equipment, and arrested Margaret Sanger and her helpers. Carlo Tresca, the well-known editor of the Italian anarchist paper *Il Matello,* was arrested at about the same time for advertising a book called *L'arte di non fare i Figli* (The Art of Not Making Children), an attempt to disseminate birth control information to Italian immigrants.

Despite their knowledge, and the respect they had in the community, midwives aroused the wrath of the medical establishment. Lillian Wald argued that American attitudes toward midwifery demonstrated a real contempt for immigrant culture:

> Perhaps nothing indicates more impressively our contempt for alien customs than the general attitude taken toward the midwife. In other lands she holds a place of respect, but in this country there seems to be a general determination on the part of physicians and departments of health to ignore her existence and leave her free to practice without fit preparation despite the fact that her services are extensively used.

Midwives were depicted by the medical profession as a remnant from the age of barbarism, and high rates of infant mortality were often blamed on the midwife's "ignorance" and filthy living conditions rather than on conditions of the Lower East Side itself. It was believed that "Americanization" would mean the end of a need for the midwife's services, and her replacement by a trained doctor in a hospital setting.

Many social workers had a different image, however. On the insistence of social workers and nursing organizations that recognized that the use of midwives was not just a barbaric remnant of another culture but the established preference of immigrant women, the Bureau of Child Hygiene in 1906 assigned its nurses the task of inspecting the bags of licensed midwives to make sure of the quality of their instruments, and to give them medicine to wipe out *opthalmia neonatorum,* a disease that led to blindness in newborns.

If social workers and nursing organizations looked for ways of improving the viability of midwifery, doctors and hospitals were preparing to take the entire birth process out of traditional hands. The promise of painless childbirth through the use of narcotics was the medical profession's answer to midwifery: "Just as the village barber no longer performs operations, the untrained midwife of the neighborhood will pass out of existence under the effective competition of . . . painless wards." The doctor/hospital was eventually successful in routing the midwife from her customary position, and by the 1930s most women were having their children in hospitals under the direct supervision of male doctors. While narcotics may have killed their labor pains, and the hospitalization of birth made a dent in infant mortality rates, one of the most significant aspects of this change was that the act of birth was isolated from the community of women.

But this was not entirely due to the medical profession. As immigrant women became more familiar with American culture, they began to prefer the services of the doctor. Emma Goldman noticed that immigrant women who "had risen in the scale of material Americanism" soon began to turn to doctors. Adriana Valenti's childbirth experience was a cross between two cultures: she had her children at home, but used the services of a doctor instead of a midwife. And in recalling her mother's extensive experience with childbirth, she felt that the high cost of hospital birth and doctors' fees was to blame for the decline in large families. Exaggerating the facts to make a point, she said, "When I was born the midwife got $5. Now I heard someone say that today when the wife gives birth, the doctor charged $4,000. You know how many babies my mother would have had for $4,000? None!"

Another cultural confrontation occurred over the issue of nursing and infant care. Immigrant mothers nursed their babies on demand. In addition, lactation was believed to be a form of birth control, so babies were nursed for a considerable length of time, sometimes up to eighteen months. In the Jewish tradition, intercourse with nursing women was forbidden by law and Jewish women often used nursing to avoid pregnancy. As a Yiddish proverb put it: "If the wife is afraid of getting pregnant, she lets her husband think she's still nursing."

The turn-of-the-century American apostles of "scientific motherhood," obsessed with what they called "good habits," were appalled by the irregularity of immigrant nursing habits. Elsa Herzfeld put it this way:

> The babies were nursed irregularly. If the mother was working or "goes out for the day," she nurses the baby at meal times and during the night. Irregular artificial feedings supplement the nursing. In the case of the non-wage-earning mother, the nursings are equally irregular. The child is nursed when it cries or whenever the mother thinks it necessary, day or night. The clock is not consulted.

Good habits were thought to be the crucible of character, and mothers were trained to inculcate these habits in their infants from birth. Nursing on demand was perceived as irregular, contrary to notions of a proper upbringing that created people capable of adapting themselves to the machine age. Social workers applied these standards to immigrant mothers; clock time was a gauge used to determine the level of assimilation. The popular *Infant Care*, a manual, published in 1914 and widely distributed to middle- and working-class mothers' clubs, stressed that the "baby should be nursed regularly, by the clock, from the very first, and should have nothing between meals, save water, to drink." In the interests of standardization, mother and child were expected to suffer through long bouts of crying; endurance was the key to success. Yet luckily for the children, the mothers preferred to feed them on demand, despite the criticisms of proponents of scientific mothering.

Even so, working conditions, undernourishment, long hours of work at home, and excessive stress created difficult nursing situations. The mother's milk was often inadequate to meet the needs of the infant, and artificial bottle feedings were used as a supplement. The lack of nourishment during pregnancy and nursing often affected the supply and quality of the mother's milk. In the Old World mothers had poor but simple diets, but here mothers were "so poorly nourished before the baby arrives that it comes into the world half-starved: the mother must often do work, the bottle is much simpler and frequently she does not have enough milk to properly feed the child." A study of bottle-fed babies stated: "In Manhattan, 12,500 mothers of the poorer classes are forced to rely upon bottle feeding for their infants—two main reasons for this material impotency are physical disability due to improper nourishment and disease, and industrial employment due to abject poverty."

An additional problem was contaminated milk. Milk in New York City was graded according to quality: the higher grades were more expensive and sold in bottles, while the cheaper grades were sold as "loose milk," taken from large open buckets in grocery stores and carried home in pails and glasses. The stores had little refrigeration and the milk was contaminated with bacteria that could cause illness and death in young children. John Spargo, in an article on the milk question for *Survey* magazine, argued that high rates of infant mortality were linked to dirty milk: "One-third of all babies die before five years old of diseases chiefly connected with the digestive tract and a considerable percent of diseases are definitely known to be caused by milk." Yet in the end it was a question of money: the higher and more sanitary grades of milk were simply too expensive for most women to buy.

In 1908, in a response to this situation, social workers set up clean milk depots in poor neighborhoods where bottled milk, free from bacteria, was sold at reasonable prices. It was a constant struggle to maintain the milk depots: year after year, "Baby Week" campaigns were run to raise money for them. In 1911, after much pressure, New York City authorized "the municipalization of fifteen milk stations and so satisfactory were the results that the next year the appropriation permitted more than a trebling of this number." Lillian Wald argued that in the neighborhoods where there were milk depots there was a sharp decrease in the infant mortality rate. Yet there were still not enough depots to satisfy the need for clean milk.

In any case, the milk stations were only a partial solution. The responsibility for unbottled, dirty milk was ultimately in the hands of the commercial dairies. *Survey* reported that a long fight with the dairy industry had resulted in the establishment of new standards for the production and pasteurization of milk that recognized pasteurization to be of primary importance if milk was to be safe. Nevertheless, pasteurization was being abused by dealers who "poured dirty milk into the machines."

The problem was complicated by the lack of adequate refrigeration at home. Even if milk was bought in bottles, there was no way to keep it cold—in the summer it would go bad by mid-morning. Most immigrant mothers had small iceboxes that had to be supplied with ice bought daily from the iceman. Since a small amount of ice cost between five and ten cents, few women could afford to buy more than small quantities.

The social workers who established milk depots included mothers' clubs and classes as part of their program. Although the classes at first focused on the milk question, they quickly turned into a general program for teaching immigrant women scientific motherhood: "When breast feeding has been found impossible, they [mothers] have been taught the value of many other things: of keeping the milk cold; of feeding the babies regularly; of throwing away the deadly pacifier; of peeling off the long red bands which swathe and infest the little baby." In the campaign to change immigrant mothering, pacifiers and swaddling clothes became bones of contention. Social workers and child care "experts" thought that pacifiers represented "an extremely bad habit," a habit for which "someone else is entirely responsible. The baby does not teach himself this disgusting habit."

Anzia Yezierska fictionalized this tension in a story called "The Free Vacation House," which was about a poor Jewish mother desperately trying to go on vacation with her children in the country. She applied to a charity organization, which sent a social worker to investigate her case:

> I hear a knock on the door and a lady comes in. She had a white starched dress like a nurse and carried a black satchel in her hand. I am from the Social Betterment Society, she tells me. You want to go to the country. Before I could say something she goes over to the baby and pulled the rubber nipple from her mouth and to me she say you must not get this child used to this; this is very unsanitary. Gott in Himmel, I beg the lady. Please don't begin with that child or she'll holler her head off. She must have that nipple.

Enrico Sartorio observed the same conflict between immigrant mothers and social workers in Italian communities:

> Italian families complain about the blunt, aggressive way in which some social workers burst into their homes and upset the usual nature of their lives, undressing children, giving orders not to eat this or that, not to wrap up babies in swaddling clothes and so forth. The mother of five and six children may be inclined to think with some reason, that she knows a little more about how to bring up children than the young looking damsel who insists upon trying to do it.

The confrontation over the pacifier, swaddling clothes, irregular feeding habits, and so on, was an area of cultural collision in which customary motherhood was confronted by the new techniques of scientific mothering. The tension between immigrant women and the representatives of industrial culture was not over the need to change the external conditions of motherhood in an urban slum environment, but over how and what knowledge was to be incorporated into the rhythm and patterns of daily life. These difficult conditions often led to extreme frustration, as exhibited by the mother in "The Free Vacation House":

> Then I looked around me in the kitchen. On one side was a big washtub of clothes waiting for me to wash. On the table was a big pile of breakfast dishes yet. The baby was beginning to cry for the bottle. Aby [one of the six children] was hollering and pulling me to take him to kindergarten. I felt that if I didn't get away from here for a little while, I could land in the crazy house, jump from the window or go to the country with the charities.

If one set of diseases devastated the lives of young children, another set—like tuberculosis and scarlet fever—ravaged the adults. Immigrants called tuberculosis the "workingman's disease" or the "tailor's disease." It was, as Lillian Wald noted, "pre-eminently a disease of poverty" created by "underlying economic causes, bad housing, bad workshops, undernourishment and so on."

The garment industry was particularly responsible for its spread. Small factories with no light or air, small apartments with no windows or ventilation, the homework system, and industrial dust, dirt, and grime made the Lower East Side a breeding ground for a disease that caused prolonged illness and death, and upset the precarious economy of many immigrant families. It was also responsible for acute suffering within the family. One immigrant father who had been tubercular for years wrote a poignant letter to the "Bintel Brief" column of the *Jewish Daily Forward:*

> I am the father of a three year old girl, a clever, pretty child who attracts everyone's attention. All who know my child hug and kiss her. I may not. . . . Every time I kiss the child I feel my wife's eyes on me, as if she wanted to shout "murderer"! but she doesn't utter a word—only her face reddens. I feel that a battle is going on within her: she compresses her lips and keeps silent. She tries to keep the child away from me though she doesn't want to hurt me. My wife's suffering deepens my pain.

Disease was also spread by the continuation of traditional customs in an environment that made no provision for them. For example, Jewish women, as part of their religious duties, were required to take *mikveh* baths:

> Women are required to use the pools regularly within seven days of menstruation. The Hebrew law is very strict regarding the method of using these baths and states that after a thorough cleansing, the person should immerse herself in a purified plunge filled with uncontaminated water or water that has not been polluted by human beings.

On the Lower East Side, *mikveh* baths were usually located in the basements of tenements in congested areas where it was impossible to change the water, which was used by hundreds of people and became a breeding ground for disease. The bath cost five cents, and it was five cents more for a shower. Since people usually did not have the extra nickel, the showers were not used. Despite the fact that the Lower East Side *mikveh* bath did not comply with the standards of "the Mosaic laws," their abolition was strongly opposed by the Jewish people who bathed there.

The attempt to find clean air and water encountered the same obstacles. Immigrant women knew about the value of fresh air and clean water, but it cost money to get to the country, or even to parks in the city. The parks had been built for the middle and upper classes and were far away from the Lower East Side. In a story for *Survey* magazine, Annie O'Hagan reconstructed the attempts of a tenement house mother trying to give her youngest child the benefits of fresh air:

> In pursuance of her resolution to procure sunlight and fresh air for Tobias without paying for it by separation from him or the rest of her tribe, her life was very strenuous. She got up at dawn to push her baby carriage through garbage-laden streets. There wasn't a park available to her. All day, as she did her own and

other people's wash, she tried to get the baby out in the fresh air, but there was little fresh air to be found.

Most adult diseases were treated at home. Social workers did a house-to-house canvas in 1904–1905 and discovered that "in the East Side district, 90 percent of sickness is cared for at home. Even such grave diseases as typhoid and tuberculosis are nursed at home. Ancient prejudices against going to the hospital persist in these districts." At the same time, social workers recognized that the hospitals were "ignorant of the home conditions from which their patients come and their patients distrust dispensaries and hospitals."

Immigrant women, lacking adequate medical advice, occasionally used folk medicine in an attempt to eradicate illness. One Jewish woman remembered that when she was very sick as a child her mother adopted her own medical practice: "My mother had me urinate and rubbed it on my forehead and my fever subsided. Another time I had fever so my mother ripped the top of my ear and let the blood flow and the fever subsided, too." Another woman remembered a cure for burns:

> My mother was very badly burned by hot water. So the grandma took some lima beans and put them in a pan on the gas stove and practically burned them. She then chopped them and put them through a sieve. It looked like powder. She put it on the burned area and it coated and cleaned the burn. The burn never showed.

The women also resorted to prayer. Fabbia Orzo's mother claimed to be cured by a miracle:

> St. Anthony was her favorite saint and she had reasons to believe in St. Anthony. My mother was crippled before her youngest son was born. She couldn't walk. Three months after she gave birth she couldn't walk until she prayed to St. Anthony. One day a parade for St. Anthony went past her window. My mother prayed that she be able to walk to the window and see the parade for St. Anthony walk by. She said if this happened she would go to church no matter where it was to pray for the saint, and pay her respects. She did walk those few steps to the window and from then on she regained her health.

Mike Gold, in his autobiographical novel *Jews Without Money,* told of another form of folk healing. During the summer months it was common to find children sleeping in the streets outside their apartment buildings. One such night, a Fourth of July, Gold was falling asleep in his bedding on the street when someone threw a lighted firecracker that exploded on his pillow and burned him. He then became subject to recurrent nightmares and lost weight, and the family consulted doctors whose cures proved to be of little help. His mother took the advice of a neighbor and called in "the Speaker-Woman, Baba-Sima":

> There were many such old women on the East Side. They were held in great respect. . . . Baba Sima called one summer night as I lay pale and exhausted by the dark mental shadows. She was a humpbacked old crone in kerchief and apron

with red rheumy eyes and protruding belly. . . . She turned me on my stomach and with a blunt knife traced magic designs on my back, mumbling over and over in singsong. . . . I was left irritable and skeptical. This foreign hocus pocus did not appeal to me, an American boy. . . . "My dear," said my mother, "this is a famous Speaker. . . . She knows more than many doctors. . . . She is sure to make you well."

Through the use of spells, incantations, and rituals, he was cured of his nightmares. The Speaker-Woman practiced a kind of primitive ritualistic psychiatry:

The East Side worshipped doctors, but in nervous cases or in mishaps of the personal life, it sometimes reverted to medievalism. Lovers sought philters of the old Babas, to win victory over a rival in love. Deserted wives paid these women money to model little wax figures of their wandering husbands and torture them until the false one returned. . . . That greedy, dirty, foolish old woman knew some deep secrets, evidently. She had cured me.

Money and time were components of that "ancient" prejudice and distrust of hospitals. Hospitals were not located within walking distance, and finding carfare was a problem. Time was also a problem: immigrants could not afford to stay away from work for even short amounts of time. Further, the hospitals cost money and sickness could easily absorb a family's entire meager savings, even with the aid of a mutual-benefit society; prolonged illness sometimes forced a family to apply for relief.

Even public clinics and dispensaries took enormous amounts of time, and provided little relief:

Most immigrants were unwilling to go to public dispensaries. Crowded rooms, hasty examinations and prescriptions that gave no relief were some reasons for that feeling. Some people had to wait half a day before their prescriptions were filled and could not afford the time to go again; others found to have contagious diseases had merely been told to go away.

Dispensing personnel frequently told people that the dispensary could not cure the disease and that they should go to a doctor's private office at a high price per visit.

Sometimes doctors came into the neighborhoods, brought either by the public schools or the Board of Health, to vaccinate children and perform minor operations. Vaccination was a yearly event, yet its purpose was never explained to the community: both agencies and doctors assumed that its value would be intuitively understood, and neglected to communicate the medical meaning clearly. Deeply suspicious, many immigrant parents believed that vaccination was poison, and, according to one newspaper account, "vaccination is always accompanied only by force in the Lower East Side."

On one occasion, in 1908, neglect and suspicion erupted into violence. The doctors descended on the schools to vaccinate and, this time, to surgically remove the children's adenoids, since it was believed that this would prevent illnesses. Although parental consent was required, most parents misunderstood what they had signed. Word spread. As the New York Tribune reported:

"Rioting women and children, by the thousands, swept into a senseless panic by an absurd story that children's throats were being cut by physicians in various East Side schools, swarmed down on these buildings . . . in great mobs . . . intent on rescuing their children and companions." The women, described by the *Tribune* as "voluble Yiddish women of luxuriant flesh," cried out that "their children were being murdered and buried in the school yard . . . [and] stoned the school houses, smashed windows and door panes." The *Tribune* attributed this riot to "ignorant, excitable Jews, fearing Russian massacres here, knowing nothing of American sanitary ideas." Events like this did little to improve the condescending attitude of the medical profession, or the ability of the women to understand the value of American medicine.

Given this lack of communication, and the immigrants' resistance to hospitals in general, social workers began to establish health care centers and visiting nurse services to help care for the sick in their homes. In this case, social workers recognized cultural practices while doctors did not:

> In the home, the largest proportion of sickness has been and will be cared for. . . . If the municipality assumes the obligation to adequately care for sickness and to prevent it when possible, measures must be taken to render service in the home. It is idle to argue that if the city provided hospitals, the people, when sick, would go to these hospitals.

They also instigated antituberculosis campaigns, argued for more sanitary working conditions in the garment industry, and agitated for new tenement house legislation that would require better ventilation and more air space.

In the final analysis, however, most of the diseases of the Lower East Side were produced by industrial conditions, and their cure was therefore dependent on better conditions and access to money. Immigrants, through lodges, mutual-benefit societies, and local unions, employed doctors who spoke the same language and whose fees were considerably lower than those of American doctors. But there were never enough of these to deal with the enormous amount of sickness. A group of concerned Lower East Side doctors confronted this situation directly when they organized a free medical visiting service during the garment strike of 1916:

> We have seen babies die because their parents had no money for a doctor and our volunteer service came too late. We have seen men suffer because they had no carfare to go to the hospital. We doctors don't complain for ourselves. These are our people. We are glad to give them our medical services freely in their great need. But hunger is a disease we cannot cure. Money is the only medicine that can save them.

If social workers and official public agencies experienced great difficulty curing the health problems of the immigrants, there was another group of "medicine men" who had few scruples about taking advantage of the health problems of the ethnic communities. Beginning in 1911, under the truth-in-advertising legislation, quack doctors and salesmen of fake and patent medicine were driven out of national magazines and high-class metropolitan dailies and found "refuge in the small town papers and especially the foreign press. The foreign-language press, it was estimated, derived 36% of their advertisements from quack practitioners and patent medicine interests." Disreputable doctors advertised in these papers, relying on the fact that most immigrants trusted their own newspapers.

The advertising consisted of all kinds of quick cures for immigrant illnesses. The ads appealed to ethnicity as the basis of trust. In 1920, *Survey* reported that the same doctor, writing ads in several papers, appealed to "my Rumanian brothers," or to "my sick Lithuanian brothers"—the nationality changed with the language of the paper—or, in a message to the Italians, "Sick Italians, don't be discouraged. Thousands of your countrymen have found health and happiness by going to see Dr. Landis." Or they appealed to a common language, "You can hold a conversation with me in your own tongue. . . . Here we speak Hungarian." The *Survey* article claimed that "the type of appeal is more vivid and dramatic in Italian, Hungarian and Polish papers, while in Swedish, Lithuanian or German, more matter of fact."

Those responsible for the ads were quick to spot what the hospitals and doctors missed: that ethnic groups preferred to rely on their own people when sick. Quack doctors made use of community interdependence for their own pecuniary benefit, while the foreign press acquiesced in return for needed revenues. The same study reported:

> The foreign language press cannot afford to give up bad types of advertising unless they can get something remunerative to replace it. One small foreign language paper refused quack patent ads to an amount of $1500 a month because its people were being exploited and victimized. As a result, it could barely pay expenses but the editor declared he felt at peace without stained money. It has, however, gradually resumed much of what it had once refused.

The remedies offered by quack doctors and patent medicine men offered little relief to those who lived in the beleaguered tenement districts, and instead compounded the problem of finding reasonable medical care from doctors who shared a common language. Few professional Italian or Jewish doctors had emigrated and the American medical profession was largely unsympathetic to the health needs of the new immigrants. This situation helps explain the desire of Jewish and Italian parents to have their sons enter the medical profession. If this desire accepted the patriarchal assumptions of a predominantly male profession, it also corresponded to the needs of a community faced with illness and disease. Both experience and tradition assumed that the best medical care could be obtained from members of the community itself. After all, who else would heal the sick?

REVIEW QUESTIONS

1. What were the most significant health problems that immigrant women had to deal with?

2. Why did most immigrant women prefer to have midwives instead of doctors attend the birth of their children? How and why did this attitude change?

3. Advocates of Americanization were convinced that immigrants would benefit from surrendering the customary beliefs and practices they brought with them from Europe because they were likely to be old-fashioned and rooted in superstition, while American ways were modern and scientific. What evidence does this selection provide for and against that view?

4. Much of the evidence in this selection comes from accounts by social workers. From this evidence, what would you say their attitude was on the question of New World versus Old World ways?

5. One of the standard views of immigrant life is that first-generation immigrants tended to hang on to the values and beliefs of the old country while their children, who were born and grew up in the United States, were eager to shed their parents' ways and embrace American ones. Does the evidence in this selection support that view or not?

6. To what extent were the health-care problems and practices of immigrant women a result of their relative poverty?

FOR FURTHER READING

The literature on immigration and the lives of immigrants in the United States is massive. General accounts include Philip A. M. Taylor, *The Distant Magnet: European Emigration to the U.S.A.* (1971); three books by Oscar Handlin, *The Uprooted* (2nd ed., 1973), *Children of the Uprooted* (1966), and *Immigration as a Factor in American History* (1959); Alan M. Kraut, *The Huddled Masses: The Immigrant in American Society, 1820–1921* (1982); and Roger Daniels, *A History of Immigration and Ethnicity in American Life* (1990). Moses Rischin, *The Promised City: New York's Jews, 1870–1914,* and Irving Howe, *World of Our Fathers* (1976), deal specifically with the Lower East Side of New York, as does the book from which the preceding selection was taken, Elizabeth Ewen, *Immigrant Women in the Land of Dollars: Life and Culture on the Lower East Side, 1890–1925* (1985). Thomas Kessner, *The Golden Door: Italian and Jewish Immigrant Mobility in New York City* (1977), focuses on the same ethnic groups. Hasia Diner, *Erin's Daughters in America* (1983), concerns the lives of Irish immigrant women. For more information on the settlement house movement, see two books by Allen F. Davis, *Spearheads for Reform: The Social Settlements and the Progressive Movement, 1890–1914* (1967), and *American Heroine: The Life and Legend of Jane Addams* (1973). The most complete treatment of anti-immigrant feelings in the United States is John Higham, *Strangers in the Land: Patterns of American Nativism* (1955). Linda Gordon, *Women's Body, Women's Right: A Social History of Birth Control in America* (1976), is a general history. Those who wish to know more about Margaret Sanger, the pioneer of the movement for birth control in the United States, should consult her *Autobiography* (1938).

The Jacob A. Riis Collection, Museum of the City of New York

Americanizing immigrant children—saluting the flag at school.

8

Immigrant Children at School

SELMA BERROL

The huge wave of immigration that flowed into the United States from the mid-1880s until the outbreak of World War I affected nearly every important aspect and institution of American life. One such institution was certainly the school.

Like many other facets of American life, public education changed rapidly in the late 1800s and early 1900s. In 1870, half the children in the United States received no schooling at all, the average length of school attendance was only four years, and 20 percent of the population was illiterate. By 1900 public school attendance had doubled, and illiteracy had been reduced by half. It was still true, however, that adults averaged only five years of schooling and that less than half of those eligible had ever attended high school.

A variety of pressures produced these results. In the South, for example, the demand of ex-slaves for education was largely responsible for the initial creation of a system of tax-supported schools. Elsewhere, while some, including many businessmen, questioned the relevance of "book learning," changing economic realities put a progressively higher premium on education as a method of personal advancement. If nothing else, it was believed that schools could teach workers-to-be the disciplined habits they would need in order to do their jobs properly.

The presence of immigrant children intensified demands for the expansion of public education. Their sheer numbers added greatly to the need for more school buildings, teachers, and supplies when such resources were already being strained. Perhaps even more important was the widespread belief that public schools could "Americanize" the immigrants, smoothing their path to full membership in American society and, in the process, alleviating problems that might arise from having a large, undigested alien lump in the nation's midst.

Immigrants' attitudes toward education were diverse. Many hoped it would provide the means to begin the climb up the socio-economic ladder. Others, however, thought compulsory school attendance deprived them of the labor and income of their children and was part of an effort to strip them of their native language and ways of life. The following selection is based on extensive interviews of those who were among the immigrant children attending public schools during the early years of this century. The variety of their attitudes indicates the clash of views about public education that existed at the time, and not only among immigrants.

At the start of the twentieth century, when immigration from southern and eastern Europe was at its peak, thousands of "little aliens" entered the public and parochial schools of large American cities, making them more congested than they had ever been before. Jam-packed classrooms and the resulting half-time schedules exemplified one way that the immigrant child's school experience differed from those of other American children. The neighborhoods in which they lived were old and their schools had been built for smaller populations. Thus, when the number of foreign-born children in the "ghettoes" increased, many schools were forced to go on half-day sessions or to seat two children at a desk made for one or sometimes to do both. Sadie R. recalled that on her first day of school she had to sit in a seat with another girl "and put an arm around her waist so I shouldn't fall off."

The *Jewish Daily Forward,* speaking for many working-class Jews, reported that the poorest children on the Lower East Side of New York attended the worst schools. In one school on Henry Street eighty children were crammed into a room built for forty; another windowless classroom held seventy. In some schools, a teacher might face as many as one hundred children a day and, given the limitations on human strength, not convey much knowledge to any of them.

Some immigrant children were turned away entirely because of overcrowding, postponing their entry into school and possibly shortening their entire school experience. This was also true for children who entered the United States at a later age than usual. Since most children finished their schooling by the age of twelve, the child who could not be admitted at the normal age of five or six and whose parents could not do without the income he or she could earn as a teenager might have little more than a primary school (grades one through three) education.

School records in urban-immigrant districts showed great variations in the ages of students in any given grade, a circumstance not true of the schools that native-born children attended. A second-year class in a school that served an immigrant district resembled an ungraded one-room school found in rural areas; it might contain seven-year-olds, ten-year-olds, and occasionally a twelve-year-old. The disparity resulted from policy adopted by most school districts that received immigrants. A foreign-born child was placed at the level indicated by his or her ability to speak, read, or write English. Thus, a ten-year-old who knew little English would be assigned to a classroom with children three or four years younger.

Most of the time a child who knew no English would be placed in a "sink-or-swim," total-immersion class when first entering school. After six months a student who did not "sink" would graduate to a class appropriate to his or her ability to cope with English. Bilingualism was not an option, and as a result many of the children schooled under this policy recall that their initial experiences were intensely traumatic. Isidor B., escorted by a neighbor to kindergarten in the Bronx, recalled his terror when she left and he realized that he could not understand what anyone around him, including the teacher, was saying. Edward Bok, a Dutch immigrant who later became the editor of the *Saturday Evening Post,* said that he did not know "a single word of English" when he entered school, an uncomfortable position he shared with Leonard Covello, who was to become a schoolmaster in "a great city" (New York City) when he grew up. Native-born children, of course, also did not know how to read and write English, but their ability to understand simple directions was one of the differences that set them apart from many immigrant children.

Language difficulties for immigrants were a problem that could be alleviated only with the passage of time, but the intense crowding that marked the schools in immigrant districts could have been relieved immediately. Most large cities had a long-established tradition of neighborhood schools; when residential patterns shifted, some schools were underutilized. At the turn of the century there were usually empty seats in classrooms in parts of the city outside the immigrant districts. Busing, however, was unpopular with immigrant parents and often unacceptable to parents at the receiving schools, many of whom had left the poorer areas where most of the newcomers lived partly to avoid immigrants.

Wherever immigrant children appeared, teachers and administrators did all they could to get them into school and to keep them there until they were old enough to leave school legally. In some places that meant completion of the sixth grade, in others the eighth year. Success was difficult to achieve. Primarily for economic reasons, parents of every ethnic background were often forced to send a child to work at the earliest possible age. Sometimes the work was part-time but very demanding. Several former students, for example, described selling newspapers form 4 A.M. to 7:45 A.M. and then again at 4 P.M. Vicenzo M., in Syracuse, New York, had such a schedule but was able to cope. Harry Roskolenko, however, who followed a similar schedule on New York City's Lower East Side, slept selectively in class, staying "partially awake during history and English lessons" but not during civics, arithmetic or "most of everything else."

Sometimes the work done by foreign-born children was full-time, possibly at home doing piecework or, in the case of girls, attending to the household so the mother could earn some much-needed money. It was not difficult for a child to find work; small jobs could be obtained at the docks and errand boys were always in demand. The absence of birth certificates, a common situation for children born abroad, made it easier to fool the truant officer or another authority figure, especially if the child was tall for his or her age.

Although most immigrant children did not want to avoid school, the acute discomfort some experienced in the classroom led them to evade the compulsory-education laws as much as possible. As Eva Morawska said in her book on the east central European immigrants in Johnstown, Pennsylvania, children from foreign homes who attended the public schools in that community between 1890 and 1940 recalled "recurrent feelings of embarrassment and inferiority to the American children caused by [their] difficulty with the English language . . . foreign dress . . . and unpronounceable names."

For many reasons, boys and girls of the immigrant generation and many of their children did not attend school for very long. In many cases it was the schools themselves, and especially the teachers in them, that were to blame. Then as now, the teacher was central to the entire school experience, and then as now, many were not equal to their task.

During these years, most immigrant children faced an unmarried woman, usually although not always a WASP or an Irish Catholic, who had completed a teacher-training program at a normal school. In addition to differences in background, age, and training, these teachers, like most human beings, differed in personality and ability. If the perceptions of most of their former students are to be trusted, however, they were alike in one very important way: They were antagonistic to their students. One after another, the men and women who were once immigrant children discussed the hostility that they felt emanating from the front desk. Some youngsters felt this early in their school careers. Samuel C. described his first-grade teacher as "cold and forbidding," an image reinforced by her habit of calling on her six-year-old charges by their surnames and requiring an instant response to her commands. Alfred Kazin wrote that his teachers "grimly, wearily, often with ill-concealed distaste, watched against their students relapsing into savage Brownsville boys."

Other students had other complaints but all revealed unfavorable memories of those who had instructed them. Mike T., whose given name was distinctly Serbian, recalled that "at school I went as Tomas . . . because the teacher would not pronounce or spell my own." A student of Slovenian background in a Pittsburgh public school, Stanley N., echoed this, recalling that his teachers, despite his corrections, continued to mispronounce his unfamiliar surname, which made him angry and contributed to his decision to drop out of school at twelve. Rosemary P., also from Pittsburgh, was told that she "talked funny" by her first high-school teacher and, to avoid further embarrassment, she spent a precious twenty-five cents on a self-improvement pamphlet and locked herself in the bathroom to "practice English" in secret until she could "pronounce properly the difficult 'th' sound."

Rightly or wrongly, former students recalled some painful experiences. Tanya N., for example, got into trouble on her first day of school:

> My mother gave me a bagel and an apple which I brought to school with me. My teacher was talking and I didn't understand a word she said. I got bored so I bit into my bagel. The teacher's face looked a little angry, so I thought something was wrong, but I didn't know what was wrong. I just kept eating the bagel and after a few minutes the teacher went over to me, took me by the hand, walked me to a corner of the room [and] sat me up on a very high teacher's chair. I took my bagel with me. She put a dunce cap on my head and the children began to laugh. I didn't know that it was a dunce cap. I learned later.

Food was often a problem. During Passover, Jewish children substituted matzo for their usual bread sandwiches. As anyone who has ever tried to manage a matzo sandwich would expect, a terrific mess resulted and led to harsh criticism from the teachers assigned to patrol the lunchroom. In general, lunch, brown-bagged from home, caused particular difficulty. Italian mothers made Italian-style lunches, but WASP teachers said that American foods were healthier. One interviewee told Leonard Covello that he threw his lunch away "rather than ruin his reputation" with his non-Italian peers and his teachers.

Some teachers did not hesitate to use humiliation in order to teach. Sadie R. recalled such an incident when she was learning English at a Lower East Side school:

On one occasion in the lower grades . . . I raised my hand and the teacher said, "What is it, Sadie?" "Can I leave the room?" I say. She said, "Yes, you can leave the room." So I picked myself up and I go and she said, "Where are you going?" And I said, "I asked you and you said I could leave the room." And she said, "I said you *can* leave the room, but you didn't ask me whether you *may* leave the room!" I was so embarrassed with the whole thing, I never forgot the difference between can and may.

Alfred Kazin, as well as others, remembered his teachers as always being angry; often their anger resulted in physical punishment. Felix B., in a Chicago school in 1915, said that he "wanted to stay out of school because every time my work was wrong, the teacher hit me." His classmate, Edward R., had a slightly different experience: When he could not do the assigned work, his teacher used "proxy punishment" and encouraged his fellow students to hit him. Edward Bok recalled being "hit hard" as a pupil in the Philadelphia public schools; Sol L. said his New York City first-grade teacher struck him "with a pointer if he talked at the wrong time" because "talking was illegal and hitting was common." In his next grade, the treatment got worse. A Miss Bower broke a ruler on him for reading under the desk.

Harry Roskolenko recalls being hit by his teachers and the school principal, possibly because he fell asleep in class, something Leonard Covello reported was not unusual. Jerre Mangione and Sam R. agreed that they feared their teachers because, as Sam said, "they would send you up to the principal and the principal would beat the hell out of you." Paul W. said that the nuns who taught him "seldom used the ruler to measure anything except the distance between a long overhead swing and the [offending] student's hand." Parents did not complain because usually they did not know. Most of the memoir writers never told their fathers or mothers, fearing that another beating would result; parents typically believed that for good or ill authority had to be respected.

Many immigrant children, especially girls, were well behaved and suffered no punishments. As a result, they had good memories of their teachers. Mary Antin was an example; at twelve, recently arrived from Russia, she entered the Chelsea, Massachusetts, public schools to find that her teachers "were patient, persevering, sweet and ready to help her at any time." She had special praise for a Miss Dillingham, who gave her private tutoring in the pronunciation of *v* and *w*. Other children, especially girls, had similar memories. Sadie R. recalled a loving first-grade teacher who "put me on her lap after school and [would] teach me English words."

Rose J. loved her fifth-grade teacher, Miss Bliss, partly because she had never known a real person with that surname but had seen the word only in books. She cared even more for her sixth-grade teacher, who was "beautiful and young" and encouraged her interest in music. Hannah T. remembered a teacher who "would help me, hug me and nurture me. My mother was not a nurturer." Rose J. agreed: "I loved my teachers . . . I always sought a surrogate mother because my own was not demonstratively an affectionate person."

On the other side of the United States, Jade Snow Wong, later to become an author and ceramicist, also found her American teachers to be very kind. Her third-grade teacher appreciated her ability and allowed her to skip a grade, and her next teacher was "loving." Harry Roskolenko recalled one teacher: "a grand lady . . . a beautiful woman [who] smelled of heaven . . . , had small hands and seemed much concerned with him." He adored her and paid her the highest tribute in his power to bestow—he did his homework that year. . . .

Teachers of immigrant children were "representatives of a different, ineluctably more attractive way of life" to the young girls they taught. Apparently to everyone's satisfaction, immigrant children learned WASP etiquette along with WASP speech and dress from their teachers, who also brought culture into their lives. Rose J. cited her attraction to music and "things cultural," which she would not have had without the teachers who set her an example to follow. She learned to love music in appreciation classes. "I had a fabulous memory," she reported and thus recognized all the songs and operatic excerpts that were played. As a result, "I won all the prizes."

More down-to-earth training was also part of her education. Girls in the upper grades of elementary school attended home-economics classes, later favorably recalled. Mary F. told her interviewer: "I didn't know what the [table] utensils were for. We'd set the table and Miss Themig [said] to me 'You don't have a butter knife there,' so I took a knife and put it down. She then said . . . [no], 'that is an ordinary knife.' " Mary did not mind the correction because she learned that there was a special knife for butter.

These girls discovered, however, that their mothers did not always respond happily to such lessons. One mother, told by her ten-year-old daughter that her cooking was not American enough and that she should use a cook book, asserted her supremacy in the kitchen in no uncertain terms; others welcomed the new knowledge as a window to the outer world. That, of course, was the reason for introducing home economics into the curriculum and also why it caused trouble for many girls. The recipes used in these classes, for example, involved mixing dairy and meat products and using pork. This created difficulty for both Orthodox Jewish girl students and for those from less observant but nonetheless traditional Jewish homes. No concessions to religious law were made, however. On the theory that immigrant cuisines would not produce healthy new Americans, young girls were taught to prepare and value American foods, including bacon and ham.

While their female peers were involved in the demonstration kitchen, boys were attending workshops. The reasoning behind workshops for boys differed somewhat from that behind home economics. Although most immigrant children were not expected to remain in school long after the legal school-leaving age, boys in particular were expected to leave quite early. Thus knowing a trade would have great value. Some of the memoirs indicate that the children liked workshop classes and took great pride in "bringing home a project from carpentry class," but others felt that such lessons had little long-term value. As with so many issues in immigrant history, reactions varied with ethnicity. Some Jewish parents, for example, considered learning manual skills a waste of time better spent in preparing for a profession, but others, notably Italians and Slavs, welcomed the opportunity for their children to learn skills that might enable them to enter a higher echelon of manual work.

In all areas of the curriculum, a good memory was much prized. Leonard Covello memorized the states, capital cities, poetry, wise sayings, and "memory gems," which by themselves were intended to create a better memory. Good handwriting was another highly rated skill. Edward Bok recalled his inability to learn a Spencerian style of writing, which led to the principal's hitting his hand with a rattan rod hard enough to cause swelling. Bok does not specify the kind of paper he was told to use, but other sources indicate that at the start of the first grade, wide-lined paper was used. The lines soon grew narrower; a sample of Thomas S.'s writing as a student in the second half of first grade (1B) was done on paper with normal line spacing.

Handwriting was not considered an individual trait. Many respondents recall the horizontal chart that adorned their primary-school classrooms showing the only correct way to write the letters of the alphabet in upper and lower case. Students also did exercises to improve muscle control and thus produce the clearest possible writing. From an inspection of one valuable source, materials collected by the recently created Board of Education of the City of New York and presented at the Paris Exposition in 1900, this practice paid off. Many second graders and even more third graders wrote with a clarity that many adults would envy.

But what were they saying in this eminently legible handwriting? Some wrote poetry and many wrote short essays. Hyman G., age nine, in the second grade at P.S. 75, Manhattan, gave us a sample of the former:

> Dear Rain, without your help, I know
> The trees and flowers could not grow
> My roses all would fade and die
> If you stayed up behind the sky

His classmate, Max A., provided a mini-mini-essay reflecting weather changes: "The birds are going South. It is too cold here."

Max's topic reflected another subject many former students recalled, most with great pleasure. Nature study was introduced into urban schools on the theory that city children, especially if they grew up in the "congested districts," would barely know what a tree looked like. In some schools such study took the form of gardening. Isidore B. remembered the elaborate ceremonies surrounding Arbor Day at his Bronx school, and Mary F., from a third-grade class in Brownsville, Brooklyn, described her experience on a nature trip: "We traipsed over to New Lots Avenue and there was this huge wilderness under the El [elevated trains] and [the teacher] gave us all kinds of implements but our job was to weed. And we weeded and we got burrs in us and we planted." Mary may have been more enthusiastic than most. She also planted seeds on her own and "used to pick up manure [for fertilizer] in the street." Most children liked physical education, but few schools in immigrant neighborhoods were equipped to hold such classes. As a substitute, Sophie Ruskay said, teachers held an exercise period when, with the window partially open, the children were ordered to "breathe in; breathe out" and to do simple exercises.

Gardening, cooking, carpentry, and physical education were not taught in every school because they were often seen as unnecessary frills. Everyone agreed, however, on the basics; arithmetic, grammar, spelling, and speech were thoroughly taught.

In retrospect, given the crowding and the problems of poverty, poor health, and adjustment presented by immigrant children to the schools, it is amazing to see how much was attempted on the elementary level. How well the schools succeeded is another matter, but judging from what the children said about the teaching methods, there was certainly no lack of trying. Charlie M. explained how he learned to read: "We had a book, story books, a progressive reader. We didn't have a formalized reading method. We had a primer. In the primer were stories: 'the sky was falling down.' We children actually repeated that story with the teacher, so we learned it by repeating it. We would match the words we had learned with the words in the book, and this way we acquired a vocabulary."

Leonard Covello, although in a different school, learned by a similar method: memorizing assigned word lists. Children at P.S. 188 on New York City's East Side learned the English words for the parts of their body by physically locating them. This led one small newcomer to say "Dis ist a piece of mine head" when the teacher patted her hair and asked what part of her body was being touched.

Phonetic methods, later used to teach reading, do not appear in the recollections of those interviewed, but recitation certainly does. Over and over, the children tell us that they were required to recite, often standing at attention. Henry Klein, who graduated from P.S. 4 on the Lower East Side, liked this approach and said that he was always ready with answers in arithmetic, history, geography, and grammar. If he also enjoyed the regular Friday tests, however, he was unusual; most children dreaded them. Tests of various kinds were an integral part of schooling. Teachers would dictate words, which children were expected to write well and to spell correctly. There were also daily oral drills and frequent spelling bees. Mistakes in spelling, wherever they occurred, might lead to a special assignment—writing each misspelled word ten times or more.

Americanization was at the top of the public-school agenda. Although immigrants had been coming to America since the colonial era, the years from 1880 to 1920 saw extraordinarily heavy immigration from areas of Europe previously underrepresented in the American population. The volume and "foreignness" of the new immigrants gave rise to much concern among those whose ancestors had come earlier. "Balkanization" was much feared; ethnic separatism was much deplored. The public school was seen as the agency best equipped to provide the remedy: assimilation. As a result, the central purpose of schools in immigrant neighborhoods became Americanization. Through reading and writing the national language and learning the national heritage and value system, the "little aliens" were expected to become socialized in American ways.

This goal was complicated because in most urban neighborhood schools children of the same ethnic background could speak to their peers in their own first language. Recognizing this, Julia Richman, the district superintendent of the Lower East Side schools from 1903 to 1912, forbade the use of Yiddish anywhere in her domain and enforced the rule by directing teachers to wash out offending mouths with kosher soap.

Unable to change the ethnic configuration of their classes, teachers took the advice of one expert and attempted to "wrest" the immigrant children in their care from their foreign backgrounds by a host of different methods, both negative and positive. They began with names. In Morreville, Pennsylvania, Slavic names were "adapted" for the teacher's convenience; in Boston, Philadelphia, and New York, first names might fall prey to the Americanizing teacher. Sadie would become Sylvia, Becky, Rebecca, and so on. Some of the newly named youngsters seemed to like the change, but others were confused because at home they continued to be called by their original names. One memorist said that when her school friends called at her home and asked for her under her American name, her parents told them no one by that name lived there.

Methods of Americanization, although they varied with individual teachers, were insensitive. Several of the Russian Jewish students who were interviewed years later remembered the inspections they were subjected to by school nurses and teachers who assumed that because they were poor they were also dirty. The nurse's inspection visits were purposely irregular; when she entered the classroom "the insides of the little immigrant daughters would begin to slide—slide" because the examination was done in groups of five in front of the class, and the public humiliation if one was found offensive was almost unbearable.

Dozens of times each day, teachers sought to "Americanize" their immigrant children into "little citizens." As the children learned the three Rs, for example, their primers, textbooks, and assignments were used to inculcate love and pride in their adopted land. History, especially American history, occupied a central place in the curriculum, with civics and geography in only a slightly lower spot. Harry L. remembered that "American holidays and Puritan roots were emphasized: We had a textbook about Puritans, pictures of Puritans with big hats and Thanksgiving and so on, and then about Betsy Ross and George Washington, and those things we learned." Other memoir writers agreed that they were taught a history that left them with "strong positive feelings about the United States."

Given their mission, the public schools ignored and often derogated the first culture of the students they were teaching. With the exception of an occasional settlement-house resident, "immigrant gifts" were not much prized. Parents did not protest. Most accepted the Protestant exercises that began the public-school day as well as the highly nationalistic American history taught in the classroom. Although most parents certainly wanted to preserve at least some aspects of their home culture and language, they seemed to agree that the public school was not obligated to do this for them. Instead they relied on the home or on an additional ethnic or religious school, for which they paid tuition, to teach the language and culture of their ethnic group.

Authors Jade Snow Wong and Maxine Hong Kingston followed this path, attending and enjoying Chinese school after public-school classes were over. Both described the long hours that they spent in the afternoon and evening classes as strengthening their feelings of self-worth, which had been somewhat damaged by classmates, and to a lesser extent, by teachers, in public school. Kingston also recalled the differences in children's behavior in the two schools. Children who were withdrawn and passive in their American classes became raucous and wild in Chinese school; depression and silence gave way to gaiety and chatter in an atmosphere where they felt at home.

Exhausting as attending two schools might be, ethnic schools did lessen the painful feelings of marginality frequently expressed in the memoirs and interviews of those recalling immigrant childhoods. Which model were they to follow? Their parents' behavior and ideas or the teachers'? Harriet Pawlowska's father, for example, left Poland, as most immigrants did, to earn a better living. He remained proud of his native land, however, and wanted his children to feel the same way. As a result, Harriet expected to see a large nation called Poland on the map when she first studied geography and was extremely puzzled when she could not find it. Papa had never told her that as a physical entity, his beloved land had ceased to exixt at the end of the eighteenth century. Whom was she to believe? Patriotic Papa or the map? Where did the child belong? Was he or she an American or something else? Or, as Jerre Mangione's father said, was the answer "half and half"?

Immigrant children became aware of this duality from their first day of school because many of them were meeting Americans for the first time. One such child, Samuel O., likened going from his own street to school to a trip to another planet. For some, it was a hostile planet; for others, the problems came from home; for still others, there were no differences. Rosemary P.'s reminiscence exemplifies what Samuel meant. As with so many other children of her time, the 1930s, she learned to read from the Dick and Jane series, and, as for so many other immigrant youngsters, the contrasts between the idealized life portrayed in the primer and her own thoroughly Slovenian family created conflict:

> I became ashamed that my parents spoke "funny"; that we laughed too loud; that we drank homemade wine; that our walls were papered in flower patterns; that we grew our own vegetables; that my father raised chickens in our garage; . . . that he repaired all our shoes in the basement; that my mother never sat down to dinner with us (she cooked, served and ate when everyone was finished); that our clothes and our curtains and towels were homemade, some of them out of feed bags from the local granary; that stockings and worn clothing were never thrown away but given to my uncle who transformed them into rag rugs.

Classroom procedures helped create feelings like Rosemary's. Two Jewish girls remembered a handkerchief problem. "I had a cold," recalled Mary F., "and I had a rag with which to blow my nose, but no handkerchief." Her teacher was "really disgusted" and made it clear that a rag was no substitute for a handkerchief. Rose K. reported that her teacher "came to school with stacks of clean handkerchiefs" and would call students up to her desk to blow their noses. On hygienic grounds the teachers could not be faulted, but at the same time their attitudes increased the problem of marginality for their students by making them doubt the customs of their homes.

Such doubts led to fear of exposure and feelings of inferiority such as those recalled by the Slavic interviewees in Morreville, Pennsylvania, who discussed the past with Ewa Morowska years later. Italian children interviewed by Leonard Covello echoed this, describing their shame at being Italian, their embarrassment at dressing "Italian style," and their envy of those "boys and girls fortunate in not having Italian parents." In view of such feelings it was not surprising to learn that many youngsters changed their first names and said that they came from Rome instead of Sicily. Covello himself said that he was nervous from 9 A.M. to 3 P.M. while he attended an integrated school and was much relieved when he and his family moved and he changed to a de facto segregated school in Italian East Harlem. There he no longer felt that he lived "in a different world," feelings also expressed by other immigrant children who were uncomfortable in schools where they were a minority but who bloomed when they attended a school where differences in speech, dress, food preferences, and other activities did not matter. As we have seen, this was also true for the children in the after-school Chinese classes described by Jade Snow Wong and Maxine Kingston. . . .

Clearly, segregation brought the security that the newly arrived child needed. In a class where almost everyone came from a similar background, childish bigotry, evidenced by name-calling and physical assault, was less likely. There was also less embarrassment if one's dress and school supplies indicated that one's family could not afford better, because in a "ghetto" school everybody's parents were poor. Several memoir writers, usually women, who attended integrated schools recalled that their inability to match the wardrobes of their Americanized peers caused them to leave school at the earliest possible age.

Richard Gambino, on the other hand, was unhappy in a school where Italians were in the majority because as a child who did well, he was "tormented" by his peers. He laid the blame for this on the conflicting messages Italian children were getting from school (do well) and at home (school is not important, don't bother). Certainly it was difficult for a child to be a high achiever in the face of hostility from his parents and his peers, and if he tried to be one, his feelings of marginality could only increase.

Several of the interviewees, however, recalled that their parents' attitudes helped them to endure these feelings. Some mothers and fathers told their children to overlook the school's efforts to change their culture and cuisine and to concentrate on what was to be gained by "going along." As Isidore B.'s father asked rhetorically, "Do you want to be an expressman [truckman] when you grow up? No? Then don't pay attention to anything else, just study!" Sam S.'s father gave another reason for his son to "go along." When Sam showed his dislike of school by being fresh to his teachers, his father was forced to come to school, thus losing a much-needed half-day's pay.

Some parents went further. Max W., born in Chicago in 1908, told his interviewer that his mother and father valued education so much that "the fact that [their] child was . . . celebrating the birth of Jesus and making Christmas decorations" was acceptable because it was "part of [his] education." When President William McKinley was assassinated, Jewish children sang "Nearer My God to Thee" along with their Christian classmates, and there is no evidence that anyone protested. William D' Antonio's parents took a middle course. Although they were Catholics, they sent their son to a public school where the Protestant version of the Lord's Prayer was recited every day but told him not to say the words. Jewish youngsters, without instructions from home, did something more inventive. They substituted their own, sometimes hostile words for the original verses in hymns and Christmas carols.

A few of the immigrants interviewed did not recall any difficulties. Thomas N., for example, says that he got the same messages at school as at home— work hard, respect your elders, learn as much as you can; as a result, he did not feel any marginality. Only the physical setting was different; the values were the same, and thus what he learned in school reinforced what he had already learned at home. Shirley K. also felt no conflict, but for quite a different reason. Her father urged total Americanization on his wife and children. Play baseball, the American game, he told his sons; join the Girl Scouts of America, he told his daughters. In his heart he may have wanted the Russian-Jewish food of his childhood, but he insisted that his wife prepare the broiled meats and bacon and eggs that Americans ate. Although he was more comfortable in Yiddish, he forbade its use in his home. With such a model, his daughter asked, who could resent Americanization at school?

There were other immigrant children who also welcomed Americanization, even against their parents' wishes; yet many more did not. Viewed from an adult's perspective, American public education might seem a homogenizing experience; certainly, this was the intent. Teachers and administrators were charged with tutoring their students in many of the same broad, general lessons and with instilling in them similar ideals and behavior. But from the child's eye view, education was diverse and disparate. Schooling meant one thing to immigrant children, quite another to native-born students. The experiences *among* those young immigrants differed as well, depending on a multitude of factors—not only their own personalities and inner resources but also their backgrounds, the teachers they faced, and the views they heard when they returned home each evening.

Thus the public school, the one institution that most of the children had in common, stands as a convincing reminder that we shall begin to understand the history of American childhood only when we accept the complexity and diversity of the children themselves and of their lives.

REVIEW QUESTIONS

1. Compare the educational experiences of immigrant and native-born children. What are the main differences? What are the main similarities?

2. What did immigrant children find that was positive in their school experiences? What were the most important negatives?

3. From what the selection says about curriculum, teachers' behavior, and demands placed on the students, what seem to have been the main purposes for public education? Did immigrant children get what they were intended to get out of their education?

4. Why were immigrant children so likely to attend private ethnic schools in addition to regular public schools? What did they gain from these schools that the public schools did not provide?

5. What was the relationship between work and school for immigrant children? Which was more important? How did they juggle the competing demands on their time?

6. Some of you may have a first language other than English or may have attended schools with students whose first language was not English. What similarities and differences are there in your (their) school experience compared to that of the immigrant children described in this selection?

FOR FURTHER READING

Most of the literature on immigration cited for the previous selection is also relevant to this one. In addition, consult the following books on education: Lawrence Cremin, *The Transformation of the School* (1961), and *American Education: The Metropolitan Experience* (1988); Marvin Lazerson, *Origins of the Urban School* (1971); David Tyack, *The One Best System: A History of American Urban Education* (1974). The author of this selection, Selma Berrol, has treated immigrants' education more fully in her book *Immigrants at School* (1978), and Paula S. Fass deals with the same subject in *Outside In: Minorities and the Transformation of American Education* (1989).

African American migrants making their way north.

9

African-American Migration

FLORETTE HENRI

Throughout much of the twentieth century, African Americans abandoned the cotton fields and small towns of the South for the industrial cities of the North. In the last decade of the nineteenth century and in the first of the twentieth, 200,000 African Americans came North. Between 1910 and 1920, a half-million more came, and larger and larger numbers migrated North in succeeding decades. They came, as Florette Henri makes clear in the essay that follows, for a number of reasons: some came to sightsee and never returned South; some came to escape the violently racist attitudes of the South; some came to enjoy the economic opportunities the North afforded. African Americans who came to the North were motivated by the same search for opportunity that drew rural and small-town whites as well as the "new" immigrants to the cities—the millions of jobs for able-bodied men and women made available by a vibrant and ever expanding industrial economy. For many, a job even at the lowest of ranks in the factory provided an income higher than they could earn as sharecroppers or tenant farmers.

Many parallels can be found between the migration of African Americans from the South to the cities of the North and the "new" immigration to the United States by southern and eastern Europeans between 1880 and 1924. Both groups were abandoning a system of landholding where they were at once tied to the land and landless—

African Americans as sharecroppers in a system of tenant farming and sharecropping, the Europeans as peasants in a feudal land system. There are other parallels as well: both groups settled, for the most part, in the big cities, not in the rural areas of the country; both were relegated to the unskilled levels of the industrial work force; and both created urban ghettoes as a shield from a strange, and even hostile, environment. But one important difference between these two groups of migrants remained: no white ethnic group had to overcome the barriers of color that confronted the African American.

[The] story of movement in the black population says clearly that many blacks did not sit quietly in one place waiting for things to change under them; that, in fact, they shared in the general American pattern of mobility. But early migrations were dwarfed by the surge of black people northward after 1900, and especially after 1910. According to various contemporaneous estimates, between 1890 and 1910 around 200,000 black Southerners fled to the North; and between 1910 and 1920 another 300,000 to 1,000,000 followed. . . .

What precipitated the mass migration of that period is succinctly expressed in this verse:

> Boll-weevil in de cotton
> Cut worm in de cotton,
> Debil in de white man,
> Wah's goin' on.

Drought, then heavy rains, and the boll weevils that flourish under wet conditions had ruined cotton crops in 1915 and 1916. Tenant farmers and croppers were desperate. Too, injustice, disfranchisement, and Jim Crow—"debil in de white man"—grew more severe and galling each year, until life in the South was intolerable for a black man. And at the same time, finally, there was a reasonable hope of escape from this suffering because of the Great War, as it approached and while it was going on. At precisely the time war production needed all the labor it could get, immigration was sharply curtailed, dropping from 1,218,480 in 1914 to 326,700 in 1915, to under 300,000 in 1916 and 1917, and finally to 110,618 in 1918—less than 10 percent of the 1914 figure. If immigration had continued at the 1914 rate, almost 5,000,000 more immigrants would have entered the United States by the end of the war, and war production could probably have employed almost all the workers among them. It seems reasonable to believe, therefore, that even if one ac-

---

cepts the top figure of 1,000,000 black migrants during that period, they and the immigrants who did manage to enter the country during the peak production years could not have filled the void. Such friction, then, as developed between black and white workers was probably not based on economic competition so much as on racism.

Woodson claims that even before the unskilled and semiskilled black laborers went North, there was a substantial movement in that direction by educated and professional-level black people—the group that [W. E. B.] DuBois named the Talented Tenth—who could no longer bear the violence, intimidation, and suppression that were part of everyday life in the South. The increasing callousness of the Republican administrations of Roosevelt and Taft badly shook their faith in the party of liberation. The Brownsville incident of 1906, when President Roosevelt and Secretary of War Taft arbitrarily punished 167 black soldiers, may have been final proof that blacks were deserted by the federal government and must look after themselves. These political facts may have motivated some of the poor, uneducated blacks also to leave the South, although by and large they clung to their faith in the party of emancipation. When Ray Stannard Baker asked a black man why he was leaving Atlanta (after a riot there in 1908) for Washington, D.C., the answer was: "Well, you see, I want to be as near the flag as I can."

According to several contemporaneous studies of the motives of migrants, most blacks left the South simply to be able to feed themselves and their families. George Edmund Haynes, one of the Urban League founders, reported in 1912 that of southern black migrants in New York City, 47.1 percent had come for better jobs. In a 1917 study made for the Secretary of Labor, again the economic motive came first. In the light of what has been said in previous pages about the condition of southern blacks, a rundown of all the reasons given in that study is interesting:

> 1. low wages: "The Negro . . . appears to be interested in having some experience with from four to six times as much pay as he has ever had before" even if, in buying power, 50¢ to $1 a day in the South should equal $2 to $4 a day in the North;
> 2. bad treatment by whites—all classes of Negroes are dissatisfied with their condition;
> 3. injustice and evils of tenant farming—difficulty of getting a planter to settle accounts, about which his word cannot be questioned; also, the high prices charged by planters and merchants for necessary supplies;
> 4. more dissatisfaction than formerly with these conditions, in the light of the world movement for democracy.

Poor pay was the leading reason for migration in a survey of 1917 in the *Crisis,* followed by bad treatment, bad schools, discrimination, and oppression. Abram L. Harris, an economist and informed student of Negro migrations, concluded that all the movements away from the rural South, from the

Civil War on, were "fundamentally the result of the growth of machine industry, and of the lack of economic freedom and the non-assurance of a margin of subsistence under the one-crop share system of the agricultural South."

There were undoubtedly some migrants who moved about simply for adventure or to see new places. Out of the 400 interviewed by Epstein, 85 said they were just traveling to see the country. Gilbert Osofsky in his Harlem study speaks of some who were just wanderers, criminals, hoodlums, or adventurers. But most evidence shows, as Louise Venable Kennedy wrote in her study of Negro urbanization, that blacks move about for the same reasons as other American groups—for jobs, education, better conditions—and not because of a racial trait of rootlessness, as many believed. John Daniels in his 1914 book on black people of Boston spoke of the "excessive migratoriness which is inherent in the Negro character." He added, "Obstacles in the environment are not opposed by a quality of rootedness," explaining why almost 2,000 blacks left Boston between 1900 and 1910. But such an attack on character was hardly necessary to explain why numbers of blacks left Boston. Daniels himself mentions a notable decrease of interest and tolerance on the part of white Bostonians. Even more important was the scarcity of any but menial jobs in nonindustrial Boston. Howard Odum, also, spoke of migratoriness as a race characteristic of blacks, claiming that they have little attachment to home, siblings, or parents. Dillard, however, said that migration was motivated by an effort to improve their condition of living, and as such deserved "commendation not condemnation." And the Atlanta *Constitution* stated bluntly: "The Negro does not move North because he is of a restless disposition. He would prefer to stay in his old home if he could do so on a wage basis more equitable to his race."

The industrial cities were magnets. To farm workers in the South who made perhaps $.75 a day, to urban female domestics who might earn from $1.50 to $3.00 a week, the North during the war years beckoned with factory wages as high as $3.00 or $4.00 a day, and domestic pay of $2.50 a day. As the Dillard report pointed out, blacks longed to get more money into their hands, even if more went out of them; and though living was higher in the North, it was generally not 400 percent higher, as wages might be. A migrant who had gone to Cleveland wrote that he regularly earned $3.60 a day, and sometimes double that, and with the pay of his wife, son, and two oldest daughters, the family took in $103.60 every ten days; the only thing that cost them more than at home, he said, was the rent, $12 a month.

In Pittsburgh in 1918, black migrants were earning between $3.00 and $3.60 a day; only 4 percent of them had earned that much in the South. A 1919 study showed that only 5 percent of migrants in Pittsburgh earned less than $2.00 a day; 56 percent of them had earned less than $2.00 a day in the South. A migrant working in a Newark, New Jersey, dye plant made $2.75 a day plus a rent-free room, and the company had paid his fare North; back home he would have earned less than $1.00 for a long day's work on a farm.

Tenant farmers in the Deep South often made less than $15 a month; in 1920, the average annual income of a rural Negro family in Georgia was $290. Even where there was some industry, as in the foundries around Birmingham, unskilled workers got a top of $2.50 for a nine-hour day, while the same sort of worker could make $4.50 a day in Illinois. In Haynes's survey of Negro migrants in New York City, the great majority reported earning from 50 to 100 percent more than they had in the South.

In the complex of motives active upon most migrants it is hard to assess the weight of better educational opportunities for their children. Letters of potential migrants to Emmett Scott and others often speak of this motive. One such letter, written by a representative of a group of 200 men in Mobile, said the men didn't care where they went "just so they cross the Mason and Dixie line" to "where a negro man can appreshate beaing a man" and give his children a good education. Southern politicians of the Vardaman stamp were constantly trying to reduce the little schooling black children got. As governor of Mississippi, Vardaman told the legislature in 1906: "It is your function to put a stop to the worse than wasting of half a million dollars annually"—the cost of black schools—"to the vain purpose of trying to make something of the negro which the Great Architect . . . failed to provide for in the original plan of creation." The black man had no vote, and without a vote he was not likely to enlist any politician in the cause of black education. When Powdermaker's study of Mississippi was made in the 1930s, black schooling was still brief and inadequate; she found fifth-grade children, in that grade because of automatic promotions, who could not read; and she found black parents, especially mothers, with a burning desire to give their children an education at whatever sacrifice to themselves.

Also, it is hard to assay a motive like wishing to appreciate being a man, or wanting to go "where a man's a man" or any place "where a man will Be anything Except a Ker . . . I don't care where so long as I go where a man is a man." The theme is repeated over and over again, and it is a difficult thing to say, a hurtful thing, much harder than simply saying one wants better pay. But it was possibly the overriding reason for leaving the South. W. T. B. Williams, the writer of the report of the Dillard team and its only black member, pointed out that although better pay was most frequently named as a reason for migrating, "the Negro really cares very little for money as such. Cupidity is hardly a Negro vice." He quoted a Florida woman as saying: "Negroes are not so greatly disturbed about wages. They are tired of being treated as children; they want to be men."

Southern blacks were tired of "bene dog as [if] I was a beast"; of never, never being addressed, as they must always address the white man, with a title of respect. Powdermaker says that in Mississippi whites will address a black grade school teacher as "doctor" or "professor" to avoid the Mr., Mrs., or Miss; the consistent withholding of those titles endowed what is a mere polite form with such symbolic force that blacks felt the values of the whole system were concentrated in that Mr. or Mrs. or Miss, and not to be called so meant to be outcast by the system. The sense of being outside the society was reinforced by the equally consistent practice of better-class whites of addressing even the meanest, most illiterate white laborer or loafer as Mr., a cheap way of flattering him into docility by giving him, through the magic of the title, assurance that he was a white man and that as such he shared the superiority of other white men to blacks. This was most damaging to the black man's sense of who he was; because if he, a respectable black, perhaps well educated and fairly prosperous, was not treated like even the dregs of white society, then perhaps he was a different species, not a man at all.

In the many bitter complaints of blacks that they were never Mr. in the South although the white man always was, and in the boast of a migrant writing home that in the North you didn't have to "sir" the white men you worked with—in these there is the cry of the dispossessed and disinherited, a summing up of all the reasons for the black migration. A black minister in Philadelphia put it this way to Ray Stannard Baker: "Well, they're treated more like men up here in the North, that's the secret of it. There's prejudice here, too, but the color line isn't drawn in their faces at every turn as it is in the South. It all gets back to a question of manhood."

Scott said that fear of mob violence and lynching were frequently alleged reasons for migrating, and Booker T. Washington had said that "for every lynching that takes place . . . a score of colored people leave . . . for the city." In the statements of migrants themselves, however, these reasons are not mentioned nearly so often as jobs, pay, justice, better living, and education. Charles Johnson came to the conclusion that persecution, and its ultimate expression in lynching, were not nearly such dominant stimuli to migration as the hope of economic betterment. He claimed that many black migrants—almost 43 percent of them—had gone not North but Southwest, mostly to Arkansas, Oklahoma, and Texas—where economic opportunities might be better but where mob violence was far from uncommon; and that Jasper County in Georgia, and Jefferson County in Alabama, both with fearsome lynching records, had increases rather than declines of black population during the migration period. Kennedy's findings indicated that insecurity of property and life was more likely a supporting cause of migration than a fundamental one, underlying the frequently named reasons of social and educational inequities, humiliations, and insults. In Dutcher's analysis of changes during the 1910–20 decade is the statement that "social grievances appear never to have been sufficient of themselves to produce any considerable movement of the Negro population," and that economic betterment had much greater force. It is amazing, if true, that fear of lynching should not have been a chief reason for flight, considering that ninety-three blacks were lynched in 1908, and fifty, sixty, seventy, or more each year (except 1917) from then until 1920; but the fear may have been too terrible to be given expression in so many words.

Also, there appears to have been a generation gap that made for different motives among older and younger blacks. Many of the older generation, although desperately in need of financial succor, were not so rebellious against "keeping their place." But their sons, who had some schooling, who could read, did not take kindly to the old customs. They were not going to endure being knocked about and beaten on the job "to an extent hardly believable," as the Labor Department reported, and hit with anything that came to the white man's hand, a tool or a piece of lumber. Particularly they resented abuse when their women were with them, and black women were so terrified of what their men might do and what might happen to them as a result, that often the women defended themselves rather than expose their husbands or male friends to danger. A young black said to his father, who was trying to persuade him not to migrate to Chicago: "When a young white man talks rough to me, I can't talk rough to him. You can stand that; I can't. I have some education, and inside I has the feelin's of a white man. I'm goin'.". . . .

Those who had left early wrote home about freedom and jobs in the North. Labor agents came South recruiting for the big industrial companies, especially the railroads. The Chicago *Defender* carried northern help-wanted ads and detailed accounts of southern lynchings in its "national edition," widely read in the South, thus both pulling and pushing black people. The idea of "exodus" became surrounded with religious fervor. Many believed that God had opened a way for them to escape oppression. Scott described a group of 147 Mississippi blacks who, when they crossed the Ohio River to freedom, knelt, prayed, and sang hymns; they stopped their watches to symbolize the end of their old life. "Exodus" was a matter of excited secret discussion among southern blacks. Anyone who advised against going was suspected of being in the pay of whites. If a black businessman opposed migration, his customers began to vanish; a minister who preached against it from the pulpit was stabbed the next day. Rumors of jobs and of transportation to them increased unrest. Incautiously, many blacks sold or gave away their belongings and followed any crowd of migrants without an idea of their destination. Some rural areas emptied out so thoroughly that one old woman complained she hadn't enough friends left to give her a decent funeral.

"I should have been here twenty years ago," a man wrote back from the North. "I just begin to feel like a man. . . . My children are going to the same school with the whites and I don't have to humble to no one. I have registered. Will vote in the next election and there isn't any yes Sir and no Sir. It's all yes and no, Sam and Bill." A man wrote from Philadelphia telling of good pay, $75 a month, enough so he could carry insurance in case of illness, and added that there you "don't have to mister every little white boy comes along" and that he hadn't heard "a white man call a colored a nigger" since he'd been North; what was more, he could sit where he chose on the streetcars— not that he craved to sit with whites "but if I have to pay the same fare I have learn to want the same acomidation"; still, this far from rootless wanderer would always "love the good old South," he said. A Columbia, South Carolina, Negro paper reported that a migrant brother had come home for a visit with "more than one hundred dollars and plenty of nice clothes." All this was hallelujah news to the home folks. They could easily ignore the occasional cautionary letter, like one from a Cleveland migrant who warned of loafers, gamblers, and pickpockets and said the city streets weren't safe at night. An unnamed but allegedly widely respected black educator is reported to have said: "Uncle Sam is the most effective [labor] agent at this time. All who are away are writing for others to come on in, the water's fine."

Stimulating the urge to "vote with their feet," as the migration was sometimes called, were the solicitations of northern labor agents. In 1916, the first year of large-scale movement, most agents were representing railroads or the mines. Baker reported: "Trains were backed into several Southern cities and hundreds of Negroes were gathered up in a day, loaded into the cars, and whirled away to the North." For example, in February 1917 a special train was sent to carry 191 black migrants from Bessemer, Alabama, to Pittsburgh at a cost to a coal company of $3,391.95. So great was the excitement, Baker said, that Negroes "deserted their jobs and went to the trains without notifying their employers or even going home." Between 75,000 and 100,000 got to Pennsylvania that way, Baker said, many of them to work for the Pennsylvania and Erie railroads, and still more for the steel mills, munitions plants, and other heavy industries. As might be expected, men so hastily and haphazardly gathered up included a good share of shiftless characters, and in addition, the companies had not prepared for their sudden arrival the necessary housing or facilities; because of this combination of circumstances, many of the labor recruits drifted off the job before they had worked out the railroad fare the companies had advanced.

Some of the labor agents were salaried employees of large industrial companies, and these included some blacks. Others were independent employment agents who charged the migrants from $1.00 to $3.00 for placing them in jobs, and collected from the companies as well if they could get anything. Often the labor recruiters gained access to Negro quarters in the cities where they worked by disguising themselves as salesmen or insurance agents. There were probably some honest men among them, but others were flagrantly unscrupulous in their promises. An agency soliciting workers in the Birmingham and Bessemer areas advertised in such phrases as: "Let's go back north where there are no labor troubles, no strikes, no lockouts; Large coal, good wages, fair treatment; Two weeks pay; Good houses; We ship you and your household goods; All colored ministers can go free; Will advance you money if necessary; Scores of men have written us thanking us for sending them; Go now while you have the chance." Some of the "agents" were downright crooks who collected fees from men wanting to migrate and then failed to be at the depot where they were supposed to rendezvous with their clients. Such was the fate of 1,800 Louisiana blacks who paid $2.00 each to an agent who promised them jobs in Chicago but never made good on the promise. The hardship was greatest when men had quit their jobs in the expectation of leaving the South. Micheaux described one agent who, after collecting $3.00 from a man, sent him to several places in search of imaginary jobs; in the end, the agent refused to refund more than $1.00, although he had done nothing for his client. Another racket was to induce ignorant black girls to sign contracts they could not read that obligated them for the cost of their journey plus a placement fee; in many cases the agents were recruiting for brothels, although what they promised the girls was domestic service.

Alarm spread throughout the white South as farm laborers and city menial and domestic help drifted off in twos, twenties, and two hundreds. State laws and city ordinances were passed to oust or curb the agents who were taking most of the workers. In the light of complaints against the agents by a number of migrants, it seems believable that licensing laws for agents were meant at first to protect black workers as well as their white employers. In South Carolina, for example, an 1891 law requiring all labor agents to pay $500 for a license might simply have been aimed at assuring the reliability of the man promising work out of the state; but when in 1907 the fee was raised to $2,000 it was due simply to panic on the part of whites who saw their cheap labor force dwindling. According to Scott, a license cost $1,000 in Jacksonville, under penalty of a $600 fine and 60 days in jail; in Alabama the state, city, and county fees totaled from $1,000 to $1,250; in Macon, a license cost $25,000, and the applicant had to be vouched for by 10 local ministers and 35 local businessmen, which seems not so much regulatory as prohibitive, as the Atlanta *Constitution* called such licensing. In Montgomery, recruiting labor for out-of-state jobs was punishable by a $100 fine and 6 months at hard labor on a convict gang. Force was not infrequently used to prevent the taking of blacks North, Scott says. Labor agents were arrested. Trains carrying migrants were stopped, the blacks forced to return, and the agents beaten. Blacks might be terrorized or lynched on suspicion of trying to leave the state. "But they might as well have tried to stop by ordinance the migration of the boll-weevil," Baker said; by ordinance, or by hitting them on the head, one by one.

Robert Abbott, editor and publisher of the Chicago *Defender* and himself a migrant from the "Negro town" of Yamacraw, was the loudest single voice calling for the northward flow of black labor, but not the only one. Many other Negro papers also encouraged migration, Baker reported. The Richmond *Reformer* spoke out against Jim Crow, segregation, and living conditions "like cattle, hogs or sheep, penned in" as evils that black people in the South must continue to endure "until they rise up in mass and oppose it openly"; self-respecting Negroes, said the Timmonsville (South Carolina) *Watchman*, should take a hint from a recent lynching and "get away at the earliest possible moment." But it was Abbott who fleshed out the vision of escape, who gave it a definite and dramatic form—even a birthday: the Great Northern Drive of May 15, 1917. Carl Sandburg wrote in the Chicago *Daily News:* "The Defender more than any other one agency was the big cause of the 'Northern fever' and the big exodus from the South." A Georgia paper called the *Defender* "the greatest disturbing element that has yet entered Georgia." The U.S. Department of Labor said that in some sections the *Defender* was probably more effective in carrying off labor than all the agents put together: "It sums up the Negro's troubles and keeps them constantly before him, and it points out in terms he can understand the way of escape.". . .

Abbott put out a "national edition" of his weekly, aimed at southern blacks. It carried in red ink such headlines as: 100 NEGROES MURDERED WEEKLY IN UNITED STATES BY WHITE AMERICANS; LYNCHING—A NATIONAL DISGRACE; and WHITE GENTLEMAN RAPES COLORED GIRL. Accompanying a lynching story was a picture of the lynch victim's severed head, with the caption: NOT BELGIUM—AMERICA. Poems entitled *Land of Hope* and *Bound for the Promised Land* urged blacks to go North, and editorials boosted Chicago as the best place for them to go. Want ads offered jobs at attractive wages in and around Chicago. In news items, anecdotes, cartoons, and photos, the *Defender* crystallized the underlying economic and social causes of black suffering into immediate motives for flight. Repeated stories of those who were leaving the South or who were already in the North conveyed the excitement of a mass movement under way and created an atmosphere of religious hysteria; the *Defender* called the migration the "Flight out of Egypt" and the migrants sang "Going into Canaan." The more people who left, inspired by *Defender* propaganda, the more wanted to go, so the migration fed on itself until in some places it turned into a wild stampede. Even illiterate people bought the paper, as a status symbol. A black leader in Louisiana was quoted as saying, "My people grab it [the *Defender*] like a mule grabs a mouthful of fine fodder." Sandburg wrote that there was in Chicago "a publicity or propaganda machine that directs its appeals or carries on an agitation that every week reaches hundreds of thousands of people of the colored race in the southern states.". . .

Abbott enlisted the aid of two very mobile groups of black people, the railroad men and the entertainers. Chicago was the end of the North-South railroad lines, and a great junction. Hundreds of Pullman porters, dining-car waiters, and traveling stage people passed through it, some of them on their way to remote whistle-stops in the South. The *Defender* paid many of them to pick up bundles of the newspaper in Chicago and drop them along their routes at points where local distributors would meet the trains, get the bundles, and circulate them. In a town where the *Defender* was unknown, the porters would give copies away to any black person they saw. Stage people took bundles of papers and distributed them free in the theaters. The well-known concert singer Sissieretta Jones, who was called the "black Patti" in the patronizing style of the day, asked the ushers in theaters where she performed to give out free copies to all comers.

By such devices the circulation of the *Defender* soared to 283,571 by 1920, with about two-thirds of its readers outside Chicago. This was by far the largest circulation any black newspaper had ever achieved. If each copy reached five readers, a reasonable guess, about 1,500,000 blacks saw it.

Abbott's master stroke in materializing a migration that in 1916 was more rumored than real was the setting of a date, a specific month and day in 1917, for what the *Defender* called "the Great Northern Drive." The incendiary message spread that on May 15 railroad cars would back into the stations of southern towns prepared to carry North any who wanted to go, at a very low fare. The word struck southern blacks with messianic force. There was to be a second coming of freedom on May 15, and it behooved everyone to be ready. . . .

They went with whatever possessions they could carry, "wearing overalls and housedresses, a few walking barefoot.". . . Although it is hard to see how they took their goats, pigs, chickens, dogs, and cats along, as he claims, they certainly must have carried provisions for their long, long journeys, a thousand miles or more for many of them, days and nights of travel with no prospect of any creature comforts along the way. To Chicago from Savannah was 1,027 railroad miles; to New York from San Antonio, 1,916 miles; to Cincinnati from Jacksonville, 822 miles; to Newark from Vicksburg, 1,273 miles; to Detroit from New Orleans, 1,096 miles; to Cleveland from Mobile, 1,046 miles. Some stopped at Chicago for a time before going to their destinations, but most went straight through: from Florida and Georgia to Pennsylvania and New York; from Alabama, Mississippi, Tennessee, and Louisiana to Illinois and Michigan. Most of these people had probably never been more than 20 miles from their homes. . . .

One cheap way to travel was in a group. The *Defender* encouraged the formation of "clubs" of ten to fifty persons and arranged special fares and travel dates with the railroad companies. Many people wrote to the newspaper that they could bring "about 8 or 10 men" or "a family of (11) eleven more or less" or "15 or 20 good men" or "25 women and men," and so on up to "300 or 500 men and women" and finally "as many men as you want." Some of these correspondents sent stamped return envelopes and asked the paper not to publish their letters—"whatever you do, don't publish my name in your paper"— or asked that, if an answer was sent by wire, there should be no mention of the number of people because "if you say 15 or 20 mans they will put me in jail." "This is among us collerd," says one letter offering to bring 20 men and their families.

With so many concerned for secrecy, many must have been too frightened to write at all. They never revealed the presence among them of labor agents. Migrants described how they had to slip away from their homes at night, walk to some railroad station where they were not known, and there board a train for the North. If they were found to have tickets, the police confiscated them. If three or four blacks were discovered together it was assumed that they were "conspiring to go North" and they would be arrested on some trumped-up charge.

For migrants to New York from a coastal city in the South—and most of those who went to New York were from the South Atlantic states—the cheapest and most direct passage was by boat. Steerage fare from Virginia, from which most New York migrants came, was $5.50 or $6.00, including meals. The Old Dominion Line ran boats twice a week from Virginia to New York, and the Baltimore, Chesapeake & Atlantic Railway ran steamers from Baltimore, Washington, and as far south as Florida. By train it would have cost at least $7.50 from Norfolk to New York City, without meals. So the boat was a good buy, although blacks might find themselves in a separate section of the vessel with the household pets of white travelers.

Toward the end of the peak migration period another category of southern blacks settled in northern cities: soldiers returning from France. Rudolph Fisher, a writer of the period, spoke in a short story of a family of Waxhaw, North Carolina, whose son "had gone to France in the draft and, returning, had never got any nearer home than Harlem." There were many such men whose fare, in a roundabout way, had been paid by Uncle Sam. "How're you gonna keep 'em down on the farm, / After they've seen Paree?" a popular song asked.

The rapid flow northward of black people, especially from 1916 when war production went into high gear, aroused much concern and discussion among whites and blacks, North and South. The word "exodus" was apparently so current that Octavus Roy Cohen used it as both noun and verb in his spurious Negro stories of the early twenties: "the merrymakers exodusted" from a party, he wrote; and, there was a "complete exodus from Decatur." Census figures show that in 1900 only 15.6 percent of black people (1,373,996) lived in a state other than that of their birth, whereas in 1910 the percentage born elsewhere had increased to 16.6 (1,616,608), and in 1920 to 19.9 (2,054,242). Of the 300,000 to 1,000,000 blacks estimated by contemporaries to have gone North, almost all went to urban centers. In 1900, 22.7 percent of Negroes lived in cities, North and South; in 1910 this had increased to 24.4 percent, and in 1920 to 34 percent, in numbers totaling more than 3,500,000. By 1920, almost 40 percent of the black population in the North was concentrated in the eight cities of Chicago, Detroit, New York, Cleveland, Cincinnati, Columbus, Philadelphia, and Pittsburgh, although those cities contained only 20 percent of the total northern population. The city with the most dramatic percentage increase in black population between 1910 and 1920 was Detroit, by an astounding 611.3 percent; Cleveland came next with a 307.8 percent increase; then Chicago, 148.2 percent; New York, 66.3 percent;

Indianapolis, 59 percent; Cincinnati, 53.2 percent; and Pittsburgh, 47.2 percent. In numbers Chicago gained nearly 65,500 black residents, New York 61,400, and Detroit 36,240.

A question that immediately comes to mind is: what did these southern people know how to do that would earn them a living in the North? Since so much of the South was rural, it is amazing the number of occupations represented by the migrants whose letters are in the Scott collection. But indications are that about half the migrants came from towns, a Labor Department survey found. The largest number said they wanted work as laborers at unspecified common labor, with some longshoremen, stevedores, freight handlers, stokers, miners, packers, and warehousemen; many of these men had experience in southern industries such as lumbering, railroading, iron and steel foundries, sawmills, and turpentine stills. The next largest category was the semiskilled or skilled craftsman: plumbers and roofers, painters and plasterers, cleaners and pressers, hotel waiters, brickmakers and bricklayers, machinists and machinists' helpers, caulkers, carpenters, woodworkers, cabinetmakers, mailmen, auto workers, engineers, blacksmiths, glaziers, lumber graders and inspectors, foundry workers, and a large number of molders. The majority of women who wanted to migrate, and some of the men, sought menial or domestic jobs: cooks, laundresses, baby nurses, housemaids, butler-chauffeurs, janitors. Among the businesses represented by migrants were insurance man, barber, hairdresser, laundry owner, merchant, and packer and mover—memorably, the moving company owner who called himself "the Daddy of the Transfer business" of Rome, Georgia. In the much smaller class of professionals and white-collar workers the majority were teachers, including the Alcorn College graduate who was four feet, six inches tall and weighed 105 pounds—a woman, presumably, as were many of the teachers who wanted to leave the South. There were also a sixty-three-year-old graduate of Howard University Law School, an eighteen-year-old artist and actor, and a fifteen-year-old cartoonist; also printers, a college-educated bookkeeper, and a stenographer-typist. Many of the educated class expressed their willingness to do any kind of work, even common labor, if only they could get jobs in the North. Only a few who wrote of their wish to migrate described themselves as farmers, and two of these wanted to go to Nebraska and Dakota to farm. But probably many of those who were looking for laborers' jobs were tenant farmers, sharecroppers, and farm workers; and probably also many other rural people could not write or were afraid to, so we do not know about them—they simply disappeared off the farms and took their chances of finding work in northern cities. Baker says that whole tenant-farming areas of Georgia and Alabama were emptied of prime-age workers. A small number wound up in the tobacco fields of Connecticut, but the great majority must have gone to industrial cities. The black rural population of the South dropped by almost 250,000 between 1910 and 1920.

As the trains and boats pulled out week after week and month after month, the South began to hurt from a loss of the black labor force, especially the Deep South. For the first time in their history, Mississippi and Louisiana showed a decrease in Negro population between 1900 and 1910; and between 1910 and 1920 Mississippi suffered a loss of 129,600 blacks, Louisiana a loss of 180,800. In that decade the black population of the East North Central states increased by 71 percent, and that of the Middle Atlantic states by over 43 percent, although the national increase was only 6.5 percent.

Contemporary estimates by observers such as Baker and Epstein of a million or so migrants seem wildly out of line with the 500,000 figure to be calculated from 1920 census figures, which were not available to them, but it may be that their estimates were more nearly correct than figures arrived at from census returns. For one thing, it has been and remains a fact, substantiated by recent studies by the Census Bureau of its own operation, that black males are significantly undercounted. . . .

If there was finally a black Joshua it was Robert Abbott, blowing the trumpet call of jobs through a rolled-up *Defender;* his troops were the Pullman porters and road shows, with labor agents as mercenaries. Half a million blacks followed behind. Where the metaphor breaks down is that their Jericho was a dirty, crowded, sickly, dangerous city ghetto, which must often have seemed scarcely worth the trouble of getting to.

But the getting there was a tremendous feat of initiative, planning, courage, and perseverance—qualities never appearing in any catalogue of Negro traits drawn up by white people, yet here demonstrated incontestibly not by one or two "exceptional individuals," as blacks were called who did not fit the stereotype, but by at least five hundred thousand perfectly average southern Negroes. They were not passive reactors, waiting for something to happen to them; they made it happen.

REVIEW QUESTIONS

1. Which African Americans, according to the author, tended to come North first—and why?

2. Outline the motives that brought about this mass migration and then find similarities and differences (from your text) between these motives and those of the immigrants from Europe.

3. Were there migratory patterns in the movement from the South to the North and, if so, what were they?

4. Offer a generalization about the following: (a) the attitudes of the African Americans toward the South and to the North once they arrived; (b) the means

through which they earned their livelihood in the South and in the North; and (c) the temperament of those who came North.

5. And finally: What role did Robert Abbott play in the Great Migration—and with what motives?

FOR FURTHER READING

John Hope Franklin, *From Slavery to Freedom: A History of Negro Americans* (1978), is a basic general history. While some of his conclusions have been questioned, C. Vann Woodward's *The Strange Career of Jim Crow* (1974) remains a compelling account of the system of racial oppression that southern African Americans tried to escape by moving to the North. In addition to the book from which this selection is taken, Florette Henri, *Black Migration* (1975), a general history of the movement of African Americans to the North is provided by Carole Marks in *Farewell—We're Good and Gone: The Great Black Migration* (1989). The following books deal with what African Americans found in specific cities after they had arrived in the North: James Borchert, *Alley Life in Washington* (1980); James R. Grossman, *Land of Hope: Chicago, Black Southerners, and the Great Migration* (1989); Kenneth Kusmer, *A Ghetto Takes Shape* (1976); Gilbert Osofsky, *Harlem: The Making of a Ghetto* (1966); Allen H. Spear, *Black Chicago* (1967). Nicolas Lemann takes the story of the migration up to recent times in *The Promised Land: The Great Black Migration and How It Changed America* (1991).

PART III

THE TENSIONS OF PROSPERITY

As the Republican candidate for the presidency in 1920, Warren Gamaliel Harding promised the American people "not nostrums but normalcy." Under his leadership and that of his Republican successors, the idealism of the Progressive era and the moralistic fervor evoked by Woodrow Wilson gave way to a more prosaic and less exalted vision of American life.

But the 1920s, in retrospect, were neither prosaic nor exalted. The maturing of the American economy of mass production and mass consumption produced social changes and social divisions. Many of those committed to the values, social practices, and institutions of native, rural, nineteenth-century Protestant America began to wonder if "progress" was a virtue or a vice. Others—largely the "new" immigrants and middle-class city dwellers—saw little value in maintaining the older, agrarian, puritanical way of life, enjoyed the changes taking place, and looked forward to more.

The issues that polarized the nation were many and bitterly contested. In addition to the "Red Scare" of 1919 and the controversy that surrounded the Sacco-Vanzetti case, the nation debated immigration policy. Nativists wanted an end to unrestricted immigration and to make certain that most future immigrants to the United States would be Anglo-Saxons rather than Southern and Eastern Europeans. The Immigration Act of 1924 made both these demands law. Other controversies concerned the teaching of evolution in the public schools and the fitness of a Catholic for the office of president of the United States. John T. Scopes was sentenced to jail for teaching evolution to his students in Tennessee in 1925; and the defeat of Alfred E. Smith in the presidential campaign of 1928 can, in part, be attributed to the nation's distrust of Catholics.

The following selections offer a sense of the American experience of the 1920s. The first concerns the Ku Klux Klan, an organization that grew out of and exploited the racial, religious, ethnic, and political prejudices of the time. The second describes the lives of Mexican-Americans in the Southwest in the 1920s. The last shows how the floods of consumer goods pouring out of American factories changed American homes and the lives of the housewives who worked in them.

A legacy of bigotry and violence—for today and tomorrow.

10

The Ku Klux Klan in Indiana

KATHLEEN M. BLEE

The 1920s were marked by strong social divisions and conflicts between various segments of the American people: between native-born Americans and immigrants, city dwellers and rural folk, African Americans and whites, religious fundamentalists and modernists, Protestants and members of other faiths. To these divisions can be added powerful antiradical feelings, disputes over the wisdom of Prohibition, and generational conflicts, particularly the concern of many parents that the moral code they had been brought up to believe in was being rejected by their children. These conflicts combined to create a widespread feeling that traditional American ways, institutions, and values were under threat and that action to protect them was urgently necessary.

These feelings found expression in a number of ways, one of them being the reappearance of the Ku Klux Klan. The Klan had been first organized at the end of the Civil War. Originally intended as a social club for ex-officers of the Confederate Army, it quickly became a secret terrorist organization devoted to maintaining white supremacy throughout the South by means of violence and intimidation directed toward African Americans and their white supporters. As an organization, the Klan largely disappeared in the 1870s, although Klan-like activities continued. The organization was revived in 1915, however, and by the early 1920s it had attained a large membership and, in some parts of the United States, considerable political influence.

The new KKK was similar to the original in some ways. Both were secret organizations, both restricted membership to white, native-born Americans, and both adhered to a philosophy of white supremacy. There were also differences. The old KKK had existed only in the South, while the new one found many if not most of its members in the North. (Its political impact was greatest in Indiana, Oregon, and Colorado, and the state with the largest Klan membership was probably Ohio.) The new Klan also added Catholics, Jews, and foreigners to its list of enemies. And its mode of operation was different. It was less secretive than the original Klan, and while it occasionally used violence, far more often it relied on political and economic pressure to secure its ends.

There was one other difference between the old and new Klans that the following selection makes clear: women were an important part of the new one. They had a separate organization of their own, the Women's Ku Klux Klan (WKKK), which worked alongside the KKK. Some of the most prominent Klan spokespersons were women, among them Helen Jackson and Daisy Barr, mentioned in the following selection. The stated goal of much of the KKK's social and political agenda was the protection of Protestant women from the supposed threats directed against them by foreigners, Catholics, African Americans, Jews, and even, on occasion, native-born Protestant men. All in all, women played a major role in many of the KKK's most important activities.

The KKK achieved the height of its power in the 1920s by posing as the defender of traditional American moral values at a time when they were supposedly under attack by a variety of alien forces. Thus, when it became known that some prominent leaders of the organization were guilty of a variety of economic and sexual misdeeds, the resulting scandal came as a crushing blow. Of course, the KKK did not disappear—it still exists—but never again did it achieve the breadth of support and influence that it had had in the early 1920s.

To many who enlisted in the fiery crusade of the 1920s Klan, racial, religious, and national antagonisms were *moral* issues. The Klan, its leaders and members insisted, did not preach hatred and intolerance of any group. It sought

From Kathleen N. Blee, *Women of the Klan.* Copyright © 1991. Reprinted by permission of the University of California Press.

only to defend traditional moral standards against the seductive allurements of modern society. And thus the Klan battled those groups—primarily Jews, Catholics, and blacks—who it claimed promoted vice and immorality. . . .

Many white Protestant women heard the Klan's message about morality and embraced it readily. Klanswomen across the country marched under banners proclaiming We Stand for True Godliness, Purity, and Loyalty; We Are the Foe of Vice, the Friends of the Innocent; Love Thy Neighbor as Thyself but Leave His Wife Alone; and Wife Beaters Beware. Women's Klan chapters often described their mission in self-righteous terms, as safeguarding public virtue and as keeping "the moral standards of the community at a high plane." The underlying message of klannish morality was effective, too. Klanswomen and Klansmen across the country responded to the Klan's appeal and launched a frenzied assault upon "immoral" Jews, Catholics, and blacks.

The Klan's morality campaigns succeeded in normalizing fear and hatred of minorities. When the second Klan attacked racial, ethnic, and religious groups, it did so by portraying them—especially minority men—as ruthless beasts who operated outside the moral code that shaped civilized life. In this way, the Klan deepened an existing perception among white Protestants that nonwhites and non-Protestants were strange, alien, and inexplicable. Disguising a viciously racist, anti-Semitic, and anti-Catholic agenda as a moral crusade was particularly effective in homogeneous white Protestant communities in which racial and religious minorities posed no immediate economic or social competition to the majority population. It allowed the Klan to denounce Jews, Catholics, and blacks as evil, even as devils, and as a potent threat to white Protestant moral values. . . .

Indiana was a particularly fertile field for the bigoted appeal to morality used by . . . Klan spokespersons. That it was may seem odd, for Indiana in the 1920s was one of the most racially, culturally, and religiously homogeneous states. The history of racism and intolerance in Indiana, however, suggests that the Klan's appearance in the state simply made visible deep racist and bigoted attitudes that many of the state's white native-born Protestants had long held. Indiana's tradition of racism, anti-Catholicism, and moral vigilantism fit well into the Klan's political agenda. . . .

Morality crusades . . . were the Klan's entrée into many communities in Indiana. The 1920s Klan was extraordinarily successful in bringing a wide range of white Protestants who feared liquor or sexual promiscuity or gambling into an organized political force with common targets: nonwhites, immigrants, and non-Protestants. The call to morality fired political passions while obscuring white Protestants' real differences in sentiments toward sexuality, alcohol, and leisure time activities. A resident of Indianapolis recalled the excitement of joining the Klan's crusade: "It gave people a feeling that they were doing the right thing . . . really felt like they were doing the Christian duty."

Klan recruiters portrayed themselves as a movement of righteous Protestants beleaguered by forces of immorality. Thousands of cards were distributed on street corners and in churches and lodges by Klanswomen and Klansmen seeking new recruits for the crusade. Each small calling card bore the terrifying message:

> Remember, every criminal, every gambler, every thug, every libertine, every girl ruiner, every home wrecker, every wife beater, every dopepeddler, every shyster lawyer, every K of C [Knight of Columbus], every white slaver, every brothel madame, every Rome-controlled newspaper—is fighting the KKK.

The Klan's claims to support women's rights and its efforts to recruit women did not prevent it from directing its morality crusades in Indiana to Klansmen and urging them to fight on behalf of white Protestant women. It invoked women to justify nearly every action that the Klan took against vice and corruption. When the Klan fought against prostitution, gambling, "bawdy houses," pool halls, dog and horse racing, and slot machines, it did so in the name of women who faced financial ruin by wayward or erring husbands: in gambling houses, "men are robbed, by shrewd house men of their weekly payroll, and their poor wives and children must suffer hunger and real need in order to please these bands of thieves."

The Klan claimed to oppose liquor for the same reason: women were vulnerable to physical abuse and economic ruin at the hands of drunken husbands and fathers. Klan chapters threatened, raided, and assaulted bootleggers and moonshiners and condemned those (outside the Klan) who used alcohol. Some Indiana chapters even gathered evidence for the arrest of local druggists who sold alcohol-based preparations. Despite its self-portrayal as an antiliquor group, KKK klaverns often protected bootleggers and moonshiners, raiding only those who did not pay for the Klan's protection.

At least initially, campaigns against vice were popular. Across Indiana, Klan members were recruited by local elites who introduced the group as a community reform organization. The Klan placed ads in local papers announcing its "clean-up campaign" and warning officials of repercussions if they failed to take action against gambling houses and liquor. Too, the Klan's ability to define itself as the major barrier to vice appealed to Protestant clergy, who recruited for the Klan from among their congregations.

Klan chapters frequently threatened those it regarded as violators of the moral code through letter or visit. Physical attacks on offending persons were less common since the Klan's reputation for violence made threats extremely effective. A resident of rural Warren, Indiana, recalled that "in spite of no record of violence there was a general feeling of fear, mystery, and power associated with the Warren Klan. Young girls were warned never to get into a car with men—especially men wearing white hoods!" . . .

There were few standards for selecting Klan victims. Women and men who were hostile to the aims of the Klan or who were not native-born white Protestants were the most likely targets. Even Klan members, however, might be singled out by fellow Klansmen or Klanswomen for not living a proper klannish life. One such incident in Williamsburg, Indiana, involved a Klansman who was accused of spending money on illegal liquor in lieu of providing adequately for his wife and children. After an evening visit by his Klan brothers the man changed his ways. A former Klansman from west-central Indiana explained that the Klan was able to make use of powerful political connections to locate its victims. "They used to take men that would leave their wives and not provide for their wife. They would get a hold of that fellow and sometimes horsewhip him." Asked how the Klan got its information, he said, "Well, a lot of lawyers were members of the Klan and the judge and those people. They were members of the Klan."

Another aspect of the Klan's moral code concerned the chastity of white Protestant women themselves. Like its predecessor, the second Klan vowed to defend women's sexual purity. The impetus for this aspect of the Klan's moral crusade came primarily from the KKK, although the women's Klan was occasionally involved.

Young women were the particular objects of male Klan protectiveness. The KKK press roused intense public fear with suggestions of a vast sexual traffic in young white women, alleging that tens of thousands of girls were snatched into a sexual netherworld each year. The northern Indiana Klan attempted to stop a scheduled boxing match near Chicago on the grounds that Jack Johnson was a professed "negro white slaver." Making a similar appeal, a Klan pamphlet posed this chilling question to potential recruits: "Do you know that annually there are 50,000 girls, from approximately 50,000 American homes, whose virtue is sacrificed upon the altar of vice? [That] there are thousands of girls of foreign birth who were once sent to this country's shores and sold as slaves to the godless passions of men?"

Klansmen's vigilantism in defense of girls' virtue, though, often mixed with other concerns, such as fear of female sexuality and attention to the interests of local elites, as in this story related by a southern Indiana former Klansmember.

> The Klan asked a chap by the name of Neth who was a minister . . . to leave town and he did. . . . In addition to being a minister of the church, he taught two or three classes in high school. . . . But this high school girl, she decided she kind of liked Neth, and so she was always a'hanging around, and the real problem was the girl was just pretty much of a tramp, anyway you'd figure it. So, but . . . nevertheless her dad was a rather prominent businessman in town and so on, and they thought that Neth and this girl was a gettin' too thick and so they advised him to leave and he did.

Many Klan actions, in which both Klansmen and Klanswomen participated, were aimed at curbing the sexual temptations of young women and men. Two areas were of particular concern: dance halls and automobiles. Both allowed young people a measure of privacy away from the watchful eyes of parents and other adults. Both gave young people a chance to indulge in liquor and sex. Both, the Imperial Wizard warned, subjected the weak to unnecessary and dangerous "seductive allurement."

In town after town in Indiana the Klan tried to make a public issue of dance halls and other "vile places of amusement." In some areas the Klan appealed to local authorities to intervene for the sake of public morality and the protection of town youth from sexually suggestive dances. An Indianapolis Christian church minister, later a Klan lecturer, generated much publicity by condemning as "immoral" the mayor's support of public dancing. In Hammond, Indiana, the Klan announced that it would monitor all dance halls, pool halls, picture shows, and other places of amusement for the town youth in order that the "moral conditions" of such places (and presumably also of the youth who frequented them) be improved. In taking this action, the Hammond Klan claimed, it was responding to protest from an aroused citizenry, citing complaints from local women about "brazen male mashers" and impassioned "love grips" in the "cheaper movie houses" of the town. Similarly, in South Bend the Klan engineered a police raid on a local liquor establishment and claimed, in an article entitled "Klan Plays Part of Good Samaritan to Modern Magdalene," that three white teenaged girls were being held prisoner there.

In other Indiana towns the Klan acted more directly, destroying and burning buildings that permitted youth dancing. The Pittsburg, Kansas, chapters of the KKK and WKKK summed up the feelings of many Indiana Klansmen and Klanswomen when they demanded the closing of all public dance resorts since "most of the cases of assault between the sexes have followed dances where they got the inspiration for rash and immoral acts." Many times, the condemnation of dance halls only thinly veiled anti-Semitic attitudes. The Klan implied and sometimes openly declared that Jews benefited financially from places of amusement and thus were responsible for the "misuse of girls" and "promiscuous petting" that these places encouraged among the young.

Automobiles offered an even more direct threat to the moral standards of young persons. Often, the Klan's first public action in a community would be a campaign to "clear the highway of spooners." Parties of masked and hooded Klansmembers (presumably, but not certainly, men) patrolled highways and back roads in search of young couples in parked automobiles. In some communities Klan delegations simply reported to parents and police the names of those found parked at the sides of roadways. In other areas couples caught in an embrace faced a more immediate punishment, including threats and beatings by night-riding Klan posses. The Klan's fervor made people fearful of using the roadways in many areas. Indeed, the Klan's enthusiasm for breaking up "petting parties" by searching all cars on highways caused several motor clubs to blacklist the entire state.

The Klan reserved its greatest terror for nonwhite men who were "involved with" white women. To the Klan of the 1920s, dating and marriage across racial or ethnic lines evoked the same images of white female exploitation and usurpation of white men's privileges that fueled the Reconstruction-era Klan. Nonwhite, foreign-born, and non-Protestant men who were caught with white women faced fierce reprisals by the Klan, including whipping, beating, kidnapping, and even lynching. White women who consorted with Jewish, immigrant, or black men met similar fates. In Muncie, Indiana, a Klanswoman even accused blacks and Catholics of a conspiracy, claiming that Catholics had discovered a powder that would bleach the skins of black men so that they could marry white girls.

Although the Indiana Klan presented itself as an agency of moral reform, the Klan's real message was clearly different. At the same time as it proclaimed itself the force of morality and sexual purity, the Indiana Klan offered audiences graphic tales of female enslavement and sexual exploitation, usually by Catholic priests but also by black and Jewish men.

Typical of such stories was the Klan's attack on a photoplay picture it described as "coarse, degrading, and insulting to the white race." In fact, the Klan's fury over the play centered on its "tendency to create aspirations in the lives of negro people." As was true in much Klan propaganda, it referred to illicit sexual aspirations and to black men: "the revolting spectacle of a white woman clinging in the arms of a colored man is simply beyond words to express." To make the threat of black men's sexual aspirations more threatening, the Indiana Klan press charged that when the picture played in Texas, a bulletin board adjoining the theater bore the message, "White-skinned ladies will flirt with black-skinned men when their husbands are away."

Similarly, the Indiana Klan justified its anti-Semitic attitudes as a defense of Gentile womanhood against the avarice of Jewish men. Jewish businessmen, according to the Klan, were attempting to destroy the very foundations of Christianity by seducing and raping Protestant girls. A typical Klan publication argued that its anti-Semitic policies were simply giving voice to the disgruntlement of many Protestants who "are tired of the outrages inflicted upon innocent girls by Hebrew libertines."

The most common target of the Indiana Klan, however, was Catholics. Anti-Catholic lectures, stories, and books that proliferated in the 1910s were recycled with few changes by the Klan a decade later. The Klan circulated thousands of copies of an alleged Knights of Columbus initiation that was the secret blueprint for a Catholic takeover of the country. In the purported pledge, aspiring Knights of Columbus promised to "wage relentless war, secretly and openly, against all heretics, Protestants, and Masons." The document detailed the Catholic initiates' vow: "Burn, waste, boil, flay, strangle and bury alive these infamous heretics; rip open the stomachs and wombs of their women and crash their infants' heads against the walls in order to annihilate their execrable race [or] secretly use the poisonous cup, strangulation cord, the steel of the poiniard, or the leaden bullet."

The most powerful anti-Catholic allegations made by the Indiana Klan concerned sexual practices of priests and nuns. Klan publications and lecturers described an international network of convent prisons that enslaved young Protestant women, exacting forced labor and sexual favors from the girls and turning them into compliant Catholic adults. According to . . . the WKKK, Romanists prevailed upon innocent Protestant couples to sign over their children to the religious upbringing of Catholics. Occasionally, boys were the alleged target of Romanist avarice, as in the tale of fifty-two boys snatched from a Methodist Episcopal orphanage by a Catholic-incited police raid and placed in Catholic homes from which they fervently endeavored to escape. But it was mainly Protestant girls who were alleged to be ensnared by Catholic institutions, allowing the Klan to claim that it was safeguarding the virtue of 100 percent females.

Indiana Protestant preachers commonly adopted the klannish term for the Roman Catholic church and titled lectures on the Klan's battle with the Catholics "The Beast vs. the Invisible Empire." In Muncie, Indiana, the Lynds' *Middletown* reported that "local Klansmen vowed they would unmask 'when and not until the Catholics take the prison walls down from about their convents and nunneries.'" One of the Lynds' informants, indicating a copy of a common Klan periodical, declared, "Look at this picture of this poor girl— look at her hands! see, all those fingers gone—just stumps left! she was in a convent when it was considered sinful to wear jewelry, and the Sisters, when they found her wearing some rings, just burned them off her fingers!"

To make initial contact in a new territory, the Klan sent lecturers posing as former nuns and former priests to titillate audiences with details of Romanist sexual depravity and to prepare the way for the Klan's troupe of Protestant minister-lecturers. The tactic was so successful that the same "nun" and "priest" lecturers returned to areas over and over, drawing massive crowds. Lurid stories of Catholic depravity were rumored in public and discussed openly and in great detail in assemblies restricted to Klan members.

The Klan's genius at self-promotion was evident in its Indiana lecture tours. Publicly distributed Klan newspapers described the "torture and abuse of Protestant girls in the Roman Catholic hell holes" of Catholic convents that observers would relate since the girls themselves demurely declined to reveal intimate details of their abuse in a public forum. Memories of the sexual tales spread by the Klan are still fresh in the minds of former Klansmembers and contemporaries of the 1920s Klan movement in Indiana.

> They were saying that the Catholic priests and nuns were having sexual relationships and they'd kill the babies. They'd have abortions. All that kind of stuff. They ripped the stomachs of the nuns open and would take the baby. All that kind of business. Just horrible things.
>
> They would never come out and say things but they would imply a lot of things. And, then you would draw your own conclusions about how the Catholics and priests and nuns behaved. In fact, you know, the convent at Huntington and the friary was right there. Of course, the friary didn't belong to the Catholics anymore. But, there actually was an underground passage between the two. And, of course, the whole community made a lot of that.

> Where the [convent] academy was, they had their own graveyard to bury
> their dead from the babies that was born to the girls there in that thing. . . . I was
> curious where the graveyard was [but] I didn't ask anybody.

One of the most successful Klan emissaries was Helen Jackson, billed as an
"escaped nun." Jackson traveled across the country, regaling her sex-segre-
gated audiences with tales of sexual horrors behind convent walls. She
claimed to have firsthand knowledge of infanticides and abortions forced on
nuns by the priests who fathered their babies. Displaying little leather bags,
Jackson told her riveted audience that these were used to dispose of the convents' murdered newborns and aborted fetuses. In small towns of the West
and Midwest, she regaled thousands of avid listeners with tales of Catholic
sadomasochistic practices, including one incident in which a cross was
burned on her own back. One informant recalled an anecdote of convent life
from Helen Jackson's speech: "When they misbehaved, they were soaked in
the bathtubs where, they didn't have kotex in those days, it was just cloth that
was washed out in tubs and soaking with those pots. That was the most
hideous thing, it just hit me."

Jackson's autobiography, *Convent Cruelties,* was sold at Klan rallies. . . . It
also was advertised in Klan publications, with a suggestive cartoon of a girl being whipped by nuns. Provocatively subtitled—"A providential delivery from
Rome's Convent Pens: a sensational experience"—the volume traced Jackson's alleged imprisonment by sadistic Catholic officials in a convent in Detroit, Michigan, and in a House of the Good Shepherd in Newport, Kentucky.
Jackson maintained that she was constantly humiliated by other nuns, forbidden any contact with the outside world, subjected to torture by immersion in
cold water, forced to drink vile substances, and ordered to work unceasingly
at ironing and embroidery. She also claimed that she had witnessed the tortures and imprisonment of other girls, some of whom were Protestants ab-
ducted into the Romanist slave den. Appended to the volume were affidavits
from other "escaped nuns" who provided their own tales of imprisonment
and abuse in Catholic convents and homes.

Helen Jackson frequently traveled with L. J. King, who billed himself as an
"ex-Romanist." King had made his living for years on the anti-Catholic lecture
circuit, claiming to be a former priest. Like other anti-Catholic evangelist lecturers of the 1910s, King specialized in highly emotional harangues. With his
audiences separated by sex, King regaled the crowd with horrid tales of
Catholic sexual tortures dating from the European Inquisition. In modern
times, King thundered, these same perversions continued, fostered by priests
whose "unnatural" pledge of celibacy drove their sexual desires in depraved
directions.

In the early 1920s L. J. King enlisted in the Klan and joined forces with
Helen Jackson on the Klan lecture circuit. King's propaganda—on the impli-
cations of the unmarried clergy and the sexual exploits of the mysterious
Catholic church—was ideal for the Klan's anti-Catholic agenda: "Every priest

and nun connected with the [school] system is chained to a life of celibacy in defiance of nature and clad in a strange, unsanitary costume."

Jackson and King held revivals on behalf of the Klan in many small towns in Indiana, setting up headquarters in a local restaurant or hotel and meeting nightly for two or three weeks—as long as a month—drawing crowds of hundreds and even thousands. In a single visit the pair would deliver lectures with titles such as "My Visit to the Nunnery at St. Louis, Missouri," "See Bottle Convent Booze," "The Fruits of the Confessional," and "Priest Hans Smytt Murders Two Girls." On the Klan circuit, King expanded on Jackson's personal account, regaling audiences with highly detailed tales of imprisonment in convents and sexual debauchery between Catholic nuns and priests. He described convent dungeons with bolted doors, iron-barred windows, and high massive walls that imprisoned hapless girls, making suicide their only escape.

King and Jackson vividly described the grotesque tortures to which nuns were subjected for the sexual pleasure of priests, including tales of nuns confined in coffins filled with human excrement. A favorite legend recounted by the pair was the tale of Maria Monk and the nunnery of the Hôtel-Dieu in Montreal, a famous anti-Catholic diatribe dating to the early nineteenth century. Indeed, nearly all my respondents recalled owning a copy of Maria Monk's story, and most could recount its "awful disclosures" of convent life, including the murder of illicitly conceived infants.

> It was a horrible tale. My grandmother and I read it when we were in Florida one winter. And, she laughed about it. She thought it was horrible too, but she let me read it, and it was just a horrible thing. It was just like all these things they had in that messy newspaper [*Fiery Cross*]. You know, incredible things.

Jackson and King were expert at picturing even innocuous Catholic rituals as sordid and perverse. Their stump speech on the "abomination of secret auricular confession" is an example. King exclaimed that the secret confessional of the Catholic church was nothing more than "a school of licentiousness, seduction, and adultery." Priests encouraged innocent young girls to participate in confidential sexual fantasies in the confessional by means of suggestive questions whispered outside the hearing of male relatives or husbands. Secret confessions also provided the pretext for illicit love making between priest-confessors and nuns in convents, leading to abortion or infanticide.

King's lectures and his annual, *The Converted Catholic and Protestant Missionary*, included many stories of women victimized in Catholic rectories, homes, and convents. These ranged from innuendo of sexual torture and intrigue to case histories of girls condemned to a life of drudgery, deprivation, and cruelty in convent "prisons." Before her lectures, Jackson would read from letters by local Klan chapters that charted successes in liberating Protestant girls from "Rome's slave pens" and encouraged others to free girls imprisoned in their localities. The traffic in white women, King seethed, was increasing "to fill up the place of poisoned, deluded, outraged, starved, raped, and murdered victims of priestcraft in the nunnery, to feed the lust of the adulterous bachelor, overfed, drunken priesthood of the Romish fake."

The magnetism of King's and Jackson's oratory is evident in the account that the daughter of an active Indiana Klanswoman and Klansman gave of how her parents "practically broke out in tears about some of the things that were being taught to the children in the school . . . all these things that went on in the priest's home and the nun's home and all these babies that were buried underneath the mother's houses."

Even girls who avoided the terror of the convent life, the Klan suggested, were not safe. Jackson, King, and other Klan lecturers charged priests with attacking girls in school dormitories and in church sanctuaries; with being drunk, stupid, or intolerant; and with gambling and promoting law breaking. Sometimes the finger of blame pointed toward priests in general; at other times it accused particular priests or convent schools.

The Klan's success in bringing sexual morality into the political agenda gave it great public credibility (and an enormous following) among white Protestants who applauded the Klan's efforts to subvert the immoral intentions of Catholic clergy, Jewish businessmen, and black and immigrant men and to uphold morality within white Protestant families. Tales of sexual perversity also normalized hatred of the Klan's enemies. The Klan's accounts of sexual depravity among Catholic clergy and the wanton sexual exploitation of youngsters by priests and nuns led many white Protestants to view Catholics as far removed from accepted standards of moral and ethical behavior.

When the Klan had established Catholics as strange and inexplicable beings, few stories about them seemed implausible. And the Klan was expert at generating rumors for gullible audiences. In reaction to news that the 1917 U.S. dollar bill was covered with secret Catholic symbols, loyal Klan members dutifully tore off a corner of the bill where the pope's picture was said to be hidden. Indiana Klan members heard, and often believed, accusations against the Catholic church that ranged from plotting the assassination of President Abraham Lincoln, to fomenting World War I in order to strengthen the papacy, to leading the massacre of American Indians.

As befitting an organization built on xenophobia, Klan propaganda was hysterical on the topic of the Italian pope and Vatican City. The pope, known in Klan parlance as the "dago on the Tiber," was identified with the biblical Delilah, putting the Samson of the United States to sleep in order to carry out her evil plans. Many Klanswomen and Klansmen in Indiana firmly believed that the arrival of the pope as emperor of the United States was imminent. Rumors circulated that a palace was being built in Washington, D.C., to allow the pope to oversee his empire.

A major theme of the Klan's anti-Catholicism was that of a church under foreign leadership. Catholics in the United States—citizens as well as immigrants—were accused of being spies for the Vatican. The police forces of the major cities, the Klan asserted, were dominated by Catholics who owed their allegiance to the pope in Rome. The Klan's opposition to the World Court was based on a similar belief—that the Vatican would manipulate the World Court as a tool for "romanizing" America and forcing "papist aliens" into the United States. Ignoring its own hierarchical structure, the Klan argued that the strict lines of authority in the Catholic church were antithetical to democracy and individual freedom. Catholics, according to the Klan, came from the lower classes and criminal elements of Europe and were forced to do the bidding of the pope.

Typical of the way that many Protestants in 1920s Indiana regarded Catholics is the account given by a woman in Muncie when attempting to convince an interviewer for the Lynds' ethnographic work, *Middletown,* to join her in the local Klan. She insisted that the pope started the first Klan in order to divide and conquer Protestants, a convoluted logic meant to underscore the malevolent intentions of the Catholic empire.

> It's about time you joined the good people and did something about this Catholic situation. The Pope is trying to get control of this country, and in order to do it, he started the old Klan to stir up trouble among the Protestants, but instead of doing that he only opened their eyes to the situation, and now all the Protestants are getting together in the new Klan to overcome the Catholic menace.

The Catholic fraternal order, the Knights of Columbus, was a frequent target of Klan propaganda, which typically insisted that the Knights were the secret military arm of the pope. According to the Klan, the Knights planted Catholic girls in Protestant homes as maids and child helpers who then filed weekly reports with the Vatican on the activities and conversations of Protestant families.

Protestants in Indiana also commonly believed that Catholics were arming themselves for a massacre of non-Catholics, using guns and ammunition stockpiled in the basements of Catholic churches. Rumors circulated throughout the state that Catholics buried a rifle under the local church each time a Catholic boy was born, for his later use to defend the papal empire that would rule the United States by the time the child grew to manhood. A woman in central Indiana recalled that "stories floated here that the Catholic church, that the basement was really an armory, getting ready for a revolution . . . the Catholic church was getting ready for a civil war in this country, they were going to take over the government." . . .

Often a fine line separated the Klan's goodwill campaigns from its political terrorism. This was most obvious in the Klan's goodwill activities for hospitals and public schools. When the WKKK and KKK made philanthropic gestures toward public schools or raised money to build Protestant hospitals, they warned Protestants that Catholics and foreigners had invaded the most basic institutions of public life. The crusade of nearly every WKKK chapter to present flags and Bibles to the public schools of their county and to build Protestant-only hospitals in communities then dependent on Catholic hospitals roused images of Catholic teachers secretly indoctrinating Protestant youth or Catholic doctors and nurses insisting on religious conversion in exchange for hospital treatment.

WKKK chapters competed among one another to bring Protestant values to the public schools. When one WKKK klavern presented a Bible to every public school in the township, another donated a Bible to every school in the county, or a flag *and* a Bible to every school. Some schools received copies of *Stories of the Bible* together with their flags and Bibles. Others received multiple copies of new Bibles for the use of their students or placards with the Ten Commandments for every schoolroom.

The way schools received their Bibles, flags, and books was important. The favored manner of donation was a public ceremony of presentation and acceptance. The WKKK of Coal City succeeded in this endeavor: it presented its gifts to the school principal on stage during intermission of the school play. Less successful was the WKKK of Terre Haute whose presentation involving one hundred Klanswomen was marred by the school board's refusal to allow the Klanswomen to don robes for the ceremony.

Many Indiana Klan chapters received favorable publicity by announcing lavish fundraising drives to assist or build local Protestant hospitals. Although few, if any, such fundraising promises were fulfilled, the WKKK and KKK made lavish predictions that it would collect sums of $50,000 and more for hospitals and schools in Indiana's cities and towns. If nothing else, these fundraising drives replenished the treasuries of Klan locals and realms.

Another deft publicity tactic pioneered by the men of the Klan and then adopted in identical form by the women's Klan was the church visit. Within a three-month period thirteen WKKK chapters reported making church visits in small Indiana communities, involving between five and seventy women. In a church visit, robed and masked Klanswomen would interrupt a Protestant service, stride up the center aisle, and present the minister with a sum of money. Ostensibly the money was for church work, in keeping with the Klan's pledge of militant Protestantism, but money easily found its way to the minister's personal funds. The minister's role was to act surprised, if pleased, by the visit of the Klanswomen. Often the drama was prearranged with cooperating ministers who viewed the proffered purse as payment for espousing Klan doctrines from the pulpit.

While the school, hospital, and church campaigns of Indiana's WKKK and KKK chapters demonstrated the Klan's muscle, they delivered the message in indirect terms. Other political actions by Klanswomen more directly abused and harassed the enemies of the Klan. WKKK chapters in Indiana bombarded public schools with protests and calls to reform a school system that Klanswomen insisted was permeated with foreign, Catholic, and even Bolshevik influences. Klanswomen fought to remove Catholic encyclopedias from public school libraries, campaigned against the teaching of German (the language of the wartime enemy), and constantly pressured for a cabinet-level Department of Education to monitor and shore up the public school system and thereby undermine parochial education. Women of the Klan in many Indiana counties met with township trustees to urge compulsory Bible reading in public schools.

Klanswomen in Indiana also were active in the effort to "cleanse" public schools of the corrupting influence of non-Protestants. The innocent minds of Protestant children, Klanswomen insisted, were being filled with Romanist doctrines. A number of Indiana's WKKK klaverns worked to have Catholic teachers, even Catholic school superintendents, fired. The Anderson WKKK, for example, mounted an effort to get two Catholic teachers fired. After being bombarded with letters from the women's Klan demanding her resignation, one teacher left town. The other teacher resigned after "several other small incidents happened," but she refused to leave town. In Muncie the Klan worked to remove a Catholic teacher with thirty-seven years' experience but without success. . . .

Though the Klan could elect members and supporters in Indiana, its electoral efforts were less effective than another political tactic: the boycott. This technique drew on women's traditional role as manager of the family's consumption. A boycott brought even the act of shopping into the fight for racial and religious supremacy. It infused the ordinary tasks of Klanswomen's lives with political content. Acting individually but with a collective direction, Klanswomen could force Jews, Catholics, or blacks out of their communities or into financial bankruptcy. Indiana Klanswomen avidly took to the task.

Daisy Barr set the tone for the WKKK's crusade of selective shopping in weekly addresses to Indianapolis Klanswomen. At each meeting, attended by as many as fifteen hundred women, Barr read the roll of Indianapolis WKKK and KKK members who were engaged in local retail or service trade. These businesses and products had the WKKK seal of approval. These, and only these, were to be patronized by Klanswomen; all others were "Catholic or Jew" (or "alien") and should be rejected. Barr was particularly indignant about "Jew-owned" stores and claimed that "Jews had 75 percent of the money of the United States." This situation would change, however. "When the women should be as strongly organized as the men," she raged, "THEY WOULD HAVE THE POWER AND THEN GOD HELP BLOCK [Jewish businessman] AND HIS SLACKER SON. THERE WILL BE NO JEWISH BUSINESS LEFT IN INDIANAPOLIS."

Organizing Klanswomen as consumers had an immediate and phenomenal effect. Businesses with Jewish owners, ranging from large department stores to small shops and professional services, went bankrupt throughout Indiana. Jewish professionals and business owners fled communities in which they had lived for decades.

The consumption campaign of the WKKK gave many communities their first indication of the strength of women's klaverns and the extent of pro-Klan sentiment among local women. Shopping at one place over another allowed women to exercise considerable political clout without overstepping even the most conventional definition of their roles as mothers and wives. Moreover, the political content of the act was elusive. Women could act on racist, anti-Semitic, or anti-Catholic sentiments in a completely invisible fashion. It was not necessary to attend klaverns, become an official WKKK member, or even discuss the Klan to participate in the Klan's economic crusade. Shopping, after all, involves myriad subjective choices about quality, price, and convenience—any woman could justify her selections, if need be, without revealing sympathy with the goals of the Klan. For many women in Indiana who declined to join the WKKK because of fear of being identified with the Klan or because of reluctance to be involved with a political movement, the economic strategy of the WKKK was perfect.

The diffusion of information about approved and boycotted businesses operated through a shadowy network of Klanswomen and Klan sympathizers. Informal conversations among women—dismissed as insignificant gossip by contemporary men and Klan historians—fueled one of the Klan's most powerful weapons. Rumor did not spread randomly; the WKKK used tightly organized bands of Klanswomen to ensure its dispersal across the state. The impact of the "poison squad of whispering women" . . . was profound. Women's poison squads could spread stories to every corner of the state within twenty-four hours. Even when the story in its entirety was known to be false, doubts lingered, as a woman in central Indiana attested: "Many of the rumors possibly had a degree of truth in them so you could not deny it all but it was not the truth as it was told."

In its political efforts, the WKKK relied on the patterns of daily activities of Indiana women. Women visiting friends and relatives or stopping to chat with acquaintances at shops or schools and over the proverbial back fence passed information about who *owned* what and who *sympathized* with what. Women needed not identify their own sentiments to pass on information; the assumption that women's conversation was personal, not political, shielded women from accusations and attacks by anti-Klan forces. Some women heard the information and dismissed it as inconsequential. To receptive ears, however, the implications for action were clear.

Few rumors seemed too farfetched. In 1923 North Manchester was swept by a rumor that Negroes were coming north in great numbers, a rumor purportedly based on sighting one local man traveling in the South. Another rumor spread by the women's Klan in North Manchester proved embarrassing to the organization after it was made public. The incredible nature of this tale indicates not only the Klan's striking ability to disseminate rumors but also the immediacy of fears about a papal assault on Indiana:

> Some Klan leader said that the Pope was coming to take over the country, and he said he might be on the next train that went through North Manchester. You know, just trying to make it specific. So, about a thousand people went out to the train station and stopped the train. It only had one passenger train and one

passenger on it. They took him off, and he finally convinced them that he wasn't the Pope. He was a carpet salesman. And so they put him on the next train and he went on to Chicago.

The organized gossip of Klanswomen spread poison about Jews, Catholics, and others opposed to the crusade of militant Protestantism. Tales about the personal life, merchandise, and political allegiances of the town's outsiders destroyed the Klan's enemies without a trace. Since gossip left no visible traces on the participants, it created no trail for those opposed to or victimized by the Klan. Indeed, the political power of gossip lay precisely in its apolitical character. There were no reports to seize, no meetings to invade, no publications to refute. One might guess at its existence from its consequences, but even those were hard to measure on the local level. Did a department store go out of business because of an invisible boycott or because of poor management or shoddy goods? Did a Jewish family leave town because of actual economic pressure or because of its exaggerated fear of such pressure? Did stores and businesses go bankrupt, or did they simply move to areas of greater financial potential? Only in retrospect did the pattern of business closures and out-migration by Jewish owners across Indiana communities become clear. Only in retrospect, and by looking closely at the lives of women, can we reveal the political character and the economic power of these networks of gossip. . . .

To victims, the Klan's power and tactics were confusing as well as destructive. Catholics and Jews who had been at least partially integrated into the social, cultural, and commercial life of the community now found themselves inexplicably labeled as outsiders and enemies. One woman gave an account of the Klan's boycott of her (Catholic) family's grocery store, made more ironic by the fact that the men's and women's Klans met in a room above the grocery.

> I blame the Klan indirectly for my father's death. . . . It just broke his heart to have people shun him, pass right in front of our door, our grocery store door and go upstairs and not look at him. Not look in our store, and he was never able to take that and he used to say, what did I do, and nothing changed on his part, he was the same person. . . . I don't think he minded losing the customers so badly . . . but the fact that he lost friends and he just was never able to accept that.

Although rumors and gossip were the most effective weapons, the Klan employed more visible mechanisms to direct the power of purchasing. The *Fiery Cross* published a "who's who" roster of Catholic businessmen, complete with names and addresses of their business establishments. No loyal Klanswoman need wonder what actions the list encouraged.

Klan members developed an organizational policy of "vocational klannishness" in which Klan members pledged to conduct "trading, dealing with, and patronizing Klansmen in preference to all others." The Klan planned to publish a National Service Directory that would list all businesses in the United States owned by Klansmembers who took out a $35 membership in the National Service Corporation. This project was never completed, but local klaverns issued their own directories and the Indiana Klan compiled a listing that covered all cities in the state. Shopkeepers supplemented these directories with advertising that broadcast the owner's political sympathies. Shopkeepers who joined the KKK or WKKK received placards for their store windows that read TWK—Trade With a Klansman. Those who belonged to the National Service Corporation received a round red, white, and blue sign to display in their businesses.

Klan papers as well as local non-Klan papers carried numerous ads openly proclaiming the klannish sympathies of local business owners. Rarely were these ads subtle. The *Franklin Evening Star* ran one such advertisement:

> Every person in Johnson County is invited
> to join the KKK Keystone Kleaning Kompany
> "keep klothes klean" campaign

The Klan's claim to represent 100 percent Americans provided merchants with another advertising ploy. Evans's American Cafe in Kokomo promised the "best 100% 25-cent meals in state," Indianapolis barber shops declared their employees to be 100 percent American, underwriters in Logansport promised insurance that was 100 percent safe, a Haughville company guaranteed 100 percent service in delivering ice, coal, and wood, and an Indianapolis jeweler urged Klan couples to examine its 100 percent workmanship before purchasing a wedding ring, adding that it would give a 10 percent discount to any 100 percent American. The *Fiery Cross* even published its own business directory in every issue, with ads for Klan-owned companies, professional services, and evangelical preachers. The issue for June 1, 1923, for example, contained notices for hotels, furniture stores, realtors, seed stores, and many other businesses:

> Columbus, Indiana, Hunter Repair Shop—Everything for a Ford, 100% shop operated by 100% man with 100% workmen. We want 100% American business.
>
> Marion, Indiana, Chiropractor—Dr. O. G. McKeever, for 100% service.

The tactic of vocational klannishness affected workers as well as merchants and professionals. Employers sympathetic to the Klan, or fearing Klan reprisals, advertised for 100 percent American employees and refused to hire Catholics, Jews, blacks, new immigrants, or people of "poor character." For its own members, the Klan served as a quasi–employment service. The state headquarters sent directives to all field officers of the KKK and WKKK in Indiana, indicating employment situations for 100 percent women and men. The *Fiery Cross*, like commercial newspapers, listed notices of "Situation Wanted" or "Employees Wanted" separately for women and men.

Workers who were Catholic, Jewish, or suspected of anti-Klan leanings often discovered vocational klannishness by being suddenly fired from their

The following selection deals with Chicanos living in northern New Mexico and southern Colorado. Initially their communities consisted mostly of an interlocked network of small, rural villages, but economic pressures forced them into increased contact with and dependence on the economic and social institutions of the larger society. In the process they encountered economic, social, and cultural dilemmas little different from those faced by Chicanos in other parts of the United States. Like others, they tended to be confined to hard, unskilled, and low-paying jobs, to suffer from serious health problems, and to lack educational opportunities. The picture was complicated by the tendency of Anglos to lump together all Chicanos, whether immigrants or American citizens, and to regard them all with prejudice.

It was early spring when they began to arrive. In the lingering chill twenty thousand Chicanos settled over the beetfields, five here, ten there. To house them, farmers rousted the hens from the chicken coops and took the last of the grain out of the storage shacks. Most of the shacks had only one or two rooms to shelter the large families—families had to be large to make a living working beets—and throughout the twenties, most shacks provided "utterly inadequate" shelter at that. Investigators continually testified that they found shacks located "with no attention to adequate sanitation, toilet facilities, sleeping room, or water supply." Without shade, the shacks became hotter than the fields; often they had no screens. The surroundings were dirty barnyards and corrals.

If they worked on the western edge of the South Platte Valley, due north of Denver, Spanish Americans could look up from the five miles of rows they tended per acre (each averaged ten acres per season) and, looking across the plain, be soothed by the sun setting over the mountains, a reminder of home. But if they worked in the long stretch of the valley to the east, there was nothing to relieve the eye from the endless rows and level terrain; they were alone on the plain, alone in the Anglo north, with nothing to remind them of the mountains, the villages, the relatives, the gardens, and the churches of home. This frontier demanded from them a new life, a new way of living. To understand their life as it evolved in the 1920s, it is necessary first to set it in the context of the regional community, then to examine the factors that conspired to make the creation of a stable community in the north difficult—including the impact of the migration on Chicanas, the community builders—and finally to analyze new strategies as they emerged in the north.

With spiraling intensity, old and new factors combined in northern New Mexico to deprive Hispanics of land and livelihood, to drive them into increased dependency on the networks and settlements, and the success, of the regional community. Each new disaster of the 1920s, natural or man-made, meant reduced resources to meet the next. Hispanic vigilante groups like the Manos Negras continued to cut fences that blocked access to traditionally communal pasture and to burn barns of Rio Arriba County's Anglo and Hispanic commercial farmers, but such efforts to resist the trend had little impact. There also continued a depressed cattle market; limited access to Anglo-controlled credit; equal division of dwindling holdings among heirs, which left each with smaller and smaller parcels of land; and an average crop failure in some parts of northern New Mexico reaching 59 percent. In addition to these older factors, a 1924 Pueblo Lands Act resulted in the eviction of nearly three thousand Hispanics and Anglos. At the same time, Texans and Oklahomans with enough capital to stake a homestead invaded the region. They disrupted the Hispanic villages and demanded services such as moving a high school from a Hispanic settlement to their own settlement or building expensive irrigation projects that would increase the tax burden on the financially strapped Hispanics just when a 1926 state tax law made land that had been tax-delinquent for three years subject to foreclosure and sale for back taxes.

These events ensured that a rapidly escalating proportion of Hispanic village families increased their reliance on wage labor or, like farm folk all over the country, left the villages altogether. Many headed for such larger towns of New Mexico as Grants and Albuquerque. Others departed for the state's coal-mining areas, Gallup and Raton, and for railroad shops and Colorado's coal mines. But the largest contingent set out for the beetfields, where push and pull came together.

Colorado's sugar-beet industry provided approximately 20,000 jobs each season, while the state's railroads employed only about 5000 Chicanos for maintenance of way, and its coal mines just over 3000. Moreover, to ensure an ample labor supply, Great Western Sugar Company, Colorado's largest, spent lavishly on recruitment campaigns throughout the decade, as much as ninety dollars per family recruited, or $250,000 in a single year. The company focused with particular intensity on the already vulnerable areas of southern Colorado and New Mexico, until the two states' share of the recruited Chicano labor rose from approximately 65 percent in 1923 to approximately 85 percent in 1927.

According to one ex-villager, recruiters claimed "you'd rake in the money," and they distributed brochures that led Hispanics to expect a garden plot for each family, decent housing, a water supply, and a friendly employer who might provide milk and eggs at cost. While it is true that a few of the Chicano beet-labor houses, more of them toward the end of the decade, were sturdy and weatherproof, that some farm owners and tenants had houses and sanitation little better than their labor did, and that farm labor conditions in other parts of the nation, notably in the South, were little if any better than those in Colorado, nonetheless, for the majority of Chicanos in the 1920s, life in Colorado's beetfields did not fulfill recruiters' promises. A simple description of conditions and attitudes there reads like a harangue against the agricultural system of the time.

Most of the farmers seemed to agree with Americanization teacher Alfred White, that "the peon has always lived like a pig and he will continue to do so." National Child Labor Committee investigator Charles Gibbons found that "the local people . . . feel they are giving the Mexican all he deserves; in fact one frequently finds the opinion that they (residents) are performing an act of charity in allowing the Mexican to work for them, and therefore any kind of a house will do for them to live in." Most growers and even investigators were convinced that whatever the conditions in Colorado, they represented an improvement over Hispanic and Mexican villages.

Most Chicanos, on the other hand, saw little if any improvement. They had come north, to the margins of the Hispanic regional community, to better their condition. Though often bitterly disappointed in what they found, many could not afford to turn back. An exasperated Chicana living in a one-room shack with her family of twelve demanded, "How can you expect folks to live decently when given a place like that?" The Chicanas tried desperately to turn these shacks into homes, despite their long hours in the fields and the meager furnishings they could bring with them. The migrants used boxes as tables and cupboards, and often slept on the floor. Mary Vela remembered that her mother stayed up all night to clean when they moved. Another mother made her own paste and pasted a two-room shack with newspapers for decoration and warmth; her daughter remembered, "[W]e would lay there and read all the news there was in the newspapers."

As to the work itself, there were some Anglo school children and a few Anglo women who, not needing to provide their entire support from the beets, contracted small acreages, an amount easily managed in workdays of reasonable length. A local lawyer assured investigators that "children are in much better conditions in the open fields and the open air than they would be in their homes. In general," he asserted, "this summer outing is looked upon by the children as a frolic." But Mary Vela recalled beetwork as "backbreaking and heavy. During the harvest we'd work 18-hours days." At least one Spanish-speaking woman lost two sons to a kidney disease exacerbated by long hours of stooping over the fields. Thinning the beets in the early summer required crawling, and topping them during the harvest required stooping, and it was all, according to investigator Paul Taylor, "disagreeable . . . dirty . . . monotonous and repetitive." Even C. V. Maddux, labor commissioner at Great Western Sugar Company in the 1920s, warned that "a man who is highly-strung could never work beets, because there are five miles of row to every acre. . . . He could not see the end."

Great Western Sugar remained the recruiter and not the direct employer of beet labor, but it taught its agricultural fieldmen Spanish, retained files on each of the laborers it recruited, and mediated in grower-labor disputes. As the roving villagers created new and reinforced old paths connecting the village economy to the large one, Great Western Sugar, by centralizing and expanding its recruiting and labor services, increased its control over the labor and the labor market on the Anglo-Chicano frontier, and so its power in the regional community.

The sugar companies together with the growers set the wages of beet labor, a crucial factor not only for Hispanic life in the north but for the possibilities of the regional community. Yet the laborers' cost of living did not enter into the companies' calculations. They simply promised to procure beet labor at the farmers' agreed rate per acre. Under the set rates, a Chicano beetworker earned only about $250 each season. Meanwhile, the cost of living in Denver for a family, according to the Colorado Industrial Commission, was $1,197.78 per year at minimum comfort. For Chicanos wintering in rural areas, the cost may have been slightly less, but not 75 percent less. Chicanos quickly came to see in the family system of labor not the promise of vastly increased wealth, but simply survival.

And even survival was questionable. "Families" under this system sometimes included distant cousins, neighbors from the home village, or even subcontractors. With more than six working members, at least four of them adult men, such a family could contract as many as 60 to 80 acres and make between $1500 and $2100 per season. But there were few such families, fewer, in fact, than 5 percent of the whole. Investigating the South Platte area in 1924, Sara Brown found earnings from beets for over half the contract families with children amounted to less than $900. Forty percent of Brown's families earned less than $700 for the season. In other beet-producing areas of Colorado, beet-labor families earned even less. Having promised to provide cheap labor to the growers, sugar companies had indeed fostered a family system where, according to one pair of investigators, "instead of paying one laborer a bare subsistence wage, the labor of father and several children is secured at this rate." But family earnings of seven hundred dollars did not provide even subsistence, except, perhaps, during the months of labor.

Clearly such low wages demanded some kind of supplement, and it was here that the village strategy of migration and the beet industry's labor strategy intersected. Credit, relief, or the beet laborer's own farm in southern Colorado, New Mexico, or Mexico could supplement beet wages in the absence

of winter work. Each of these alternatives informally subsidized the beet industry by making the low wages possible, but in some ways, perpetual migration seemed the most desirable to all parties. . . . Having at the end of the beet
season an average of approximately $150, "plenty to get them out of the coun-
try," as one farmer observed, and spending approximately two-thirds of it on
returning to the village, a beet-labor family would have fifty dollars to pay
taxes on the farm and supply cash needs throughout the winter. In turn, the
farm that could not support the family year round might provide the missing
six months' subsistence. This semi-autonomous cultural retreat fit the mytho-
logical image of the vanishing "Mexican" whose "homing instinct" saved the
Southwest from "the terrible mistakes which have been made in the southern
states . . . a civilization of masters and servants." In Colorado, growers sent the
"servants" home when they were not wanted, in an extended echo of a day
work system rather than live-in help. This migratory pattern permitted members of each culture to deny their membership in and responsibility for the
other, and allowed farmers to keep the doors to Mexican reserve labor open.

The number of Chicanos who either lacked the farm to which to return or
lacked the means to get there belied the comforting myth. Mexican nationals
in particular, unlike most Spanish Americans tended to come from landless
families. But both groups settled in the north in greater numbers than during
the war. The resident Chicano population of northeastern Colorado more
than doubled relative to the total population and more than tripled in absolute numbers between 1920 and 1927 alone. Approximately one-third wintered in the open fields and the rest in towns. In Denver their number grew
from approximately two thousand to over eight thousand. Expanding earlier
settlements in Denver, Spanish Americans clustered west of the city center, in
the vicinity of West Colfax between the Platte River and Cherry Creek, and
also to the north along the east coast of the river. To the northeast of this latter area were the Mexicans, perhaps a fifth of the total Chicano population in
the city. These were poor parts of the city, multiethnic, with rooming houses,
the unemployed, and the transient. Among these last, Denver's Chicanos fit
well. Over three-quarters of the families from each section left Denver each
spring for seasonal labor. By 1929, such Chicano clusters, however transient,
made it clear that the "Mexicans" disappearing from the fields after harvest
had not moved very far. . . .

Hispanics found the traditional agricultural ladder to ownership full of
broken rungs. Landowners hesitated to lease farms to Hispanics. One who
did complained, "People around here blame me for leasing to Mexicans and
so displacing the whites." But even a lease proved at best a rickety, inadequate
vehicle. Few Chicanos would follow their predecessors, the German-Russian
immigrants, to farm ownership. Chicanos arrived with smaller families than
the German-Russians, and with an unwillingness to keep the women and children in the fields for the same long hours. Moreover, they came at a time

when land values had escalated while beet-labor wages had not and when the move to ownership had generally dwindled. It was, in fact, only the lack of movement between tenancy and ownership that reconciled Anglos to Chicano lessees at all. As one farmer's wife explained, "There is no danger from the Mexicans. They won't save enough to buy land." Without land ownership it would be difficult for Hispanics to convert the periphery of one Chicano regional community, the outermost edge of the network system, into the center of another, the node of a new set of networks.

What year-round residences Chicanos could buy consisted of town lots and even these were not easily acquired. "Dealers in real estate," Paul Taylor revealed, "carry out the policy of separating Mexicans in northeastern Colorado." And even a modest $250 mortgage on a lot in a Chicano enclave, with the family paying only twelve dollars a year, outran beetworker resources. One former beetworker remembered an Anglo realtor in Greeley in the late 1920s who "was working the Spanish real good, he *lived* off the Spanish," providing loans and repossessing partially paid-up houses. A reluctant Anglo host society joined with the dynamics of the beet industry to keep most Chicanos transient and hovering on the margins of society.

Nor did the Great Western Sugar Company's compromise of company-financed colonies impinge markedly on this system. Faced with increasing recruiting costs, the company, unlike the farmers, wanted a larger resident population. In colonies they provided land lots Chicanos could buy as house sites. While the colonies did allow a number of Chicano families to winter in the north each year, the high turnover and lapsed payments proved them not much more affordable for Chicanos than noncompany housing. In addition, the company colonies themselves emblemized the system which kept the Chicanos safely (for the Anglos) marginal and had as its aim the preservation in Chicanos of a perpetual and distinct laboring force. Their one- or two-room distinctive adobe structures stood on lots devoid of shade or farmland, a mile or two outside of Anglo towns or literally across the tracks.

For those Chicanos who did succeed in purchasing such a home, it offered a measure of stability and avoided a winter in the often leaky, overcrowded, and unsanitary farm buildings and Denver shacks. But it offered scant if any aid to gaining subsistence or even acceptance into Anglo society. It had little in common with owning land in the village. For Chicanos, ownership of a home on the periphery of an Anglo community and unaccompanied by ownership of productive land could mark not upward mobility, but confinement to a seasonal laboring class.

When these Chicano colonists and settlers no longer disappeared each winter below some imaginary border, the Anglo townspeople erected their own borders. They used the burning crosses of the Ku Klux Klan, so popular elsewhere in Colorado in the 1920s, to mark the edges of the adobe colonies, and used signs in restaurants, barbershops, and movie theaters bearing such inscriptions as "White Trade Only" and "No Mexican Trade Wanted," which made it impossible for Hispanics in towns like Greeley and Brighton to buy so much as a hamburger. The rhetoric of a "Mexican invasion" continued virtually unabated both in the national popular press and in Colorado. And Hispanic colonists remembered vividly nearly sixty years later the indignity of having an Anglo doctor arrive unannounced to take blood samples for Wasserman tests to detect syphilis. "That's how bad they wanted to get rid of us," recalled one. Spanish Americans had difficulty registering to vote, and local Anglos continued to "wish the Mexicans were not there."

It was ironic that the local growers simultaneously protested the invasion of their neighborhoods by "Mexicans" and petitioned Congress to retain unrestricted Mexican immigration. It was ironic, also, that at the same time Great Western Sugar was erecting its colonies, its representative vigorously contended that "the Mexican eventually returns south of the Rio Grande," having "ebbed and flowed into agriculture and industry as needed for the past fifteen years, with good results to all interests concerned." Colorado's Congressman, Charles Timberlake, even denied that the company had built any houses for Mexican labor. The public and the private face of the industry, its social and its economic needs, had become increasingly disparate under the strain of reinforcing the myths which perpetuated the labor system.

Local Anglos and sugar company officials came up with new myths, or applied old ones, to justify the developments. Although the local Anglos gave the colonies unattractive names—the one in Eaton was called "Ragtown"—the vice president of Holly Sugar Company informed a Senate committee that "Mexicans" were "content to conduct their own community life apart from other races," and Robert McLean claimed that segregation was "due quite as much to the clannishness of the Mexican, as to the opposition of the American." Mexican segregation, it was implied, was by their own choice. When the Fort Collins hospital relegated its Hispanics to the basement, "there were always some real good reasons why they did it," remembered Arthur Maes, "'more at home' . . . 'we can serve them better' . . . 'they can talk to each other in the same language.'"

Many Chicanos—not consumers of the myths—resented the implications of such segregation. Some Hispanics remembered that people were considered "better" if they lived outside the colony, and that the colonies' lack of modern sanitary facilities helped give some colonists the attitude of "If I ever get a chance, I'll move out of this place." But the isolation from Anglo life, the Anglo prejudices, and the low wages reinforced each other and created, as one investigating team expressed it, "a vicious circle." "From this circle," they concluded, "few can escape through their own efforts."

For during winter it was not only the housing situation that created an unstable life for Hispanics. As a rule, the majority of beetwork families who wintered in the north found no work at all between beet seasons. And those whose family members did find jobs, including mothers who did laundry and domestic service, averaged less than $300 in earnings for the winter. Most earned less than $200. The sugar company itself admitted that in northern Colorado "the growers, generally speaking, have been less inclined with the Mexican than with the German-Russian to afford opportunities for extra work." As with those reluctant to lease land to Chicanos, these growers hesitated to displace regular Anglo winter farm labor. In the area's small industrial sector, too, it seemed to some Chicanos that unless jobs were so temporary or so bad that Anglos did not want them, Hispanics could not get them. The Mexican Welfare Committee of the Colorado State Council of the Knights of Columbus concurred, reporting in 1928 that only about 150 of the 7,000 men in northern Colorado employed in industry outside the mines and railroads were "Mexicans," and these, the Committee revealed, "were on rockpiles and at work no other laborer [would] do." Some Chicanos left their families in the north and migrated for winter work, becoming sheepherders in Colorado or Wyoming or going to coal mines or to Pueblo's steel mill. But in this way, they were not replicating the migrant patterns and village systems as much as extending them, since their life in the north centered not on a stable village core, but on a transient migrant settlement, marginal to both Anglo and Hispanic worlds.

Even the number of summer field-labor jobs fluctuated, offering no security for the resident laborer. The beet acreage harvested in a single sugar factory district could go up or down by as much as 75 percent from one year to the next. The beetgrower a Chicano family had worked for one summer may not have been in beets the next. And even if the grower stayed in beets, he might choose newly recruited labor over resident labor, or Mexican over Spanish American. Mexican immigration provided only one-quarter of beetfield labor, but it provided the valve which allowed sporadic large increases in beet acreage, and thus in demand for labor without commensurately increased wages.

The use of Mexican labor affected Hispanic community-building in the north even beyond the lowered wage rates. According to Taylor, the sugar company often brought the labor north a month early to avoid the increasingly strident competition among recruiters as summer approached, and tried to place the recruits on spring railroad work to allow them to support themselves until beetwork began. This employment service brought the two groups, resident and migrant Chicanos, into direct competition even before the beet season. With Mexicans posing the most immediate and visible threat to the Spanish Americans, the latter did all in their power to dissociate themselves from the former and to assert their prior claims to services and employment as citizens and particularly as veterans. One Spanish American told investigator B. F. Coen that Mexicans "aren't any good. You'll only find one out of every 100 that's a 'sitter' [citizen] and I don't think it's right." Spanish Americans also blamed the Mexicans for the new restrictions posted in barber and other shops. Living under the same conditions, Spanish Americans and Mexicans usually resided in separate colonies, rejected each other's company, and fought when mixed. Enrique Lopez recalled of his youth in Denver, "the bitterest 'race riots' I have ever witnessed—and engaged in—were between the look-alike, talk-alike *surumatos* [Mexicans] and *manitos* [Spanish Americans]."

Even a few Anglos made distinctions between the two groups, endowing Mexicans with a character more docile and less educated, and allowing Spanish Americans "more fiery blood in their veins" and more Anglo habits which made them "less passive in their attitudes toward social and civil rights." On the whole, those who made such distinctions placed the Spanish Americans above the Mexicans, and the Spanish Americans certainly placed themselves there. Some of the children of Mexican immigrants began to adopt the term "Spanish American" to describe themselves as well, but most of them heartily resented the condescending attitude of the Spanish-speaking from Colorado and New Mexico and labeled them "comprado," or "bought," for having remained in the United States after 1848 instead of leaving for Mexico. They taunted them with Anglo discriminations, calling them people without a country.

Infuriatingly, most Anglos continued in daily practice to make no distinction among them at all. "During the war," complained one citizen of Anglo attitudes, "we were Spanish Americans; now we are just Mexicans." Anglos referred to the "Mexican, or his cousin the Spanish-American" as people "who easily merge" on United States soil, and in one area officials expressed their chagrin that not one of the local "Mexicans" had showed up at citizenship classes, apparently unaware that the majority of local Hispanic residents were already citizens, by birth. To most Anglos, as one investigation team discovered, both groups "are called 'Mexes' or 'Greasers' and are regarded as foreigners." This amalgamation continued the trend begun at least during World War I of excluding Chicanos from the United States polity both as foreigners and as a separate "race." . . .

As for immigrant groups and minorities elsewhere, education was supposed to provide the compensating factor. The Great Western Sugar Company touted educational benefits as lending "a humanitarian impulse" to their proposals that beetworkers remain over the winter. Even economist Paul Taylor believed that "despite interrupted attendance, as good or better education advantages are offered in the beet area than in the places from which the workers came." Certainly public education in Hispanic northern New Mexico continued in the 1920s to be plagued by lack of funds, short school terms, and underqualified teachers. Of the Spanish American parents who moved north, approximately one-quarter were illiterate in any language, one-half in English, and one-third had had no schooling. For their children, they wanted more. They kept fewer of their school-age children in the fields than the German-Russians did, though it meant they made less money, and when

Hispanic mothers worked beets it was often so children could attend school. "They want me to go to school so that I won't have to work beets," explained a Spanish American boy, and one girl's parents promised her a better job if she went to college.

Hispanic children, however, often remained skeptical of their future possibilities, "because," as the college-bound girl put it, "the Americans won't give me a chance." They had some reason for doubt. Teachers who said, "Oh, why don't you go back to the god-damned beet fields," did not instill confidence. A more sympathetic teacher reported that the Anglo children, also, "feel as hostile to the Mexican children on the playground as they do toward Negros in Gary, Indiana." And so did their parents. A school superintendent of Weld County insisted that "the respectable white people of Weld County do not want their children to sit alongside of dirty, filthy, disease-infested Mexicans in schools." Chicano school children found that, indeed, Anglos would not sit next to them, taunted them with phrases like "dirty Mexicans" and "greaser, greaser, sitting on an ice-cream freezer," "wouldn't want us ever to touch them," and made fun of their food until the Hispanic children hid away to eat. The state's constitution, written within recent memory of the Civil War, forbade segregation, but de facto segregation, particularly with the erection of company colonies at some distance from town and with the mid-term entrance and departure of beetworking children, was relatively easily achieved. Northern schools may have been better equipped than those in Hispanic villages, but the atmosphere was definitely more hostile, and the degree to which Hispanics would benefit remained in doubt.

Even when schools welcomed Chicano children, or were at least neutral, the necessity of family labor kept many children from attending. The work of children under sixteen, according to one 1925 study, contributed nearly one-third of the total contract labor's seasonal beet earnings. Most children working in beets were between ten and fourteen years old, but even six-year-olds sometimes spent their days thinning beets. Schooling for these children represented a substantial and sometimes impossible sacrifice for the whole family. A few Hispanic children managed to get through grammar school by asking for advance work each March and doing extra work all winter, but even for these children, high school, which demanded a set number of credits, was impossible. Almost universally, parents cared about education, but sometimes the alternative to child labor was starvation; Margarita Garcia remembered of her parents, "There was not much they could do. I guess we were so close to them, we didn't insist."

Missing approximately one-third of each school year, though regular in attendance once they enrolled, four-fifths of the Chicano children fell behind in school, almost two-thirds of them, by 1925, three years behind. Often they had lost interest in school activities and had little in common with their classmates. As a result, Chicanos in the north stayed in school little longer than those who remained in Hispanic villages. Most left school before sixth grade, and while the number of more advanced students rose in the 1920s, still only a handful enrolled in high school.

Faced with economic pressures and hostile neighbors, many Chicano families simply did not enroll their children in school. To many Anglos, this seemed the best solution to the educational dilemma, better than segregated schools or special classes. A former school board member asserted. "They're needed in the fields and the school don't do them any good anyway." Officials in the South Platte Valley granted illegal school exemptions to Chicano beet-working children and tended to turn a blind eye to those not applying. One confessed, "[W]e never try to enforce the compulsory attendance laws on the Mexicans. We just wink at the law." And Great Western Sugar, despite its claims for education, perpetrated myths that justified this denial of duty. The company claimed that "while beet children may be absent for several weeks each year from their classes in geography and spelling," they learned not only "industry and thrift," but "the craft of their fathers," a blessing for "people whose social and intellectual state may be below the standards of our ideals."

Underneath the justification ran other concerns. "If every child has a high school education," sugar company representatives demanded, "who will labor?" If the Anglo farmer was to keep his own children in school, he had to hire someone else to do the work. "[I]t is believed that a cheap labor supply is necessary for this industry," reported investigators in the Arkansas Valley, "and that the Spanish-American or Mexican is the one to furnish it. Too regular school attendance would not be compatible with this." The marginalization of Chicanos was no haphazard social development. Great Western Sugar's C. V. Maddux explained, "We no longer want settlers to occupy vacant land. . . . What we want is workers to work for the settlers who came before." Fred Cummings, a beetgrower from Fort Collins, elucidated, "[N]o man can accumulate anything in this world until by some means or device he is enabled to enjoy the benefit of some other man's labor." That Anglo farmers well understood the developing situation was revealed even further by one South Platte school official who feared, "[W]e are building up a caste system that inside of two generations will be worse than India ever dreamed of." Far from liberating the next generation of Chicanos from their backbreaking toil, the educational system of the north, better endowed than that of the Hispanic villages, seemed for the majority geared only to perpetuate the Chicanos as marginal agricultural labor. . . .

With Chicanas unable to recreate the stable village core that sustained social harmony in the villages, and with Chicanos marginal economically and socially to the Anglo community, it was unclear what sort of community Hispanics could create on the northern Colorado frontier. Indeed, Anglos tended to be pessimistic about the ability of Chicanos to adjust to life in northern Colorado at all. Inheriting a legacy of disdain for seasonal workers and migrant laborers, which labeled their relationship to farm labor as "excrescences upon its fair face," Anglos were disposed to agree with a Weld County sheriff that "a Mexican is a 'natural born liar, thief, and gambler.'" Visions of lawless and irresponsible hordes, visions unanchored by statistics, floated in the public imagination. The colonies were seen as potential dens of iniquity, where "the dancing girl and the wine-cup are star attractions." Their inhabitants appeared in local papers almost solely in criminal context, with their ethnicity prominently featured.

Chicanos did commit some crimes. Most involved petty theft—stealing from coal bins—or revolved around prohibition: moonshining and drinking and selling liquor, activities popular among Chicanos in both New Mexico and Colorado, but hardly peculiar to them. Anglos, however, even those with the most direct contact with Hispanics, consistently and greatly distorted the scale of lawbreaking. The official line held that prosecution of Chicanos accounted for three-quarters of Weld County court cases. An investigation in 1924 revealed instead that even including appearances as plaintiffs, Chicanos accounted for only 6 percent of the total county court cases and 10 percent of the justice of the peace cases, a figure not disproportionate to their number in the county's population. Conspicuous in their "otherness" and their poverty, Chicanos found themselves subject to these myths and to arrest, according to contemporary investigators, "without a clearly defined case or cause against them." Where a fee system ruled, constables and other officers whose income depended on fines and costs advised their victims to plead guilty.

In terms of relief and family stability, fears had also exaggerated the reality. Hispanic divorces in Weld County occurred at a lower rate than either Anglo divorces in that county or Hispanic divorces in southern Colorado or New Mexico. Few Hispanic children spent time in either the state home for dependent children or the state Industrial School for Girls. And the proportion of relief accounted for by Hispanics, while slightly greater than their proportion of the population at large, remained well under 20 percent, less than the proportion of Hispanics among the lowest-income groups. On the whole, concluded one investigator, impoverished Anglos in northern Colorado "indicated a much poorer social adjustment proportionately than did the Spanish-speaking group." It is possible that, after northern trauma, divorcées, single and deserted mothers, and delinquent children all fled back to the Hispanic homeland. It seems more consistent with the evidence, however, that despite frequent migration, low income, and severe discrimination, solidarity and not disorganization characterized Chicano families in the Anglo north. These families proved stronger than the forces which buffeted them on the edge of the regional community. . . .

As the Hispanic presence became more established, the coal camps, the Hispanic section of Denver, and the beet colonies all became foci of Chicano communities whose inhabitants' social needs were met from within rather than from the villages of the regional community. Of these, the Chicano enclaves in Denver, growing in size and becoming more stable during the 1920s, were among the largest and most articulated. When Arthur Maes's father died in 1927, the second winter after the family had come from New Mexico to northern Colorado to work beets, his mother was unable to survive in Fort Lupton. She took the family to Denver where they had spent the previous winter, as she "knew the community in the Bottoms," and it was the only place she had any friends. Whereas other towns in the area had at most one Hispanic realtor or cleaner to represent the community in the business world, Denver had tamale shops, some family stores, and the occasional scion of an upper-class New Mexican, southern Colorado, or Mexican family. Yet even Denver hardly compared in the scale of its Hispanic community to Trinidad, and the majority of its Hispanic residents were seasonal laborers.

Like many of the coal camps, the Chicano sections of Denver were distinctly unlovely. Robert McLean and Charles Thomson described one in 1924 as "a district which looks as if both God and Denver had forgotten it . . . the mongrel off-spring of a deserted village and a city slum" with "no paving, sidewalks, no sewers." Nevertheless, the concentration of Chicanos made possible some early attempts at organization on ethnic lines, including not only the Anglo sponsored missions such as Jerome Park Mission and the First Spanish Methodist Church, but the Sociedad Protectora, a mutualista [mutual aid society] in the Lawrence Street area originating in 1921, the Cruz Azul for Mexicans, the Spanish-American Club—a cultural association whose president was a former Mexican consul—and the Spanish-American Citizens Association, the latest of these organizations and one which in 1931 intended to organize the estimated 15,000 Spanish American citizens in Denver and the vicinity for industrial, political, and social justice in all public affairs.

Denver was not unique. Larger than other enclaves, its Hispanic communities garnered more elites and Anglo attention, but they shared many of the same strategies and problems as the colonies and barrios across northeastern Colorado. The nascent Chicano community in the north was not yet entirely centered on a single site, despite the hostility of the environs. And while many Hispanics in northern Colorado wintered in Denver, more lived outside it, and many moved from winter to winter among the towns, the company colonies, and the city and had, by the late 1920s, relatives scattered across the area.

First erected in 1924, the Great Western Sugar Company's beet-labor colonies soon became not only the more stable clusters the company desired, but, like Denver, centers of Hispanic community organizing. Unlike Colorado Fuel and Iron, the sugar company allowed its control to lie loosely on these colonies. It retained the right to dispossess undesirables as long as it held the leases, and it contributed to church and community buildings, but the colonies were not closed camps, not located at the workplace, and not polyglot. Within them, colonists bought not just houses, but the land on which they stood. And ironically, their very isolation from Anglo society helped foster their development as something more than transient labor camps.

As with racial and immigrant enclaves elsewhere, the colonies' homogeneity relieved some of the pressure to assimilate. Residents had, as one investigator found, "their own favorite dishes," and no one encouraged them "to abandon their native language for American." Though economically dependent on the Anglo world, they retained, as had the villages, some social and cultural autonomy. Here, perhaps, those who did remain year after year could re-create the regional community in truncated and more vulnerable form. The barrio could be a new core.

By the late 1920s, some colonies increasingly resembled the interrelated villages. Chicano couples met and courted there, among the "meticulously tended lawns, and the watered and swept earthen patios," that one colonist remembered. They held dances and even fiestas in the colonies. The women, recalled one early settler, "had their own clubs," and sewing, cooking, mutual aid, and church groups, and in January 1930, it was their efforts, in part, which culminated in a new Pentecostal Assembly of God Church built by colonists in the Greeley colony.

From this more cohesive base, colonists and other settlers began to shift to more aggressive strategies in intercultural matters. The regional community, with its migrant patterns, was in some sense a strategy of retreat, as was the high turnover that embodied Chicano protest at conditions in beetwork. In the same vein, Mexicans consciously decided against citizenship, rejecting the second-class status they believed it would bring. A Mexican in the South Platte Valley declared, "To hell with the United States. We don't have to be slaves in Mexico." But as retreat to the villages became increasingly impracticable and more stable communities evolved, direct protests occurred. At least one Chicano in Weld County filed a civil rights case in 1927 against Greeley restaurant proprietors who ejected him on the grounds that he was a Mexican. World War I veterans among the colonists also early asserted the colonists' rights in the community at large in regard to voting and discrimination. Their membership in local American Legion branches provided virtually the only organized non-charitable social link between ethnic groups and bolstered their legitimacy as spokesmen in each.

As the sense of neighborhood in the colonies grew, resistance began to take more collective forms. Chicano boycotts in Greeley and Johnstown led to the removal of discriminatory signs from the shop windows, at least temporarily, in 1927. Though less successful, a committee of Chicanos also protested the establishment of separate school rooms for Chicano children. By the end of the decade, like Denver, the colonies and mining towns had their own Hispanic groups and mutualistas. Some accepted both Mexican and Spanish Americans, others only one or the other. Some of the colonies even organized into self-governing bodies under commissioners of their own choosing. In 1928 the Greeley colony, for example, drew up "articles of association for the management of colony affairs," including police and sanitary regulations, and filed them with the county police. This was, perhaps, the ultimate declaration of an autonomous community on the Anglo-Hispanic frontier. These Hispanics created room for themselves and committed themselves to permanent residence without committing themselves to assimilation.

REVIEW QUESTIONS

1. The author of the selection uses different terms in referring to people of Mexican ancestry living in the United States. From the context, determine the precise definitions of "Chicano," "Chicana," "Hispanic," and "Mexican" as the author uses them. Check newspapers, television, and other sources to see whether she uses these terms in the same way as others do. Although Deutsch does not use the term "Latino" or "Latina," try also to find out what these terms mean.

2. Describe the strategies Chicanos employed to enable them to live on the low wages provided by the sugar-beet companies.

3. Compare the Chicano communities in western cities like Denver to those of European immigrants in eastern cities described in earlier selections. What are the main similarities and differences with regard to employment, housing, education, the attitudes of the dominant population, and attempts to foster or resist assimilation into the dominant culture?

FOR FURTHER READING

Rodolfo Acuña, *Occupied America: A History of Chicanos* (1981), is a general history of people of Mexican ancestry in the United States. Albert Camarillo, *Chicanos in a Changing Society* (1979), and Mario T. Garcia, *Desert Immigrants: The Mexicans of El Paso, 1880–1920* (1981), deal with particular cities, Santa Barbara, California, and El Paso, Texas, respectively. Carey McWilliams, *Factories in the Field: The Story of Migratory Farm Labor in California* (1939), and *Ill Fares the Land: Migrants and Migratory Labor in the United States* (1942), are early and still illuminating examinations of migrant labor. Jacqueline Jones, *The Dispossessed: America's*

Underclass from the Civil War to the Present (1992), also has much to say about migrant labor in general. Mark Reisler, *By the Sweat of Their Brow: Mexican Immigrant Labor in the United States, 1900–1940* (1976), tells part of the story of Mexican immigration to the United States. James D. Cockcroft, *Outlaws in the Promised Land: Mexican Immigrant Workers and America's Future* (1986), discusses the same subject in more recent years. David Reimers, *Still the Golden Door: The Third World Comes to America* (1985), covers recent immigration from Mexico along with that from other lands.

This modern
'ice man'
calls once –
with Frigidaire –
and the ice
stays always

Be Sure it *is* a Frigidaire!

THERE are now more than two hundred thousand users of Frigidaire Electric Refrigeration. And these users are telling their friends and neighbors that Frigidaire has brought to their homes and places of business a measure of convenience and economy unequaled by anything they have ever known.

You have heard of Frigidaire—of the constant, dependable and economical service it renders, of the *better* way in which it keeps all foods, of the convenience of the ice it makes and the desserts it freezes.

You are probably thinking *now* of electric refrigeration for your own home. Be sure, when you *do* buy, that you get a genuine Frigidaire. Look for the name itself—you'll find it on every Frigidaire. It identifies the product of General Motors. It is your assurance that you will enjoy the combined advantages which only Frigidaire can give.

There is a wide range of Frigidaires built complete with metal cabinet, finished in white Duco, lined with seamless porcelain enamel. They are priced as low as $245. Frigidaire mechanical units for installation in the standard makes of iceboxes, as low as $190. All prices f. o. b. Dayton. Any Frigidaire may be purchased on the GMAC deferred payment plan.

DELCO-LIGHT COMPANY, *Subsidiary of General Motors Corporation*, Dept. V-34, DAYTON, OHIO

Frigidaire
ELECTRIC REFRIGERATION

BE SURE IT *IS* A FRIGIDAIRE ~ PRODUCT OF GENERAL MOTORS

The 1920s saw the introduction of modern appliances into the American home.

12

Women and Housework in the 1920s

RUTH SCHWARTZ COWAN

Except for a sharp but short-lived economic downturn early in the decade, the 1920s were quite prosperous. Productivity and real wages—that is, the amount of goods and services that a person could buy with an hour's labor—both rose. New industries such as radio and aviation became prominent and profitable. Older industries such as automobile production, the movies, and advertising enjoyed rapid growth. People spoke of "The New Era" in the nation's economic life, in which mass production was linked to mass consumption in such a way as to generate uninterrupted growth and general prosperity and ensure that depressions would become relics of the past. That optimism was proved erroneous when the stock market crash of 1929 signaled the start of the worst depression the nation had ever endured.

Still, the prosperity of the 1920s, temporary as it may have been, had permanent effects on the way Americans lived, in large part because the primary driving force behind the decade's economic growth was spending on consumer goods. The introduction and widespread use of installment-plan buying, time-purchase plans, and other forms of consumer credit permitted millions of Americans to acquire the automobiles, radios, and other glittery new gadgets that a flourishing mass-production economy was turning out for their delight.

That avalanche of new consumer goods had a dramatic impact on the American home. There were significant differences between social classes in "typical" household furnishings, and the impact of the new mass-consumption society was much greater on urban than on rural America. Still, by the end of the 1920s the majority of Americans—rural and urban, and of all social classes—lived in homes that were quite different from those of their parents or grandparents. The following essay by Ruth Schwartz Cowan focuses primarily on how the definitions and the conduct of housework changed during the 1920s, but it also provides clues as to how American life in general was transformed by industrial technology and new buying habits.

In the twentieth century, the proliferation of household technology has dramatically altered women's lives but has not in the least mitigated the assignment of housework to women. When the twentieth century opened, the vast majority of American women spent most of their waking hours feeding, clothing, cleaning, and sustaining themselves and their families; eighty years later, as the century is drawing to a close, the vast majority of American women are still spending many of their waking hours feeding, clothing, cleaning, and sustaining themselves and their families, albeit with markedly different tools. . . .

While it is no doubt true that every family is unique, it is also true that, at any given time and place, families living within the range of a certain standard of living confront similar material conditions in their homes and similar public attitudes about what distinguishes a "good" or a "decent" home from one that is neither. Each of us may bring a unique combination of psychic and social factors to our work; but, in any given time or place, depending upon the class to which we belong, women tend to organize their kitchens in more or less the same way and to read the same magazines, newspapers, and books. If our work, at least part of the time, is housework, then no matter how different we may be from each other, our work processes will be fairly similar. Hence, although it is difficult for a historian to learn much about *what* individual women and men felt about the work that was (or was not) being done in their homes, it is somewhat easier to learn *how* that work was being done. Between 1900 and 1940, the differences in the work processes of housework between those who were rich and those who were poor, were striking—so striking, indeed, that they remained engraved, consciously and unconsciously, on the minds and in the behavior of later generations. . . .

The second generation of twentieth-century women came to maturity during the First World War, bore their children during the Roaring Twenties, and struggled to keep their households functioning during the dreary years of the Depression. Enormous technological and social changes occurred between their mothers' time and their own; and these changes began—but only just began—to alter not only the work processes of housework but also the fundamental differences between women of the two great social classes.

Material Conditions for Those Who Were Still Living Comfortably

During the 1920s and the 1930s, a housewife of the more prosperous classes did not regularly work for wages, despite the fact that she was better educated than her mother had been and more likely to have worked for a few years before marriage. Only one in forty of the "business class" housewives who were studied by Helen and Robert Lynd in Muncie, Indiana ("Middletown"), in 1925 had worked for wages in the previous five years. The typical comfortable housewife of this generation lived in a house that was fairly similar to the one in which she had been raised (if she were lucky enough to have been the daughter of a prosperous father); it was spacious, perhaps a bit smaller than her parents' had been, lacking a spare bedroom or an old-fashioned parlor, but not much smaller; and it was equipped with many of the same modern conveniences (telephones, hot and cold running water, indoor plumbing, gas and electricity). By the end of the 1920s, the daughter was likely to have had one or two appliances that had not been available to her mother (perhaps an electric washing machine, or a refrigerator, or an automobile); but, even more significantly, she would have acquired the conveniences and the appliances earlier in her marriage, when her children were still young and the burden of her work was heaviest, and when her household routines (which are very resistant to change) were first established. In 1926, 80 percent of all the affluent households that were studied by market researchers in thirty-six American cities had vacuum cleaners and washing machines. More than half of all the households in the United States had an automobile by 1930, and every single one of the business-class households of Muncie had one by 1925. When the Lynds returned to study Muncie again in 1935, 40 percent of all the households whose assessed value was over two thousand dollars (a sum the Lynds regarded as the dividing line between adequate and inadequate housing) had a refrigerator.

Taken together, the vacuum cleaner, the washing machine, the refrigerator, and the automobile had profound implications for the reorganization of work in the households of the prosperous. Possession of an electric washing machine meant that a "decent" housewife could do her wash at home and by herself without undue drudgery; these early washing machines did not go through their cycles automatically and did not spin the clothing semi-dry (they had electrically powered wringers), but they did eliminate a good deal of the hauling and the hand wringing that had once made laundry work inconceivable for a woman of "status." The vacuum cleaners of the day were heavy instruments; but since they could be wheeled, they eliminated not only the drudgery but also the stooping that had once been associated with heavy cleaning and thus eliminated the perceived necessity for a servant to undertake it. Vacuum cleaners also cleaned more thoroughly than brooms and thus made it possible for the young housewife to dispense not only with the horrors of spring cleaning but also with the women whom her mother had hired to help with it. The young housewife's refrigerator reinforced the tendency—which had actually commenced when either her basement or her mother's had been converted from a storage room to a furnace room—to purchase foodstuffs in small, rather than large, quantities and to dispense with delivery services provided by the retailer. The automobile served only to accelerate that trend as well as to create a host of other transportation services (such as taking children to parties and to doctors) that women of an earlier generation had not provided for their families. The average comfortable housewife of the generation before the First World War had done some of her housework herself and managed the labor of other people who did the rest of it; the average comfortable housewife of the generation that came to maturity after the war managed more appliances than people.

The availability of appliances and conveniences was one—but not the only one—of the factors that stimulated this reorganization. One study of the relationship between the acquisition of household appliances and the organization of household work in this period reported that, while most of the families of students at Mount Holyoke College had acquired four or five major appliances in the decade between 1919 and 1929, and 96 percent of the families had also decreased the amount of household help that they employed, only a small fraction of these attributed the decrease solely to the acquisition of the appliances. The other families were probably responding to a new set of demographic factors (namely, a severe contraction in the available supply of servants) and to a new set of ideological factors (namely, new attitudes articulated in women's magazines and advice books during the 1920s). . . .

The supply of servants was shrinking for many reasons. The European conflict and, after that, the immigration restrictions of the mid-1920s drastically reduced the influx of foreign-born young women, who had previously constituted the largest portion of the servant population. In addition, the expanding economy of the 1920s increased the opportunities in factories for women without skills. In Indiana, for example, the ratio of servants to households was 1 in 20 in 1920; and the business-class wives of Muncie reported that they employed approximately half as many servant-hours as their mothers had done, at roughly five times the wages (salaries for people in the middle-income ranges had roughly doubled in the same period). Only one quarter of the seven hundred urban households of college-educated women that were studied carefully by the United States Department of Agriculture in 1930 employed a domestic servant, as did only 17 percent of the three thousand middle-class families studied a year later by President Hoover's Conference on Home Building and Homeownership—percentages that would have been astounding twenty years earlier. . . .

"Really doing it yourself" had once been considered demeaning, but attitudes were changing. In the early decades of the century, women's magazines had repeatedly offered advice to housewives who were, for one unfortunate reason or another, coping with their homes singlehanded, but the emphasis in those articles had been on the word *unfortunate.* The housewife was told, for example, that if help was scarce, it was easiest to serve children the same food adults were eating, although clearly it would be better for the former's digestion and your temperament if they ate with a nursemaid in the nursery; with luck, the servant shortage would soon pass. "Decent" housewives were never depicted, in those years, as doing the heavy work of their households themselves; when instructions for proper laundry work or sanitary cleaning were proffered, a tell-tale "instruct your laundress" or "see that your maid" would always slip through. In the years after the First World War, as advertisements for refrigerators, washing machines, and vacuum cleaners replaced those for iceboxes, laundry tubs, and brooms, servants disappeared from the advertisements—to be replaced by housewives, neatly manicured and elegantly coiffured, but housewives nonetheless. In those same years, the language used in the nonfiction material in women's magazines also underwent a subtle change, coming to imply that housework was to be thought of no longer as a chore but, rather, as an expression of the housewife's personality and her affection for her family. Laundering had once been just a task to be finished as quickly as possible; now it was an expression of love. The new bride could speak her affection by washing tattle-tale gray out of her husband's shirts. Feeding the family had once been just part of a day's work; now it was a way to communicate deep-seated emotions:

> When the careful housekeeper turns from the preparation of company dinner to the routine of family meals, she will know that prime rib roast, like peach ice cream, *is a wonderful stimulant to family loyalty,* but that it is not absolutely necessary for every day.

Diapering was now a time for building a baby's sense of security, and cleaning the bathroom sink became an exercise for the maternal instincts, protecting the family from disease.

Clearly, tasks of such emotional magnitude could not be relegated to servants. The servantless household may have been an economic necessity for people in the 1920s and the 1930s; but, for the first time, that necessity was widely regarded, at least in the public press, as a potential virtue. And whether or not she regarded it as a virtue, the average comfortable housewife of this generation learned to organize the work in her household without the assistance of servants or with far fewer hours of assistance than her mother had had. Where a servant had been replaced by a vacuum cleaner, the comfortable housewife was spending more time than her mother had spent getting the floors and the rugs into shape; where a laundress had been replaced by a washing machine or a deliveryman by the household automobile, a housewife was spending time and energy on chores that, in her mother's day, had been performed by other people. No matter how a household chose to slice the cake of available resources in the interwar years, every decision to "do it my-self" was a decision to increase the time that the housewife would spend at her work. In households that were prosperous, the labor saved by labor-saving de-vices was that not of the housewife but of her helpers. This is the most salient reason that every time-study of affluent housewives during these years (and many such studies were done, as these were the years in which home econo-mists, like so many other Americans, were fascinated by "efficiency studies") revealed that no matter how many appliances they owned, or how many con-veniences were at their command, they were still spending roughly the same number of hours per week at housework as their mothers had. The most com-prehensive of those studies, covering fifteen hundred urban and rural house-holds, in the years 1924–25 and 1930–31, found a range of hours spent in housework from a high of sixty-one (for rural farm homemakers) to a low of forty-eight (for college-educated urban women living in large cities)—figures that were not markedly different from those reported by Leeds and Wood-bury twenty years earlier.

This second-generation prosperous housewife had also expanded certain aspects of her job description, which could not be mediated by technology at all—namely, those aspects having to do with the care of her children. Infant care was much more complex than it once had been, because in an effort to combat infant mortality (which had been scandalously high in the United States in the pre-war period)*—mothers were watching scrupulously over their children's diets, weighing them several times a day, and repeatedly car-rying them to physicians' offices for checkups. Child care no longer consisted of teaching young children to read, write, and add and in seeing to it that children were adequately clothed and regularly fed; it now also involved at-tending child-study meetings, becoming involved in the local schools, reading books and magazines about children, supervising them in playgrounds, and transporting them to lessons and social events.

> I accommodate my entire life to my little girl. She takes three music lessons a week and I practice with her forty minutes a day. I help her with her school work and go to dancing school with her.

> My mother never stepped inside the school building as far as I can remember, but now there are never ten days that go by without my either visiting the chil-dren's school or getting in touch with their teacher. I have given up church work and club work since the children came. I always like to be here when they

---

*The infant mortality rate was 100 per 1,000 live births in 1915 (one of the highest in the Western world), 71.7 in 1925, and 55.7 in 1935. By comparison, in 1978 it was 13.8.

get home from school so that I can keep in touch with their games and their friends. Any extra time goes into reading books on nutrition and character building.

I put on roller skates with the boys and pass a football with them. In the evenings we play cards and on Sundays we go to ball games. My mother back East thinks it's scandalous.

Experts repeatedly suggested that a mother was the single most important person in a child's life, and that the child raised by nursemaids was a child to be pitied. The young boy raised by servants would never learn the upright, go-getting resourcefulness of the truly American child, would never become a useful member of the egalitarian republic, and would probably fail in the business world; his sister, deprived of the example of her mother, would not know how to manage the myriad appliances of the modern kitchen, would never learn how to decorate a pineapple salad or wash silk underwear in an electric machine, and might thus never be able to capture a husband. Even more worrisome was the thought that children raised by nursemaids might never reach adulthood because they would be tended by persons who were unfamiliar with the latest medical and nutritional information. Mothers were being asked to take more of a hand in the rearing of their children, and many mothers were responding to the challenge.

Thus, the comfortably situated housewife of the interwar years expended most of her time and energy, just as her mother had, in the interests of her family. Even during the worst years of the Depression, she continued to run her household "decently"; her husband was still employed, the family was not on relief; they still owned their own home, and they still kept it up; the interior was orderly, the meals arrived regularly, the children stayed in school, the family went to church, their health—whatever strain they were under—remained reasonably stable.

But something subtle had changed. Emily Post summed it up better than anyone else when she added a new chapter to the fifth edition (1937) of the famous etiquette book that had first appeared in 1915. This chapter dealt with the problems faced by "Mrs. Three-in-One"—the woman who had to be guest, waitress, and cook at her own dinner parties. Like her mother she understood the rituals of gracious entertaining, knew how to make guests comfortable in her home, knew precisely which foods should be served on which occasions, knew how to reflect the status of her household in her own behavior. But unlike her mother, either because of inclination or circumstance, she was also a manual laborer: she had to chop the onions, roll the pastries, manipulate the cooking times, arrange the platters, carry them to the table, carve the roast, remove the dirty plates, pour the coffee—all the while appearing as if she were not doing any of these tasks. As part of the process of reallocating the time she spent in household work, she had ceased managing the labor of others and had substituted her own. This transformation, which might properly be called the "proletarianization" of the work of economically comfortable housewives, did not occur overnight. Its fullest effects would not be felt until the next generation had reached maturity, but the handwriting was on the wall. In an effort to sustain the standard of living to which an earlier generation had been accustomed, the prosperous housewife of this generation started down the path of "doing it herself," the implications of which would not become entirely clear until her daughter had completed the journey.

Material Conditions for Those Who Were Still Struggling to Make Ends Meet

Meanwhile, during these decades, many Americans—in fact, still the majority of Americans—were struggling, as their parents had, to maintain their families at something over the level of mere subsistence. The fabled "prosperity" of the 1920s was more apparent than real, more intermittent than continuous, for the families of industrial workers, small farmers, day laborers, and skilled craftsmen. Industrial productivity—particularly of consumer goods—multiplied during the 1920s and then multiplied again. Automobiles were appearing in ever more front yards, radios proliferated, the number of pages devoted to advertisements in newspapers and magazines trebled and then quadrupled. In communities across the land, however, more than half of the households were still living below—and, in some cases, far below—what was then defined as the minimum standard of "health and decency." Helen and Robert Lynd calculated, for example, that in Muncie in 1924, $1,920.87 was required to achieve this standard for a family of five (the estimate included the cost of rent, food, fuel, clothing, insurance, union dues, and other such items as well, significantly enough, as one full day per week of paid household help), and that somewhere between 70 percent and 88 percent of all the households in town, in that year did not attain it. Similarly, in 1926, in Zanesville, Ohio, 70 percent of all families had incomes below $2,000. Wages for skilled and unskilled workers and prices for agricultural goods were indeed better in the 1920s than they had been in any previous decade; but the problem, for the families of men so employed, was that good wages and prices could not be depended upon to be continuous: factory workers were likely to be laid off at a day's notice when business was slow; farmers had good seasons but also bad ones; day laborers were paid only during certain seasons of the year; illness and accident could strike at any moment and, in the absence of guaranteed sick leaves and adequate workmen's compensation, could cripple a family for substantial periods. A nationwide study conducted by economists at the Brookings Institution in 1929—when the boom had presumably been booming for close to a decade—revealed that 59 percent of the nation's families appeared to be living below a minimally decent standard; needless to say, that figure went up, rather than down, during the next decade.

There were, to put it simply, still more "uncomfortable" people than "comfortable" ones during the supposedly gay 1920s, and there were considerably more during the depressing 1930s. During the 1920s, sheer subsistence may not have been as much of a problem as it had been for an earlier generation; but families still found that, periodically, they needed two incomes in order to get by. Fifty-five out of 124 "working class" wives studied by the Lynds in Muncie had worked for wages between 1920 and 1924: "the mister was sick and I had to"; "it takes the work of two to keep a family nowadays"; "we are always needing extra money."

Admittedly, some of that extra money was being spent on goods and services that would have been totally out of reach twenty years earlier. The hard-pressed housewife of the 1920s was not investing in luxuries (although some contemporary critics accused her of doing so); but when times were good, she and her husband were trying to create for themselves the standard of living to which more prosperous families had become accustomed before the First World War. With the help of building-and-loan associations, these families were buying their own houses; in Zanesville, for example, where 70 percent of the households earned less than two thousand dollars, 79.9 percent of them were owners rather than renters of their dwellings. The houses in which the second generation of hard-pressed housewives lived were neither spacious nor elegant (a typical one would have been a four-room, one-story bungalow), but they were likely to be wired for electricity (73.7 percent of the houses in Zanesville), outfitted with running water (90 percent), perhaps a bathroom with indoor toilet and a tub (60 percent), piped gas (96 percent), a gas range (89.6 percent), and a telephone (69 percent); and if things had gone particularly well for the family, or if there was more than one continuous breadwinner, there might even be a car (48 percent of the families in Zanesville had one at a time when only 30 percent of the families were living above the poverty level). Those social critics who disparaged these expenditures (because "money was being wasted on luxuries," or because "the pressure to conform and to consume is everywhere more intense," or because "people are today so willing to put themselves into debt to satisfy expanded wants") were uniformly members of the more comfortable classes. From the point of view of those who had known the discomforts of poverty in their youth, these amenities were not so much amenities as basic decencies too long withheld. To own one's home meant to be out from under the thumb of a landlord who could evict a family at a moment's notice; to have electric lights meant an end to eyestrain, kerosene explosions, and the need to clean lamps; to have running water, an end to exhausting labor; to have a toilet, and end to the discomfort of a privy on a snowy night and to typhoid fever in the summer; to have a telephone, the possibility of easy communication with members of one's family; to have a gas range, the end to coal dust all over the kitchen; to have an automobile, the possibility of a Sunday in the country (is that luxury?) and also, of finding a job on the other side of town in case the plant close to home shut down (is *that* a luxury?).

In the period after the First World War, the diffusion of these amenities, combined with public health measures that were becoming more prevalent (purification and inspection of milk, water treatment plants, sewers for poor neighborhoods, diphtheria inoculations, regular refuse collection, fortification of certain foods with vitamins, certification of meat and poultry supplies) meant that the standard of living for this generation was considerably higher (or rather the standard of death and illness considerably lower) than it had been for their parents. Nationwide, the infant mortality rate continued to fall—in part, at least, because milk and water ceased to be contaminated; and physicians learned how to control diarrhea, tuberculosis, congenital syphilis, and diphtheria (which had all been major killers of infants). Some of the dreadful epidemic diseases that had either killed or debilitated adults and older children in an earlier generation (cholera, typhoid fever, smallpox) were virtually eradicated by the 1920s; and other diseases (such as tuberculosis, rickets, syphilis, and dysentery) were vastly diminished in their destructive power: in Chicago the death rate from typhoid fever had gone as high as 174 per 100,000 per population in the latter years of the nineteenth century, but was down to 2 per 100,000 in the 1920s; tuberculosis, which had been the second most prevalent cause of death in the United States in 1900, had declined to tenth by 1930, and the death rate from tuberculosis dropped by an incredible one third (from 150 to 98) just in the four years between 1918 and 1922; Salversan was being widely used to control syphilis, and cod liver oil (however awful it may have tasted) and fortified flour and margarine (whatever natural food buffs today may think of them) were just as widely used to control rickets. All of this, needless to say, went a long way toward easing a poor housewife's concern about the health of her family and toward relieving her, as her mother could not have been relieved, of the difficult work of caring for those who were ill.

The trouble was that neither the amenities nor the public health measures did much to lighten the burden of her other chores. While the hard-pressed housewife may have entered the twentieth century in terms of electricity, running water, and pasteurized milk, she had not entered it in terms of birth control. In 1924, for example, the Lynds found that in Muncie all of the business-class housewives approved of the use of contraceptives, but that only half of the working-class housewives did. Thus, not surprisingly, only one business-class home among those the Lynds studied had six or more children, but there were seven such working-class homes. In the 1920s, although the birth rate was dropping nationwide, the poor continued to have markedly more children than the "comfortable." In the 1930s, although the birth rate in urban areas dropped off markedly for all classes of the population, that in rural areas—where many such housewives lived—was as high as it had ever been. Nothing is, of course, better calculated to increase the burden of housework than the presence of children, especially small ones. When there are eight or nine mouths to feed (or even five or six), cooking is a difficult enterprise, even if it can be done at a gas range; and the drudgery of laundry (especially if there are diapers) is not greatly eased by having the hot water come out of a tap instead of a pot. The electric appliances that would have made some aspects of housework markedly easier simply remained too expensive for those who were still struggling to make ends meet. Even when electric service was available, an electric washing machine cost between sixty and two hundred dollars (a month's wage for a workingman), and only the more expensive models would have been truly labor saving, since the less expensive ones had small tubs, which had to be emptied and filled manually, and hand-cranked wringers. Small wonder, then, that in 1926 only 28 percent of the homes in Zanesville had electric washers, and that the vast majority of them were in affluent homes. What was true for the washer was true also for the vacuum cleaner (only 52.6 percent of homes, of whom slightly more than half were affluent homes) and mechanical refrigeration (.4 percent).

In any event, in both the 1920s and the 1930s, a substantial number of poor housewives were either rural or black or both and thus lacked access to amenities, public health measures, and appliances. Among the tenant farmers that Martha Hagood studied in 1934 in Tennessee, only eight out of two hundred households could afford electric service (although the area in which they lived was considered progressive in rural electrification), and not a single one had running water—at a time when 83 percent of all urban and rural non-farm residences were electrified. In "Plainville," a rural town studied by James West in 1940, only three homes had bathrooms, and they belonged, respectively, to the funeral director, the veterinarian, and the mayor. The Farm Housing Survey, undertaken by the United States Department of Agriculture in 1934, revealed that, for example, only 20 percent of the farmhouses in Missouri had a kitchen sink with a drain, that only 7 percent of those in Kentucky had a bathroom, that only 25 percent of those in the state of Washington (which was considered a particularly prosperous agricultural state) had flush toilets, and that only 17 percent of those in Ohio (which was also fairly prosperous) had electricity. On farms across the land, the birthrate was still high, the average length of life still low, the "old-fashioned" diseases still appallingly prevalent, and various discomforts, both of body and of mind, were part and parcel of daily experience.

Even the hard-pressed housewife who had access to amenities, and had invested in appliances, could not be certain that they would be there when most needed. The washing machine, the car, and the living-room furniture were all likely to have been bought on installment plans, the house carried a mortgage, and the utility companies presented their bills monthly. Thus, in bad times, when her husband was out of work or disabled, and she was forced into the labor market—precisely the time when she dearly needed her washing machine to do the laundry or her car to reduce her trips to market—the family was more than likely to have fallen behind in its payments; and, as a result, the electricity might be turned off or the car repossessed. The Lynds described the technological condition of working-class homes, under the best of conditions, as a "crazy quilt":

> A single home may be operated in the twentieth century when it comes to ownership of an automobile and vacuum cleaner, while its lack of a bathtub may throw it back into another era and its lack of sewer connection and custom of pumping drinking water from a well in the same backyard with the family "privy" put it on par with life in the Middle Ages.

To make matters even worse, the hard-pressed housewife of this generation had begun to read—as her mother probably had not—many of the magazines that were addressed to her more affluent contemporaries; and the daughters of both classes were taking the same home economics courses in school. Through these various sources of information, such a housewife learned about ways to feed her family, furnish her home, do her laundry, and otherwise conduct her daily life—ways that were approved of by "experts," and that would have been totally foreign to her mother: nutritionally balanced meals, carefully structured family budgets, four-hour intervals between infant feedings, cabinets and extensive work surfaces in kitchens, completely tiled bathrooms, percale sheets, and many, many more. Unfortunately many of these products were very expensive; and if the price was not beyond the hard-pressed housewife's means at a particular moment, it may well have been beyond her ability to plan for. How do you make out a budget when you cannot predict what your income will be next month? How do you feed an infant on a four-hour schedule when you have a toddler who eats all the time, a husband who gets his breakfast at six in the morning and returns home hungry at seven at night, and a school child who eats at seven, at noon, and at five o'clock?

If inability to rearrange her life in the "recommended" fashion were not enough to make the struggling housewife feel inferior, the women's magazines were delivering yet another message deliberately calculated to make her feel even worse: to wit, that if her family were not socially accepted, if her children and her husband were not healthy, if her home were a breeding ground for germs, if she herself looked old and tired before her time, or if her babies failed to gain weight—or, worse yet, if they died—she was entirely to blame, since remedies for those conditions were easily at hand and easy to apply. If such a notion had ever crossed her mother's mind, it was at least not confirmed, over and over again, on almost every printed page. In her mother's day, when copywriters composed advertisements for soap or sheets or sealing wax, they thought in terms of the ingredients in the product, or the cleanliness of the factory where it was made, or the various ways in which a clever housewife could use it. In the years between the wars, they thought about "guilt" and did so intentionally, because psychologists were telling them that "guilt," "embarrassment," and "insecurity" would sell goods faster than any other pitch. Thus, the hard-pressed housewife was being told that if she failed to feed her babies special foods, to scrub behind the sink with special cleaners, to reduce the spread of infection by using paper tissues, to control mouth odor by urging everyone to gargle and body odor by urging everyone to bathe, to improve her children's schoolwork by sending them off with a good breakfast, or her daughter's "social rating" by sending her off to parties with polished white shoes—then any number of woeful events would ensue, and they would all be entirely her fault: not God's will, and certainly not a result of the greed of capitalists or the cupidity of public officials. This message was reiterated so frequently, and the visual material accompanying it was so blatant, that it could not have failed to make an impression on such a housewife and, at the very least, to undermine her self-confidence. Small wonder, then, that some of these housewives went out to work even when their husbands had steady jobs: with the additional cash, these wives could at least purchase the clothing, the cosmetics, the appliances, and the sundries that the magazines were suggesting would so markedly improve a family's way of life and a mother's own peace of mind.* "I began to work during the war," one housewife in Muncie reported,

> when everyone else did; we had to meet payments on our house and everything else was getting so high. The mister objected at first, but now he don't mind. I'd rather keep on working so my boys can play football and basketball and have spending money their father can't give them. I have felt better since I worked than ever before in my life. . . . We have an electric washing machine, electric iron, and vacuum sweeper. I don't even have to ask my husband anymore because I buy these things with my own money.

Older cultural values may have suggested that a working wife was a sign of economic distress and social disorganization in a family (which no doubt is why many "misters" didn't approve of their wives going out to work, and why many wives avoided such work), but newer cultural values suggested that it was the responsibility of both parents to improve the standard of living of their children; and some women no doubt concluded, as had the mother just quoted, that they could achieve this aim faster and more surely with cash in their pockets then with bread dough on their hands.

Thus while the comfortably situated housewives of this generation were slowly marching down the road to proletarianization, their less comfortably situated contemporaries were heading toward greater productivity. Improvements in technological systems were having the same effect on the households of people with small incomes as they have in giant factories and offices: an increase in the goods or services that can be produced for the person-hours that are being expended. Low-income housewives worked very hard in the interwar years. None of the working-class wives of Muncie reported spending less than four hours a day on cooking, cleaning, and laundering (marketing and child care were not even inquired after), and most reported seven or more hours a day, seven days a week. Yet for some of those housewives, some of that hard work was paying off, some of the time. If a hard-pressed mother of this generation had more cash than her mother had had, then her children ate better than she had as a child; since more fruits and vegetables were available, fresh and cheap, at more seasons of the year, their diet was more varied and more healthful. If she and her husband had managed to buy a house, then it was, like as not, more spacious than the one in which she had been raised, and it was better ventilated, warmer in the winter and cooler in

---

*Whether women of the lower economic classes worked for "pin money" or out of real economic necessity is a question that has been endlessly debated, one commentator's pin money invariably turning out to be another commentator's "real necessity." The most recent analyses of working women in the interwar years are no exception: Winifred Wandersee sees married women's workforce participation as a result of the "pursuit of luxury"; while Alice Kessler-Harris sees it as an effort to maintain or to improve a family's standard of living. Kessler-Harris seems to me to be right; the "rising expectations" of this period were the expectations of working-class people that they had a right to the same conveniences and amenities that had long been associated with the standards of the more comfortable classes. What Wandersee seems to regard as luxuries were washing machines, automobiles, additional changes of clothing, a four-room apartment, and a chance for children to stay in school longer than their parents had.

the summer, and more likely to have running water and a toilet. With the running water and a hot-water heater and a sewing machine, she could keep her children cleaner, better dressed, more comfortable, and possibly even healthier than she had been as a child, without spending much more time than her mother had spent in the doing of it. She certainly could not afford to pay the wages of human servants; but when times were good, she was beginning to invest in electrical appliances and she knew that they, too, could increase her productivity: that a washing machine meant the ability to change the sheets every week or underwear every day, and a vacuum cleaner meant that dust could be kept from accumulating in the house.

Conclusion

In the years between the two world wars, there were still many differences between the two great segments of the population—not the least of which was that, for those who were poor, any gain in their standard of living in one year was likely to be lost in the next. In some communities, at some times, the gap between the standard of living of the two classes was as great as it had ever been: the poor still begot many children and took them out of school early, still lived with filth and ate in their kitchens, still suffered ill health, lost their teeth and smelled bad, still handed down their clothes and took their shoes from the ragpile. But in other communities, at other times, the ability to live at a minimum standard of health and decency was no longer the privilege only of those who were affluent. Public health was improving, housing conditions were better than they had been, various amenities and conveniences were becoming more widely diffused; and even those who were poor in relative terms could profit from some of these changes. All of them worked together to make hard-pressed housewives more productive and less uncomfortable than their mothers had been and to make their housework bear fruit in improving the health and the prospects of their families. The gap between those who could afford to live "decently" and those who could not may have been as wide as ever; but in the years between the wars, the average housewife of less than modest means was living, at least some of the time, at a higher standard than her mother had been able to attain. Looking back, we can readily understand why she, and her daughter in the next generation, believed that gas ranges, pasteurized milk, electricity, washing machines, fortified margarine, and vacuum cleaners had played a significant role in this accomplishment. We can also understand why these women continued to believe not just that their place was in their homes but that the work that they did there had enormous value. Small wonder then that these women, and their descendants, accepted the yoke of women's work in the home and viewed the modern tools with which they did it as liberating, rather than as oppressive, agents.

REVIEW QUESTIONS

1. According to Cowan, what were the main differences between the households of the relatively prosperous and those of the people who were "struggling to make ends meet"?

2. What were the main differences between living conditions in homes in rural America and those in urban America?

3. How did the definition of the housewife's proper role change during this period for both groups Cowan discusses? What factors are responsible for these changes?

4. One of the traditional ideas about the 1920s is that there was a "revolution in manners and morals" during the decade that involved, among other things, changes in women's roles and in notions about what constituted proper feminine behavior. From the evidence in this selection, does it seem to you that such a "revolution" occurred? Why or why not?

5. What major changes in the lives of Americans were brought about by the growth of a mass-consumption society in the 1920s?

6. Cowan points out that even when they had jobs outside the home, women remained primarily responsible for doing the housework. How do you explain this? Today, with a much larger percentage of women holding jobs outside the home, they are still primarily responsible for it. How do you explain that?

FOR FURTHER READING

Frederick Lewis Allen's account of the 1920s, *Only Yesterday* (1931), remains lively and informative more than 60 years after its publication. William E. Leuchtenberg, *The Perils of Prosperity, 1914–1932* (1958), and Ellis W. Hawley, *The Great War and the Search for a Modern Order, A History of the American People and Their Institutions, 1917–1933* (1979), are more scholarly. George Soule, *Prosperity Decade: From War to Depression, 1917–1929* (1947), is the standard economic history of the decade. For accounts of how ordinary Americans were living, see two books by Robert S. Lynd and Helen Merrill Lynd, *Middletown* (1929), and *Middletown in Transition* (1937), detailed studies of life in Muncie, Indiana. The lives of women in the 1920s are discussed in Dorothy M. Brown, *Setting a Course: American Women in the 1920s* (1987), and J. Stanley Lemons, *The Woman Citizen: Social Feminism in the 1920s* (1973). Susan Strasser, *Never Done: A History of American Housework* (1982), covers much the same ground as the book from which this selection was taken, Ruth Schwartz Cowan, *More Work for Mother* (1983).

PART IV

DEPRESSION AND WAR

The stock market crash of 1929 signalled the beginning of the end of the prosperity of the 1920s. For the next three years the economy declined steadily until, during the winter of 1932–33, the United States was at the low point of the worst depression it had ever suffered. With the benefit of hindsight it is possible to see that the causes of the Great Depression of the 1930s are to be found in some of the economic conditions and practices of the 1920s, including the tendency to use business profits for speculation rather than reinvestment, declining prices for agricultural goods and declining income for farmers, and a maldistribution of income that sent too much money flowing into too few pockets producing a steady erosion of purchasing power. The stock market crash and declining demand generated a crisis of confidence among American businessmen, and they responded by cutting back production and laying off workers. Naturally, this resulted in further declines in purchasing power, still lower demand levels, further cutbacks in production, more layoffs, and on and on in an ever-downward spiral. The nation's problems were further complicated by the continuing dominance of a political philosophy that severely limited the role of government in reacting to the nation's needs because it saw such action as contrary to the Constitution and American traditions.

The situation began to change with the election of Franklin Roosevelt to the presidency in 1932. Roosevelt brought a new activist approach to Washington, inaugurating the New Deal, a massive array of government programs that tried to alleviate the suffering the Depression was causing and generate economic recovery. In the meantime, however, the problems remained acute: an unemployment rate that ranged as high as 25% according to conservative estimates, continuing business failures, thousands upon thousands of mortgage foreclosures on homes and farms, widespread homelessness, and so forth. The first selection in this section describes the impact the Great Depression had on the lives of ordinary Americans, and the second focuses on some of the relief programs the New Deal created in its attempts to combat the Depression.

The anti-Depression programs of the New Deal won the wholehearted support of a considerable majority of the American people, but the fact remains that these programs were only marginally successful in bringing the country out of the Depression. Conditions in 1939 were better than they had been in 1932 but not as good as they had been in 1929. It was the start of World War II that provided the economic stimulus that finally ended the Depression once and for all. Suddenly, unemployment vanished, to be followed almost immediately by a serious labor *shortage* as the United States entered a war that everyone was convinced would be won in our factories even more than on battlefields. The noneconomic effects of the war were equally great. The third selection in this section deals with some of the social consequences of the war. The last takes a close look at one particular policy that resulted from the war, the so-called GI Bill of Rights.

In the short span of roughly fifteen years, the United States lived through two of the greatest crises in its entire national existence: the worst depression it had ever endured and the largest foreign war it had ever fought. Each had permanent effects in changing and remaking the nation. Together, their influence was massive.

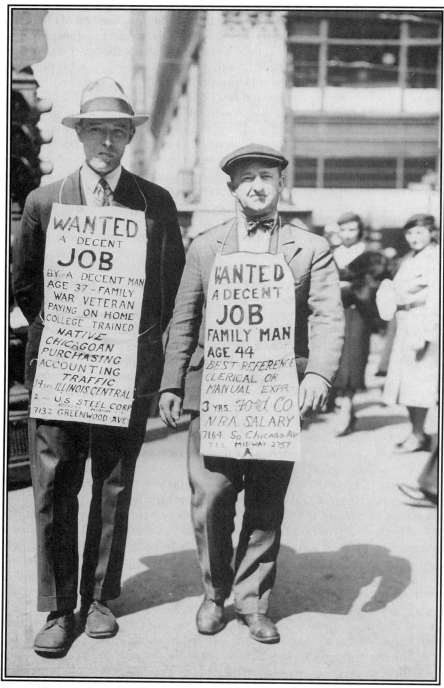

Carrying a sandwich sign in the hope of putting food on the family table, 1934.

13

The Nation Confronts
the Great Depression

CAROLINE BIRD

Karl Mannheim, one of Europe's greatest sociologists, has stressed the importance of trying to understand human behavior as a response to an experience shared by members of a particular generation. Several historical examples of an experience that served to influence the outlook of an entire generation can be cited: the bitterness and anger experienced by southern whites as a consequence of their defeat at the hands of the North in the Civil War and the humiliation of the Radical Reconstruction that followed; the disillusionment of the generation that went to war in Europe trying to fulfill Woodrow Wilson's promise to "make the world safe for democracy"; and the susceptibility of the German people to the glorious future offered them by Adolph Hitler and his Nazi regime after their defeat in World War I and their postwar social and economic agonies. The Great Depression of the 1930s was a similarly traumatic experience for millions of Americans left without jobs and, in some instances, without food or shelter. These Americans shared a common generational experience: hunger and want, an unemployed father, no money for recreation or schooling, and a constant fear of what their economic future might be.

The pervasiveness and the duration of the Great Depression are unparalleled in the history of the American people. The stock market crash of 1929—which wiped out the hopes and the savings of all but a few—only served as the first act of a drama that was to last for more than a decade. By the early thirties, hundreds of banks were failing, tens of thousands of businesses were going bankrupt, and millions of Americans were being added to the unemployment rolls each month. Industrial production by 1933 fell to pre–World War I levels, farm prices plummeted to unprecedented lows, and foreclosures were common experiences as the farmer lost his land and the city dweller his home.

While the pursuit of material wealth has always been central to the American ethos, one may find a causal relationship between the deprivations suffered by the generation of Americans who grew up in the 1930s and their frenzied postwar pursuit of material comforts— new suburban homes, annual editions of chrome-decorated automobiles, and credit cards for every occasion. The Great Depression, as this selection by Caroline Bird makes amply clear, created an "invisible scar"—and a lasting one.

You could feel the Depression deepen, but you could not look out of the window and see it. Men who lost their jobs dropped out of sight. They were quiet, and you had to know just when and where to find them: at night, for instance, on the edge of town huddling for warmth around a bonfire, or even the municipal incinerator; at dawn, picking over the garbage dump for scraps of food or salvageable clothing.

In Oakland, California, they lived in sewer pipes the manufacturer could not sell. In Connellsville, Pennsylvania, unemployed steelworkers kept warm in the big ovens they had formerly coked. Outside Washington, D.C., one Bonus Marcher slept in a barrel filled with grass, another in a piano box, a third in a coffin set on trestles. Every big city had a "Hooverville" camp of dispossessed men living like this.

It took a knowing eye—or the eye of poverty itself—to understand or even to observe some of the action. When oranges fell off a truck, it wasn't always an accident; sometimes they were the truck driver's contribution to slum kids. A woman burning newspapers in a vacant lot might be trying to warm a baby's bottle. The ragged men standing silent as cattle, in a flatrack truck parked on a lonely public road, might be getting the bum's rush out of town. In the Southwest, freight trains were black with human bodies headed for warm

---

weather. Railroad dicks shooed them off at stations. Deming, New Mexico, hired a special constable to keep them out of town. When the Southern Pacific police ordered the men off the train, the special constable ordered them back on again.

Everyone knew of someone engaged in a desperate struggle, although most of the agony went on behind closed doors. The stories were whispered. There was something indecent about them. A well-to-do man living on the income from rental property could not collect his rents. His mortgages were foreclosed, and his houses sold for less than the debt. To make up the difference, he sold his own home. He moved himself and his wife into a nearby basement and did odd jobs for the people upstairs in exchange for a room for some of his six children. He mowed lawns, graded yards, and did whatever common labor he could find in order to pay for groceries, until his health broke down under the unaccustomed work. The doctor told him that he needed an operation and would have to rest for a year afterward.

A 72-year-old factory worker was told that he could no longer be employed because he was too old. He went home and turned on the gas. His 56-year-old widow, who had worked as a proofreader before developing heart trouble, sat alone staring at their few sticks of furniture for three days after her husband's death. Then she too turned on the gas. The neighbors smelled it in time and saved her life.

Neither the property owner nor the widow was an uncommon case. They merely were lucky enough to be among the Hundred Neediest Cases chosen by *The New York Times* for 1932. Unlike the hardship cases of the 1960s, who are often urgently in need of psychiatric help, these people were in trouble only because they were physically sick and had no money. By the charitable standards of the rich at that time, they were regarded as the "deserving poor," as distinguished from the undeserving poor, who were thought to be unwilling to work or to save.

If the "deserving poor" had been few, charitable help might have sufficed. But there were too many, and more all the time. In December 1929, three million people were out of work. The next winter, four to five million. The winter of 1931–1932, eight million. The following year, no one knew exactly how many, but all authorities agreed that additional millions were unemployed. In 1965, unemployment is a "problem" when one in twenty is idle. In the fall of 1932, *Fortune* thought that 34 million men, women, and children— better than a fourth of the nation—were members of families that had no regular full-time breadwinner. Estimates differed, but none included farmers unable to make both ends meet, in spite of the blessing of seven-day, sunup-to-sundown employment, or factory hands who were making out on two or three days' work a week.

There were too many in want to hide. There were too many in want to blame. And even if the poor were shiftless, a Christian country would not let them starve. "Everyone is getting along somehow," people said to each other. "After all, no one has starved." But they worried even as they spoke.

A few were ashamed to eat. The Elks in Mt. Kisco, New York, and Princeton University eating clubs were among the organizations that sent leftovers from their tables to the unemployed. A reporter on *The Brooklyn Eagle* suggested a central warehouse where families could send their leftovers for distribution to the needy. John B. Nichlos, of the Oklahoma Gas Utilities Company, worked out a leftover system in detail and urged it on Hoover's Cabinet. It provided:

> Sanitary containers of five (5) gallons each should be secured in a large number so that four (4) will always be left in large kitchens where the restaurants are serving a volume business. The containers should be labeled "MEAT, BEANS, POTATOES, BREAD, AND OTHER ITEMS." Someone from the Salvation Army with a truck should pick up the loaded containers every morning and leave empty ones. The civic clubs, restaurants, the proprietors and the workers should be asked to cooperate in order to take care of all surplus food in as sanitary a way as possible. In other words, when a man finishes his meal he should not (after lighting his cigarette or cigar) leave the ashes on the food which he was unable to consume.

Many more fortunate people turned away from the unemployed, but some tried to help in the traditional neighborly way. A Brooklyn convent put sandwiches outside its door where the needy could get them without knocking. St. Louis society women distributed unsold food from restaurants. Someone put baskets in New York City railroad stations so that commuters could donate vegetables from their gardens. In New York, Bernard Macfadden served six-cent lunches to the unemployed and claimed he was making money. In San Francisco, the hotel and restaurant workers' union arranged for unemployed chefs and waiters to serve elegant if simple meals to the unemployed.

But there was more talk than help. A great many people spent a great deal of energy urging each other to give, to share, to hire. President Hoover led a national publicity campaign to urge people to give locally and to make jobs. At the suggestion of public-relations counsel Edward L. Bernays, the first President's Emergency Committee was named "for Employment" (PECE) to accentuate the positive. In 1931 it was reorganized more realistically as the President's Organization for Unemployment Relief (POUR). Both undertook to inspire confidence by the issuing of optimistic statements; POUR chairman Walter Gifford told a Senate committee offhandedly that he did not know how many were unemployed and did not think it was the committee's job to find out.

Local groups responded by pressing campaigns of their own to "Give-A-Job" or "Share-A-Meal" until people grew deaf to them. Carl Byoir, founder of one of the country's biggest public-relations firms, declared a "War against

Depression" that proposed to wipe it out in six months by getting one million employers to make one new job each.

Results of such appeals were disappointing. Corporation executives answered the pleas of PECE and POUR by saying that they had no right to spend stockholders' money hiring men they did not need. Even in New York City, where the able and well-supported Community Service Society pioneered work relief, there were enough hungry men without money to keep 82 badly managed breadlines going, and men were selling apples on every street corner. Newspapers discovered and photographed an apple seller who was formerly a near-millionaire.

The well of private charity ran dry. A Westchester woman is said to have fired all her servants in order to have money to contribute to the unemployed. "Voluntary conscription" of wages helped steelworkers weather the first round of layoffs in little Conshohocken, Pennsylvania, but the plan broke down as there were more mouths to feed and fewer pay envelopes to conscript. Local charities everywhere were overwhelmed by 1931, and the worst was yet to come.

Kentucky coal miners suffered perhaps the most. In Harlan County there were whole towns whose people had not a cent of income. They lived on dandelions and blackberries. The women washed clothes in soapweed suds. Dysentery bloated the stomachs of starving babies. Children were reported so famished they were chewing up their own hands. Miners tried to plant vegetables, but they were often so hungry that they ate them before they were ripe. On her first trip to the mountains, Eleanor Roosevelt saw a little boy trying to hide his pet rabbit. "He thinks we are not going to eat it," his sister told her, "but we are." In West Virginia, miners mobbed company stores demanding food. Mountain people, with no means to leave their homes, sometimes had to burn their last chairs and tables to keep warm. Local charity could not help in a place where everyone was destitute. . . .

A Quaker himself, Hoover went to the American Friends Service Committee. The Philadelphia Meeting developed a "concern" for the miners. Swarthmore and Haverford students ventured into the hollows, winning the confidence of suspicious miners. They systematically weighed the children, so they could feed those in greatest need first. Hoover gave them $2,500 out of his own pocket, but most of the contributions seem to have come from the Rockefellers.

"No one has starved," Hoover boasted. To prove it, he announced a decline in the death rate. It was heartening, but puzzling, too. Even the social workers could not see how the unemployed kept body and soul together, and the more they studied, the more the wonder grew. Savings, if any, went first. Then insurance was cashed. Then people borrowed from family and friends. They stopped paying rent. When evicted, they moved in with relatives. They ran up bills. It was surprising how much credit could be wangled. In 1932, about 400 families on relief in Philadelphia had managed to contract an average debt of $160, a tribute to the hearts if not the business heads of landlords and merchants. But in the end they had to eat "tight."

Every serious dieter knows how little food it takes to keep alive. One woman borrowed 50¢, bought stale bread at 3½¢ a loaf, and kept her family alive on it for 11 days. Every serious dieter knows how hunger induces total concentration on food. When eating tight, the poor thought of nothing but food, just food. They hunted food like alley cats, and in some of the same places. They haunted docks where spoiled vegetables might be thrown out and brought them home to cook up in a stew from which every member of the family would eat as little as possible, and only when very hungry. Neighbors would ask a child in for a meal or give him scraps—stale bread, bones with a bit of good meat still on them, raw potato peelings. Children would hang around grocery stores, begging a little food, running errands, or watching carts in exchange for a piece of fruit. Sometimes a member of the family would go to another part of town and beg. Anyone on the block who got hold of something big might call the neighbors in to share it. Then everyone would gorge like savages at a killing, to make up for the lean days. Enough people discovered that a five-cent candy bar can make a lunch to boom sales during the generally slow year of 1931. You get used to hunger. After the first few days it doesn't even hurt; you just get weak. When work opened up, at one point, in the Pittsburgh steel mills, men who were called back were not strong enough to do it.

Those who were still prosperous hated to think of such things and frequently succeeded in avoiding them. But professional people could not always escape. A doctor would order medicine for a charity case and then realize that there was no money to pay for it. A school doctor in Philadelphia gave a listless child a tonic to stimulate her appetite and later found that her family did not have enough to eat at home.

A reporter on *The Detroit Free Press* helped the police bring a missing boy back to a bare home on Christmas Day, 1934. He and his friends on the paper got a drugstore to open up so they could bring the boy some toys. *The Detroit Free Press* has supplied Christmas gifts for needy children every year since.

A teacher in a mountain school told a little girl who looked sick but said she was hungry to go home and eat something. "I can't," the youngster said. "It's my sister's turn to eat." In Chicago, teachers were ordered to ask what a child had had to eat before punishing him. Many of them were getting nothing but potatoes, a diet that kept their weight up, but left them listless, crotchety, and sleepy.

The police saw more than anyone else. They had to cope with the homeless men sleeping in doorways or breaking into empty buildings. They had to find help for people who fell sick in the streets or tried to commit suicide. And it was to a cop that city people went when they were at the end of their rope and did not know what else to do. In New York City, the police kept a list of the charities to which they could direct the helpless. In 1930 they took a census of needy families, and city employees started contributing one percent of their salaries to a fund for the police to use to buy food for people they found actually starving. It was the first public confession of official responsibility for plain poverty, and it came not from the top, but from the lowest-paid civil servants, who worked down where the poor people were.

Teachers worried about the children who came to school to get warm. They organized help for youngsters who needed food and clothing before they could learn. Sometimes Boards of Education diverted school funds to feed them. Often the teachers did it on their own. In 1932, New York City schoolteachers contributed $260,000 out of their salaries in one month. Chicago teachers fed 11,000 pupils out of their own pockets in 1931, although they had not themselves been paid for months. "For God's sake, help us feed these children during the summer," Chicago's superintendent of schools begged the governor in June. . . .

Men of old-fashioned principles really believed that the less said about the unemployed, the faster they would get jobs. They really believed that public relief was bad for the poor because it discouraged them from looking for work or from taking it at wages that would tempt business to start up again. According to their theory, permanent mass unemployment was impossible, because there was work at some wage for every able-bodied man, if he would only find and do it. Charity was necessary, of course, for those who were really disabled through no fault of their own, but there could never be very many of these, and they should be screened carefully and given help of a kind and in a way that would keep them from asking for it as long as possible. . . .

The view persists. In 1961, the mayor of Newburgh, New York, cut off relief to make the unemployed find jobs. In 1965, it was thought that raising the minimum wage would hurt the poor by pricing them out of jobs.

Thirty years earlier, respectable folk worried about the idea of public relief, even though accepting the need for it. On opinion polls they agreed with the general proposition that public relief should be temporary, hard to get and less than the lowest wage offered by any employer. In the North as well as in the South, relief stations were closed at harvesttime to force the unemployed to work at getting in the crops, for whatever wages farmers offered.

It was a scandal when a relief client drove an old jalopy up to the commissary to lug his groceries home. In some places, a client had to surrender his license plates in order to get relief, even if the old car meant a chance to earn small sums to pay for necessities not covered by relief. Phones went, too, even when they were a relief client's only lifeline to odd jobs. It was considered an outrage if a woman on relief had a smart-looking winter coat, or a ring, or a burial-insurance policy, or a piano. She was made to sell them for groceries before relief would help her. The search for hidden assets was thorough. One thrifty family in New York was denied relief "because it does not seem possible for this family to have managed without some other kind of assistance."

When a woman on relief had triplets, newspapers pointed out that for every 100 children born to self-supporting parents, relief parents produced 160. It was hard even for the social workers to see that big families were more apt to need relief. Almost everybody thought relief caused the poor to become irresponsible and to have children they could not support—if, in fact, they did not have babies deliberately in order to qualify. . . . During the Depression, if some way could have been found to prevent married couples on relief from indulging in sexual intercourse, there would have been those who would have demanded it.

People who took public relief were denied civil rights. Some state constitutions disqualified relief clients from voting, and as late as 1938 an opinion poll showed that one out of every three Republicans thought this was right. In some places, village taxpayers' organizations tried to keep the children of tax delinquents out of the local schools. People suspected of taking public relief were even turned away from churches.

During the first and worst years of the Depression, the only public relief was improvised by cities. Appropriations were deliberately low. If funds ran out every few months, so much the better. The poor would have to make another effort to find work. Every program was "temporary." In most cases, this was sheer necessity. Cities could not afford otherwise. Their tax bases were too narrow. Some of them had lost tax money when banks folded. Detroit could not collect property taxes because landlords could not collect the rent from their unemployed tenants. Bankrupt Chicago was living on tax anticipation warrants doled out by bankers. Some well-heeled citizens refused to pay their taxes at all. Cities cut their own employees, stopped buying library books, and shot zoo animals to divert money to relief. . . .

Cities had to ration relief. In 1932, family allowances in New York City fell to $2.39 a week, and only half of the families who could qualify were getting it. Things were worse elsewhere. In little Hamtramck, Michigan, welfare officials had to cut off all families with fewer than three children. In Detroit, allowances fell to 15¢ a day per person before running out entirely. Across the country, only about a fourth of the unemployed were able to get help, and fewer than that in many cities. Almost everywhere, aid was confined to food and fuel. Relief workers connived with clients to put off landlords. Medical care, clothing, shoes, chairs, beds, safety pins—everything else had to be scrounged or bought by doing without food. Those on relief were little better off than those who couldn't get it. Private help dwindled to six percent of the money spent on the unemployed.

Still, Hoover kept insisting, no one starved. In May 1932, Hoover's Secretary of the Interior, Dr. Ray Lyman Wilbur, reassured the National Conference of Social Workers meeting in Philadelphia. "We must set up the neglect of prosperity against the care of adversity," he philosophized. "With prosperity many parents unload the responsibilities for their children onto others. With adversity the home takes its normal place. The interest of thousands of keen and well-trained people throughout the whole country in seeing that our children are properly fed and cared for has given many of them better and more suitable food than in past good times."

Social workers were indignant. "Have you ever seen the uncontrolled trembling of parents who have starved themselves for weeks so that their children might not go hungry?" social worker Lillian Wald demanded. Others told how fathers and even older brothers and sisters hung around the street corners while the younger children were being fed, for fear they would be tempted to eat more than their share. The social workers knew the facts. They also knew newspaper reporters. In 1932, the public began to listen.

"Mrs. Green left her five small children alone one morning while she went to have her grocery order filled," one social worker reported. "While she was away the constable arrived and padlocked her house with the children inside. When she came back she heard the six-weeks-old baby crying. She did not dare touch the padlock for fear of being arrested, but she found a window open and climbed in and nursed the baby and then climbed out and appealed to the police to let her children out."

Eviction was so common that children in a Philadelphia day-care center made a game of it. They would pile all the doll furniture up first in one corner and then in another. "We ain't got no money for the rent, so we's moved into a new house," a tot explained to the teacher. "Then we got the constable on us, so we's movin' again." Philadelphia relief paid an evicted family's rent for one month in the new house. Then they were on their own. Public opinion favored the tenant. An eviction could bring on a neighborhood riot.

Landlords often let the rent go. Some of them needed relief as much as their tenants, and had a harder time qualifying for it. In Philadelphia a little girl whose father was on relief could not get milk at school, under a program for needy children, because her father "owned property." Investigators found some unemployed tenants sharing food orders with their landlords. In the country, where poor farmers had been accustomed to paying their taxes in work on the roads, tenants who could not pay their rent sometimes did the landlord's road work for him.

It was not true that "no one starved." People starved to death, and not only in Harlan County, Kentucky. The New York City Welfare Council counted 29 deaths from starvation in 1933. More than fifty other people were treated for starvation in hospitals. An additional 110, most of them children, died of malnutrition.

A father who had been turned away by a New York City welfare agency was afraid to apply for help after public relief had been set up. Social workers found one of his children dead; another, too weak to move, lay in bed with the mother; the rest huddled, shivering and hungry, around the desperate father.

A New York dentist and his wife died rather than accept charity. They left a note, and then took gas together. "The entire blame for this tragedy rests with the City of New York or whoever it is that allows free dental work in the hospital," the note read. "We want to get out of the way before we are forced to accept relief money. The City of New York is not to touch our bodies. We have a horror of charity burial. We have put the last of our money in the hands of a friend who will turn it over to my brother."

Health surveys were made to pound home the fact that poor people are sicker than the well-to-do. Doctors, nurses, teachers, and social workers warned that privation was ruining the nation's health. In 1933, the Children's Bureau reported that one in five American children was not getting enough of the right things to eat. Lower vitality, greater susceptibility to infections, slower recovery, stunting, more organic disease, a reversal of gains against tuberculosis—all were freely predicted. Medical care for the poor was sketchy. Doctors were hard hit financially, and they did not always live up to the Oath of Hippocrates. Frequently, the poor were afraid to call a doctor because they did not have money. New York City surgeons sometimes demanded cash in advance or delayed operations until the family could get money together.

Middle-class people put off the doctor and the dentist. "Illness frightens us," John Dos Passos writes of his Depression days at Pacific Grove, California. "You have to have money to be sick—or did then. Any dentistry also was out of the question, with the result that my teeth went badly to pieces. Without dough you couldn't have a tooth filled." Hospitals could never fill the private rooms that helped to pay for their charity cases, with the result that they had fewer patients than they do now, but sicker ones. They learned to be tough in admitting people who could not pay.

The harder the middle class looked, the more critical poverty seemed. It did not seem possible that people could stand lack of regular food, unstable homes, medical neglect. The Depression would leave its mark in the future. "If we put the children in these families under a period of malnutrition such as they are going through today, what sort of people are we going to have twenty years from now?" Karl de Schweinitz of the Philadelphia Community Council asked a Senate committee in 1932. "What will we say at that time about them?" . . .

. . . The Depression did not depress the conditions of the poor. It merely publicized them. The poor had been poor all along. It was just that nobody had looked at them. The children of Depression grew up to be bigger and healthier than their parents, who had enjoyed the advantages of a prosperous childhood. World War II recruits were more fit in every way than doughboys drafted in World War I. The death rate did not rise in the Depression. It kept going down. The health record of the Depression parallels that of rapidly industrializing societies everywhere: infectious diseases dropped, but mental illness, suicide, and the degenerative diseases of an aging population rose. . . .

. . . The poor survived because they knew how to be poor. The Milbank Foundation found more sickness among the poor than among the well off, but they also found that the newly poor were sicker more often than those who always had been poor. In the 1960s, social work provided steady jobs for people who often were close to poverty themselves. In the 1930s, charity was work for middle- and upper-class volunteers, who were charmed and awed by the techniques for survival that they discovered.

A family eating tight would stay in bed a lot. That way they would save fuel, as well as the extra food calories needed in cold weather. The experienced poor, particularly the Negroes, knew about eating the parts of the animal normally rejected. And the poor generally did not spend as much money on food as their middle-class advisers thought they should be spending.

The poor worked at keeping warm. A family with no money for the gas company would economize by cooking once a week. When it was cut off, they would cook in the furnace. They gathered scrap wood to keep the furnace going. They saved by heating only the kitchen. When fuel was low, the experienced poor would sneak into a movie house. Even if they had to spend ten cents to get in, they could sometimes keep out of the cold for two double features. When the electricity was turned off, some men found ways to steal current by tapping a neighbor's wire.

Shoes were a problem. The poor took them off when they got home, to save them. Do-it-yourself shoe-repair kits were popular with the middle class, but if you could not afford the dimestore item you could resole a pair of shoes with rubber cut from an old tire, or wear rubbers over a wornout sole. Clothes were swapped among the family. One mother and daughter managed to get together an outfit both could wear. They took turns going to church.

The poor whose lives were laid bare by the Depression lived in the same world of poverty that Michael Harrington has recently described in *The Other America,* and Oscar Lewis in his studies of the working classes in Mexico. They lived for the present without much thought for their own past or future. They ate literally from hand to mouth. Even when they had a little money, they did not lay in stocks of food. They paid high interest rates on what they bought or borrowed, and seldom got their money's worth. Their world was small, limited to the people they saw every day, and they did not venture out of it. A trip to the relief office was a daring undertaking. They had few friends. They did not read. Without outside contacts, they could not organize or revolt or escape.

A year after his defeat by Roosevelt, Hoover—who had repeated so many times that no one was starving—went on a fishing trip with cartoonist "Ding" Darling in the Rocky Mountains. One morning a local man came into their camp, found Hoover awake, and led him to a shack where one child lay dead and seven others were in the last stages of starvation. Hoover took the children to a hospital, made a few phone calls, and raised a fund of $3,030 for them. . . .

The Depression gave the middle classes a double vision of the poor. They did not give up the notions that the poor should have saved or that they did not want to work, or that their poverty was their own fault. These were concepts hard to change. While firmly holding to these ideas, however, they saw contradictory facts before their eyes. When the Depression forced them to scrutinize the condition of the working people, they could see that wages were too low and employment too intermittent for most wageworkers to save enough money to see them through emergencies, or old age, even if banks had not failed. A favorite cartoon of the times pictured a squirrel asking an old man sitting on a park bench why he had not saved for a rainy day.

"I did," said the old man.

REVIEW QUESTIONS

1. What would you consider the major socioeconomic differences (for example, in employment) between the 1930s as described by Caroline Bird and the 1990s? Are there segments of American society today experiencing the conditions described by Bird? Who? Where?

2. What services, institutions, and agencies has our nation established—during and since the Depression—to prevent the kind of suffering described by the author? Could this nation enter another depression similar to the one of the 1930s? Why or why not?

3. What impression do you get of the frame of mind of the millions of poor and the unemployed? How does the author account for the divergent responses to the Depression by various socioeconomic segments of American society?

4. Explain how each of the following institutions and groups responded to the plight of the American people during the Depression: (a) newspapers; (b) industrialists; (c) social agencies; (d) landlords; and (e) political leaders.

5. Some historians have suggested that many Americans may have accepted the sufferings of the Depression out of a feeling of guilt—an acceptance of the notion that their unemployment and their inability to provide the basic necessities for their family were consequences of their own deficiencies rather than the results of defects in the economic system of the nation. Does this idea—the passivity of the nation in the face of joblessness and hunger—seem to be borne out by this essay? Or do the American people appear to have been hostile or angry or rebellious during the Depression? If so, at whom? If not, why not?

FOR FURTHER READING

The Great Depression of the 1930s started with the stock market crash of 1929. John Kenneth Galbraith's *The Great Crash* (2nd ed., 1989) is a readable account of what happened, why, and what its consequences were. David Burner, *Herbert Hoover* (1979); Donald J. Lisio, *The President and Protest: Hoover, Conspiracy, and the Bonus Riot* (1974); and Albert Romasco, *The Poverty of Abundance: Hoover, the Nation, the Depression* (1965), all deal with the Hoover administration. Frederick Lewis Allen, *Since Yesterday* (1939), and Robert S. McElvaine, *The Great Depression: America, 1929–1941* (1984), are general histories of the decade. Charles Jellison, *Tomatoes Were Cheaper: Tales from the Thirties* (1977), and many of the essays in Isabel Leighton, ed., *The Aspirin Age: 1919–1941*, talk about aspects of life during the period that conventional history books often ignore. Studs Terkel, *Hard Times: An Oral History of the Great Depression* (1970), is a collection of recollections of the Depression. Robert S. McElvaine, ed., *Down and Out in the Great Depression: Letters from the Forgotten Man* (1983), uses letters to government agencies to provide insights into the hardships people faced.

One of hundreds of murals painted by artists working for the WPA. Its focus on how ordinary working people built America is characteristic of American art in the 1930s.

14

Work Relief in the Great Depression

EDWARD ROBB ELLIS

The social and economic crisis that gripped the American nation in 1933, the year Franklin D. Roosevelt came to office, was, in many ways, more serious than any other crisis since 1861, when Abraham Lincoln came into the White House on the eve of the Civil War. By 1933, the stock market crash had turned into a full-fledged depression: World War I veterans marched on Washington and were dispersed by federal troops; one-quarter of the work force was unemployed; farmers were halting foreclosures on their land by threats of armed violence; and in the cities, a rising tide of radical protest appeared to be equally imminent. Only within this context of economic deprivation and social tension can one understand the depth and breadth of the legislation of the New Deal—and the contribution made by that singular figure in the history of the American nation in the twentieth century, Franklin Delano Roosevelt.

The New Deal program of social and economic reform, launched by Roosevelt in 1933, endured until 1939, when World War II broke out in Europe. This program massively reformed our country's institutions and way of life to a far greater degree than had the unrealized reforms demanded by the Greenbackers and Populists in the late nineteenth century or those enacted into law by the Progressives in the early twentieth. In addition to New Deal efforts to promote recovery and reform of the nation's economic institutions, the reformers of the 1930s

launched an unprecedented program of relief for the poor and the unemployed. In contrast to the sociopolitical philosophy of Herbert
Hoover, whose "rugged individualism" consigned relief programs to
private philanthropy, Franklin Roosevelt accepted the notion that ultimately—if all else proved inadequate—clothing, housing, and feeding
the nation's poor was the responsibility of the federal government.

The relief programs funded by the federal government can be divided into two basic categories: *direct relief,* funded by the federal
government and administered by the states and the cities, and *work
relief,* funded by the federal government and administered out of
Washington. As the next selection makes clear, work relief was both a
controversial and significant element of the New Deal. By the end of
the decade, however, millions of Americans had found succor
through one of the relief programs sponsored by the New Deal: the
multifaceted Works Progress Administration (WPA), the conservation-
oriented Civil Conservation Corps (CCC), and the National Youth Administration (NYA), a program for high school and college students.

Harry Hopkins loped into the federal security building in Washington, D.C.,
twisting his scrawny neck from side to side and barking orders at the assistants
trying to keep up with him.

The previous day, May 22, 1933, President Roosevelt had named him the
administrator of the Federal Emergency Relief Administration. His lips taut,
his movements jerky, Hopkins scurried down a hall, saw a desk that had not yet
been moved into the room that was to become his office, flopped down into
the chair behind it. Oblivious to the confusion swirling about him and raising
his voice to be heard over the clatter of heels in the corridor, the former social
worker began dictating telegrams to the governors of all forty-eight states. . . .

Harry Lloyd Hopkins was born in Sioux City, Iowa, on August 17, 1890, the
fourth of David and Anna Hopkins' five children. His father was a harness
maker; his mother taught school. After Harry became the most influential
man in the United States government, next to Roosevelt himself, he continued to boast about his humble origins—sometimes to the annoyance of his
friends. Frances Perkins thought this a sign of insecurity—that he always felt
inferior to others despite what she considered to be his superior mind and
character.

When Harry was two years old, his family moved to Nebraska. By the time he was eleven the Hopkins' had settled in Grinnell, Iowa, a folksy town with a strong Methodist flavor. From his mother, a zealous Methodist, he got his strong sense of righteousness, while from his father he inherited geniality and wit. As a boy Harry scrubbed floors, beat carpets, milked cows and toiled on nearby farms like other underprivileged young people. In 1908 he entered Grinnell College, a small institution with a high reputation for scholarship. He made only average grades, seldom revealing the probing intelligence which later caused Winston Churchill to dub him Lord Root of the Matter. . . .

In 1912, after graduation, he headed for the East Coast. One of his professors, who was connected with a Manhattan settlement house named Christodora House, had won his appointment as head of a summer camp for boys across the Hudson River in New Jersey. When camp was over, he began working in Christodora House itself, located on Manhattan's Lower East Side, and there the naïve youth from the Corn Belt met Jewish boys for the first time in his life. He was amazed to see gangsters stroll into settlement dances and street bullies fighting with broken bottles.

Over the next few years Hopkins developed into a social worker and an executive of social agencies, slaving sixteen hours a day, organizing boys' clubs, plodding up tenement stairs, listening to the laments of the underprivileged, making pioneer surveys of unemployment. Humble and sincere, he was able to get along with all kinds of people. With the stench of the slums constantly in his nostrils, he made a slight turn to the political left and seemingly was registered for a while as a Socialist—a matter of some concern after he entered the federal government. And after his divorce he suffered so much personal strain that he had himself psychoanalyzed. . . .

"Dole" had become an emotionally charged word ever since the advent of the Depression. Throughout the Thirties people criticized the dole or praised the dole, often in a slipshod way since they did not bother to define the term and applied it to a variety of conditions and plans. Their arguments frequently ended in semantics—a debate over the meaning of meaning. . . .

Franklin D. Roosevelt, for his part, tried to balance idealism with practicality. As governor of New York he had said that "to these unfortunate citizens aid must be extended by government, not as a matter of charity, but as a matter of social duty." Nonetheless, while still governor, he had also said: "The dole method of relief for unemployment is not only repugnant to all sound principles of social economics, but is contrary to every principle of American citizenship and of sound government. American labor seeks no charity, but only a chance to work for its living."

Harry Hopkins agreed with Roosevelt. He detested direct relief. Work relief, said Hopkins, "preserves a man's morale. It saves his skill. It gives him a chance to do something socially useful." Both the President and his key relief administrator were keenly aware that the Federal Emergency Relief Administration was a quick thrust at a massive problem calling for greater leverage. On November 27, 1934, Roosevelt wrote to a friend: "What I am seeking is the abolition of relief altogether. I cannot say so out loud yet but I hope to substitute work for relief. . . ."

The heavily Democratic Seventy-fourth Congress opened its first session on January 3, 1935, and one day later the President delivered his annual message. After reporting that more than $2 billion had been spent in direct relief, he went on to say: "The federal government must and shall quit this business of relief. I am not willing that the vitality of our people be further sapped by the giving of cash, of market baskets. . . ."

Roosevelt then announced that he intended to establish a new relief system. . . . This new program, the President added, would be guided by the following principles:

1. All work to be as useful and permanent as possible.
2. Relief wages to be higher than those paid under the FERA and CWA, but not so high as to discourage men from taking jobs in private industry.
3. More money to be spent on wages than on materials. . . .

On April 5, 1935, the Senate and House passed a joint resolution giving the President the relief money he had sought—$4 billion in new funds and $880,000,000 unused from previous appropriations. This $4.8 billion was the largest peacetime appropriation in American history. One day later the bill was signed by the Vice President and the Speaker of the House and put on a plane bound for Jacksonville, Florida. Roosevelt, who had been fishing off the coast, came back to port, boarded a north-bound train and on April 8 signed the measure to the contrapuntal clickety clack of train wheels. . . .

On May 6, 1935, the President issued an executive order establishing the Works Progress Administration. As of that date no one could foretell that, with one change of name, it would continue in existence until June 30, 1943—eight years and two months.

The WPA was designed as the key agency in the government's entire works program, which came to include a total of forty federal agencies. It withdrew the federal government from the field of direct relief, leaving that responsibility to the various states and cities. Roosevelt flatly said that the principal purpose of the WPA was to provide work.

Hopkins began this new job with his usual demonic energy. At one of the first WPA staff meetings he raised the question of whether women should be paid the same wages as men. Everyone said no. Everyone, that is, except Hopkins' assistant administrator, Aubrey Williams, who said he thought women should be paid equal wages with men.

"Oh, you do?" Hopkins barked. "What makes you think you could get away with it?"

Williams said he did not care whether he could get away with it or not.

"Do you know who disagrees with you?" Hopkins persisted. "The secretary of labor—a woman!"

"Pay 'em the same!" Williams said doggedly.

Hopkins, who was testing his assistant, baited him further until Williams became silent and glum.

Then Hopkins ended the session with the words: "Well, fellows, thank you very much. Aubrey's right about this, and that's what we'll do."

As the others walked out, Hopkins turned to Williams, smiled a lopsided smile and asked: "What's wrong with those other fellows?"

The WPA paid wages slightly higher than the grants for direct relief but lower than wages prevailing in private industry. There were exceptions, however, for the WPA refused to lower its rates to meet the substandard ones prevailing in certain districts, notably in the South. For wage-fixing purposes the country was divided into four regions. Monthly rates of pay in each region varied according to the character of the work and to the population. Unskilled work paid as little as $19 a month while professional and technical jobs paid up to $94 a month—and sometimes slightly higher.

The nerve center of the WPA—and thus of the nation's entire works program—was located in the Walker-Johnson Building in Washington at 1734 New York Avenue, NW, a few blocks from the White House. It was a dirty, shabby old place with a blind newsdealer on its front steps. Upon entering it one smelled antiseptic odors and then rode in an elevator so rickety it was frightening. But Hopkins, who detested elegance, felt this was what a relief office should be like. . . .

In the aggregate the WPA did spend a great deal of money, but, as has been indicated, individual wages were hardly lavish. In December 1935, WPA workers averaged $41.57 a month. Between 60 and 70 percent of those on the rolls were unskilled workers.

But among the skilled workers were accountants, architects, bricklayers, biologists, carpenters, chemists, dentists, draftsmen, dieticians, electricians, engravers, foresters, firemen, geologists, gardeners, hoisting engineers, housekeepers, instrument men, ironworkers, jackhammer operators, janitors, kettlemen, kitchen maids, librarians, linotypers, locksmiths, lumbermen, millwrights, machinists, musicians, nurses, nutritionists, oilers, painters, plasterers, plumbers, patternmakers, photographers, printers, physicians, quarry men, quilters, riveters, roofers, roadmakers, riggers, sculptors, seamstresses, stonemasons, stenographers, statisticians, teamsters, truck drivers, teachers, tabulators, upholsterers, veterinarians, welders, woodchoppers, waiters, watchmen, X-ray technicians—and others.

During its more than eight years of existence, the WPA employed 8,500,000 different people in more than 3,000 counties and spent in excess of $11 billion on a total of 1,410,000 projects. It was by far the biggest employer and spender of all the New Deal agencies. WPA workers built 651,087 miles of highways, roads and streets; constructed, repaired or improved 124,031 bridges; erected 125,110 public buildings; created 8,192 public parks; built or improved 853 airports. Besides its immediate importance to the people who worked on this massive program, Americans were using and enjoying some of these facilities one-third of a century later. More than anything else, however, the WPA was an escape hatch from the trap of the Depression.

Early in the program Roosevelt had warned: "It must be recognized that when an enterprise of this character is extended over more than three thousand counties throughout the nation, there may be occasional instances of inefficiency, bad management, or misuse of funds." Cases of this kind did, of course, occur. A few Senators, Congressmen, governors, state WPA directors and small-time politicians tried to enrich themselves and enhance their power by means of the WPA.

Harry Hopkins was incorruptible and, for a man who liked to spend money, strangely economy-minded in some ways. Loathing organizational charts and fossilized bureaucratic procedures, he ran the national organization with the smallest possible staff and the smallest possible overhead. He got help to the people as directly and quickly as possible. "Hunger is not debatable," he liked to say. "People don't eat in the long run—they eat every day.". . .

The New Deal did more to promote culture than any previous administration in the history of this nation. . . .

The WPA's arts division consisted of four separate programs. As overall supervisor of them Harry Hopkins chose Jacob Baker, liberal in his tastes and a believer in experimentation. The music program was headed by Nikolai Sokoloff, conductor of the Cleveland Orchestra and a frequent guest conductor of many other symphony orchestras throughout the nation. The art program was directed by Holger Cahill, an art critic, authority on folk art and an outstanding museum technician. The theater project was headed by Hallie Flanagan. The writers' program was headed by Henry Alsberg, an editorial writer for the New York *Evening Post* and a foreign correspondent for liberal magazines.

Alsberg told Hopkins that the WPA could make a lasting cultural contribution to the nation if the men and women employed by the writers' project were put to work preparing a series of guidebooks about the states, one for each state. He pointed out that the latest issue of Baedeker's guide to America had been issued in 1909—so outdated that it advised Europeans planning to visit this land to bring along matches, buttons, and dress gloves. Agreeing, Hopkins gave Alsberg the word to launch the American Guide Series. . . .

Alsberg began hiring unemployed writers and editors, librarians and photographers, until at last he had 7,500 people at work. A director was named for each of the forty-eight states, and they, in turn, received the help of local reporters, historians, genealogists, librarians and businessmen. Each did his part in the massive chore of researching, writing, editing and publishing the state guidebooks, and soon copy was pouring into the Washington headquarters at the rate of 50,000 words a day. . . .

One of the greatest accomplishments of the writers' project was its historical records survey, instituted in 1936. Relief workers took inventories of local public records stored in city hall cellars, library lofts and courthouse garrets. They indexed old newspaper files. They made abstracts of court cases containing nuggets of local history. They examined business archives, looked through church records, studied tombstones to verify vital statistics. The perfection of microfilm had made it possible for them to photograph, and thus to preserve, millions of pages crumbling into decay. They measured, sketched, diagrammed and photographed 2,300 historic buildings.

In 1937 the American Guide Series became a reality with publication of the first of the set, a book about Idaho. By the end of its life the project produced 378 books and pamphlets—a volume for each of the forty-eight states, 30 about our major cities, others about historic waterways and highways, such as *The Oregon Trail.* Various commercial and university publishers issued these works, with royalties either paying for everything except labor costs or going into the federal treasury.

In a *New Republic* article Robert Cantwell said of the writers' project: "The least publicized of the art projects, it may emerge as the most influential and valuable of them all." Nearly one-third of a century later the American Guide Series continued to be a prime source of information for every serious writer of American history.

Musicians were suffering even before the beginning of the Depression. The popularity of radio, the advent of talking movies and the death of vaudeville had thrown 50,000 musical performers out of work. After the Crash there were few Americans who could afford music lessons for their children, so music teachers lost their pupils or had to cut their fees for the few who remained. Music publishers, recording companies and manufacturers of musical instruments earned less or suffered heavy losses. To most of these people the federal music project, under Nikolai Sokoloff, came as salvation.

Established in July, 1935, the music program put musicians to work in orchestras and bands, in chamber music and choral and operatic groups throughout the nation. Forty-five cities obtained their own WPA symphony orchestra, while 110 other cities got orchestras with more than thirty-five players. Just before the start of a concert by a WPA orchestra in Florida, a violinist apologized to the audience on behalf of his colleagues and himself for the quality of their concert. He explained that their fingers were stiff because of their previous relief job—working on a road gang.

When the music project was at its peak it supported 15,000 people. They gave a total of 150,000 programs heard by more than 100,000,000 people, many of whom had been unfamiliar with anything but popular songs. Each month more than 500,000 pupils attended free music classes. WPA musical groups relieved the boredom of hospital patients. Project workers dug out and recorded American folk music—the Cajun songs of Louisiana, the Indian-flavored songs of early Oklahoma, the British-born ballads of Kentucky mountaineers, the African-inspired songs of Mississippi bayous.

Although the program was designed to help performers more than composers, since the former outnumbered the latter, it established a composers' forum-laboratory. Before the project was terminated, 1,400 native composers produced 4,915 original compositions—some bad, many mediocre, a few hailed by music critics as "distinguished." One prominent critic, Deems Taylor, wrote in 1935: "It is safe to say that during the past two years the WPA orchestras alone have probably performed more American music than our other symphony orchestras, combined, during the past ten."

Thanks to this project, music became democratized in this country. In about the year 1915 there had been only 17 symphony orchestras in the United States; by 1939 there were more than 270. Europe's leadership in the musical world, together with its snobbish aloofness, had been shattered.

The WPA art project was set up by Holger Cahill on "the principle that it is not the solitary genius but a sound general movement which maintains art as a vital, functioning part of any cultural scheme."

All a person had to do to get on the art project was to obtain proof from local authorities that he needed relief and that he had once had some connection, however tenuous, with the world of art. As a result, of the more than 5,000 people ultimately hired, fewer than half ever painted a picture, sculpted a statue or decorated a building with a mural. This does not mean that the art program was a boondoggle. While creativity flowered among the great artists—Jackson Pollock, Aaron Bohrod, Ben Shahn, Willem de Kooning, Concetta Scaravaglione, Anna Walinska and the like—those with limited talent taught free art classes, photographed historic houses, painted posters and designed stage sets for the federal theater project. Others maintained sixty-six community art centers which attracted a total of 6,000,000 visitors.

In addition to the invaluable and enduring artworks produced by the most gifted relief workers, the art project left all of us a monumental *Index of American Design*. This part of the program was directed by Constance Rourke and gave employment to about 1,000 artists. Wishing to find and preserve specimens of early American arts and crafts, they ransacked New England farmhouses, museums, antique shops, historical societies, Shaker barns, and California missions. They photographed or painted every treasure they discovered—embroidered seat covers, oil paintings, watercolors, carved figureheads, antique quilts and samplers, weather vanes and such. Collectively, these artists produced 7,000 illustrations of every variety of native American art.

On May 16, 1935, the phone rang in the Poughkeepsie, New York, home of a small, red-headed middle-aged woman named Hallie Flanagan. When she answered it, she heard Jacob Baker, the head of the WPA's four arts program, saying that he was calling from Washington. "Mr. Hopkins wants you to come to Washington to talk about unemployed actors," Baker said. Miss Flanagan was in charge of Vassar College's Experimental Theatre. She knew Hopkins, for they had grown up together in Grinnell, Iowa, and attended the same college. . . .

Actors, as Miss Flanagan knew, were suffering severe hardships. Like musicians, many had lost their jobs with the death of vaudeville and the birth of the talkies. No one knew for sure just how many performers were out of work. Actors Equity said there were 5,000 unemployed actors in New York City alone, while WPA officials put the nationwide total at 20,000 to 30,000 people. In Harlem black entertainers were kissing the Tree of Hope, a local talisman, for luck.

In 1931 two-thirds of Manhattan's playhouses were shut. During the 1932–33 season eight out of every ten new plays failed. The Shuberts had plunged into receivership. In 1932 no less than 22,000 people registered with Hollywood casting bureaus. *Variety* had reduced its price from 25 to 15 cents. . . .

On July 27, 1935, Miss Flanagan was sworn in as administrator of the new federal theater project. The ceremony was held in a Washington playhouse called the old Auditorium, a vast hulk of a building now abuzz with rushing people, whirring electric fans, riveting machines and cement-slapping plasterers. She sat down in a new cubicle and conferred with her staff of four about the possibility of getting at least 10,000 theater people back to work within a short time.

Since Broadway was the heart of the American theater, Miss Flanagan wanted an especially able man to direct the New York City unit of her project, and her choice was Elmer Rice. The forty-three-year-old Rice had proved himself as a playwright, stage director and novelist. With the deepening of the Depression, his plays had shifted from realistic reporting to social and political themes. Rice already had sent Hopkins a letter outlining a plan for the establishment of a national theater, but he hesitated about accepting Miss Flanagan's offer because he was about to begin writing another novel.

"What could we do with all the actors?" he asked her. "Even if we had twenty plays in rehearsal at once, with thirty in a cast, that would keep only a fraction of them busy."

Badly wanting Rice, she grabbed at a straw and impulsively said: "We wouldn't use them all in plays. We could do *Living Newspapers*. We could dramatize the news with living actors, light, music, movement."

This idea appealed to Rice, who cried: "Yes. And I can get the Newspaper Guild to back it!". . .

Elmer Rice was paid $260 a month on the theory that he worked thirteen days at $20 a day, but actually he worked from early morning until late at night every day of the month, including Sundays. It amused him to get nasty letters accusing him of making a fortune on a soft government job. Sometimes he opened press conferences by saying to reporters: "Well, what do you vultures want to swoop down on now?"

At first jobs were limited to entertainers on home relief rolls, but this excluded many who had been too proud to ask for help. Miss Flanagan and Rice managed to get this rule modified. She watched in horror as a man applying for work went mad and beat his head against a wall. A famous clown was taken on the WPA rolls, became so excited at the chance to work again that on the opening night of the show he suffered a stroke from which he never recovered. . . .

Into the project flocked young men and women who later became celebrated actors—Joseph Cotton, Orson Welles, Arthur Kennedy, Burt Lancaster, Arlene Francis, Ed Gardner, Rex Ingram, Canada Lee, Howard da Silva, William Bendix, Bil Baird. Another employed by the WPA, but not on the theater project, was Robert Ryan, who worked as a paving supervisor.

At its peak the program gave work to 12,700 theater people in twenty-nine states. Besides the actors themselves, there were producers, directors, playwrights, stagehands, electricians, propmen—all the crafts found in stage work. Hopkins had told Miss Flanagan: "We're for labor—first, last and all the time. WPA is labor—don't forget that." He insisted that $9 of every $10 be spent on wages, leaving only about $1 to meet operating costs. Nine out of every 10 people hired had to come from relief rolls. Wages averaged $83 a month, although some actors were paid up to $103.40 a month for performing in New York City. According to the place and circumstance, admission to WPA shows was free, or cost 10 cents, 25 cents, 50 cents, and in rare instances as much as $1.

The federal theater project presented many different kinds of shows—Negro drama, dance drama, children's theater, puppet and marionette shows, a documentary about syphilis, classical drama, modern drama, foreign language drama, musicals, Living Newspapers, pageants, vaudeville, circus, religious drama, spectacles, opera, and radio programs. . . .

George Bernard Shaw let the WPA stage his plays at $50 a week, writing to Miss Flanagan: "As long as you stick to your fifty-cents maximum for admission . . . you can play anything of mine you like unless you hear from me to the contrary. . . . Any author of serious plays who does not follow my example does not know what is good for him. I am not making a public-spirited sacrifice; I am jumping at an unprecedentedly good offer."

Eugene O'Neill released his own plays on similar terms, telling reporters: "The WPA units can present important plays before audiences that never before have seen an actual stage production. The possibilities in this respect are thrilling. . . . These units are translating into action the fact that the government has an obligation to give a reasonable amount of encouragement and assistance to cultural undertakings."

Sinclair Lewis had been offered a lot of money by commercial theater producers to make a play out of his novel *It Can't Happen Here.* Instead, he offered it to WPA. The red-headed writer told reporters: "I prefer to give it to the federal theater for two reasons: first, because of my tremendous enthusiasm for its work and, second, because I know I can depend on the federal theater for a non-partisan point of view."

Lewis and his collaborators began their rewrite work in the Essex House on Manhattan's Central Park South—but not at government expense. Much newspaper space was given to the fact that this famous author was working on a play for the WPA. Some editorial writers and readers felt that his study of the rise of an American dictator was Communist-inspired, or the result of Fascism, or a plot to reelect Roosevelt, or a scheme to defeat him. Huey Long had been dead only about a year, so New Orleans officials would not book this show into a city where the late dictator still had many friends. *It Can't Happen Here* became so controversial that before it premiered, the nation's newspapers printed 78,000 lines of pro and con comment about the production.

On October 27, 1936, the play opened simultaneously in twenty-one theaters in seventeen states—the most multiple and extensive first night in the history of the American theater. From Bridgeport and Cleveland, Miami and Birmingham, Detroit and Indianapolis—from each of the several cities came reports that audiences had received the play with wild enthusiasm. In its first few weeks it drew more than a quarter million spectators.

In the New York *Times* Brooks Atkinson wrote: "Mr. Lewis has a story to tell that is calculated to make the blood of a liberal run pretty cold. . . . *It Can't Happen Here* ought to scare the daylights out of the heedless Americans who believe, as this column does, that it can't happen here as long as Mr. Lewis keeps his health."

A smash hit, the play was presented here and there across the country for a total of 260 weeks. . . .

The federal theater project was sponsored and patronized by unions and schools, colleges and universities, Catholics and Jews, Protestants and civic groups, industrial and philanthropic organizations. It brought the living theater to youths who never before had seen flesh-and-blood actors. In the *Federal Theater Magazine* a writer described this huge audience in these words: "We're a hundred thousand kids who never saw a play before. We're students in colleges, housewives in the Bronx, lumberjacks in Oregon, sharecroppers in Georgia. We're rich and poor, old and young, sick and well. We're America and this is our theatre.". . .

Earlier, while the government was setting up the Civilian Conservation Corps, Eleanor Roosevelt lamented that it did nothing for girls. She wanted single, jobless women brought together in urban clubs somewhat similar to CCC camps, but got nowhere. Trying to go it alone, she held a series of meetings in her Manhattan home with a group of about thirty underprivileged young people.

Ensnared in the Depression, few young men and women could afford to attend college, while at the same time they found it increasingly difficult to get jobs. Between 1920 and 1930 college attendance had more than doubled, but from 1932 to 1934 college enrollment fell by 10 percent. High schools, colleges and universities slashed their budgets and cut the salaries of teachers, many of whom went for months without getting a paycheck. By the spring of

1935 a total of 3,000,000 people between the ages of sixteen and twenty-five were on relief—an average of 1 in 7. Even more distressing was the fact that many youths became transients; on a single day in May, 1935, the WPA's transient service counted 54,000 of them registered at its camps and shelters.

Besides the intrinsic misery of this situation, it was also politically dangerous. One confused young man said: "If someone came along with a line of stuff in which I could really believe, I'd follow him pretty nearly anywhere." In Germany and Italy millions of youths had harkened to the evil music of those corrupt pipers, Hitler and Mussolini.

Here in America the President's wife felt it would be wise to create a kind of junior CCC or WPA to help young people and give them a sense of direction. Perhaps such a program could be set up as a subdivision of the WPA. She explained her plan to Harry Hopkins and his assistant, Aubrey Williams, who liked it so much that they expanded on it and outlined what became the National Youth Administration. However, they hesitated about presenting the idea to the President. Hopkins told Mrs. Roosevelt: "There may be many people against the establishment of such an agency in the government, and there may be bad political repercussions. We do not know that the country will accept it. We do not even like to ask the President, because we do not think he should be put in a position where he has to say officially 'yes' or 'no' now."

One night Eleanor Roosevelt entered her husband's bedroom as he was about to go to sleep. When he saw the expression on her face, he smiled and said: "Well, well—what new program is hanging fire?"

She described the idea for the National Youth Administration, frankly adding that Hopkins was unsure of the wisdom of pushing it.

The President asked: "Do you think it is right to do this?"

"It will be a great help to the young people, Franklin. But I don't want you to forget that Harry Hopkins thinks it may be unwise politically. Some people might say it's like the way Hitler is regimenting German youths."

This, as Mrs. Roosevelt may have intended, was a challenge to the President.

"If it is the right thing to do for the young people," he said, looking up at her, "then it should be done. I guess we can stand the criticism, and I doubt if our youth can be regimented in this way or in any other way."

On June 26, 1935, President Roosevelt issued an executive order creating the National Youth Administration. Its purpose was to administer a relief and unemployment program for young women between the ages of sixteen and twenty-five, for young men of this age who were physically unsuited for CCC labor, for the children of rural families, for those no longer attending school regularly and for needy students who wanted to finish their educations but lacked the means. The NYA was set up as a part of the WPA. As executive director of this new agency the President appointed Aubrey Williams. . . .

Now he [Williams] faced an enormous task. The first fiscal year Williams had $41.2 million to spend, and in 1936 he got $68 million more. Because the president wanted the NYA to be as decentralized as possible, separate administrations were set up in each of the forty-eight states and a special one in New

York City, owing to its size. These forty-nine administrations were supplemented by district and local directors, together with advisory committees throughout the nation.

Just about the time of the creation of the NYA, a twenty-six-year-old Texan by the name of Lyndon B. Johnson suffered a shock. For nearly three years he had worked in Washington as secretary to Representative Richard M. Kleberg of Texas. Johnson, an aggressive young man, pretty much dominated his boss, and when Mrs. Kleberg told her husband that the boy was planning to run against him in the next election, the enraged Congressman fired his secretary. Johnson scurried to Representative Maury Maverick of Texas with the sad news that he was just out of a job. Maverick, who liked Johnson, knew that President Roosevelt was about to name forty-eight state NYA directors.

On easy terms with Roosevelt, Maverick went to him to say he knew just the man to direct the Texas NYA—Lyndon Johnson. The President was agreeable until he learned that Johnson was only twenty-six years old. He scoffed that he would not give such an important position to a child, but the Texas Congressman persisted. "After all," said Maverick, "you need someone who's honestly interested in helping his own generation work their way through high school and college and improve themselves, rather than sit around unemployed." In July, 1935, President Roosevelt named Lyndon Baines Johnson the head of the NYA in Texas.

Johnson, who hero-worshiped Roosevelt then and thereafter, flew from Washington to Texas and opened state headquarters of the NYA on the sixth floor of the shabby Littlefield Building in Austin. Then he flew back to the national capital to attend the first nationwide meeting of state NYA directors, called into session by Aubrey Williams on August 20, 1935. Johnson was not shy about telling reporters that he was the youngest of all the state directors and was delighted when this news item was published in newspapers from coast to coast. Also making a good impression on Williams, he obtained more funds for Texas than had originally been allocated to it. . . .

During the twenty months that Lyndon B. Johnson served as state director of the NYA in Texas, he helped 18,000 students by giving them money to go to school and by arranging part-time work in colleges at 35 cents an hour. He also aided 12,000 out-of-school youngsters, seeing that they learned trades and did useful work on public projects. Since Texas was the biggest state in the union, Johnson spent much of his time traveling, and the contacts he made were of use to him in furthering his political career.

In the spring of 1937 he decided to run for Congress. When the news reached Aubrey Williams in the national capital, Williams called the White House and spoke on the phone with Presidential aide Tommy Corcoran.

"Tommy," said Williams, "you've got to get the President to make this guy Johnson lay off running for the Congressional seat down in Austin. He's my whole youth program in Texas, and if he quits, I have no program down there."

Corcoran spoke to Roosevelt, who gave him orders to make sure that Johnson stuck to his NYA job and forgot about running for Congress. But before

Corcoran could locate Johnson to relay this word from on high, LBJ had quit his NYA post and filed for Congress.

Richard M. Nixon, who succeeded Johnson as President in 1969, also bene-fited from the New Deal. In September, 1934, Nixon arrived in Durham, North Carolina, to enter Duke University's new law school. Having been grad-uated second in his class from Whittier College in California, the twenty-one-year-old student had been given a $200 tuition grant; to keep it he had to maintain a B average at Duke. Because of the Depression, his family was able to send him only $35 a month. To supplement this grant and allowance, Nixon accepted aid from the National Youth Administration, earning thirty-five cents an hour for doing research in the law library. . . .

With three other students he rented a room in a ramshackle farmhouse a mile from the campus and set in the midst of tall pines. They shared two double beds in a big room heated by an old iron potbellied stove. Their quarters lacked any lights, so Nixon studied in the law library. It was also without water, so he showered in the university gym. He used his trunk for a closet, could afford only secondhand books and paid twenty-five cents a meal in a boardinghouse.

Helen Gahagan Douglas, with whom Nixon later feuded politically, was a member of the California state committee of the NYA. Eric F. Goldman, who developed into a noted historian and educator, got through Johns Hopkins University at Baltimore with NYA help. Raymond Clapper was another who had reason to be grateful to the NYA. After Clapper became a famous colum-nist, he wrote that "some of our leading citizens who are so violently opposed to institutions like the National Youth Administration are not so opposed to subsidizing college students for football teams."

Arthur Miller, who subsequently won renown as a dramatist, got NYA aid while attending the University of Michigan. Of those days he later wrote:

> I loved the idea of being separated from the nation, because the spirit of the na-tion, like its soil, was being blown by crazy winds. Friends of mine in New York, one of them a *cum laude* from Columbia, were aspiring to the city firemen's exam; but in Ann Arbor I saw that if it came to the worst a man could live on nothing for a long time.
>
> I earned $15 a month for feeding a building full of mice—the National Youth Administration footing the bill—and out of it I paid $1.75 a week for my room and squeezed the rest for my Granger tobacco (two packs for thirteen cents), my books, laundry and movies. For my meals I washed dishes in the co-op cafeteria. My eyeglasses were supplied by the Health Service, and my teeth were fixed for the cost of materials. The girls paid for themselves including the one I married.

While still in college, Miller wrote several plays. In the spring of 1938 he was graduated, and two months later he was on relief. Then he returned to his hometown, New York City, where he joined the federal theater project. Be-fore the project could present his first play, though, its activities were ended.

A sampling of 150 NYA work projects for out-of-school youths showed that the young men and women employed on them engaged in 169 types of work. Among other things, they installed floodlights in airports, built athletic courts, beautified parks, made brooms, canned vegetables and fruits, took care of infants, cleaned bricks for reuse, cleaned lagoons, cleared land, clipped newspapers in libraries, cooked for lunchrooms, excavated for artifacts, made furniture, worked as nurses, laid pipes, planted grass and so on.

In Fort Morgan, Colorado, fifty-two NYA boys converted a dump into a public recreation ground with 40 acres of grass, shrubs, trees and a new 5-acre swimming pool. At Gloucester, Massachusetts, rubber-booted NYA youths took eggs from lobsters to restock a federal fish hatchery. On the Onondaga Indian reservation in New York State some Indian boys working for the NYA chopped down trees, shaped logs and built a summer camp for children. At the Fort Valley Normal and Industrial School in Georgia a group of Negro boys and girls, few of whom had finished grade school, were paid by the NYA as they were trained in farming, homemaking, and various trades. In the Flint-Goodridge Hospital in New Orleans black NYA girls helped regular staff members in every department of the hospital.

Under NYA rules the youths were to work no more than eight hours a day, forty hours a week or seventy hours a month. They earned from $10 to $25 a month, depending on prevailing local wage standards. What did they do with these meager earnings? First they helped their families. Then they bought themselves new clothes, since they had worn nothing but hand-me-down clothing for years. Telling what the NYA meant to him, one boy said: "Maybe you don't know what it's like to come home and have everyone looking at you, and you know what they're thinking, even if they don't say it, 'He didn't find a job.' It gets terrible. You just don't want to come home. . . . But a guy's gotta eat some place and you gotta sleep some place. . . . I tell you, the first time I walked in the front door with my paycheck, I was somebody!". . .

However, to some Americans who ate three square meals a day without the help of the government, the overall program of the Works Progress Administration seemed less than noble. One of the popular pastimes was telling WPA jokes like the following:

"A farmer asked a druggist for 'some of that WPA poison. It won't kill squirrels, but it will make them so lazy I can just stomp them to death.' "

"A WPA worker sued the government because he hurt himself when the shovel he was leaning on broke."

"Why is a WPA worker like King Solomon? . . . Because he takes his pick and goes to bed."

"I hear Harry Hopkins is planning to equip all of his WPA workers with rubber-handled shovels."

"Don't shoot our still life—it may be a WPA worker at work."

"There's a new cure for cancer, but they can't get any of it. It's sweat from a WPA worker."

Some of these jokes were thought up by professional comedians, but at last the American Federation of Actors ordered all its members to stop poking fun at the WPA. . . .

As has been said, the WPA employed 8,500,000 people in 1,410,000 projects in more than 3,000 counties at a cost of more than $11 billion. Naturally, in a program of such magnitude there were bound to be inequities and injustice, scandals and corruption. Campaigning by WPA staff members in Pennsylvania, Kentucky and Tennessee in the 1938 Congressional elections led to adverse comment and passage of the Hatch Act of July, 1939, curbing "pernicious political activities" by federal appointees. President Roosevelt discharged at least one state WPA director and began keeping a closer eye on the others.

Harry Hopkins was loved and hated by relief workers and politicians according to how well the WPA treated them. While he certainly had personal preferences in which he indulged, he was totally honest and therefore beyond the reach of provable scandal. Except for betting on the horses and lifting a glass of champagne with rich friends, he maintained his modest way of life. None of that $11 billion ever found its way into his pockets. . . .

In 1939 the Works Progress Administration had its name changed to the Works Projects Administration, and it continued in existence until June 30, 1943.

This vast, long-lived agency created enduring public works, helped the United States prepare for the approaching war, increased purchasing power and left grateful memories among millions of Americans who, without it, might have lost their lives, their hope of salvation, their faith in their country.

REVIEW QUESTIONS

1. What impression do you get of Franklin Delano Roosevelt in the following areas as a result of reading this essay: his temperament, his social outlook, and his accomplishments?

2. What was the reasoning behind the establishment of these cultural programs by the New Deal? On what grounds were these programs criticized—and which ones came in for the greatest criticism? Do you feel these criticisms were justified? If so, why; if not, why not?

3. What was the total cost of the WPA program, and how many Americans benefited from it? Do you consider this cost excessive? If so, why; if not, why not?

4. Given a depression similar to that of the 1930s, would there be a controversy *today* over the need for work relief for the unemployed? If so, why; if not, why not?

FOR FURTHER READING

The amount of historical literature on Franklin Roosevelt and the New Deal is staggering. A good general introduction is William E. Leuchtenberg, *Franklin D. Roo-*

sevelt and the New Deal (1963). The last two volumes of Arthur Schlesinger, Jr.'s three-volume work *The Age of Roosevelt* (1957–1960) are more detailed. Paul Conkin has written a brief, thought-provoking criticism of the New Deal in *The New Deal* (1967). Joseph Lash, *Dealers and Dreamers: A New Look at the New Deal* (1988), is more sympathetic. Geoffrey Ward has written two biographical works on FDR, *Before the Trumpet: Young Franklin Roosevelt* (1985) and *A First Class Temperament: The Emergence of Franklin Roosevelt* (1989). Kenneth S. Davis has also produced a two-book account in *FDR: The New Deal Years, 1933–1937* (1986) and *FDR: Into the Storm, 1937–1940* (1993). Some of the books dealing with workers in the Depression are Irving Bernstein, *A Caring Society: The New Deal, the Worker, and the Great Depression* (1985), and *Turbulent Years: A History of the American Worker, 1933–1941* (1969); and Lizabeth Cohen, *Making a New Deal: Industrial Workers in Chicago, 1919–1939* (1991). On the WPA see Jerre Mangione, *The Dream and the Deal: The Federal Writers' Project, 1935–1943* (1972), and Karal A. Marling, *Wall-to-Wall America: A Cultural History of Post-Office Murals in the Great Depression* (1982), which shed much light on the socioartistic aspects of the New Deal era.

Culver, Inc.

A military wedding, 1944. Family allotments and full employment made early marriage possible for millions.

15

The Home Front During World War II

RICHARD R. LINGEMAN

In a number of ways, World War II was an ideal war for the American people. The United States suffered none of the devastation that was visited on other warring nations, and American casualties were relatively light compared to those incurred by Britain, Russia, Germany, Japan, or China. There was less internal dissent about the wisdom or morality of the war than for any other conflict in American history. Increased spending for defense purposes brought the country out of the depression of the 1930s and restored prosperity. There were jobs for all and even a labor shortage. It is true that some consumer goods like automobiles and large appliances were unavailable because the factories that used to produce them were converted to war production. It is also true that other goods were rationed and that wage and price controls were imposed for the duration of the war. But the vast majority of Americans put up with wartime restrictions and shortages with good humor, accepting them as part of the price of victory. The general feeling was that we were engaged in an eminently worthwhile crusade on behalf of values that all Americans believed in, a crusade, in fact, in defense of civilization itself against German Nazism and Japanese militarism, forces that could readily be defined as truly evil.

While the war was going on, the United States was transformed in fundamental ways, not all of them by design. Full employment produced a substantial redistribution of income and a degree of economic security for middle-class Americans that became the foundation of postwar prosperity. Employment opportunities for women expanded enormously under the pressures created by the scarcity of labor. The same was true for African Americans, and the increased economic security and political clout that they achieved during the war years were important factors in the postwar civil rights movement. The war also saw a trend toward marriage at a younger age and an increase in the birth rate that was to persist into the postwar years and become known as the baby boom. Finally, World War II saw the first development and use of nuclear energy, holding out great hopes for a variety of peaceful uses, but also chilling prospects about what might happen if it were ever used again as a weapon. The following selection by Richard R. Lingeman shows how the war overseas affected many aspects of life within the United States for both good and ill.

The end of Hard Times was a motley caravan observed on Route 66, near Albuquerque, New Mexico, a road that was both *via doloroso* and passage of hope in John Steinbeck's *Grapes of Wrath*. Now, by the same route, in early 1942 the Okies were returning home. They came in old battered sedans and wheezing trucks and Model T's, sometimes twelve in a car, with all their possessions strapped on the tops and sides—rockers, buckets, shovels, stoves, bedding and springs. A few of the migrants were fleeing what they regarded as the imminent invasion of California by the Japanese, but the attitude of most was summed up by the man who said: "We ain't war-scared or anything like that, but a lot of others were pulling up and clearing out—not all of 'em understand—and Ma and I figured that if we was going back, now was the time. And, besides, Ed Lou is pretty big now and there ought to be a job for him in the oil fields and maybe for me too."

There were still more than 3,600,000 men unemployed. So the migration had momentum to gain as hillbillies from Appalachia, po' whites and Negroes from the South, farmers from the Midwest, garment workers from New York City picked up stakes and swarmed to the centers of war production.

The factories were rising up out of the raw, graded earth. The year 1942 was a year of frantic construction—more than $12 billion worth of it financed by the federal government, most of that on military camps, factories and installation of heavy machinery.

Near the little town of Starke, Florida, Camp Blanding had been erected in six months of feverish building. The workers turned the little town upside

Reprinted by permission of The Putnam Publishing Group from *Don't You Know There's a War On?*, by Richard Lingeman. Copyright © 1970 by Richard Lingeman.

down. "Why, people were sleeping in the streets, in the churches, in the trees," one resident recalled. The local grocer reminisced: "I had two stores and I sold groceries to the construction gangs. Two stores and I couldn't get any help. I worked 18 to 20 hours a day. My weekend profits were unbeliev- able, but I wouldn't want to go through it again. These fellows from the con- struction jobs—these carpenters and plumbers—were getting more money than they'd ever had in their lives and they had no place to spend it except in Starke. They were always hungry and they were always buying. It went for five or six months. We all got rich.". . .

To millions who had suffered the Depression years on relief, with occa- sional spells of odd jobs, this meant a time of opportunity, a time to pick up stakes and head to the war production centers, where there were steady jobs and good money to be had. In times of depression people tend to crawl into their holes and lick their wounds: in good times they head for the money. Es- timates of the number of Americans who left their homes to seek work else- where—in a different county, a different state or even a different region— ranged as high as 20,000,000. Probably the true number will never be known, but the Census Bureau attempted to capture the figures as best it could, be- fore the time was irretrievably gone. Based on a sample of 30,000 persons, the bureau took a demographic snapshot of the nation in March, 1945, and com- pared it with the prewar period. The Bureau estimated that by 1945, 15,300,000 persons were living in counties different from those in which they lived at Pearl Harbor; 7,700,000 of these migrants were living in a different state and 3,600,000 in a different part of the country. . . .

A major source of this migration was the farm, where, most agrarian econ- omists agreed, there were about 2,000,000 too many people in 1940. Between Pearl Harbor and March, 1945, nearly 5,500,000 people left the farms to live and work in the city (another 1,500,000 went into the armed forces). So effec- tively did the war siphon off the surplus that there were severe labor shortages on the farms, and in 1943–44, farm deferments were drastically increased by Selective Service. Women, city teen-agers, Axis war prisoners, interned Japan- ese-Americans and even GI's were pressed into service to help out with the harvest (a time when an additional 3,000,000 laborers are needed). The grip of the agriculture depression, which had held since the early twenties, was at last broken, and farmers' profits soared to record highs. With all this farm prosperity, a reverse migration trend was also operative, for some 2,500,000 people moved from nonfarm to farm areas, presumably to take up farmwork. Still, the farm population suffered a net loss of nearly 17 percent, not count- ing those in the armed forces. . . .

The greatest percentage of the immigrants settled in the immediate envi- rons of the city or cities, rather than inside the cities. This was reflected in the mushrooming growth of war worker towns and federal housing projects laid out where there were only rural fields before or, even worse, the ubiquitous

"New Hoovervilles"—trailer camps, tent settlements, shanty towns, "foxhole houses" and all other temporary conglomerations of people which sprang up over the countryside, often as satellites of the new war plants which had been erected on unused land. What this further meant was that these settlements were often located outside the service ambit of city and township governments. They were in a jurisdictional limbo, and there was no local government unit to take responsibility for them: further, many of the small towns to which they were often closest, hence most directly affected, lacked the resources with which to help them, even if they had wished to. Most of the migrants were nonvoting, nontaxpaying, nonhomeowning—in effect, political pariahs.

The geographical flow of the migration was strikingly skewed. Between April, 1940, and November, 1943, thirty-five states showed a net *loss* in total civilian population. The thirteen states that gained did so in numbers varying from California's 1,020,000 to Delaware's 7,240, but the geographical pattern was clear: By far the largest gainer was the Far West—the three coast states of California, Washington and Oregon, in that order, and to a much smaller degree, Arizona, Utah and Nevada. Next to the Pacific coast states, were three South Atlantic states: Maryland, Florida and Virginia. (In a class by itself was the District of Columbia, which gained 162,469 people; the federal government was also a booming war industry.)

The people went to the Far West because the opportunity was there, and the opportunity was there because the war money went West: California alone, with 6.2 percent of the population had by 1944 received war contracts totaling $15.8 billion, or 9.7 percent of the total for the nation. More than half the wartime shipbuilding took place in the three Pacific coast states, and nearly half the airplane manufacture. Because of its location on the sea and the existence of a prewar aircraft industry, California logically helped itself to a large chunk of this production. When the war ended, an estimated 1,000,000 war workers would be out of work, but till then California was truly the Golden State. All told its population increased by almost 2,000,000 between 1940 and 1945. Per capita income rose apace, reaching $1,740 annually, the highest in the nation. Here was the real gold rush in California's colorful history.

In sum the general pattern of the great national migration seemed to be this: Deep South po' whites to the shipyards around the Gulf crescent and in the Hampton Roads—Newport News—Norfolk complex and, farther North, to the Michigan manufacturing complexes.

Southern Negro sharecroppers and tenant farmers to the shipyards and factories of the West Coast; up the East Coast and to the factories of the Middle West.

Arkies, Okies, Tennessee, Kentucky and West-by-God-Virginia hillbillies to Illinois and Indiana and Michigan or to the southern oilfields and shipyards.

Kansas, Nebraska, Iowa, North and South Dakota plowboys to the great aircraft factories of the West Coast.

New York and other urban small-manufacturing workers to the Mid and Far West.

They came in cars, driving their rubber down to the rims and then paying exorbitant prices for used tires or retreads en route; or, more likely, they sat up or stood in the aisles for days and nights on crowded trains; or they packed their few working clothes into cardboard suitcases, made dust down the red dirt roads of the backwoods South to the crossroads store, and there waited for the bus to take them on the long trip to Pascagoula or Mobile or New Orleans. . . .

Everyone, on the move. Young wives with colicky babies, making the long journey to join their husbands at this new war job. Lone men, creased and weathered by work, and pink-cheeked young farm boys, migrating West because they heard there was plenty of work out there, sitting in the dark loneliness of the bus at night, only the glow of the orange spark of their cigarettes for company, their thoughts set free to range back and forth in time and space from regret to hope, over the vast American landscape of shadowy, empty hills and somber forests and little towns, their dark windows staring like empty-skulled eye sockets. In the next seat might be another man, he too sitting staring out at the landscape at night, he too coming from somewhere but off to somewhere else. The low voices hummed in talk of "where-are-you-going?" and "what's-it-like down there?". . .

Men were picking up stakes and moving on. Some left signs on the doors of closed businesses, letting their customers and friends and the whole world (and maybe even God) know that they had vamoosed, flown the coop, skedaddled, made tracks, hit the road, up and went. Signs that read like the one on the door of Joe's Country Lunch in Alabama:

> Maybe you don't know there's a war on. Have gone to see what it's all about. Meanwhile good luck and best wishes until we all come home. (Signed) Joe.

Or that of Lem Ah Toy, Chinese laundryman of Seattle:

> Go to war. Closed duration. Will clean shirts after clean Axis. Thank you. . . .

Signs, signs. Cocky, patriotic signs. The whole country, it seemed, was bursting out in a springtime of patriotism. . . . On bar mirrors in small dusty roadside taverns were soap-scrawled fighting slogans, like:

SLAP THE JAPS OFF THE MAP!
TO HELL WITH THE JAPS!
REMEMBER PEARL HARBOR!!!. . .

Young girls sitting in soda fountains adorned themselves with the unit patches of their boyfriends, sergeant's stripes or lieutenant's bars; the soda fountain they were lounging in purveyed such patriotic combinations as:

Blackout Sundae, Commando Sundae (War Workers, Get Your Vitamins the Delicious Way), Flying Fortress Sundae, Morale Builder and Paratroops Sundae (Goes Down Easy). In more and more windows hung service flags: red border, surrounding a white rectangle in which were one or more blue stars. Gold ones were making their appearance too. ("THE WAR DEPARTMENT RE-GRETS TO INFORM YOU THAT YOUR SON. . . . " The papers printed names on casualty lists, but never gave total killed and wounded until mid-1942.) Along with the service flags in homes and places of business, small towns had erected Honor Roll signs, with lengthening lists of names and branches of service of their local boys. . . .

At last the journey would near its end, and the migrant would catch a glimpse of the city of his destination: "snowy plains where great manufacturing plants jut up among their parking lots like mesas in the desert . . . mills that smear the sky with brown smoke out of tall cylindrical chimneys. . . ."

In green, gently rolling farmland, long, low dull-red brick factories rose up where bulldozers had scraped the land bare. Walter Wiard owned a farm and orchard in an area near Ypsilanti, Michigan, known as Willow Run after a stream that meandered through it on its way to the Huron River. In early 1941, Walter Wiard's land lay next to the site the Ford people had chosen for their new bomber plant, and the Ford people came to him and offered him a nice price for the land. Then Wiard watched as the giant groundbreaking machines went to work. Later he remarked: "It took me twenty-nine years to plant, cultivate and make that fine orchard. It took those tractors and bulldozers just twenty-nine minutes to tear it all down.". . .

So the workers arrived at the towns and cities where the war plants had risen and got off their crowded buses and walked the streets looking for a job, which was easy to find, and a bed, which was not. They might have landed in LA or San Francisco or Detroit or Pascagoula or Buffalo or Mobile. . . .

San Diego, once a quiet coastal town, was inundated with a lusty gang of workers and servicemen. For a new dry dock the Navy dug a hole that seemed as deep as the Grand Canyon, and one old resident described it as "a hole that you could have dumped most of this town [into] when I first saw it 70 years ago." Another graybeard, shaking his head in wonderment, recalled, "We used to go to bed by ten, or anyway, by eleven. Now some theaters and cafes never close! I remember it was like that in the Klondike. Now when boatloads of sailors hurry ashore, and all those soldiers from Fort Rosecrans and Camp Callan swarm in on payday, this town goes crazy. In one day they eat 50,000 hot dogs! Even shoe shine boys get the jitters. Sherman's Cafe has ten bars, and a dance floor so big that 5,000 of 'em can dance at once." Ten years before, exactly 6 men worked in San Diego's one aircraft factory; now there were 50,000. Any innocent tourist who decided to sit for a moment on a park bench would find himself approached by a series of people wanting to hire him to do some kind of job. . . .

Consider the town of Beaumont, Texas, which needed an incinerator. Next door to the Pennsylvania Shipyards stood a giant garbage dump which exhaled a miasma that could be smelled miles away when the wind was right. With the nauseating smells came flies. An official of the shipyards described what the flies were like: "The flies we get from the dump in the executive offices are so thick that it is almost impossible to concentrate on our duties. Twice a day the rooms are sprayed and the dead swept out with a broom. As soon as it gets warm we have to send people around the yard to spray the men on the job, or they would be eaten up by mosquitoes and flies."

The incinerator had been approved by the Federal Works Administration, and work had been begun. Then the WPB [War Production Board] refused the town a priority on a needed bit of equipment worth about $14,000. And so work stopped, and a half-finished incinerator stood in the midst of the stench and rotting garbage, a monument to government shortsightedness, while the stink grew and the danger of typhoid increased apace. . . .

Housing was an immediate and frequently insoluble problem for the migrant war workers. The government and private builders, largely with federally insured mortgage money, built a total of $7 billion of new housing, much of it temporary—barracks, trailers, demountable homes, dormitories, and the like. The NHA [National Housing Agency] calculated that it had to provide new or existing housing for 9,000,000 migratory workers and their families. To do this, it built and it scoured up existing vacant rooms and houses with the assistance of local community groups. Existing housing took care of 600,000 workers and their families. Over and above this, private companies built something more than 1,000,000 new units and the federal government 832,000 for a total of 1,800,000 units or housing for about 5,000,000 people: housing for at best 7,000,000 out of 9,000,000 migrants was provided; the remaining 2,000,000 presumably had to scour up their own shelter.

These bare statistics do not of course reflect the flesh and blood of the housing situation—the thousands who had to live in trailers, converted garages, tents, shacks, overpriced rooms, "hot beds," even their own cars during the early part of the war; the rent gouging that went on, even though rents were regulated by the Office of Price Administration; and the difficulties people with children had, especially the wives of servicemen who followed them to their training camps.

Landlord hostility to the newcomers was endemic in this sellers' market. An ad in a Fort Worth, Texas, newspaper revealed it: "Fur. Apt., no streetwalkers, home wreckers, drunks wanted; couple must present marriage certificate." On the West Coast, which had had an influx of more than 2,000,000 newcomers, it was chaotic. In San Francisco people lived in tents, basements, refrigerator lockers and automobiles. A city official reported in 1943: "Families are sleeping in garages, with mattresses right on cement floors and three, four, five to one bed." In Richmond, where the Kaiser shipyards were located, people were living under conditions that were worse than the Hoovervilles of the Depression. A trailer camp in San Pablo was crowded with people in trailers, tents and shacks; there was no sewage, and children waded about in a stagnant pond. A family of four adults and seven children lived in an 8-by-10-foot shack with two cots and one full-sized bed. A war housing project at Sausalito offered good living conditions for 4,500 people with self-government, low rentals and health insurance; but when a 90-mile-an-hour gale hit the area in January, 1943, all the tarpaper roofs of the temporary housing blew off. . . .

The philosophy underlying the governmental housing program was that "the government doesn't belong in the housing business," which meant that private housing interests were deferred to. In San Francisco, for example, which had a population increase of 200,000, local realtors had initially opposed war housing, saying there were 10,000 vacancies in the area. They were fearful of the competition, of course, but then, when the housing situation reached crisis proportions, they did a turnabout and blamed the federal government for not building enough war housing. And though they had relented on allowing government housing, they were adamant in their demands that only temporary housing, which could be torn down after the war, be built, lest property values suffer. This insistence that war workers be given only temporary or demountable housing was widespread and reflected not only the real estate man's pocketbook talking but also fear that the outsiders would stay after the war. As a result (and also because of the shortage of building materials), much government housing was jerry-built—instant slums, they might be called. . . .

One of the better federal housing projects was that erected near the Willow Run bomber plant. Because of opposition on the part of the townspeople in nearby Ypsilanti and the Ford Motor Company to a planned permanent residential area known as Bomber City . . . and material shortages, construction of alternate, temporary units was proposed and finally got under way in 1943. The first units—a dormitory for single workers called Willow Lodge—were open for occupancy by February, 1943. There followed trailer homes and prefabricated units for families, which were completed in August 1943. In all there was housing for about 14,000 workers—or one-third the number working at Willow Run plant at peak production.

By wartime housing standards these units were luxury housing, although they were not much to look at, being row upon row of gray, monotonous, flat-roofed buildings. The residents often had difficulty locating their own quarters. One lady always marked her house by a bedspring leaning against the adjoining unit. So much did she come to rely on the bedspring that she forgot the number of her own dwelling, and so one day, when inevitably, the bedspring was removed, she spent hours searching for her place. . . .

Most of the married workers with families overcame these minor hardships at Willow Run and turned it into a stable community. Still there were problems that could have been predicted among such a large and fluid population, many of them unmarried immigrants from the South. One reporter was critical of the "lack of wholesome recreational facilities and the generally drab social environment of Willow Run" which "stimulated private-party types of entertainment, featured by heavy drinking and promiscuous sex relations among fun-starved workers."

The center of the "promiscuous sex" was, not surprisingly, the Willow Lodge dormitory, which the FPHA [Federal Public Housing Agency] had opened to unmarried workers of both sexes. The result: "Professional gamblers and fast women quickly moved in for a clean-up." The co-ed policy was quickly dropped, however, and tenant policing, in cooperation with the FPHA, cleaned up the budding Gomorrah. . . .

Roving youngsters with nowhere to go were widespread. In Mobile, there were more than 2,000 children who didn't go to school at all, and one high school with an enrollment of 3,650 had a total of 8,217 absences during a single month. One movie theater owner joked with the local lady truant officer: "Miss Bessie, why don't you bring your teachers down here? My place is always full of children.". . .

Some towns, even without federal assistance, made an effort to set up day-care centers and nursery schools in a variety of ways, and the unions and war industries made an even greater contribution, the latter prodded by the labor shortage and the need to attract women workers, the former by a doctrine of demanding work rights. On the other hand, there was a distinct strain of prejudice against working mothers, who were regarded as selfishly materialistic; forgotten was the desperate need for them in the plants, the fact that many were servicemen's wives who needed to supplement their allotments, and the desire of others to take advantage of an opportunity to save up some money for the future. One of the leaders in the opposition to women working was the Catholic Church, which in many areas opposed nursery schools and day-care centers. . . .

Not unrelated to the shortage of day care, the overcrowded schools, the entry of youngsters into industry, and the lack of parental supervision was an increase in the incidence of crimes committed by teenagers (a term that came into wide currency during the war, along with juvenile delinquency). Juvenile arrests increased 20 percent in 1943; in some cities it was even higher—San Diego, for example, reported an increase of 55 percent among boys and 355 percent among girls. This was not a reflection of a nationwide crime wave, for crime on the whole—at least according to FBI figures—dropped during the war, with the exception of assault and rape. This was because the young men, who committed the largest percentage of crimes, were off in service. One of the heaviest areas of increase was among girls under seventeen who were arrested not only for various forms of "sex delinquency" such as prostitution, but also for violent crimes. In 1943 alone, the number of girls arrested for prostitution increased by 68 percent over the previous year.

Among the boys, it was largely theft and a striking incidence of acts of vandalism, destruction and violence. Some of these acts seemed a kind of acting-out of war fantasies—such as the thirteen-year-old "thrill saboteur" who put a stick of dynamite under a railroad track, lit the fuse and ran. The dynamite did not go off because he had attached no cap. He explained his action by saying he was attempting to close off all roads into the town and set himself up as "dictator."

With the girls, delinquency took the form of an aggressive promiscuity, and the lure was the glamor of a uniform. These "khaki-whacky" teenagers—some barely thirteen—were known as V-(for Victory) girls. They hung around bus depots, train stations, drugstores or wherever soldiers and sailors on leave might congregate, flirted with the boys, and propositioned them for dates. They were amateurs for the most part, the price of their favors being a movie, a dance, a Coke or some stronger drink. (A joke of the time ran: Sailor: "I'm going to Walgreen's to meet a girl." "What's her name?" "How should I know?")

The V-girls were easily recognizable in their Sloppy Joe sweaters, hair ribbons, anklets or bobby sox and saddle shoes, trying to look older with heavily made-up faces and blood-red lipstick. In Detroit the Navy had to build a fence around its armory, located in the city, to keep out not the enemy, but the bobby-soxers. In Chicago, sailors said it was worth one's life to try to walk from the Navy Pier to State Street, where the V-girls swarmed like flies. In Mobile, the girls themselves bought contraceptives for their dates, and when one druggist refused to sell them to a group of girls, he was jeered at and called an old fuddy-duddy.

The V-girls had their similarities all over the country. Some of them followed their lovers when they were transferred to another post, but many were left stranded when the boyfriend left. These often ended up working as waitresses or as barmaids in servicemen's hangouts, passing from one uniform to another.

There had always been teen-age girls who "did it," of course; war made them more visible, more independent, more mobile. One estimate had it that the V-girls represented at most only one in 1,700 out of their age group. More conservative girls, caught up in the transitoriness of wartime meetings and the glamor of a uniform, might also "do it," but they were more discreet and less promiscuous and conducted their assignations in more privacy.

The V-girl was next door to being a prostitute, yet there was about her at least a certain refreshing lack of cold professionalism. She offered a lonely GI transitory fun and excitement, devoid of the professional's matter-of-fact indifference. She could also, of course, offer him VD, for there was a higher incidence among the amateurs than among the professionals. In 1941, Congress, worried about the mother's vote, had passed the May Act, which forbade houses of prostitution near military bases. The result was that a lot of establishments were closed down and their inmates put out to walk the streets. These and their amateur competitors were found to inflict VD at a much higher rate than the house-based girls. . . .

The guardians of morality—whose view on the subject had been expressed in a 1942 *Reader's Digest* article by Gene Tunney entitled "The Bright Shield of Continence"—of course were against any kind of sex by soldiers with women other than their wives (if that) and would be shocked at the idea of brothels near Army camps where innocent young selectees would be exposed to unholy, irresistible temptation leading to inevitable corruption. (There was a similar logic running through the efforts of temperance groups to ban the distribution of beer to combat troops or its sale at PX's.)

As for the servicemen themselves, the Army traditionally liked to say that 15 percent "won't," 15 percent "will" and the remainder occasionally would succumb to temptation if the serpent insinuated itself (these figures derived from World War I). For that wavering 70 percent, the problems of finding "nice girls" in the camp towns, whether their intent was to deflower them or take them to the Sunday night meeting of the Epworth League, were often insuperable. . . .

Still, if the number of marriages and families formed is any sort of index to the degree of adherence to the American fundamental belief in marriage, the war period could be looked upon as fostering a salubrious moral climate. Beginning in 1940, as prosperity began to take hold and the Depression receded, the marriage rate began to rise abruptly—one is tempted to say alarmingly. . . .

The rush to wed was impelled as much by prosperity as it was by the war. A justice of the peace in Yuma, Arizona, a marriage town just over the California border, explained the sudden upswing in business in 1941. Not love but "aircraft did it for us," he said. "The figures began going up as soon as those boys were given employment in those plants at San Diego and Los Angeles and were taken off W.P.A. [Works Progress Administration]." Aircraft workers had been issued 90 percent of the licenses since the summer of 1941. "You see, when they were on the dole they had girls but no money. Once off the dole and once getting good money they began sending for the girls back home— girls in the Middle Western states, a great many of them. The girls wouldn't waste any time in coming in and then on weekends—we get the great rush on weekends—they'd all come hustling over to Yuma." It was the same story in Cincinnati, where weddings involving defense workers increased 51 percent; in Baltimore, where they were up 47 percent; and in Youngstown and Akron (up 17 percent) and Detroit (up 12 percent).

Of course, at that time a wife would also qualify as a dependent and men with dependents were deferred, until Congress discouraged this by establishing an allotment system in 1942. Under it, a man's wife would receive a minimum of $50 a month, $22 of which was deducted from his pay and $28 contributed by the government. To preserve family life and also perhaps to encourage a population increase to offset anticipated manpower losses in the war, the Selective Service Act deferred fathers until 1943, when manpower needs were so pressing that so-called pre–Pearl Harbor fathers were drafted.

Whether the Selective Service Act's policy was responsible or not (and we must give the parents some credit for initiative), the birthrate did go up during the war in a preview of the postwar baby boom when returning GI's set about forming families as fast as they could. Since the 1920s the birthrate, like the marriage rate, had been declining, but in 1943, it rose to 22 per 1,000—the highest in two decades. Most of these babies were "good-bye babies," conceived before the husband shipped out. Since the wife's allotment check would be increased upon the child's arrival, finances were no longer a major worry. In addition, there were compelling emotional reasons: The father, faced with the possibility of being killed in battle, was depositing a small guarantor to posterity, an assurance that someone would carry on his name, while the wife was given something to hold onto, a living, breathing symbol of their marriage. . . .

So they were married, this courageous young couple; perhaps they did know each other well and were in love, or perhaps they had met on a weekend pass and married in haste. Or perhaps the woman had eyed covetously the allotment check and looked forward to a life of some ease (and if he was killed, there was always the $10,000 to the widow from his life insurance). A $50-a-month allotment was of course not princely, but a GI overseas, with nothing else to spend it on, would usually send part of his regular pay home.

With the going rate only $50 per month per husband, a really ambitious girl might decide she needed four, five, six or more husbands to support her in any kind of style. Inevitably there developed the wartime racket of bigamous marriage for allotment checks. The girls who engaged in it came to be known as Allotment Annies. They posted themselves in bars around military bases and struck up acquaintances with lonely servicemen, otherwise known as shooting fish in a barrel. The men, desirous of the certainty that when they went off to battle, there would be a girl back home waiting for them, writing them V-mail letters, could often be had. So they married, the hero went off to war, and Annie stayed home and collected a lot of those pale blue-green checks from the U.S. Treasury Department.

A representative Allotment Annie was a hustling seventeen-year-old named Elvira Tayloe, who operated out of Norfolk, Virginia, and specialized in sailors shipping out from the large naval base there. Working as a hostess in a nightclub, she managed to snare six live ones and was working on her seventh when caught. This came about because a couple of sailors on liberty had met in an English pub, and as servicemen are wont, as the warm beer flowed, took out wallets and exchanged pictures of their gorgeous wives. Both were surprised, to put it mildly, when their pictures turned out to be identical, both of Elvira. A fight ensued over whose wife was being adulterous with whom. After the shore patrol had cooled them off, the boys joined forces, Elvira was traced and her career of cupidity brought to an end. . . .

Wartime marriage was hard, and the real miracle was that so many survived it. What the husband did overseas during off-duty hours is beyond our scope, but the girls back here were, largely, brave—and true. Not heroic; but they got by. Some, it is true, cracked up, or fell into dalliance with a representative of the local supply of 4-F's and joyriding war workers.

Life gave another portrait of the typical Army wife. Her husband is a lieutenant in India and her $180-a-month allotment makes her atypical right there, yet she adds some less dramatic hues to the portrait. She lives in a 3½-room apartment, rent $65 a month; she spends $45 a month on food for herself and the baby; she doesn't go out on dates, goes to parties unescorted and doesn't have a great deal of fun ("There's always some woman who thinks you're trying to take their man away"); sometimes at night she gets the blues and cries, but her baby son cheers her up a lot; she writes her husband a letter every day; she spends her evenings listening to the radio a lot (Guy Lombardo's is her favorite orchestra); when she hears "Soon"—"their song" in 1935, when they were married—she becomes sad. . . .

Dr. Jacob Sergi Kasanin, chief psychiatrist at Mount Zion Hospital in San Francisco, went so far as to identify a neurotic syndrome characteristic of servicemen's wives in 1945. Like many men who went overseas and cracked up before they reached combat (there were estimates that as high as one-half of the combat-trained troops avoided battle by "psyching out," getting a dishonorable discharge and the like), the wives had their own form of crackup. The physical symptoms included depression, colitis, heart palpitations, diarrhea, frequent headaches. Hardest hit were the recently married who had no children. They often developed "pathological reactions" in the form of resentment against their husband or even inability to recall what he looked like. (This was true even among fairly normal wives. One such wife decided to knit a sweater for her husband. As the months of separation drew on, her idea of her tall husband grew accordingly. He sent a picture of himself in the new sweater: it reached halfway down to his knees.) These women often had followed their husbands to his embarkation point; then in symbolic identity with him, they stayed there, and some couldn't take the loneliness, away from home, and began going to the bars, meeting other servicemen in transit. (The ratio of female alcoholics—defined as those who got into trouble with the police—to male alcoholics in Chicago was one to two, compared to one in five in 1931.)

For the more mature marriages, the ones in which the couple would pick up the pieces of their life and put them back together after long separation, there were still changes to be faced. A Navy doctor took a look at himself in the mirror one day and saw that he had grown bald and fat. He wrote about this to his wife, and she wrote back, sadly, "You will find that three years have done quite a bit to me, too."

The war, then, upset the social topography as it did the physical landscape; people met new places, new situations, new jobs, new living conditions, new ways of life, new temptations, new opportunities. There were social ills aplenty, but for all their novelty, they were perhaps the familiar ones; war simply exaggerated them and made them more visible. A sociologist writing on juvenile delinquency in *Federal Probation Officer* expressed a view that most diagnosticians of society would share:

> . . . many mothers of school-age boys and girls work in normal times; families are "broken" either physically or psychologically in normal times; children are exploited in normal times; some young people have always earned good wages and spent them unwisely; families always have moved from one neighborhood or community to another; some recreational facilities of an undesirable nature can be found in most communities in normal times. . . . Actually war does not create new problems with which we are unfamiliar. It accentuates old problems and in so doing the number of boys and girls affected is increased greatly.

One can only add that, in view of the familiarity of the problems and their increased magnitude, the governmental agencies might have done more to alleviate them. But of course, to Congress, stepped-up programs of social welfare would have smacked of "New Deal social experiments," and besides—don't you know there's a war on?

The citizenry out in the provinces who thought they had problems could take a measure of malicious satisfaction, if they wanted to, over the fact that their nation's capital was perhaps the most mixed-up, down-at-the-heels war town of them all. Its traditional industry was mainly government, of course, but everybody in the provinces knew that Washington's "bit" was doing the war's desk work—paper shuffling, tabulating, enumerating, filing. What people in Washington did was concoct complicated forms and schedules, issue directives, create agencies and, when they had some spare time, which was often, sit around and lobby, trade favors, peddle influence, gossip, boondoggle and, above all, take part in colorful feuds for the delectation of newspaper readers everywhere.

An exaggeration of course, but Washington was easy to poke fun at. It was a sort of sitting lame duck for conservative writers who gleefully pointed to whopping inefficiencies, pullulating paper work, labyrinthine bureaucracies, overlapping jurisdictions and a steady stream of executive directives. (FDR issued more executive orders during his Presidency than all previous Presidents combined.) "Washington Wonderland," they called it; "A red-tape-snarled, swarming, sweating metropolis"; "an insane asylum run by the inmates"; or in the words of a taxi driver: "the greatest goddamn insane asylum of the universe."

Overcrowding was Washington's most obvious physical symptom. Since 1940, more than 280,000 government job seekers had poured into town to hold down jobs as clerks and typists in the burgeoning wartime bureaucracy. Most of them were girls; most came from small towns all across the nation. They were drawn by the lure of higher wages—a girl could make $1,600 a year as a typist—and though they reveled in their newfound affluence, they could never get over the high prices, at which they clucked and shook their heads like tourists.

They were set down into a sort of Dogpatch with monuments, plagued by an acute housing shortage, overburdened and capricious public transportation, a cost of living that gobbled up their salaries (that government typist making $1,600 was lucky if she saved $25 in a year) and temporary office buildings that were as homey to work in as a railroad station.

Washington's housing shortage became an overused comic premise in movies and plays about the city, but to the people who lived there it was not always so funny. People paid $24 or $35 or more a month for glorified cubicles or jammed into shabby boardinghouses. They jostled for bathroom access with a herd of fellow boarders and were lucky if they could get a bath once every ten days. Landladies discouraged women tenants because they were wont to do their own laundry, request kitchen privileges and entertain gentlemen callers in the parlor. "Men, on the other hand," observed one concierge, "don't wash anything but themselves and eat all their meals out."

Hotels limited guests to a three-day stay. Hospitals had reverted to something out of Dickens; it was the practice to induce childbirth, for otherwise a room might not be available at the right time. . . .

For a family—especially a family with children—it was nearly impossible to find a place. Pathetic want ads appeared in the newspapers: "Won't someone help a refined enlisted Navy man and wife, employed, no children, to obtain an unfurnished room or two with kitchen?" Houses for sale were flagrantly overpriced, and people in Georgetown bought up old, run-down houses for $3,000, renovated them and sold them for five times what they had paid. Renting a house was dearer yet: tiny Georgetown houses rented for a minimum of $250 a month, and some larger houses in other neighborhoods that were by no means mansions were going for $1,000 a month. After President Roosevelt's death, the thought quickly occurred to a lot of people at the same time that the new President would soon be moving out of his two-bedroom,

$120-a-month, rent-controlled apartment. The switchboard at Mr. Truman's building was jammed with calls; the operator told each caller that the president had already promised the apartment to at least three people. . . .

Uniforms were everywhere, representing a rainbow of international military pageantry. At night American soldiers and sailors crowded into the little nightclubs, and Washington night life boomed as it never had before or since. As part of its hospitality to servicemen, Washington offered, in addition to man-starved G-girls ("Washington is the loneliest town," one of them said), the highest VD-contraction rate among servicemen of any city in the country. . . .

Like housing, office space was in short supply, even with the ugly new temporary buildings. The government resorted to pressuring businesses and private residents to move out, and the President spoke darkly of "parasites"— useless people occupying vitally needed space. About the only solution to the office shortage was for the government to move out of town. This it did, in part, setting up branch offices in Richmond, New York, Chicago, St. Louis, Cincinnati, Kansas City, Philadelphia and Baltimore. More than 35,000 government employees moved out, too. . . .

In 1942 the world's largest office building was completed across the Potomac near Arlington. Called the Pentagon, its labyrinthine corridors and offices housed 35,000 office workers. When people wondered what in the world the War Department would do with such an enormous building in peacetime, the President explained that it would be used to store government records and quartermaster supplies, which seemed to satisfy everybody.

REVIEW QUESTIONS

1. World War II brought an end to the widespread unemployment of the Great Depression. Is there any hint in the author's narrative of a regret on the part of the nation that it took a war—and a massive one at that—to pull the country out of the Depression?

2. What impression do you get of the spirit of the nation in its newly found prosperity and employment: a sense of dedication to the war effort? gratitude to the government for a job and a weekly income? sadness that a war was going on?

3. How did the federal government respond to the *social* needs of war workers? Was housing for workers planned as well or as extensively by the government as, for example, munitions plants or airplane factories? Support your answer with evidence from the essay.

4. Compare what Lingeman says about the behavior of teenagers during the war years with the way they behave today. What differences, if any, do you see?

5. World War II, at least as it affected the United States, is sometimes referred to as "the good war." To what extent and in what ways does this label make sense to you? In what ways does it seem wrong?

FOR FURTHER READING

The volume from which this selection was taken—Richard R. Lingeman, *Don't You Know There's a War On?: The American Home Front, 1941–1945* (1970)—is an entertaining account of life during World War II. It may be supplemented with the following general accounts: Richard Polenberg, *War and Society: The United States, 1941–1945* (1972); Geoffrey Perrett, *Days of Sadness, Years of Triumph: The American People, 1939–1945* (1973); and John Morton Blum, *V Was for Victory: Politics and American Culture During World War II* (1976). The lives of American women during the war are the focus of D'Ann Campbell, *Women at War with America* (1984); Sherna Berger Gluck, *Rosie the Riveter Revisited* (1987); and Susan M. Hartmann, *The Home Front and Beyond* (1982). Clayton R. Koppes and Gregory D. Black provide an interesting account of how American movies became a part of the war effort in *Hollywood Goes to War* (1987).

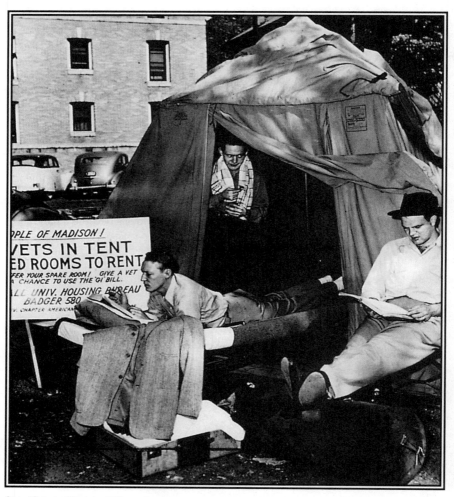

The text visible in the image includes:

PLE OF MADISON !

VETS IN TENT
ED ROOMS TO RENT

FER YOUR SPARE ROOM! GIVE A VET
A CHANCE TO USE THE 'GI' BILL.

LL UNIV. HOUSING BUREAU
BADGER 580

V. CHAPTER AMERICAN

Taking advantage of the educational benefits of the GI Bill of Rights created problems, as well as, opportunities for the veterans and the colleges they attended.

16

The GI Bill of Rights

MICHAEL J. BENNETT

Even before World War II ended in 1945, the nation was making plans for the future. One special area of concern was how to treat the people who would be released from military service when hostilities ended. There were concerns that the veterans might have difficulty readjusting to civilian life. Even more worrisome was the question of how to find jobs for all of them. Most Americans were aware that the economic stimulus of the war had finally pulled the nation out of the Depression of the 1930s, and they feared that the end of wartime spending might see a return of hard times, especially when there would be literally millions of new job-seekers flooding the labor market. In 1944 Congress passed and President Roosevelt signed into law the Serviceman's Readjustment Act, better known as the GI Bill of Rights, in an attempt to deal with or forestall some of these problems as well as to express the nation's gratitude to the veterans for a job well done.

The law extended a variety of benefits to veterans. For example, they were entitled to unemployment compensation in the amount of $20 per week for a period not to exceed 52 weeks, so that they would have something to live on while looking for a job. (It was possible to live on $20 a week at the time, although certainly not lavishly.) They received a preference—usually a certain number of points automatically added to their actual score—when they took exams for civil service jobs. They had re-employment rights, meaning that the employers for whom they had been working when they entered military service were required to give them their old jobs back if they asked for them. They were eligible for low-interest, government-guaranteed loans to buy homes or start businesses.

But the Act's most famous provision, and the one that probably had the greatest impact on the future, was the one that made it possible for veterans to begin or complete educations at schools of their choice with all the costs, including tuition, fees, and books, borne by the government, with a small stipend for living expenses thrown in so that veterans would be able to devote full time to their studies. The consequences were enormous. Not only were the lives of the veterans were changed, and so was the nation as a whole. Tens of thousands to whom a college education would have been nothing but a distant dream now were able to attend the best universities in the land. In doing so they were able to acquire the degrees and the skills that helped to make the United States into the world leader in research and technology in the postwar period. American higher education was transformed, too. Previously, with some limited exceptions, it had been regarded as something available only to the economic and social elite, but the GI Bill of Rights democratized it. Not only was college now within the economic grasp of all veterans, regardless of their social origin, it was becoming a target for the aspirations of others to whom the idea of going to college simply would not have occurred previously. The nation's experience with the GI Bill of Rights was a major step toward the idea that higher education ought somehow be available to all those who were educationally qualified, regardless of their economic circumstances.

An enormous price had been paid for peace, but, for the survivors, there were great rewards. Never before had so many people been so free economically, educationally, and socially. Astonishing numbers of people were entering and leaving the workforce. Military enrollment plunged from 11.4 million in 1945 to 3.4 million in 1946. Another nearly 2 million were discharged between 1946 and 1947, bringing military strength down to 1.5 million in 1947. At the same time, civilian employment climbed from 53.8 million in 1945 to 57.5 million in 1946, and to 60.8 million in 1947. In other words, while 10 million were discharged from military service, civilian employment increased by 7 million. In the jargon of statisticians, the labor market was "churning." Amid all those zigzagging figures, in theory as many as 7 million to 8 million were

---

out of work at all times during those two years. Indeed, almost 9 million veterans drew 52-20 benefits between 1944 and 1949, but presumably because they were counted as part of the civilian labor force, the unemployment rate was unaffected. On the other hand, they did so for an average of only seventeen weeks—less than a third of the fifty-two weeks they were entitled to.

Where were those people who were out of work but not apparently looking for jobs? A great many were in school. About 7.8 million World War II veterans, in all, enrolled in some sort of educational or training program under the GI Bill. Total college and university enrollment leaped from 1,676,856 in 1945, with 88,000 veterans attending, to 2,078,095 in 1946 with veterans accounting for 1,013,000, or 48.7 percent of the total. In 1947, veteran enrollment peaked at 2,338,226 with 1,150,000 veterans, or 49.2 percent, among them. . . .

Reality is conveyed better in individual terms, in stories about a few of the many millions whose lives were transformed during those years. One such story was that of Les Faulk of Turtle Creek, Pennsylvania. Faulk graduated from high school in May 1944 and celebrated the death of Hitler and the overthrow of the Nazi regime a year later as a Seventh Army infantryman in Germany. When Faulk had left Turtle Creek, he had a pretty clear notion of what his life would be like after the war—assuming he survived. He'd come back to the small town wrapped in industrial haze and get his old jobs back—if he was lucky—caddying at the local golf course and racking balls at Kindler's poolroom. In time, he could expect to get a "good" job stoking an open-hearth steel mill or winding copper armatures in the Westinghouse generator plant.

Faulk was one of twelve Turtle Creek High School graduates that Edwin Keister, Jr. interviewed for an article in *Smithsonian Magazine* in 1994, a class that was a microcosm of hundreds of thousands of others. The young man who left high school in 1944 expecting to become no more than a steel mill stoker or an armature winder instead spent thirty-eight years as a teacher and an elementary school principal. Les Faulk had not only gone to college, he also had acquired both a bachelor's and a master's degree and several credits toward his doctorate, even though the name on his high school diploma was "Falcocchio." That name—and his decision to change it—was significant. In those days, being the son of an Italian immigrant family with a "foreign" name could be almost as much a barrier to getting into college as a black skin. "College," as Faulk recalled fifty years later, "was for teachers' kids and the preacher's kids. For the rest of us, with names like Tarantini and Trkula, it was a distant dream."

Faulk and his classmates in Mrs. Whittum's American history class had been urged to believe that that dream, no matter how distant, could come true for them. But the hopes held out in school didn't stand up very well to the living and working conditions Faulk and his classmates grew up in. Turtle Creek was a factory town where half the male students dropped out of high school. Only 5 percent went on to any kind of postsecondary education, even barber or secretarial school, the latter being one of the few avenues to white-collar work then pursued by men as well as women. The war and the GI Bill changed everything. Faulk, like millions of other young Americans sent off to war, grew up fast in a foxhole. That alone might have made it difficult to accept what Turtle Creek had to offer when he came back home, even with a job awaiting him as an apprentice bricklayer, a job arranged by his father. That wasn't the reason he quit after one day, though, throwing away an opportunity for a skilled, well-paid, and prestigious job at the time. He had heard of the GI Bill, and he had made a decision. "I went to the poolroom and told my old boss, 'I'm going to college.' He said, 'I read that only one vet in 20 who enters college will finish.' I said, 'I'm going to be that one.'" The government had turned him into a soldier who had helped beat the best the German army had to offer; now the same government thought he had the makings of a college graduate. Who was he to argue?

Faulk wasn't alone. Among the eleven other graduates of Turtle Creek High School who joined him at the fiftieth reunion of the Class of '44 were an aerospace engineer, a federal judge, a microchip engineer, a professor of law who is also a research scientist, and an engineer specializing in military survival techniques. . . .

Chesterfield Smith signed up for prelaw at the University of Florida back in 1935, but as his wife, Vivian Parker, recalled years later, "He was just a poker-playing, crap-shooting boy who couldn't settle down." By his own account, Smith "chose the easy life in college. I'd go to school a semester and then drop out for a semester to earn enough money to return"—in style. "I'd rather drop out and work than skimp in school." He worked as a clerk in the Florida legislature, a soda jerk, a debt collector, and a candy and tobacco vendor. By the time he was drafted in 1940, though, he had managed to complete three and a half years of college. Commissioned in the National Guard, he was assigned to a field artillery unit in France beginning "about D day plus 45" and served through the Battle of the Bulge before returning to the University of Florida in 1946.

By the standards of the day, Smith had done well financially, saving $5,000 from his pay and winning another $3,000 in craps on the long voyage home. But the man who had married Vivian in 1944 before shipping out for Europe had changed when he came back in 1945. She recalled, "He was a serious man when he returned." Smith didn't give up the good life entirely; he found time to golf five days a week through law school. Financially, his carefully budgeted savings and a teaching job obtained in his second year at law school meant the couple "had more than most." But he also budgeted his time as carefully as his money. "I didn't go drink coffee or sit out on the bench and bull it all the time. I never missed a day of class. I kept a work schedule just like I had a job. If I had a paper due in three weeks, I started it right away and finished a week early. Hell, here I was, almost thirty years of age—I wanted to get that law license and get into practice and make myself some money. The idea of playing around a university for unnecessary months or years had no appeal to me whatsoever."

Twenty years later, Smith was the president of the American Bar Association and the principal partner in a Tampa-Orlando law firm. "The way I was going before the war," Smith said, "I don't think I would ever have made it through law school. But after the war, I felt I had something invested in my country— five years of my life. I said to myself, 'Boy, you've got to settle down and make something of yourself, otherwise you ain't going to 'mount to nothing.' My classmates in the '40s, after the war, we wanted to 'get on with our lives. We were men, not kids, and we had the maturity to recognize that we had to go get what we wanted, and not just wait for things to happen to us." . . .

. . . social change on a seismic scale was happening and nowhere more so than at Harvard. Harvard was the oldest elite institution traditionally preparing the sons of America's WASP families to take their places as the economic and social leaders of the country. Yet it helped pioneer the new meritocratic society that . . . the GI Bill made possible. Harvard had taken the lead a generation before under President A. Lawrence Lowell in restricting the percentage of Jewish students. But under President Conant after the war, the university began vigorously recruiting students from every ethnic and religious background and section of the country, often to the discomfort of alumni who assumed admission of their sons into Harvard Yard was part of the family patrimony. For the veterans who were unexpectedly within the walls of the Yard, it was both a disconcerting and liberating experience.

Frank O'Hara, for example, who was to become a leading literary and art figure of New York in the 1950s and 1960s, wasn't even sure the GI Bill of Rights was a good idea. He had been an enlisted man working as a sonar operator in San Pedro, California, in 1946 when a conversation with a bunkmate, Douglas "Diddy" Starr, turned to the GI Bill. O'Hara, unlike most of his fellow sailors who were singularly pleased with the windfall, was wary, according to his biographer, Brad Gooch. O'Hara had read and been impressed with an article by President Hutchins of the University of Chicago in *Collier's* arguing the bill would turn the nation's colleges into "educational hobo jungles." He was also suspicious of a bandwagon mood that assumed education was the answer to all problems. Nonetheless, O'Hara, whose father graduated from the College of the Holy Cross in Worcester, Massachusetts, applied for and was accepted at Harvard—and so far as living arrangements were concerned, might as well have been back in the Navy. "In 1946, you might as well have been living in an American Legion post as in one of the Houses," a graduating senior reminisced in the 1950 *Harvard Yearbook*. Four thousand veterans were among the record 5,435 students enrolled at Harvard in 1946, filing through registration points in Memorial Hall at the rate of 3 a minute. The spectacle of seventeen-year-old beardless youths in white buck shoes, unloading Vuitton bags from their convertibles outside the "Gold Coast" houses along the Charles River was overshadowed by the sea of older faces surging into the red brick dormitories reserved for veterans on the north side of the Yard. Double-deck bunk beds had to be moved into some dorms, and cots were set up in the Indoor Athletic Building's basketball court to accommodate latecomers.

The words "invasion" and "siege" were predictably and incessantly used by *The Harvard Crimson* as lines formed everywhere—to register, eat, get books, cash checks. The more popular lecturers spoke in classrooms where students arrived early to claim seats on windowsills. The old rules still applied. Jackets and ties were required in the Union, the dining hall, but manufacturers had stopped making blazers and white shirts during the war, and veterans couldn't afford them even if they were available at the Coop, the university's cooperative store. So military coats were cut to hip length, service-issue trousers given a quick press, and insignia cut off old khaki shirts.

O'Hara found it amazing that he was at Harvard at all, Gooch wrote. A mere three months before he had been an enlisted man on the U.S.S. *Nicholas* who, without the GI Bill, would never have been able to afford Harvard's stiff fees. Yet not all of the nuances of Harvard pleased him. He couldn't help feel the pressure of elitism, and he wasn't sure if being at Harvard meant anything to anybody except snobs. He also felt pigeonholed by being Irish even though Irish-Catholics had been the first minority admitted to Harvard back in the 1870s. There had always been a subtle rivalry between Protestants and Catholics, Gooch wrote, although it usually didn't take any more serious form than drinking contests. O'Hara was also unlike relatively sophisticated big-city and wealthy Irish-Catholics like the Kennedys. He was from a small Massachusetts farm town, Grafton near Athol, and a graduate of a parochial high school. Almost another twenty years would pass before graduates of public and parochial high schools outnumbered the products of select private schools among the undergraduates of Harvard. One acquaintance described O'Hara at the time as looking "potato Irish, lower class, with pasty skin." He was often kidded as coming from "Asshole" and told a boyhood friend from Grafton, Phil Charron, "I'm going to Harvard; they say it's the death knell of all Catholics." O'Hara reacted to the social fencing, Gooch wrote, as did many others, by developing a personal style of speech using "arch Angloisms" to both blend in and subtly mock the accents and manners of WASP culture.

Arch Angloisms weren't any part of the style of another member of the class of 1950, although his potato face did go well with the Germanic accent he has retained. Henry Kissinger [later to become Secretary of State], before being drafted into the army, had enrolled as a college student in what was often called the Jewish Harvard, CCNY. The German-Jewish immigrant had planned on becoming an accountant, like this father. "My horizons were never that great when I was in City College," Kissinger said, according to his biographer, Walter Isaacson. Kissinger, who had fled Nazi persecution in Germany with his parents, became an American citizen in the army. The naturalization ceremony at dusty Camp Croft in South Carolina had been just another event in the daily process of, as Kissinger wrote to his brother, "being pushed around and inoculated, counted and stood to attention." The erstwhile accountant returned to Germany, Isaacson wrote, as part of a

> vast democratizing force, one that transformed how Americans lived. Soldiers from small towns in South Carolina and Louisiana for the first time saw places like Paris and Berlin, turning all-American boys with hardscrabble heritages into cosmopolitan conquerors. And, on a smaller scale, the army took young refugees from Nuremberg and Furth, put them into places such as Camp Croft and Camp Claiborne, then marched them off to war in melting pot platoons, thus turning cosmopolitan allies into acculturated American citizens. For immigrant boys, such as Kissinger, serving in the war made citizenship more than a gift merely bestowed; it was an honor they had earned. Having defended the United States, they now had as much claim as any Winthrop or Lowell to feel it was their nation, their country, their home. They were outsiders no more.

Lowells and Cabots mingled quite freely with O'Haras and Kissingers and the other provincial young men tossed up on the banks of the Charles River by the GI Bill. The war, after all, had given all of them the same veneer. Kissinger himself liked to say later that his experience with "the real middle American boys" in his regiment from Wisconsin, Illinois, and Indiana "made me feel like an American." He quoted Helmet Sonnenfeld, a national security adviser, as observing, "The Army made the melting pot melt faster." Indeed, the melting-pot experience young men had undergone in the military was much more readily replicated on college campuses than in established multigenerational and ethnically dominated cities such as Boston, where veterans were sometimes suspected of getting above themselves. That was particularly true of Harvard in comparison to the Boston-Cambridge community where racial, ethnic, and religious tensions would plague the community long after they had subsided on the Harvard campus. Boston, in the late '40s, wasn't quite the city made famous by the doggerel toast of an Irish-Catholic alumnus of Boston College at the turn of the century: "Here's to Boston, the home of the bean and the cod, where the Lowells speak only to the Cabots and the Cabots speak only to God." Nevertheless, it was still a community in which the Yankees spoke rarely to the Irish; the Irish avoided conversation with their fellow Catholics, the Italians; and Jews talked with the Yankees, Irish, and Italians only on business. At the time, in fact, the Cabots were, according to a widely circulated story, suing a Jewish family named Cabotsky. The Cabotskys had changed their name so they could advertise their pharmacy as "Cabot's Drugs." Presumably the old toast had been changed to: "Here's to the home of the bean and the cod, where the Lowells speak to no one, for the Cabots speak Yiddish, by God!"

Kissinger's Germanic accent no doubt stood him in good stead on the Harvard campus and unquestionably helped him in his determination to avoid assimilation into democratic anonymity. His Teutonic tonalities served the same purpose as O'Hara's arch Angloisms. The difference was intriguing and enticing for insiders who not only accepted, but thought more highly of them for being outsiders. Kissinger had listened carefully to his first mentor, Fritz Gustave Anton Kraemer, a German refugee of Prussian background, who was his boss in the American military government of Germany. Kraemer advised him: "Go to a fine college. A gentleman does not go to the College of the City of New York." Kissinger was admitted to Harvard, however, only because the college was willing to take students whose papers were filed late, unlike Princeton and Columbia where he also applied. Isaacson attributed that to the fact that Conant, whom he incorrectly described as a driving force behind the GI Bill, had appointed an outreach counselor to make sure veterans had access to his university.

Once the bill was passed, Conant added his own support to the bill's influence in breaking down the ethnic, religious, and especially anti-Semitic prejudices on campus, although Jews entering Harvard in 1947 were usually assigned other Jews as roommates. The college administration did caution residential housemasters not to take more Jews "than the traffic will allow," for several years after the war, but the practice was discontinued by the end of the decade. So, too, was the custom of designating the names of Jews on college records with asterisks. Actual enrollment of Jews in the late '40s was about 17 percent, slightly lower than the level in the 1920s when President Lowell imposed quotas. The difference wasn't in the numbers so much as the degree of acceptance. "Harvard welcomed us with open arms," remembered Henry Rosovsky, who served with Kissinger in Germany and later became an economics professor, dean of the faculty, and the first Jewish member of the Harvard Corporation. Discrimination was a reality in some departments of the university, Isaacson observed, but it was least evident in government where Louis Hartz, a Jew, was professor of political theory and onetime chairman. . . .

Blacks especially came back from the war walking—and feeling—like free men. They took advantage of the GI Bill in the same way whites did, as individuals, not as members of a group except insofar as membership in the American Legion, the VFW, or the DAV might be helpful in negotiating red tape. Of course, blacks weren't free in the same way whites were, and it seems probable they didn't take advantage of the education benefits in the same percentages as whites. No authoritative numerical estimates of black beneficiaries are available other than an assertion, without documentation, in the *Encyclopedia of the Second World War* that 250,000 blacks were given the opportunity to go college for the first time under the GI Bill. The percentage of those who wouldn't otherwise have gone to college was certainly much higher than whites, according to Reginald Wilson, senior scholar at the American Council on Education, citing a study that "approximately 20 percent of veterans could not have gone to college without the GI Bill. I would conjecture the figure was much higher for African-American veterans. Besides, having come from families that were disproportionately poorer, most had been subjected to underfunded, segregated schools. However, when special accommodations were made and relatively open admissions policies were put in place, black veterans flocked to the colleges and universities and did well academically." At his own alma mater, Wayne State University in Detroit, Wilson recalled, "it is estimated that nearly a third of the veterans enrolled between 1946 and 1950 were African-Americans, and during those years, veterans were almost a majority of the school's students."

The northern and western colleges many blacks attended didn't keep racial census figures, at least not in any systematic fashion. Statistics for black colleges are the best indices for determining the numbers of Negroes who took advantage of the bill. In 1940, enrollment in black colleges was 1.08 percent of the U.S. college enrollment. By 1950, in a greatly expanded student population, it had almost tripled, to 3.6 percent. Overall enrollment in the Negro Land-Grant colleges after the war was 50 percent higher than before. More significantly, the number of veterans in the black colleges was double the entire 1937–38 enrollment. Partially because black colleges had been traditionally shortchanged in funding for building purposes, another federal bill, the Lanham Act of 1946, actually made proportionately more money available for construction and repair at black institutions. Acting under the law, the officers of the Commission of Education recognized the relatively large need of the Negro institutions, according to Wilson. Consequently, funds were distributed to institutions on the assumption that 33.4 square feet of construction was needed for veterans in black colleges as compared with 17.4 square feet in white schools. Nevertheless, despite the additional money for construction, black colleges had to turn away twenty thousand veterans for lack of space.

The shortage of seats was more than made up by colleges and universities in the North and West. "Black veterans with vouchers in hand, paid for by the federal government, were an attractive commodity to many institutions in the North that would not have welcomed them in vast numbers (nor could many have afforded to go before the war)," Wilson wrote. "The white colleges welcomed them and made special provisions to accommodate all of the veterans; they were given additional points on admission tests; in some instances, admission requirements were waived; they were given credit for special training received in the military; tutors were provided in recognition of the veterans being three to five years out of school; and, despite sometimes mediocre high school records, they were welcomed."

The special provisions, it should be noted, applied to many white veterans, not just blacks. As early as February 9, 1942, for example, the University of Wisconsin approved granting ten elective college credits to former enlisted men and fifteen to ex-officers. Wisconsin made other concessions, too. In March 1944, a veteran could even apply four special war credits to the sixteen high school credits needed for admission. If that wasn't enough to meet the admission requirements, a veteran could take an oral or written examination proving he was capable of college work. Credit was also given for college-level work completed in service schools and military training schools, and veterans were exempted from taking the physical education courses compulsory for other students. Wisconsin's medical school lowered admission requirements from three to two years of premed training. Refresher courses were offered in mathematics and English; a full-semester summer school was created; the engineering college operated on a trimester schedule with classes starting in March, July, and November.

The innovations and accommodations pleased some veteran students and didn't appeal to others. A navy officer, responding to a survey sent to former students by Columbia University, had mixed feelings about accelerated courses. "Education is too important to me to be rushed through," he wrote. "I want to have the feeling of leisure to do an honest job with the most valuable time of my life." A year-round trimester program would turn college into a factory, he thought. But a P-51 fighter pilot had a different attitude: "I remember how we used to think that a full year would be a tough grind, but it was probably laziness that prompted that feeling."

Robert A. Eubanks was a black veteran who wasn't the least bothered about going to college full time; he thrived on it. He was bright enough to have graduated in 1942 from high school at the age of fifteen. But he couldn't get a job because he was black and couldn't take advantage of a tuition-only scholarship to Howard University in Washington, D.C., because he didn't have enough money to live on. So he joined the army, and he heard about the GI Bill through word-of-mouth—as most veterans did—when he mustered out in 1946. Eubanks got into a year-round program at the Illinois Institute of Technology (ITT) and earned a degree in theoretical and applied mechanical engineering in 1950. Once again, his job-hunting forays ran up against whites-only hiring policies, so he stayed on at ITT, earning a master's and then a doctoral degree in 1953, all on the GI Bill. With the changing social climate after the *Brown* decision, he was able to get high-paying work in industry. Later, he was lured back to academia, first as a visiting professor at the University of Illinois. After six months, he was offered a tenured full professorship and stayed on until retirement in 1986, teaching and conducting research. "It's very hard to explain now how things were during the 1940s," Eubanks said in reflecting on this life. "The restrictions on blacks then were rough. The GI Bill gave me my start on being a professional instead of a stock clerk." . . .

As a matter of reality, with the great exception of the GI Bill of Rights, government programs to help people haven't directly given people the resources to help themselves. That was the GI Bill's greatest characteristic and accomplishment. It didn't have to appeal to shared human values and social goals by persuading people that institutions knew what was best for them. It gave the individuals the power to decide for themselves what was best for themselves and, at the same time, freed educational institutions to do what they did best, teach. It caused a silent revolution, not by the force of the state, but by using the resources of the state to encourage what George Mason spelled out in the Virginia Declaration much more explicitly than Thomas Jefferson did in the Declaration of Independence: the means of acquiring and possessing property for pursuing and obtaining happiness and safety. The GI Bill gave people the economic resources to train their minds, their most important property, and they went out and used it to pursue happiness and safety.

REVIEW QUESTIONS

1. In what specific ways did the GI Bill of Rights make higher education in America more democratic?

2. The essay suggests that some people believed that the effects of the GI Bill on American education would be unfortunate. What specific ill-effects do you suppose they were concerned about?

3. Name some of the problems that the presence of large numbers of veterans created for American colleges and universities and what adjustments these institutions made to accommodate these new students. Can you think of other problems that might have existed besides those mentioned in the selection?

4. In what ways were veterans different from their nonveteran fellow students? What special problems do you suppose they faced? Can you think of any advantages they may have had over their fellow students in their attempt to complete a college education successfully?

5. It has been said that the GI Bill of Rights may be the most successful piece of government-sponsored social policy ever enacted. Consider whether this is true in relation to other such policies as Social Security, Medicare, civil rights laws, and so forth. Can you see any negative features in the GI Bill of Rights?

FOR FURTHER READING

The books by Blum, Lingeman, Perrett, and Polenberg suggested for the previous selection all provide information about the hopes, worries, and expectations of GIs and the nation as a whole about their return to civilian life. Joseph C. Goulden, *The Best Years, 1945–1950* (1976) is an entertaining general account of the immediate postwar period. David R. B. Ross, *Preparing for Ulysses: Politics and Veterans During World War II* and the book from which this selection is taken, Michael J. Bennett, *When Dreams Came True: The GI Bill and the Making of Modern America* (1996) deal extensively with the political background of the GI Bill. Keith W. Olson, *The G. I. Bill, the Veterans, and the Colleges* (1974) is a detailed look at the impact of the Bill's educational benefits. Raymond Moley, Jr., *The American Legion Story* (1966) is a history of the nation's most influential veterans' organization, which played a crucial role in securing the passage of the GI Bill. Richard Severo and Lewis Milford, *The Wages of War: When America's Soldiers Came Home: From Valley Forge to Vietnam* (1989) compares the way the nation has treated the veterans of its major wars.

AFFLUENCE AND ITS DISCONTENTS

The material well-being of the American people in the decades since the end of World War II contrasts sharply with their poverty in the Great Depression of the 1930s. While not all Americans shared equally in the postwar prosperity, most enjoyed a standard of living far higher than that of previous generations. Furthermore, American influence abroad also reached its zenith following the end of World War II.

But the postwar decades were also marked by internal insecurities and divisions and external wars that belied the facade of confidence and contentment. In the Truman-Eisenhower years, from 1945 to 1960, the second Red Scare and the Korean War disturbed and divided the nation. Three assassinations in the 1960s, of John F. Kennedy, Robert Kennedy, and Martin Luther King, Jr., provided further proof that social and political stability did not necessarily go hand in hand with material prosperity and national power. Despite Lyndon B. Johnson's announcement of the "Great Society" and Richard Nixon's promise "to bring the American people together," developments from the mid-1960s to the late 1970s showed clearly that neither vision was being fulfilled. Instead, conflict and crisis seemed to rule. The 60s saw protest movements and bitter disagreements over the Vietnam War; the 70s, the energy crisis, and the Iranian hostage crisis. Public opinion polls showed that Americans were increasingly disillusioned with their society, particularly with their political institutions and leaders, as they showed by staying away from voting booths in increasing numbers in the 70s and 80s. On the other hand, there were indications that Americans were becoming increasingly interested in grassroots social and political movements that addressed immediate concerns close to home.

The essays in this section reflect the widely varying experiences of our nation since the end of World War II. In the first, Landon Y. Jones looks at the baby boom and the move to suburbia that postwar affluence made possible. The next two deal with two of the significant attacks on the status quo in the 1960s, the civil rights movement and the counterculture. The next examines the experiences of the soldiers who fought the Vietnam War. The following one describes recent changes in Americans' sexual behavior and attitudes, and the last offers a detailed look at one example of a local campaign by the so-called religious right, a combination of political conservatism and evangelical or fundamentalist religion that emerged to prominence in the 70s and 80s.

American Community of Builders, Inc.

Suburbia—the home of the baby boom.

17

The Baby Boom

LANDON Y. JONES

A popular television program of the 1970s was set in the 1950s. The title, *Happy Days,* reflects not only nostalgia for a previous, presumably happier era, but also the feelings of many Americans at the time. To be sure, the Cold War was an ever-present fact of life, and the prospect of nuclear destruction was terrifyingly real. There were unresolved racial tensions in the nation, McCarthyism revealed the excesses that a fear of political dissent might lead to, and many social commentators were disturbed by what they saw as a trend toward an all-encompassing and deadening conformity in American life. Yet, life for most Americans was quite pleasant. They had endured the worst depression and the largest foreign war that the nation had ever experienced, and felt, understandably, that they were due for a little enjoyment. And they were able to afford it. During World War II, there had been an unintentional and unforeseen redistribution of income, which significantly improved the economic condition of the middle class. This, in turn, became the foundation for an extended period of virtually uninterrupted prosperity. More Americans had more disposable income than ever before in the nation's history, and this affluence affected all other aspects of American society during the 1950s.

One important result was the move to suburbia. With large numbers now able to buy their own homes, Americans streamed out from the center cities in search of the traditional good life to be found in one's own house on one's own plot of land. They usually conducted the search in a ranch-style house with a picture window instead of in the rose-covered cottage with white picket fence of folklore. But while the architecture was new, the values and aspirations of those living inside were comfortably old-fashioned.

The resurgence of traditional values in the 1950s can be seen in the centrality of family life. Seldom, if ever before, had the family received as much attention or praise as it did at this time. Popular magazines praised the virtues of "Togetherness"; a family room to serve as the home's social center was almost a necessity in all new houses. Popular novels like *The Man in the Gray Flannel Suit* by Sloan Wilson showed heroes who chose family solidarity over wealth, power, and success, and women were told in all sorts of ways by all sorts of cultural authorities that they truly belonged in the home and that their proper role was to insure that their husbands and children were healthy, happy, and well-adjusted.

And, finally, there was the baby boom, an unprecedented increase in the birthrate that flabbergasted demographers who had been serenely confident that Americans would have fewer babies than before. Instead, they proceeded to have more than ever, faster than ever. In retrospect, we can see that the baby boom was closely tied to many of the social trends of the 1950s. The following selection examines some of the connections.

In the early 1950s, the huge Census Clock in Washington was clicking like a runaway taxi meter. Every seven seconds the Birth Light blinked off a new baby. Boys were arriving with familiar names like Robert, John, James, Michael, William, Richard, Joseph, Thomas, Steven, and David, making a Top Ten of favorite names that was proudly all-American. Girls were named Linda, Mary, Barbara, Patricia, Susan, Kathleen, Carol, Nancy, Margaret, and Diane. And perhaps thanks to Debbie Reynolds, "Deborah" would have a run all of her own later in the decade.

Like the steel industry, mothering was running at close to 100 percent capacity, and it was harder and harder to keep up. In January of 1952, General Electric decided to celebrate its seventy-fifth anniversary by awarding five shares of common stock to any employee who had a baby on October 15. Some public-relations whiz tried to predict the eventual number of winners by dividing the total of 226,000 G.E. employees by the U.S. crude birthrate. Unfortunately, he forgot that G.E. workers as a population were considerably more fertile than the United States as a whole, since they contained no one under 17 nor over 65. In the end, the company's guess that thirteen G.E. babies would be born amounted to underestimation on a grand scale. The workers, true to the thriving surplus economy of the era, came through with no less than 189 new G.E. babies that day.

But General Electric was not about to complain. It was investing $650 million in new plants and assembly lines over seven postwar years to prepare for the boom in babies. As early as 1948, *Time* noted that the U.S. population had just increased by "2,800,000 more consumers" (*not* babies) the year before. Economists happily predicted that the new babies would set off a demand explosion for commodities such as homes, foodstuffs, clothing, furniture, appliances, and schools, to name only a few examples. *Fortune* pronounced the baby boom "exhilarating" and with an almost-audible sigh of relief concluded that the low birthrates of the 1930s were a "freakish interlude, rather than a trend." "We need not stew too much about a post-armament depression," the magazine wrote. "A civilian market growing by the size of Iowa every year ought to be able to absorb whatever production the military will eventually turn loose."

As the economic and baby booms surged on together, the cheerleading became almost feverish. Public-service signs went up in New York City subways reading, "Your future is great in a growing America. Every day 11,000 babies are born in America. This means new business, new jobs, new opportunities." After-dinner speakers began to talk about "Prosperity by Population" and lofted tantalizing guesses of up to five million new babies a year by 1975. Financial magazines editorialized about the joys of "this remarkable boom." "Gone, for the first time in history," announced *Time* in 1955, "is the worry over whether a society can produce enough goods to take care of its people. The lingering worry is whether it will have enough people to consume the goods."

The most euphoric article of all, perhaps, was a story *Life* printed in 1958, at the height of the boom. Three dozen children were crowded onto the cover along with the banner headline: KIDS: BUILT-IN RECESSION CURE—HOW 4,000,000 A YEAR MAKE MILLIONS IN BUSINESS. Inside, the article began with another headline—ROCKETING BIRTHS: BUSINESS BONANZA—and continued chockablock with statistics and photographs about new citizens who were "a brand-new market for food, clothing, and shelter." In its first year, *Life* calculated, a baby is not just a child but already a prodigious consumer, "a potential market for $800 worth of products." Even before returning from the hospital, an infant had "already rung up $450 in medical expenses." Four-year-olds are not just sugar and spice or puppy-dog tails but rather represent a "a backlog of business orders that will take two decades to fulfill." A rhapsodic *Life* then clinched its case by visiting Joe Powers, a thirty-five-year-old salesman from Port Washington, New York. He and his wife, Carol, had produced ten children and were buying 77 quarts of milk and 28 loaves of bread a week, just for starters. Faced with examples like that of meritorious devotion to the Procreation Ethic, little wonder that some American mothers felt as if it were their *duty* to have children. Either they were pregnant or, if not, wondered whether they should be.

The baby-boom kids had kicked off in America a buccaneering orgy of buying and selling that carried all things before it. The only thing like it earlier was the Gilded Age of the post–Civil War 1870s, which the historian Vernon Louis Parrington so aptly dubbed "the Great Barbecue." Here was a feast spread out for an entire nation, and everyone scrambling for it. More food was spoiled than eaten, perhaps, and the revelry was a bit unseemly, but no one minded. Everywhere people were getting rich in a demographic debauch.

The spending boom started, literally, at the bottom. Diapers went from a $32-million industry in 1947 to $50 million in 1957. The diaper services (disposables had not yet arrived) also prospered. Mothers and fathers were paying $5 million annually (twice the preboom business) to have baby's shoes bronze-plated at L. E. Mason. Inc., in Boston. The under-five appetite, which had grown from 13 million mouths to 20 million by 1960, more than one out of every ten Americans, was consuming baby food at a rate of 1.5 billion cans a year in 1953 (up from 270 million cans in 1940).

As the kids grew up, so did the markets. Throughout the 1950s, the 5–13 age group grew by an additional one million baby boomers every year. The toy industry set sales records annually after 1940, growing from an $84-million-a-year stripling to a $1.25-billion giant. Sales of bicycles doubled to two million a year: cowboy outfits became a $75-million subindustry; space-science toys claimed another $60 million. Children's clothes became a boom market, and packaging researchers suddenly discovered the troika of "family" sizes— Giant, Economy, and Super-economy. At its peak, the juvenile market was ringing up a staggering $33 billion annually.

The rain of spending did not fall evenly on society. Rather, it was both a cause and an effect of what amounted to the opening of a new American frontier: the suburbs. Historians had already suggested that America's expansiveness during the nineteenth century was built on the common goal of settling the West. Now there was a new impetus behind the conquering of the suburan frontier: babies. The suburbs were conceived for the baby boom— and vice versa. Here in green garlands around the cities, Americans were creating new child-oriented societies, "babyvilles" teeming with new appetites, new institutions, and new values. Families who were asked why they moved to the suburbs first mentioned better housing and leisure, as if they were conforming to the old goal of a country place that began with the French aristocracy. But then, invariably, they added that they thought suburbia was "a better place to bring up the kids." The common acceptance of this goal united the suburbs. "Instead of the wagon train, where people leaned on one another as they moved across the continent," historian Daniel Boorstin remarked, "Americans in suburbs leaned on one another as they moved rapidly about the country and up the ladder of consumption." Author William H. Whyte found the same communal spirit in his examination of the mythical suburb of Park Forest. Families shared baby-sitters, cribs, lawn mowers, tea services, and baseball equipment. "We laughed at first at how the Marxist society had finally arrived," one suburban executive told Whyte. "But I think the real analogy is to the pioneers."

As an internal migration, the settling of the suburbs was phenomenal. In the twenty years from 1950 to 1970, the population of the suburbs doubled from 36 million to 72 million. No less than 83 percent of the total population growth in the United States during the 1950s was in the suburbs, which were growing fifteen times faster than any other segment of the country. As people packed and moved, the national mobility rate leaped by 50 percent. The only other comparable influx was the wave of European immigrants to the United States around the turn of the century. But, as *Fortune* pointed out, more people moved to the suburbs every year than had ever arrived on Ellis Island.

By now, bulldozers were churning up dust storms as they cleared the land for housing developments. More than a million acres of farmland were plowed under every year during the 1950s. Millions of apartment-dwelling parents with two children were suddenly realizing that two children could be doubled up in a spare bedroom, but a third child cried loudly for something more. The proportion of new houses with three or more bedrooms, in fact, rose from one-third in 1947 to three-quarters by 1954. The necessary *Lebensraum* could only be found in the suburbs. There was a housing shortage, but young couples armed with VA [Veterans Administration] and FHA [Federal Housing Administration] loans built their dream homes with easy credit and free spending habits that were unthinkable to the baby-boom grandparents, who shook their heads with the Depression still fresh in their memories. Of the 13 million homes built in the decade before 1958, 11 million of them—or 85 percent—were built in the suburbs. Home ownership rose 50 percent between 1940 and 1950, and another 50 percent by 1960. By then, one-fourth of *all* housing in the United States had been built in the fifties. For the first time, more Americans owned homes than rented them.

We were becoming a land of gigantic nurseries. The biggest were built by Abraham Levitt, the son of poor Russian-Jewish immigrants, who had originally built houses for the Navy during the war. The first of three East Coast Levittowns went up on the potato fields of Long Island. Exactly $7900—or $60 a month and no money down—bought you a Monopoly-board bungalow with four rooms, attic, washing machine, outdoor barbecue, and a television set built into the wall. The 17,447 units eventually became home to 82,000 people, many of whom were pregnant or wanted to be. In a typical story on the suburban explosion, one magazine breathlessly described a volleyball game of nine couples in which no less than five of the women were expecting.

Marketers were quick to spot what amounted to capitalism's Klondike Lode. "Anybody who wants to sell anything to Americans should take a long look at the New Suburbia," marveled *Fortune* in 1953. "It is big and lush and uniform—a combination made to order for the comprehending marketer." It went far beyond toys and diapers. In suburbia's servantless society, laborsaving devices were necessary adjuncts to having children. The number of washing machines sold in America went from 1.7 million in 1950 to 2.6 million in 1960. Sales of electric clothes dryers doubled during one two-year stretch. With a then-astonishing average family income of $6500 (compared to $3800 for everyone else), the suburbanites were creating an American way of spending organized around children and the needs they created. Retailers eagerly followed them to the suburbs, opening branch stores by the dozen and clearing the way for the later age of shopping malls.

The settlers of suburbia also brought with them beasts of burden. They had Fords in their future—and Chevys and De Sotos and Hudsons and Studebakers. The car, especially the second car, was the one indispensable suburban accessory. Car registrations soared along with the birthrate: from 26 million in 1945 to 40 million in 1950 to 60 million by the end of the decade. The number of two-car families rose 750,000 a year and doubled from 1951 to 1958. Station wagons, the housewife's version of the Willys Jeep, began crisscrossing the suburbs like water bugs, dropping off husbands, picking up children, stopping by the supermarket. "A suburban mother's role is to deliver children obstetrically once," said Peter De Vries, "and by car forever after." *Time* joked that "if the theory of evolution is still working, it may well one day transform the suburban housewife's right foot into a flared paddle, grooved for easy traction on the gas pedal and brake."

Even in those days, the automobile had seized its central place in the emotional life of the baby boom. It was the first entire generation to be driven before it walked. It was the first generation to grow up in cars, even to seek its entertainment in cars. Back in 1933 a chemicals manufacturer named Richard Hollinshead had turned a parking lot in Camden, New Jersey, into the World's First Automobile Movie Theatre. Fifteen years later, there were only 480 drive-ins in the country. But between 1948 and 1958 the number zoomed to 4000, equipped with everything from playgrounds for the kids to Laundromats for Mom. For millions of baby-boom parents, a night at the drive-in neatly solved the suburban dilemma of what to do if you couldn't get a baby-sitter. Much later, the adolescent baby boomers would find their own use for the passion pits. Here is Lisa Alther in *Kinflicks:*

> Mixed with the dialogue were the various sighs and gasps and sucking sounds from the front seats and blasts from car horns throughout the parking area as, in keeping with Hullsport High tradition, couples signalled that they'd gone all the way.

Nowhere was the postwar baby-suburb-car symbiosis more symbolically apparent than during the gasoline shortage of July 1979 in the Philadelphia suburb of Levittown, Pennsylvania. There some 75,000 people live on 7000 acres of suburb. But, for a city of such density, it is served by little mass transportation. Threatened by the loss of their cars, angry young Levittowners staged the nation's first gas riot, burning cars, stoning ambulances, and battling police. Ironically, many of the 195 who were arrested belonged to the same families who had originally settled there during the baby-boom years and who, in 1960, won the Little League World Series for Levittown.

Meanwhile, the suburbs continued to grow and prosper and create a whole new sequence of bench marks for American Studies teachers. In 1956, white-collar workers outnumbered blue-collar workers for the first time. In 1970, the suburbs became the largest single sector of the nation's population, exceeding both central cities and the farms. By 1972, the suburbs were even offering more jobs than the central cities. Everyone was enthusiastically buying "on time" (as it was called then), and the number of Americans who thought installment financing was a good thing increased from 50 percent to 60 percent in ten years.

Sociologists began to pursue the suburbanites like doctors after a new virus. The baby-boom parents were poked and prodded and examined with the kind of fascination hitherto reserved for South Sea Islanders. They were, to be sure, pioneering a life-style (the dread word first came into currency then) that would be predominant in America. Often living in small houses filled with children, they moved outside to their patios and barbecue pits and created a new, rigorously informal style. Lawn and porch furniture sales went from $53 million in 1950 to $145 million in 1960. Hot dog production likewise zoomed from 750 million pounds to more than 2 billion pounds in the decade. Everyone first-named everyone and no one criticized the neighbor's kids (at least in front of a neighbor). Books of the time began to portray a strange netherworld of rathskellers and dens, of cheese dips and cocktails (the required icebreakers in a highly mobile society), of Kaffeeklatsches and card parties, and of outer-directed husbands and neurotic corporate wives.

Some of these studies no doubt revealed more of the anxieties of the examiners than the examined. (Did ordinary citizens really have "identity crises"?) But, if there was a common message, it was of the *sameness* of suburbia. It was as if the same forces that produced prosperity and fertility also produced homogeneity. Parents had rediscovered the old verities—home, hearth, children, church. But they had also made a faith out of brand names, modular housing, and gray flannel suits. Everywhere were the same drugstores, the same franchises, the same music on the radio. The children, too, were being shaped by a world of repeatable experience. But they were not being molded by their parents or their teachers. Instead, there was another dominant presence in the early lives of the baby boomers. It was one that would forge their unity as a generation. It would mobilize them as a consumer force. It was television. In 1938, E. B. White prophesied that "television is going to be the test of the modern world and . . . in this new opportunity to see beyond the range of our vision we shall discover either a new and unbearable disturbance of the general peace or a saving radiance in the sky. We shall stand or fall by television—of that I am quite sure." In the year White wrote that, barely 2 percent of American families owned the small, flickering Philcos and DuMonts dwarfed in their elephantine cabinets. But in less than a decade, the age of television swept over us. From fewer than 6000 sets manufactured at the baby boom's outset in 1946, production leaped, almost impossibly, to 7 million a year by 1953. Eighty-six percent of American homes had television sets at the end of the decade and, by 1967, 98 percent of all homes had sets, effectively saturating the market. The exponential growth curve of television was steeper than that of any other technological innovation of the century—including the telephone, radio, and automobile.

It was also the most important new child-care development of the century, one that would redefine the environment in which Americans grew up. Some of the oldest baby-boomers remember when the first sets were lugged into their homes. But, for most, television was not an intruder in the home but what Buckminster Fuller called "the third parent," practically a family member itself. These children treated the glowing box not with the awe due a mysterious and wonderful invention but with the unquestioned familiarity of an old armchair or the kitchen sink.

Families wanted to stay home in the 1950s, and television made it easier. Aside from the growth in drive-ins, movies almost withered away during the baby-boom years. In 1946, the first year of the boom, Hollywood had recorded its biggest year ever: 400 features were released and 90 million went to the movies every week. Then in 1947, movie attendance dropped 10 percent as parents stayed home with their babies. By January 1953, when a record 50 million of them watched another baby-boom mother, Lucy Ricardo, have her baby on *I Love Lucy,* movie attendance had been cut to one-half the 1946 level, despite such lures as 3-D movies. (The first was *Bwana Devil* in 1952.) With most of its screens located in emptying downtowns instead of expanding suburbs—in New York City alone, 55 theaters closed in 1951—Hollywood lost an audience it would not even begin to reclaim until it squeezed theaters into suburban malls twenty years later.

Television, meanwhile, was giving the baby-boom children a series of vivid images that would color their memories forever. They all sang "M-I-C-K-E-Y M-O-U-S-E" with Karen and Doreen. (In those days, no one noticed that there were no black or Asian or Hispanic Mouseketeers.) They grew up glued to *Howdy Doody,* part of a vast Peanut Gallery in a national Doodyville. Mr. Bluster was a faintly disguised Ike, and as author Jeff Greenfield has observed, Clarabell was the original Yippie. Two decades later, in the aftermath of the Vietnam antiwar strife, Buffalo Bob and Howdy put together a road show that offered a burned-out student generation a return to a childhood myth that somehow seemed more real, or at least comforting, than the 1960s had been.

The baby-boom parents themselves were mirrored in nuclear-family dramas like *The Adventures of Ozzie and Harriet, Father Knows Best,* and *The Life of Riley.* Yet, on TV at least, the birthrate remained surprisingly low—evidently the bumbling Ozzie Nelsons and Chester A. Rileys were a lot more savvy about some family matters than their children ever could have suspected. (*The Brady Bunch*, with its amalgam of six children by two different marriages, was more of a postboom family that arrived ahead of its time.) Perhaps the prototypical baby-boom family was the Cleavers in *Leave It to Beaver*. Beaver Cleaver could have been penned by Norman Rockwell as a sort of Tom Sawyer relocated in Pasadena. The rumor that the actor who played Beaver, Jerry Mathers, had been killed later in Vietnam seemed cruelly symbolic of the death of the generation's own innocence. (The reality was, if anything, even more appropriate: Mathers had actually gone from selling insurance to real estate, while his klutzy buddy, Eddie Haskell, had really become a cop with the Los Angeles Police Department.)

At the same time, the television series the baby boomers watched were relentlessly programming a vision of the American family that was either unrealistic or unattainable. No one, as Jeff Greenfield has pointed out, is ever alone in Televisionland. There is little real despair. Problems can be worked out and almost always are. More TV parents are widowed than divorced. Anger is cute, rarely ugly. A child who would believe television would believe that most problems are soluble, usually within the half hour, and that sacrifices and compromises rarely involve human pain. Beaver Cleaver never had to worry that his parents would announce a trial separation. And if Ozzie Nelson had a drinking problem or was otherwise unemployable—why else was he always hanging around the house?—no one worried about it. . . .

Television also gave the baby boom its first lessons in the little dishonesties of adult life. The numbing repetition of Saturday-morning ads for candied cereals and electric toys did not turn every child into a drooling consumer. Many of them simply developed built-in truth detectors. They assumed that the commercials were less than truthful, that grown-ups lied, and made judgments accordingly. (Was Watergate really a surprise to the TV generation?) Television comedies further presented an image of domestic life based largely on trickeries. How would Lucy Ricardo hide from Ricky the awful truth of her shopping spree? Would Ralph Cramden lure Norton into his latest get-rich-quick scheme? Adult life had lost its mystery. "We grew up old," said Joyce Maynard. "We are the cynics who see the trap door in the magic show, the pillow stuffing in Salvation Army Santa Clauses, the camera tricks in TV commercials.". . .

We will now be led for the rest of this century and into the next one by the first generation born and bred on television. It would be foolish to think that television is the sole decisive factor in their lives. We still know relatively little about the way television has altered our sensibilities and our capacity to think and act. But no product of technology is more intimately involved with the people of the boom generation than television. From *Howdy Doody* to the streets of Chicago in 1968, the baby boomers sought to validate and legitimatize their life on television. Television has molded their style and controlled their daily habits. It has helped bind them to their peers while driving wedges between them and their parents. It has given them economic power and a spurious sense of omnipotence. It has given them sophistication without understanding. It has taught that self-gratification is no farther away than the off-on switch.

Now the first young generation raised on television is becoming the first generation of parents who have spent their lives with television. If we know little about how television affected them as children, we know even less about its long-term effects on adults. The baby boom is the first generation of adults whose attitudes about marriage, family, and consumption were formed during a lifetime of television use. It will eventually become the first generation of elderly people to have grown up with television. How will that life stage be altered? The worrisome question that remains is whether we will become the masters of this powerful medium—or vice versa.

REVIEW QUESTIONS

1. What social conditions existed in the late 1940s and early 1950s that might explain the origins of the baby boom? Why, contrary to all expectations, did Americans have so many children during this period?

2. What were some of the consequences of the affluence of the postwar period besides paving the road to suburbia and making the baby boom possible?

3. Like the 1950s, the current period is one in which there is a greater than usual expression of reverence for the family and the traditional values the family supposedly represents. Is this rooted in something similar to the social conditions that existed in the 1950s? In what other ways does the current period resemble that decade?

4. Several of the television shows mentioned in the article are still being shown as reruns. Watch some of them to see what they seem to indicate about the period when they were first made. What strikes you about them? How does the life they depict resemble or differ from what you are familiar with? If there are differences, are they due to differences between the 1950s and the present day or to the differences between the real world and the world as it exists on television?

FOR FURTHER READING

The following are general works on postwar America: Charles C. Alexander, *Holding the Line: The Eisenhower Era, 1952–1959* (1975); John Patrick Diggins, *The Proud Decades* (1988); Eric F. Goldman, *The Crucial Decade—and After: America, 1945–1960* (1960); David Halberstam, *The Fifties* (1993); Marty Jezer, *The Dark Ages* (1982); William L. O'Neill, *American High: The Years of Confidence, 1945–1960* (1986). Kenneth Jackson, *Crabgrass Frontier: The Suburbanization of the United States* (1985), is a general history of the development of suburbia. Herbert J.

Gans, *The Levittowners: Ways of Life and Politics in a New Suburban Community* (1967), deals specifically with the postwar period, as does William Whyte in *The Organization Man* (1956). David Riesman et al., *The Lonely Crowd* (1950), was one of the most widely read nonfiction books of the 1950s. An important cultural document in its own right, it also offers stimulating interpretations of American society. Concerning television, Erik Barnouw, *Tube of Plenty: The Evolution of American Television* (1975), is a general history of the development of the medium. Horace Newcomb, *TV: The Most Popular Art* (1974), and David Marc, *Demographic Vistas* (1984), offer interpretations of specific programs, including most of those mentioned in this selection. The book from which this selection is taken, Landon Y. Jones, *Great Expectations: America and the Baby Boom Generation* (1980), is worth reading in its entirety. It not only deals in great detail with the social factors that produced the baby boom but also takes the story of the baby boom generation forward into the 1960s and 1970s, providing interesting insights into these decades.

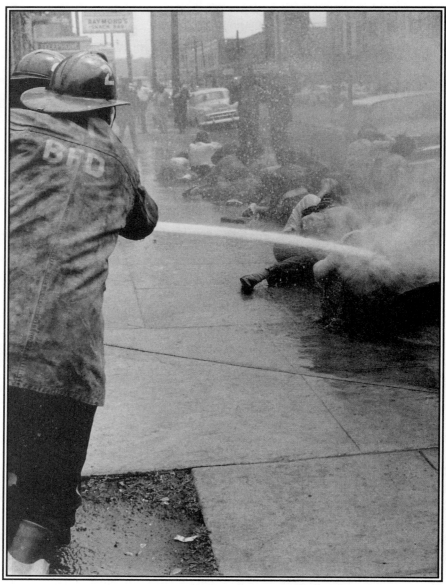

Charles Moore/Black Star

Those working for civil rights, like these demonstrators in Birmingham, Alabama, were often victims of violence.

18

The Struggle for Civil Rights

DOUG McADAM

One can make a good argument that for most of the period since World War II the single most important domestic issue in the United States has been the struggle to achieve equality for African Americans. Slavery was destroyed after the Civil War, but it was quickly replaced by a system of "second-class citizenship" for African Americans, which included segregation, denial of equal access to education, jobs, and political power, and the general assumption by the majority of white Americans that African Americans were inherently and unalterably inferior. While challenges to this system were never entirely absent, it remained remarkably intact until well into the twentieth century, particularly in the South, where "Jim Crow," a system of laws requiring racial segregation and including the nearly universal deprivation of African Americans' right to vote, was an inescapable fact of life.

Attacks on the system began to accelerate, however, during and after World War II. Two particularly important events occurred in the mid-1950s. In 1954 the Supreme Court struck a major blow against one of the most important bastions of the whole system of Jim Crow when it held that racial segregation in public education was unconstitutional. In 1955 African Americans took another significant "stride toward freedom" with their boycott of city buses in Montgomery, Alabama. This marked a turning point in the struggle for African American equality in several ways. First, it was the occasion for the rise to national prominence and leadership of Dr. Martin Luther King, Jr., who was to remain until his assassination in 1968 the most important spokesman for the idea of the civil rights movement as a moral crusade. Second, it marked the first widespread use of direct mass action by African Americans themselves, a tactic that was to be used over and over again in the civil rights struggles of the 1960s (and in the other protest movements of that decade as well). Third, it was a direct challenge to Jim Crow in the very heart of Jim Crow country.

For the next ten years, from 1955, when the Montgomery bus boycott was begun, to 1965, when President Lyndon Johnson signed the Voting Rights Act into law, the South was the major focus of civil rights activity in the United States, direct mass action was the preferred method of attack, and the primary target was Jim Crow, that massive system of racial segregation and subordination written into the laws of the southern states. While many individuals and organizations were involved in the struggle, the spearhead of the movement in the early 1960s was SNCC (pronounced "Snick"), the Student Nonviolent Coordinating Committee. Early in its existence, it turned to the attempt to build permanent political power for southern African Americans as the shortest path to the ultimate goal of racial equality. In the summer of 1964, the leaders of SNCC conceived the idea of "Freedom Summer," during which hundreds of volunteers, mostly white college students from the North, were to conduct a massive voter registration drive in Mississippi, the poorest state in the nation and the one in which the racial situation was universally regarded as the most oppressive. The following selection by Doug McAdam tells part of the story of that summer's effort, giving an insight into the kind of opposition the civil rights movement encountered and the type of courage it took to challenge the racial status quo.

For most of the volunteers, Freedom Summer began not in Mississippi, but at the Western College for Women in Oxford, Ohio. There, in mid-June, the National Council of Churches sponsored two, week-long orientation sessions for volunteers accepted for work in Mississippi. The first session was held June 14–20 and was tailored to those who were to work in voter registration. A second session, for Freedom School teachers, was held the following week.

If the volunteers had expected a languid, leisurely week in the early summer freshness of rural Ohio, they were to be disappointed. The intensity that was to mark the entire summer was very much in evidence at Oxford. It is interesting that the volunteers interviewed have retained so few specific memories of orientation or of the summer itself. They seem to attribute this to the fact that the events in question occurred nearly twenty-five years ago. In contrast, they usually have very detailed memories of events *prior* to the summer, such as when and how they heard about the project in the first place. Possibly the reason for the lack of specific memories is simply the pace of events that summer. Things happened too quickly to allow time for the reflection required to commit specific events to long-term memory. The volunteers were feeling, seeing, experiencing too much.

Some of the intensity of the experience owed to the specific activities planned for the week. The volunteers were subjected to a daunting schedule of general assemblies, section meetings, and work groups. The general assemblies brought all the volunteers together to hear what amounted to broad orientation sessions on Mississippi or some aspect of the movement. Sometimes staff members spoke at these assemblies; more often, it was invited speakers from outside the project. Established civil right leaders, such as Bayard Rustin, Vincent Harding, and James Lawson, spoke. So too did native Mississippians, trying to give the volunteers a better understanding of their state. Jess Brown, one of only three civil rights lawyers in the state, apprised the volunteers of the "unique" quality of Mississippi justice. Long-time state civil rights leader, Aaron Henry, gave a short history of the movement in Mississippi. Even the Justice Department dispatched a representative to the orientation. In a sobering and, for many, radicalizing session, John Doar warned the volunteers not to expect federal protection while in Mississippi. "Maintaining law and order," he argued, "is a state responsibility." In the weeks to come, the volunteers would have ample opportunity to see just how Mississippi exercised that responsibility.

Section meetings were more focused planning groups involving twenty to thirty people who were expected to be engaged in the same type of work during the summer. Work groups were smaller still, consisting of between five and ten people who would actually be working with one another in Mississippi. What these smaller groups lacked in drama and emotional intensity, they made up for in relevance. It was here that the volunteers met and got to know their fellow project members and were trained in the basics of their work assignments.

The power of orientation, however, derived less from this mix of planned sessions as from the informal aspects of the experience. For many of the volunteers it was the beginning of an intensely stressful, yet exhilarating, confrontation with traditional conceptions of America, community, politics, morality, sexuality, and, above all else, themselves. What the volunteers were beginning to experience at Oxford was, to use Peter Berger's term, "ecstasy," that giddy, disorienting sense of liberation that comes from "stepping outside ... the taken-for-granted routines of society." It was not so much of a case of the volunteers *choosing* to take this step, as being compelled to do so by virtue of their contact with a project staff that had itself become more radical and alienated as a result of three long years of struggle in Mississippi. If ever a group embodied the risks and rewards of an "ecstatic" way of life, it was the SNCC veterans. The volunteers were clearly fascinated by them and drawn to the way of life they represented. One volunteer interviewed by Sarah Evans "claimed that the first night of the orientation session in Oxford changed her life 'because I met those SNCC people and my mouth fell open'." In a letter home, another volunteer, Margaret Aley, described the SNCC staff in equally glowing terms:

> I've never known people like them before; they are so full of heart and life. They are not afraid to show their emotions, they cry when they are sad; they laugh and dance when they are happy. And they sing; they sing from their hearts and in their songs they tell of life, struggle, sadness and beauty. They have a freeness of spirit that I've rarely seen. But I think that's because they don't worry about maintaining the status quo. When we arrived here Saturday, I had a feeling that I didn't belong. . . . [Now] somehow I feel like I've found something I've been looking for for a long time. I feel like I've finally come home. I now have no doubt that I belong here.

Ruth Steward put the matter a bit more succinctly. In a letter to her parents, she explained that "you can always tell a CORE or SNCC worker—they're beautiful." What these statements betray is a growing identification with the activist community and with a way of life that would later be dubbed the "counterculture."

Other aspects of the orientation sessions also reinforced this sense of identification. For many, the legions of reporters and television cameramen swarming over the campus had that effect. Their presence communicated a sense of "history-making" significance that was intoxicating. Not that the hypocrisy and sensationalism of the media was lost on the volunteers. This too was a part of the radicalizing process they were undergoing. In her beautiful book describing the Freedom Summer experience, another volunteer, Sally Belfrage, wrote of how the media

> followed us into the classrooms and dormitories, around the lounges, out along the paths. They asked people to sing that song again for the American public. There was footage, yardage, mileage of every face in the place. "At the beginning it made me feel important," a boy from Utah said at lunch. "But they have a way of degrading everything they touch." "It's because we need them more than they need us," his neighbor returned, "and they know it." "It's just their job," commented a third. "Well, I feel unclean," the boy from Utah said.

Degrading or not, the volunteers' letters home are filled with entreaties to parents to "save the *Life* magazine picture for me," or to "watch CBS tonight; I may be on." Degrading or not, the media attention clearly reinforced the volunteers' sense of their own and the project's importance.

More than anything else, however, it was the volunteers' growing appreciation of the dangers inherent in the project that had the greatest impact on them. If they had not realized the extent of these dangers before orientation, they certainly did by the time they left Ohio. This was no accident. In planning the sessions, one of the overriding goals had been to overwhelm the volunteers with the savagery and violence of life in Mississippi. It was hoped that by doing so, the staff might be able to persuade the naive or those with lingering doubts to stay home. So in session after session, staff members recounted the litany of horror they had seen in Mississippi. In turn, the volunteers duly recorded these sessions in their journals or letters home. Margaret Rose wrote:

> Last night's objective narration of facts is shot to hell by a breakdown in my defensives against fear and intimidation. The straw to break the back was the narration of a white leader here (a face mangled by scars) about a near death experience on the road coming up here. Fifteen guys in 3 cars ran them off the road (normal) and all in the car experienced the intent of the group: murder. It was somehow absolutely clear. A car full of leaders. Too good to pass over. One man, an exchange professor from Pakistan in a Mississippi university, happened to say he was a foreigner and had a passport. Some small doubt cross [*sic*] the minds of one of the 15. Somehow the mood shifted. They did not murder. He said we could expect this kind of encounter. He means it.

Another volunteer wrote:

> There is a quiet Negro fellow on the staff who has an ugly scar on his neck and another on his shoulder where he stopped 45 slugs. . . . Another fellow told this morning how his father and later his brother had been shot to death. . . . I'd venture to say that every member of the Mississippi staff has been beaten at least once and he who has not been shot at is rare. It is impossible for you to imagine what we are going in to, as it is for me now, but I'm beginning to see.

Role playing sessions and lessons in how to protect oneself if attacked only underscored the growing fear the volunteers were feeling. A volunteer described the general response to one such session: "John Strickland [a volunteer] stood ashen, staring at the lad curled up on the ground. Like the rest of the crowd, he was silent. Their eyes stayed riveted to the frozen tableau of a violence that till that moment had existed for them only in grade-B movies and tabloid spreads."

But no planned simulation could ever have dramatized the dangers of Mississippi life more forcefully than the real life event that took place in Neshoba County, Mississippi, on June 21, just as the second group of volunteers were arriving at Oxford, Ohio. Less than twenty-four hours after arriving in Mississippi, one in the first group of volunteers, Andrew Goodman, climbed into a station wagon with staff members James Chaney and Michael Schwerner, and drove off to investigate a church bombing near Philadelphia, Mississippi. They never returned. Arrested in the afternoon on traffic charges, the three were held until the evening, and then released into the Mississippi night. It was the last time they were seen alive. Their burned-out station wagon was found near Bogue Chitto Swamp the next day. But it was not until August that the bodies were discovered beneath an earthen dam near Philadelphia: Chaney's showed signs of a savage beating, and Goodman's and Schwerner's, single gunshot wounds to the chest.

Back at Oxford, news of the disappearance reached the volunteers during a general assembly. Sally Belfrage describes the scene:

> There was an interruption then at a side entrance: three or four staff members had come in and were whispering agitatedly. One of them walked over to the stage and sprang up to whisper to Moses, who bent on his knees to hear. In a moment he was alone again. Still crouched, he gazed at the floor at his feet, unconscious of us. Time passed. When he stood and spoke, he was something else; it was simply that he was obliged to say something, but his voice was automatic. "Yesterday morning, three of our people left Meridian, Mississippi, to investigate a church-burning in Neshoba County. They haven't come back, and we haven't had any word from them. . . ." Then a thin girl in shorts was talking to us from the stage: Rita Schwerner, the wife of one of the three. She paced as she spoke, her eyes distraught and her face quite white, but in a voice that was even and disciplined . . . Rita asked us to form in groups by home areas and wire our congressmen. . . . We composed telegrams, collected money and sent them, and tried to rub out the reality of the situation with action. No one was willing to believe that the event involved more than a disappearance. It was hard to believe even that. Somehow it seemed only a climactic object lesson, part of the morning's lecture, an anecdote to give life to the words of Bob Moses. To think of it in other terms was to be forced to identify with the three, to be prepared, irrevocably, to give one's life.

Word of the disappearance did, in fact, force the volunteers to confront the possibility of their own deaths. Some, like Stuart Rawlings, did so dispassionately:

> What are my personal chances? There are 200 COFO [Council of Federated Organizations] volunteers who have been working in the state a week, and three of them have already been killed. I shall be working in Forrest County, which is reputedly less violent than Neshoba County. But I shall be working on voter registration, which is more dangerous than work in Freedom Schools or Community Centers. There are other factors which must be considered too—age, sex, experience and common sense. All considered, I think my chances of being killed are 2%, or one in fifty.

Others expressed their fears more emotionally. "The reality of Mississippi gets closer to us everyday. We know the blood is going to flow this summer and it's going to be our blood. And I'm scared—I'm very scared.". . .

Voter Registration

Voter registration was the cornerstone of the Summer Project. This is not to say that it was necessarily the most important part of Freedom Summer.

However, it did supply the strategic impetus to the project. It was the success of the Freedom Vote campaign in the fall of 1963 that led SNCC and COFO to approve Bob Moses' plan for an even more ambitious political project the following summer. Originally, the plan was simply to use large numbers of white students—à la the Freedom Vote—to register as many black voters as possible. However, as long as the state Democratic party was effectively closed to blacks, it was unclear how beneficial the simple registration of voters would be. To address the problem, SNCC spearheaded the establishment of the Mississippi Freedom Democratic Party (MFDP) at a meeting held in Jackson on April 26, 1964. The MFDP then selected and ran a slate of candidates in the June 2 Democratic Primaries for Senator and three House seats. Not surprisingly, all four of the MFDP candidates (Fannie Lou Hamer, Victoria Gray, John Houston, and the Rev. John Cameron) were soundly beaten. So, following the primary, they obtained and filed the necessary number of signatures to be placed on the November ballot as independents. The Mississippi State Board of Elections rejected these petitions. Thus stymied, the SNCC/MFDP leadership returned to the strategy that had served them so well the previous fall. If they were to be shut out of regular electoral politics in the state, they would conduct a mock election to challenge the Mississippi Delegation to the August Democratic National Convention to be held in Atlantic City.

For the volunteers, this meant they would be involved in two parallel tasks: persuading blacks to attempt to register as official voters and "freedom registering" voters on behalf of the MFDP. Freedom registration forms could be filled out in the applicant's home: official registration meant a trip to the courthouse. That made the latter process the much more difficult of the two. Neither, however, was easy.

Canvassing is very trying, you walk a little dusty street, with incredibly broken down shacks. The people sitting on porches staring away into nowhere—the sweat running down your face! Little kids half-naked in ragged clothes *all* over the place—this is what you face with your little packet of "Freedom Forms". . . . Unfortunateley [sic], Freedom registration is terribely [sic] remote to these people. I almost feel guilty—like I'm playing for numbers only; . . . you walk up to a porch, knock on a door and enter into another world. . . . The walls are inevitably covered with a funeral hall calendar, a portrait calendar of President Kennedy, old graduation pictures. Maybe a new cheap lamp from Fred's dollar store.

You meet an afraid, but sometimes eager, curious face—one which is used to . . . saying "Yes Sir" to everything a white man says. . . . You see their pain, the incredible years of suffering etched in their worn faces; and then if you convince them to sign you leave. You walk down the deteriorating steps to the dirt, to the next house—the next world and start in on your sales pitch again, leaving behind something which has broken you a little more. Poverty in the abstract does nothing to you. When you wake up to it every morning, and come down through the streets of it, and see the same old man on the ground playing the accordian [sic], the same man selling peaches out of [a] basket to [sic] heavy for his twisted body, the same children, a day older—a day closer to those men—after this everyday, poverty is a reality that is so outrageous you have to learn to . . . become jaded for the moment—or else be unable to function.

I work in voter registration. . . . On a normal day we roll out of bed early in the morning. We may have slept in the Freedom House, or in the home of some generous and brave farmer. . . . We study the map of the county, decide where we will work for the day. We scramble for breakfast and hit the road.

The work is long and hot. We drive from farmhouse to farmhouse. I have averaged almost 200 miles a day in the car. The roads are in despicable condition . . . where the pavement stops the Negro sections are likely to begin. And if there is not even gravel on the roads, we can be reasonably sure that we are in a "safe" neighborhood. Such is not always the case, though, and more than once we have been cursed and threatened by someone for knocking on a white man's door.

When we walk up to a house there are always children out front. They look up and see white men in the car, and fear and caution cover their expressions. Those terrified eyes are never quite out of my mind; they drive me as little else could. Children who have hardly learned to talk are well-taught in the arts of avoiding whites. They learn "yassah" as almost their first words. If they did not, they could not survive. The children run to their parents, hide behind them. We walk up, smile, say howdy, and hold out our hands. As we shake hands I tell them my name. They tell me their names and I say Mr. ————, how do you do. It is likely the first time in the life of this farmer or housewife a white man has ever shaken hands with them, or even called them "with a handle to their names." This does not necessarily bode well with them; they are suspicious. Chances are they have heard about the "freedom riders" passing through. The news is usually greeted with mingled fear, excitement, enthusiasm and gratitude. But the confrontation is more serious and more threatening. They think, if Mr. Charlie knew . . . , and they are afraid. They have good reason to be. . . . Many . . . are sharecroppers, who must turn over a third to a half of the year's harvest to a man who does not work at all, but who owns the land they till. They may be evicted, and have often been for far less serious offenses. Nearly everyone black in Mississippi is at least a year in debt. The threat of suspended credit and foreclosure is a tremendous burden. . . .

Freedom Schools

In planning for the Summer Project, the SNCC staff was smart enough to realize that the oppression of Mississippi's black population depended on more than restricting access to the political system. An elaborate array of caste restrictions and institutional inequities also contributed to the maintenance of the racial status quo. Among these was Mississippi's separate but clearly unequal school system. . . . State educational expenditures in 1964 averaged $81.66 per white student and $21.77 for each black student. The fact that Mississippi was one of only two states without a mandatory education law merely underscored the lack of importance accorded public education. So too did other bits of evidence. At the time of the fall cotton harvest, many of the black schools in the delta were routinely closed to take advantage of the cheap source of labor the students provided. Within the classroom, curriculum content was carefully controlled. State-selected textbooks glorified the "Southern way of life" and made no mention of significant achievements by black Americans. In some districts, school superintendents even forbade the history of the Reconstruction period from being taught in the black schools. The Freedom Schools were an effort to counter the obvious inequities and insidious political messages inherent in this system.

The chief architect of the Freedom Schools was veteran SNCC field secretary Charlie Cobb. Drafted in the fall of 1963, Cobb's proposal called for the establishment of Freedom Schools "to provide an educational experience for students which will make it possible for them to challenge the myths of our society, to perceive more clearly its realities, and to find alternatives, and ultimately new directions for action." To put the necessary curricular flesh on the bones of Cobb's proposal, the National Council of Churches sponsored a March, 1964 meeting in New York City. There, educators, clergy, and SNCC staff members hammered out a basic curriculum for the schools emphasizing four principal topic areas: (1) remedial education, (2) leadership development, (3) contemporary issues, and (4) nonacademic curriculum. This basic framework was modified again following the appointment of Staughton Lynd, a history professor at Spelman, as director of the Freedom School program. In a mimeographed packet sent out just before the start of the Summer Project, the prospective teachers were informed that "the kind of activities you will be developing will fall into three general areas: (1) academic work, (2) recreation and cultural activities, (3) leadership development." In effect, the second and third topic areas designated in the original proposal had been lumped together under the single heading of "leadership development." Judging from the letters and journals written by the teachers, most projects adhered to this modified framework in organizing their Freedom School programs. Most offered a variety of basic courses in "leadership development," or what came to be known as the core curriculum. This consisted of courses in the history and philosophy of the movement, current events, and black history. "Academic work" was represented by nearly as many courses as there were students interested in taking them. Offerings ranged from basic remedial courses in reading and math to a variety of specialized classes in such topics as French, science, dance, and debate. Finally, a variety of "recreation and cultural activities" served to round out the Freedom School program. Among the most notable of these activities were the establishment of student-run newspapers on several projects and the writing and performing of an original play by the students in the Holly Springs project.

By any standard, the Freedom Schools were a success. Where project staff had hoped to attract 1,000 or so students, between 3,000 and 3,500 showed up. This in the face of a lack of facilities, the fears of black parents, and considerable violence directed at the schools. In McComb, seventy-five students showed up for classes the morning after a bomb leveled the church that had been serving as their school. Classes were held on the lawn in front of the smoldering church while younger children played in the ruins. In the small town of Harmony, the volunteers and townspeople set to cleaning up and repairing four abandoned school buildings to be used as classrooms.

> Then the sheriff came with about six white men, who were introduced as the "Board of Education." If they weren't Klan men, then they were at least Citizen Council [a more moderate segregationist group] people. God, they hated us . . . they told us we should not use it [the school building]; it is county property. We told them it was private property. We are getting a lawyer and will fight in court. Meanwhile . . . we will teach in a nearby church and outside.

Predictably, the court ruled in favor of the "Board of Education." Undaunted, the community erected its own school/community center.

> Everyday this week . . . the men of the community hammered and poured cement. At noon, about 7 or 8 women all gathered at the center with fried chicken, fish, salad, gallons of Kool-Aid, and apple turnovers, and served them to the men, we teachers, and each other. It is a thing of beauty to see us all work together. . . . We are a living repudiation of the "too many cooks" theory. It should be up by Saturday, or at latest Tuesday.

Eventually construction was finished and classes were held in the new building, if only for the final week of the summer.

In the classroom, the volunteers discovered most of the frustrations teachers have always faced. Overcrowding was frequently a problem:

> It became evident quite early that we were going to have many more than the expected 75 students. We called Jackson and got a promise of more teachers— at full strength we will have 23. This was when we expected 150 students. On registration day, however, we had a totally unexpected deluge: 600 students! . . . After a while, as they were coming in, it changed from a celebration to a crisis. This is 26 students per teacher—much better than the local or usual ratios, but still not enough . . . to do all we want to in six weeks.

Complaints about a lack of "educational standards" or "academic discipline" were common as well:

> The . . . class tends to degenerate into discussion of anything from standards of Negro beauty to the Marxist view of private property. . . . They are eager to argue, in some ways less eager to learn; some days ago I was attempting to give some minimal account of certain facts, when one of the more brilliant and remarkable pupils, but somewhat headstrong, declared that no offense, but, all this was rather boring, and it would be better if other people got a chance to speak, and if we could have discussions. I often think of the difficulties which . . . we will (for these schools will be continued all year) have in making the transition from this school to one where solid academic discipline must be imposed.

Add to this list the problems of absenteeism, staff dissension, and teacher "burn out," and one might well be describing the generic teaching experience. But there was a difference. The volunteers also experienced the emotional rewards reserved for those teaching students who are there voluntarily and who are being taken seriously for perhaps the first time in their lives.

> I can see the change. The 16 year-old's discovery of poetry, of Whitman and Cummings and above all else, the struggle to express thoughts in words, to translate ideas into concrete written words. After two weeks a child finally looks me in the eye, unafraid, acknowledging a bond of trust which 300 years of Mississippians said should never, could never exist—I can feel the growth of self-confidence.

> The atmosphere in the class is unbelievable. It is what every teacher dreams about—real, honest enthusiasm and desire to learn anything and everything. The girls come to class of their own free will. They respond to everything that is said. They are excited about learning. They drain me of everything that I have to offer so that I go home at night completely exhausted but very happy in spirit because I know that I have given to people. . . . Every class is beautiful. The girls respond, respond, respond. And they disagree among themselves. I have no doubt that soon they will be disagreeing with me. At least this is one thing that I am working towards. They know that they have been cheated and they want anything and everything that we can given them. I feel inadequate to the task of teaching them but I keep saying to myself that as long as I continue to feel humble there is a chance that we might all learn a whole lot together.

In talking to the volunteers today it is clear that they *did* learn a lot from their experience as teachers. Some became more politically radical as a result of the courses they taught or the discussions they had with other teachers. Others altered their career plans because of the satisfaction they had derived from teaching. The schools, then, had an impact beyond the students; the teachers, too, were taught.

Life in the Black Community

While not discounting the time and energy the volunteers expended on their jobs, it may well be that work was the least demanding part of their summer experience. After all there was a certain familiarity about their work assignments. Many of those who taught either were studying to become teachers or had taught before. Those with no teaching experience had at least spent years going to school as students, so the classroom was hardly a foreign place to them. As for the voter registration workers, 76 percent had participated in some form of civil rights organizing prior to the summer.

Very few of the volunteers, however, had had experiences that prepared them for life in the black community. For one thing, few had ever lived in rural areas. Their letters capture a kind of bemused appreciation of the new experiences this afforded them.

Man, like I don't even believe what I just did. You really had to be there to appreciate it. I took a bath. But no ordinary bath 'cause there's no running water. No, we take this bucket out in the back yard and fill it with water warmed over a fire. It's pitch black so we shine Mr. Clark's truck lights on the bucket. Then I strip down naked and stand in the bucket to wash. That is the way you take a bath around here.

[T]here are several [chickens] and several roosters. Roosters have this habit—one sits by the window and at dawn melancholically crows in a refrain reminiscent of a man falling off a cliff. The dog outside is just thrilled by this and barks his approval. The rooster thinks about this for a while—then to show he's no party-pooper he lets go again. This sends the dog in to sheer ecstasy. A little while later they pal it up and do a duet. By this time I usually wake up for the third time convinced that someone is being murdered at the foot of my bed.

More significant and more sobering than the volunteers' introduction to rural life was their exposure to "the other America." The publicity accorded Michael Harrington's 1962 book of the same name may have made the volunteers intellectually aware of poverty, but their class advantages had insulated them from any real experiential understanding of the problem. No such comfortable distance was possible in Mississippi. The volunteers' generally optimistic, idealistic upbringing had not prepared them for the underside of the American dream.

This was the most appalling example of deprivation ever seen by any of us who were canvassing. Upon approaching the house, we were invited on the porch which was strewn with bean shellings, rotten cotton sacks, pieces of a broken stove, and other assorted bits of scrap. . . . On a drooping cot to our right as we came in the door lay a small child (six months old). The child's eyes, nose, and mouth were covered with flies. Not being able to stand such a sight, I tried to chase them away only to be met with the reply of the mother of the child. "They will only come back again."

The whole house seemed diseased, rotten, and splitting at the seams with infection. Nevertheless, the people knew what we were coming for, and the forms were filled out without our asking. . . . This is a scene that was burned into all of our minds and which will make quiet sleep impossible.

One day has passed in Shaw and the other America is opening itself before my naive, middle-class eyes. The cockroaches draw patterns across the floor and table and make a live patchwork on the bed. Sweat covers my skin and cakes brown in my joints—wrist, elbow, knee, neck. Mosquito bites, red specks on white background.

The four-year-old grandson is standing by my side. I wonder how our presence now will affect him when he is a man?

I saw other children today who bore the marks of the Negro in rural Mississippi. One had a protruding navel the size of the stone he held in his hand. Several had distended stomachs.

Is America really the land that greets its visitors with "Send me your tired, your poor, your helpless masses to breathe free"?
There is no Golden Door in Shaw.

These images had a powerful impact on the volunteers, especially those whose upbringing had failed to provide them with even an ideological awareness of the problem. One especially sheltered volunteer, raised in an upper-middle-class suburb of Chicago, remembers "crying myself to bed at night [in Mississippi]. . . . I was just seeing too much, feeling too much. Things weren't supposed to be like this. I was just a mess. I just remember feeling sad, guilty and angry all at the same time."

In the face of these feelings—especially the guilt—the warmth, openness, and acceptance the volunteers felt from the black community was both confirming and confusing at the same time. Confirming because it communicated a kind of redemptive forgiveness that assuaged the guilt many of the volunteers were feeling; confusing because they didn't feel they deserved the special attention they were receiving. It all added up to a rich welter of feelings that left a good many of the volunteers overwhelmed. In a letter to her parents, Pam Parker struggled to communicate all she was feeling:

> I am starting to ramble because there is so much in my head and heart that I want to say but cannot. It has been a big week filled with so much enthsiasm and love that I feel overwhelmed. The girls I work with . . . have accepted me completely. They have told me this in a way they have responded in class, and some have told me this directly in their essays they have written me or in actual conversations. . . . This abundance of love and gratitude and acceptance makes me feel so humble and so happy.

Even today this jumble of emotions is evident in the former volunteers' recollections of the summer. Elinor Tideman Aurthur movingly recalled the daily lunchtime ritual at the Freedom School where she taught.

> [T]he women from the church everyday would bring food for all the teachers. . . . I used to look forward to it so much, and the fact that they would give this to us everyday, you know, was just wonderful . . . they had fried chicken and deviled eggs and potato salad. . . . They would spread it out on the table and they would, it was so nice [starts to cry] . . . it was so touching . . . to be cared for . . . that [way] . . . I felt like I belonged; I felt like they liked me and they wanted me to be there and I, it was so healing, you know, knowing what the divisions were . . . and yet somehow you can heal . . . I don't mean to say that they idealized us . . . because I don't think they did, but I think there was a kind of love . . . and a kind of compassion for us that they showed. It was a daily demonstration of love and acceptance . . . they were feeding us; they were giving us nourishment.

For many of the volunteers, the most immediate purveyors of this love and acceptance were the families that housed them. Sally Belfrage describes her introduction to her summer hostess: "[Mrs. Amos] hadn't planned to house summer volunteers, but Cora Lou's guest immediately became to her another child . . . she hugged me, fed me fried chicken and cornbread and installed me in the back bedroom."

Midway through the summer another volunteer described her "home life" to her mother:

> I have become so close to the family I am staying with—eleven people—that Mrs. H. finally paid me a great compliment. She was introducing me to one of her Negro women friends and said, "This is Nancy, my adopted daughter!" I baby-sat for her one night and in general we have become very close friends. She is a beautiful mother. My favorite picture of her is sitting peacefully in a summer chair with her 2-year-old baby girl in her lap; the baby, sucking her bottle, with one hand inside her mother's dress resting on her bosom. It is such a human sight; such love oozes from this house I can't begin to explain.

The hospitality of the local families was all the more touching for the risks they ran in housing the volunteers. Sheltering the "invaders" was grounds for harassment, dismissal from a job, or worse. David Gelfand relates an incident that took place while he was living with a prosperous black family in Meridian:

> [D]uring the five or six days I was there, there had been numerous . . . threatening phone calls and his [the black homeowner's] wife was quite upset about it. And one morning he came and woke me up. I was sleeping on the couch in the living room. And we had put a single piece of hair on Scotch Magic Tape across the hood, so you always checked before you got in the car. And the tape was broken. He had checked it. And the carport was right next to the kids bedroom— ages four to twelve. . . . And so he said, "okay, let's not do anything but release the emergency break and roll it out to the road." And we did that and then opened the hood. And there were four sticks of dynamite tied [to] . . . the ignition coil.

On occasion the volunteers were reluctantly asked to leave following incidents such as this. More often than not their hosts responded with a resiliency and toughness that impressed the volunteers. In his journal, Gren Whitman recounted the following early-morning encounter with the woman in whose house he was living:

> I am writing this at 6 A.M. Just now coming down the hall from the bathroom. I met Mrs. Fairley coming down the hall from the front porch carrying a rifle in one hand [and] a pistol in the other. I do not know what is going on. . . . [All she said was] "You go to sleep; let me fight for you."

Nor was this volunteer's experience unique. In their journals, letters, or interviews, many of the volunteers recounted similar incidents. For a group not raised around guns, it was yet another eye-opening aspect of the summer, and one that would lead a number of the volunteers to rethink strongly held pacifist convictions. . . .

Confrontation with White Mississippi

During the course of the summer, COFO compiled a running chronology of "hostile incidents.". . . . The list is twenty-six mimeographed pages long and covers everything from threatening phone calls to the disappearance of the three workers. Oddly, instead of being viscerally powerful, the list is curiously unaffecting. The sheer number of incidents simply overwhelms the reader, leaving one emotionally numb to the specifics of any given incident. A summary of violence during the summer has much the same effect. So that the following statistics:

- 4 project workers killed
- 4 persons critically wounded
- 80 workers beaten
- 1000 arrests
- 37 churches bombed or burned
- 30 black homes or businesses bombed or burned

fail to inform in an emotional sense. To gain some empathetic understanding of these events, one really has to read the volunteers' own accounts of them. Only then does one begin to appreciate the combination of shock, anger, disillusionment, and fear the volunteers felt in the face of the violence and terror they were witnessing.

> I really cannot describe how sick I think this state is. I really cannot describe the feeling in my stomach when I hear a typical story of injustice. . . . I cannot describe the real courage it takes to stay down here. I cannot describe the fears, the tensions and the uncertainties of living here. When I walk I am always looking at cars and people: if Negro, they are my friends; if white, I am frightened and walk faster. When driving, I am always asking: black? white? It is the fear and uncertainty that is maddening. I must always be on guard. . . . When confronted with a crisis, then the action is clearly defined. But when I do not know what to expect, but always know to expect something, then the tensions mount and I think of courage and of how deep my commitment has to be, and I think of getting the hell out of this sick state. I live day to day. I wake up in the morning sighing with relief that I was not bombed, because I know that "they" know where I live. And I think, well, I got through that night, now I have to get through this day, and it goes on and on. Even as I write this letter we are told that our office might be bombed by an anonymous voice, "to get rid of it once and for all."

> Yesterday while the Mississippi River was being dragged looking for the three missing civil rights workers, two bodies of Negroes were found—one cut in half and one without a head. Mississippi is the only state where you can drag a river any time and find bodies you were not expecting . . . Negroes disappear down here every week and are never heard about. Things are really much better for rabbits here. There is a closed season on rabbits when they may not be killed. Negroes are killed all year round. So are rabbits. The difference is that arrests

are made for killing rabbits out of season . . . Jesus Christ, this is supposed to be America in 1964.

Tonight the sickness struck. At our mass meeting, as we were singing "We Shall Overcome," a girl was shot in the side and in the chest. We fell to the floor in deathly fear; but soon we recovered and began moving out of the hall to see what had happened. . . . When I went out I saw a woman lying on the ground clutching her stomach. She was so still and looked like a statue with a tranquil smile on her face. I ran to call an ambulance.

While the presence of so many reporters in the state muted the violence to a degree, there was still no shortage of celebrated atrocities. In Greenwood a local activist, Silas McGhee, was shot in the head while he sat in his car out in front of a local club. Three volunteers raced him to the hospital only to be told they couldn't bring him in because they didn't have shirts on. They had taken their shirts off to bandage McGhee's head. On the evening of July 8, the front wall of the McComb Freedom House was destroyed by eight sticks of dynamite. Miraculously, the workers sleeping inside sustained only minor injuries. In Hattiesburg, two days later, five voter registration workers (including a rabbi visiting from Ohio) were attacked and severely beaten by two local men armed with lead pipes. And so it went, day in and day out, an endless string of incidents that lent a brutal and frightening texture to the volunteers' lives.

Had the volunteers been in their home states, they would invariably have turned to the police for protection from such incidents. Obviously, this was not practical in Mississippi. Often the police were implicated in the very incidents they were called to investigate. For instance, it turned out that Neshoba County Deputy Sheriff Cecil Price had coordinated the kidnapping and murders of Chaney, Goodman, and Schwerner. Even acting in their official capacity as law enforcement officers, the police spared few opportunities to harass or terrorize the volunteers. The following two affidavits filed by project volunteers recount typical incidents:

On July 9, 1964 Mary Lane, George Johnson and I accompanied Phillip Moore to the Greenwood Police Station. His purpose was to swear out a warrant against one of the local whites who had beaten him on the street. While Moore was thus occupied in another room, Miss Lane (Negro), Johnson (white) and I waited in the station room. There were three officers present—Desk Sergeant Simpson, Officer Logan and another unidentified officer. Logan was not in uniform—evidently off duty.

Logan took a long knife out of his pocket and started to sharpen it, [directing] a running stream of threats at the three of us. He asked Johnson how he liked "screwing that nigger" (indicating Miss Lane). Then he said, while sharpening the knife: "sounds like rubbing up against nigger pussy." He poked the knife against my ribs a few times; then he held it out toward me, told me to put my hand on it and asked: "Think it's sharp enough to cut your cock off?" Then he looked at Officer Simpson and said "You'd better get me out of here before I do what I'd like to do." At no time did Simpson or the other officer make any move to restrain him or protect us.

Shortly thereafter, he walked over behind the desk and took out a pistol from his trousers pocket. He brandished it in our direction and spun the chamber, then tucked it in his shirt front. He walked over to the door. Miss Lane was standing about eight feet from the door in front of him with her back turned to him. He took out his gun again, pointed it at Miss Lane for a few seconds and put it in his pants pocket. Then he opened the door with his left hand and simultaneously reached out and gave Miss Lane a shove with his right fist, knocking her several feet across the room. He swore at her; then Officer Simpson joined in and told Miss Lane: "Nigger, you get your ass away from that door." Miss Lane refused to move, explaining that she wasn't in the doorway, especially since Logan had knocked her practically across the room. Both the officers shouted threats at her, threatening to throw her in jail if she didn't move.

We went out about 15 minutes later and found that the tires of my car had been slashed. We went back in and reported the vandalism to the police but to no avail.

I pulled over and stopped, even though I heard no siren and had no definite knowledge that the following car contained police . . . and waited until the man in the car arrived. He came up to the truck and told me to get out. I asked for identification. He didn't show me anything, but told me to get out of the truck. I got out . . . and he and I walked to his car. Eric also got out and we received a . . . lecture while he was writing a ticket for speeding. . . . A highway patrol car arrived. . . . A third car then pulled up, which was unmarked and contained one man not in uniform. We could tell he had been drinking because of his actions and because we could smell the liquor.

After a short interchange between him and the first man, the first man left and the third man took me back to the car of the highway patrolman. He opened the car and told me to get inside. I got inside and sat on the back seat. He told me to move over and got in. All the doors and windows were shut. He said, "I can't kill you, but you know what I'm going to do to you." I answered, "No, sir." At this time he pulled his gun out of his holster and started to hit me on the head with the gun butt. I put my hands up to protect my head and rolled into a ball on the seat. Over a period of about a minute he hit me about four times on the head and about eight to ten times on the left hand. He also hit me about three times on the left leg, twice on my right hand, and once on my left shoulder. All or this was with the gun butt. . . . Three of them then went up to Eric. They had a conversation with Eric which I could not hear and one of the men raised a gun and struck Eric, knocking him down. He got up and was knocked down again. I had been sitting in the car through all of this. I felt the blood on my face and on my arm. The man who had beaten me then came back to the car and sat down in the back seat. He picked up a flashlight and hit me across the mouth with it. I then rolled into a ball again and he put the gun to my temple and cocked it. He said, "If you move, I'll blow your brains out."

Arrest often held a special kind of terror for the volunteers. As generations of Mississippi blacks had learned, there was virtually no end to the physical and psychological brutality Southern jailers could inflict upon a prisoner. In this the volunteers achieved equality. The police accorded them the same treatment.

> Upon entering [the] cell block we were taken to "nigger bull pen." Then [we] were shoved inside and officers said, "Here they are, get 'em boys." This is very unusual practice for whites to be put into the Negro section. The Negroes expressed confusion and fear. They were moved to beat us. Five minutes later, two officers took us into a white cellblock. This was about 12:30 A.M. Wednesday. At the white cell, the officers tried to incite white prisoners to take out their aggressions on the volunteers. ("It's wooping [*sic*] time.") The officers left and white prisoners gathered about. R———opened a conversation with one, and eased some of the tension. At this point, a Mexican spoke up and R———spoke to him in Spanish to help develop a rapport. After several minutes, a Mississippian announced that he hated all niggers and nigger-lovers and that COFOers were there to be beaten by the whites. However he was going to let us go.
>
> We lay down and listened to the argument, that lasted about three hours, on whether or not to beat us up. Sporadically, police officers and trustees would enter argument, attempting to incite white prisoners to "do justice." Morning arrived without real incident.
>
> About 10 A.M. officers took us out of the cell into fingerprinting rooms. As they were fingerprinting and [taking mug shots of] me, the officers told——— sordid stories about brutality that had been imposed upon fellow COFOers since the day before . . . and that a fellow white girl worker had been brutally raped and was on her death bed. At this point R———fainted. Upon awakening, the back of his head bleeding, we both were escorted to the lobby where attorneys from COFO in Jackson were waiting. . . . Local police refused to return personal papers, mainly handwritten notes, and denied they had even taken them. . . . In a subsequent interview, FBI agents expressed no interest in the mental harassment which occurred during the 12 hours spent in jail. . . . When taken to jail, R———had been told he was being arrested on a vagrancy charge. The following morning the sheriff said there were no charges.

Even when nothing happened, the possibility that something might could turn an evening alone in jail into an exhausting experience. In a letter home, William Hodes described his feelings during just such an evening.

> So there I was: alone in a Southern jail. First thing I did was check the layout of the cell in case I had to protect myself. I pulled the mattresses halfway off the beds so that I wouldn't hit any sharp corners as I went down. I planned to stay on one of the beds in the corner, so that I could get between two beds and a wall, and make myself hard to get at, except maybe by kicking. I was very jumpy, and was terrified at every door slam, phone call, and particularly key ring jingle jangle. My pulse was . . . over a hundred the whole three hours or so that I was in jail. . . . Then I was sure they would suddenly decide to drop charges and put me out into the hostile night. That would be really bad, because I knew that trouble was brewing all over the city. I could see the big police wagon outside my cell window, all ready to go. Cops with gas masks and sheriffs with rifles jump into

cars and zoom off. I heard dogs barking, police dogs. I figured that I would refuse to leave the station until they gave me a phone call: "You didn't let me have one when I came in, so you might as well give it to me now," I imagined myself saying. Could I hit a cop to get rearrested, or would that beating be worse than the possibility of getting caught by a mob? You can see why my pulse wasn't normal. . . .

I went home to bed, absolutely exhausted. The mental strain of being in there alone was just too much. While I slept, the office was shot into.

The cumulative effect of these confrontations with the enemy was to wear the volunteers down. As the summer wore on, the physical and emotional strain grew progressively worse. "Fear *can't* become a habit," wrote one volunteer to a friend. But in fact it had. The quality of Mississippi violence—random, savage—necessitated the habit. It was a means of survival. But it was achieved at the cost of physical and psychological exhaustion. Writing late in the summer, Sally Belfrage acknowledged that "there are incipient nervous breakdowns walking all over Greenwood." Tensions within the projects only added to the strain. . . .

All things considered, it had been a remarkable summer for a remarkable group of people. As it drew to a close, the volunteers found themselves exhausted and exhilarated in equal measure. There simply had been no letup in intensity from the time they had arrived at Oxford. For the better part of two months they had been subjected to one emotionally draining experience after another. They had confronted their own mortality, experimented with new lifestyles, reveled in transcendent community, known terror, lived in poverty, felt the sting of racial hostility, and experienced the development of a radical new political consciousness. Theirs was an interesting dilemma. As much as they wanted the psychic barrage to stop, so too did they want the "high" to continue. In letters home the volunteers acknowledged the strong and conflicting feelings they were having:

All I have to do is sit and the world piles in on me. I would like something simple, to go swimming once, or see a movie, or walk in a field, or go for a drive without having to look out the back window or just to sit somewhere cool and quiet with a friend. Only once might work. . . . I'm simply exhausted. I yell at everybody. No, I don't yell at anyone at all, I only think I do, but I can't. Madness, a constant agitation, unrest. It could all be explained by fatigue. . . . But there's a strange mechanism at work on us at night . . . when the children are gone, the chicken eaten, the mass meeting over, then there are still all of us left to egg each other on, everyone full and fed up with it but somehow longing for the next disaster. . . . All I've got is a fabulous depression, split in two—I can't bear another moment of it but it's impossible to believe that it can end in three weeks. How can I leave? How can I leave people I love so much? What made me think I could accomplish anything in this length of time? There's nowhere else I want to be.

The volunteers resolved this conflict in very different ways. At least eighty decided to stay in Mississippi indefinitely. While there had been little encouragement from SNCC to do so and no official mechanism set up to retain people, these volunteers were not ready to leave in August. Their letters home reflected both their resolve and the anguish they were causing their families.

> I have been here nearly two months. I know the drudgery, the dangers, and the disappointments. I know what it's like to eat meatless dinners, to be so exhausted you feel as though you will drop, to have five people show up at a meeting to which 20 should have come. Yet I also know what it's like to sing, "We Shall Overcome" with 200 others till you think the roof will explode off the church. I know what it's like to see the organization which you have nurtured come to life and begin to function and create. I know what it's like to have a choir of little girls sing out, "Hi, Ellen," as I walk down the road and envelop me in their hugs.
>
> Only now that I know these things can the decision to stay be mature and meaningful.
>
> Furthermore, maturity does not develop from facing a familiar routine from year to year. Maturity comes from having to face new situations, from making new decisions, from coming to terms with a new world. . . .
>
> This summer is only the briefest beginning of this experience—both for myself and for the Negroes of Mississippi. So much of it will seem pointless if it ends now, or if it is taken up again in two years. A war cannot be fought and won if the soldiers take twelve-month leaves after every skirmish. . . . I have considered your parental qualms; really I have. But I'm afraid they cannot counterbalance the feelings of my duty here.

> Many people, including those who supported my going to Mississippi as part of the Summer Project, and those who believe that the Summer Project has been an important thing, have expressed shock and disapproval at my decision to go back to Mississippi, and have attempted to dissuade me from returning. I have been amazed at this response.
>
> There is a certainty, when you are working in Mississippi, that it is important for you to be alive and to be alive doing just what you are doing. And whatever small bit we did for Mississippi this summer, Mississippi did ten times as much for us.
>
> I guess the thing that pulls me back most are the people who made us a part of their community. People I knew in Mississippi could honestly and unselfconsciously express affection in a way that few people I know in the North are able to do. They did not have to be "cool" or "one up" or "careful.". . . In Mississippi I have felt more love, more sympathy and warmth, more community than I have known in my life. And especially the children pull me back.

The majority of the volunteers *did* go home. However, for many the decision to do so was just as wrenching as it had been for those who remained behind.

August 6

> I had a very hard time . . . convincing myself that I should leave Mississippi. . . . It is so necessary that people stay, especially northern white students. Holly Springs

has so much potential and could really develop into something much greater than it already is if there are the right leaders here. I would love to be a part of making the Freedom School into a real ongoing concern with the adults and kids of the community doing most of the teaching and leading themselves. However, I have come to realize that there is still a great deal that I need to learn. I feel that I still have a lot of growing up to do. But most of all I see what this kind of life can do to you and I think that I need a rest and a change of environment to prepare myself for a life-long commitment wherever I might be needed.

Even harder than the decision to leave was the painful sense of dislocation many of the volunteers felt once they were out of Mississippi. They had arrived in the state in groups, buoyed by the exhilarating sense of community they had felt at Oxford. Now they trickled out of Mississippi one by one, alone and exhausted, without ever having an opportunity to process or come to grips with all they had seen and felt. If Oxford had oriented them to life in Mississippi, nothing prepared them for life after Mississippi. For many the transition was rough. Barely three weeks after writing the previous letter, Pam Parker struggled to express how she was feeling:

> I have been putting off writing my concluding thoughts on my experiences in Mississippi because I have been unable to sort out my thoughts and feelings since leaving. I will try to at least give you a picture of the reactions of one girl on entering the free, white world of her past once again. No one can go through an experience such as Mississippi without coming out changed. I do not believe that many of those who spent their summer in Mississippi will be able to go back to their old way of living.
>
> I am out of Mississippi and glad to be out for a while. I have always loved to take walks at night but never have I felt so grateful for the opportunity to take peaceful walks as these last few days. I could sit for hours on the porch of our friends' place in New Hampshire, soaking in the peacefulness and the quiet of the countryside. I feel so relaxed . . . but I am not relaxed, not completely. I wonder if I will ever relax fully again. . . .
>
> I have found that instead of Mississippi seeming distant from my life, it and all that it exemplifies in a magnified form of our society has become unbearably real to me.

She was not alone in what she was feeling. On the very same day, another volunteer in another state echoed her sentiments: "I've felt depressed since I've returned. I don't know how much is personal, and how much it is a reaction to that place and the people I've left behind, and a heightened awareness of so much that is wrong up here." Contrast the underlying tone of these two letters with that expressed in a third letter written the same day by a volunteer who had stayed on in Mississippi:

> We were sitting on the steps at dusk, watching the landscape and the sun folding into the flat country, with the backboard of the basketball net that is now netless sticking up into the sunset at a crazy angle. Cotton harvesters went by—and the

sheriff—and then a 6-year-old Negro girl with a stick and a dog, kicking up as much dust as she could with her bare feet. As she went by, we could hear her humming to herself, "We shall overcome."

The psychic and geographic distance from Mississippi was great indeed. Even greater was the gulf between the volunteers' summer experiences and their previous lives. Bridging that gap would prove difficult for many, impossible for some. For many the old adage, "you can always go home," would prove a lie. For some of the volunteers there would be no "going home" except in a geographical sense. They had simply seen and felt too much to ever experience their world in the same way again. They had been changed in some very fundamental ways. The extent and significance of these changes would become apparent over the next few months.

REVIEW QUESTIONS

1. What were the specific obstacles that the summer volunteers faced in Mississippi in getting African Americans registered to vote?

2. Why was it thought necessary or desirable to establish Freedom Schools? What were the schools intended to do?

3. In 1964, Mississippi ranked at or near the bottom of all the states in various measures of economic health and prosperity. In addition to being among the poorest states, if not absolutely the poorest, Mississippi also probably had the worst record with regard to racial oppression and violence. What evidence do you find in the selection that these two conditions may have been connected? What other connections may there have been between poverty and racial oppression?

4. What were the effects on the volunteers, positive and negative, of their experiences in Mississippi?

5. The selection clearly shows that those involved in Freedom Summer felt a curious mixture of hope and fear about what they were doing. To what extent was this mixture of feelings prevalent in the rest of the civil rights movement of the 1950s and 1960s? To what extent were the violence and threat of violence that marked Freedom Summer characteristic of the rest of the movement?

FOR FURTHER READING

John Hope Franklin's *From Slavery to Freedom* (1978) is a general history of African-Americans. C. Vann Woodward, *The Strange Career of Jim Crow* (1974), is a relatively brief but very rich account of race relations in the South from the end of the Civil War to the recent past. Harvard Sitkoff, *The Struggle for Black Equality: 1954–1980* (1981) is a very good short history of the civil rights movement. Taylor Branch's *Parting the Waters: America in the King Years, 1954–1963* (1988) tells a part of that story in much greater detail. Martin Luther King, Jr. expressed his own views in *Stride Toward Freedom: The Montgomery Story* (1958) and *Why We Can't Wait* (1964). For another perspective on racial issues in the United States, *The Autobiography of Malcolm X* (1965) is essential reading. The history of SNCC is related by Clayborne Carson in *In Struggle: SNCC and the Black Awakening of the 1960's* (1981). There are many autobiographical accounts of life in the civil rights movement in general and Freedom Summer in particular that are valuable sources of information. Among them are Cleveland Sellers with Robert Terrell, *The River of No Return: The Autobiography of a Black Militant and the Life and Death of SNCC* (1973), by an African American man, Mary King, *Freedom Song: A Personal History of the 1960's Civil Rights Movement* (1987), by a white woman, and Anne Moody, *Coming of Age in Mississippi* (1968) by an African-American woman who was also a native of Mississippi.

Wayne Miller/Magnum Photos

The Haight-Ashbury section of San Francisco was the headquarters of the counterculture.

19

The Counterculture

JAY STEVENS

The 1960s were many things, most certainly a decade of tumult and up-heaval, marked by the emergence of a number of protest movements—the civil rights movement, the student movement, the women's rights movement, the antiwar movement, the environmental movement. Those who enlisted in these causes were, of course, demonstrating their unhappiness with the existing state of affairs and their desire to change it in some way. We may distinguish two broad types of protest or rebel-lion: One type—the civil rights movement and the protests against the Vietnam War for example—was directed toward social change through political action. The other type—for example the "consciousness rais-ing" efforts of the women's movement, trying to make women aware of the disadvantages they faced solely because of their gender—might be called cultural rebellion, in that the action was not directed so much against particular laws, policies, or institutions, but against the values and ways of thinking out of which those laws, policies, and institutions grew. The goal was not to get laws repealed or policies revised but to change the way people thought.

Another example of cultural rebellion is the counterculture. In the 1950s, a small group of artists and intellectuals known as the Beats, including such people as the poet Allen Ginsberg and the novelists Jack Kerouac and William Burroughs, had begun to argue that Ameri-can society and culture were intellectually and spiritually sterile. Throughout the 1950s the Beats were little more than a curiosity to most Americans, more ridiculed for their strange appearance or reviled for their use of drugs than listened to for their ideas. By the 1960s, increasing numbers came to share the Beats' notion that America was deeply flawed in fundamental ways and that drastic revisions were necessary. The counterculture was born out of the resulting search for alternatives to the dominant culture.

The term "counterculture" is difficult to define with precision, for the people who comprised it were a diffuse group with divergent ideas and goals. In general, however, one can say that they were united by a common belief that modern America was materialistic, overcentralized, competitive, conformity-ridden, and riddled with conflict and anxiety. In its place, they hoped to construct a new culture based on individual freedom and love. Frequently, perhaps even usually, these ideas were so vague as to be nearly meaningless, and many of those who eventually became involved in the counterculture were self-indulgent sensation-seekers. This was true in large part because of the central place drugs held in the counterculture experience. To prophets of the drug culture, such as the maverick psychologists Timothy Leary and Richard Alpert, drugs were a means by which individuals could "expand their consciousness" and achieve important insights about the universe, themselves, and their place in it. All too often, however, the drug experience degenerated into a quest for nothing more profound than a good time, immediate gratification, "kicks". In the following selection Jay Stevens tells the story of the counterculture, where it came from, what it was all about, and what happened to it.

There is no simple way to explain what went on in the Sixties, no easily identifiable event, like the assassination at Sarajevo, which one can point to and say, "there, tensions might have been growing for decades, but that's the spark that touched off the explosion." Indeed, the more thoroughly you study the Sixties, the more comforting becomes a concept like the *zeitgeist*. Strip away the decade's thick impasto of sex, drugs, rebellion, politics, music, and art, and what you find is a restless imperative to change, a "will to change," if you will, and one that could be as explanatory for the latter half of this century as Nietzsche's "will to power" was for the first.

Change jobs, spouses, hairstyles, clothes; change religion, politics, values, even the personality; try everything, experiment constantly, accept nothing as given. It was as though the country as a whole was undergoing a late adolescence, and not just the 20 million Baby Boomers whose leading edge began turning eighteen in 1964. Either that or the Boomers, the largest generation ever, possessed enough mass of their own to alter the normal spin of things.

But alter it in what direction? Somehow the satire of *Mad* magazine and the kinetic electricity of Elvis, the surreal dailyness of Beaver Cleaver and the fear of the Bomb; somehow the awful drabness of Dad in his official corporate uniform, the gray flannel suit, and the awful sameness of the suburbs, those theme parks of the good safe life; somehow all these had combined into a combustible outrage. It was an almost obscene irony, but the kids who had enjoyed the richest, most pampered adolescence in the history of the world had now decided that it was all crap. "We've got so many things we could puke," they said. "We live in the most manipulated society ever created by man."

Since infancy (or so it seemed to the Boomers) their minds had been measured, their psyches sculpted, their emotions straitjacketed, and for what? Why, to preserve the good old Corporate American Way of Life!

The corporations, so omnipotent during the Fifties, were vilified as the source of most of what was wrong with America, whether it was the imperialism that had brought on the Vietnam War or the subtler neurosis that caused people to measure their self-worth in terms of the number and quality of the consumer items they were able to surround themselves with. The same throwaway culture that the parents found convenient and liberating was dismissed by the children as ugly, trashy, and stupid when measured against the ecological cost of living in such a manner.

But the kids also realized that the corporations were only the visible tip of the iceberg, that the real menace was less tangible, although by the late Fifties it already had a number of provocative names: *the military-industrial complex, the power elite, the Garrison Society,* and—the ultimate winner in terms of usage—*the Establishment.*

What these terms attempted to describe was a conspiracy of money and power whose tentacles stretched into every nook and cranny of daily life. Corporations were members of the Establishment. But so were labor unions. Politicians were valued players, of course, but so were teachers, reporters and generals. Republicans and Democrats were merely different frequencies in the Establishment spectrum, while liberalism was nothing more than a clever way of allowing the illusion of change while maintaining the perquisites of power. Uniting these disparate elements was an overt commitment to anticommunism and American hegemony abroad, together with a domestic brand of democracy that sounded more like a well-run corporation than the noble experiment of the Founding Fathers. Instead of "the people," Establishmentarians talked about the managed and the managers, a formula that was not too dissimilar to the one followed in the Establishment's archenemy, the USSR.

Reflecting upon this woeful state of affairs, the Baby Boomers decided that not only didn't they want to be managed, but they could do without the occupation of manager as well. Norman Mailer caught their mood exactly when he wrote that "the authority had operated on their brain with commercials, and washed their brain with packaged education, packaged politics. The authority had presented itself as honorable, and it was corrupt, corrupt as payola on television, and scandals concerning the leasing of aviation contracts—the real scandals as everyone was beginning to sense were more intimate and could be found in all the products in all the suburban homes which did not work so well as they should have worked, and broke down too soon for mysterious reasons. The shoddiness was buried deep. . . ."

Of course not every Sixties kid accepted this critique. For each one who wanted to seize power, dismantle the Establishment, and redistribute the wealth, there were at least ten others who just wanted to get through school, get laid, get a job, and get out of going to Vietnam; for every kid who grew his hair long, smoked dope, listened to rock music, and proclaimed an urgent longing to make a clean break with American society, there was a corresponding kid who drank beer, worshiped the local football team, and measured his personal worth by the car he drove. The differential between silent majority and noisy minority probably varied little for the kids of the Sixties from that of their parents. But it didn't seem that way, if only because the silent majority is never news. And they are even less so when the *zeitgeist* is changing rapidly.

Compared to the quiescent teens of the Fifties, the Baby Boomers seemed a generation of Jacobins, a rude, unwashed, overeducated mob who, if not precisely endangering the State, certainly threatened one's peace of mind.

One of the difficulties in writing about the Sixties is deciding when the story began. Was it the day President Kennedy was assassinated in Dallas, a day imprinted on every Baby Boomer the way Pearl Harbor was for their parents? Kennedy was the Establishment's best salesman; with programs like the Peace Corps he almost managed to sell liberalism to the Baby Boom. But his death left a vacuum that was soon filled with anger and cynicism.

Or was it during the first freedom marches in Mississippi, when the kids learned just how loath the Establishment was to extend basic rights to the Blacks? Reflecting on what had happened to the consciousness of those kids who went South in the summer of 1964, Michael Novak later wrote: "Enough young people have been beaten, jailed and even killed while trying to bring about simple constitutional rights to American Negroes to have altered the inner life of a generation. The young do not think of law enforcement as the enforcement of justice; they have experienced it as the enforcement of injustice."

Or did it begin in the fall of 1964, when a group of Berkeley students staged a spontaneous sit-in that quickly grew into the Free Speech Movement?

The seeds of the FSM were sown in early September, when Berkeley Chancellor Clark Kerr, perhaps acting upon the liberal assumption that politics in the old sense was dead, banned all politicking outside Berkeley's main gate on Bancroft Way. For years Bancroft Way had been an ideological flea market, with groups of every persuasion soliciting funds and dispersing literature. Although Kerr's decision drew protests from nearly every student group, from the fledgling Students for a Democratic Society to Youth for Goldwater, Kerr refused to relent and in late September suspended eight students for political activities.

Then, on October 1, a young mathematics graduate student named Jack Weinberg was arrested for refusing to abandon the table he was manning for CORE—the Committee on Racial Equality. A campus squad car was dispatched and when it arrived Weinberg went limp, a technique he had acquired the previous summer during the freedom marches in Mississippi. As the security guards dragged him to the car, an outraged crowd began to form, effectively blocking the exit. For the next thirty-two hours, speaker after speaker climbed atop the car's hood, exhorting the students to seize the moment and strike. It was as though somebody had touched a match to a mood that had been building for years, not just a few weeks.

I felt "torn open, everything boiling in me," wrote Michael Rossman in *The Wedding Within the War*, his memoir of the Sixties. A colleague of Weinberg's in the Berkeley mathematics department, and a fellow radical, Rossman described the aftermath of the cop car siege as "the Tearing Loose—the active beginning of the end of my life within the old institutions."

On December 2, 1964, four hundred members of the Free Speech Movement seized Sproul Hall and held it until they were dragged out singing by hundreds of helmeted riot police. Five days later, an audience of eighteen thousand gathered at Berkeley's Greek Theatre to listen as Clark Kerr poured forth his vision of the true academic community as a "knowledge factory" whose purpose lay in creating socially productive individuals. Now this was the wrong tack to take with students who increasingly resented the factory analogy, but the real mistake came after the speech. As the meeting ended, Mario Savio, a young philosophy major who had become one of the leaders of the FSM, stepped to the rostrum. He intended to invite everyone to a mass rally where Kerr's speech could be debated, but before he could open his mouth to speak he was grabbed by two policemen and wrestled to the floor. A wave of anger swept the crowd. As Godfrey Hodgson later wrote, "one minute Clark Kerr, the champion of liberalism, had been talking about the powers of persuasion against the use of force, and the next moment armed agents of the University were choking his opponent, the symbolic representative of free speech."

The next afternoon the faculty voted 824–115 to accede to the FSM's demands. The Baby Boom had received its first taste of political power.

Not surprisingly, the facts attending the birth of the FSM were drowned in an ocean of learned speculation, as journalists and political scientists rushed to explain this momentary aberration. Although few of the commentators could see beyond their own ideological categories—Lewis Feuer, a reputed expert in left-wing political phenomena, dismissed the FSM as "intellectual lumpen-proletariats, lumpen beatniks, and lumpen agitators" who espoused a "melange of narcotics, sexual perversion, collegiate Castroism and campus Maoism"—most divined the central theme of the protest, which was a hearty dislike of the liberal ideal of a rationally managed society. It was a revolt against the depersonalization implied by the factory analogy that Kerr was so fond of, which was why the IBM card, with its ubiquitous warning "do not fold, spindle or mutilate," became the symbol of all they despised. Rossman described the target of the FSM as the Big Daddy Complex, which was his name for the species of liberal paternalism that had banished political diversity not only from Bancroft Way, but from the University curriculum as well. The motto of the Big Daddy Complex, he wrote, was the phrase "for your own good," and its "effect is to inhibit autonomous adulthood."

This last was a crucial point: instead of adopting the definition of psychological maturity that the mental health movement had proposed in the Fifties, with its emphasis on conformity and responsibility to the larger ideals of society, the Baby Boomers were moving in the opposite direction. The ability to let go, to explore the depths of one's own psyche, to conform to individual rather than social imperatives—these were the new benchmarks of psychological maturity.

Another element that the commentators completely ignored was the exhilaration that came from collective action. During the fifteen-hour occupation of Sproul Hall, life had been lived in a wholly new key. It was, to bend Maslow's term, a collective peak experience whose import lay not so much in the demands that had brought them together, as in the fact that they *were* together. The protesters had turned Sproul Hall into a carnival, with Chaplin movies on the walls and folksingers in the stairwells. "We ate terrible baloney sandwiches and then established the first Free University, conducting some dozen classes cross-legged atop the Civil Defense disaster drums stored in the basement," remembered Rossman. "People smoked grass in the corners . . . and at least two women had their first full sexual experiences under blankets on the roof, where walkie-talkies were broadcasting news to the outside." . . .

The word *hippie*, indeed the whole phenomenon of the Haight-Ashbury, first came to light in September 1965, in the course of a San Francisco *Examiner* article about a coffeehouse called the Blue Unicorn.

The Unicorn, which advertised the cheapest food in the city, was a little hole in the wall on Hayes Street, near Golden Gate Park, in the midst of a twenty-five-block district that derived its name from two intersecting streets—Haight Street, which ran in a flat line toward the Pacific Ocean; and Ashbury, a much shorter thoroughfare which climbed up Mt. Sutro and stopped. Like the Unicorn, the Haight-Ashbury was something of a hole-in-the-wall district, full of ornate but shabby Victorian houses dating back to the Teens, when so many politicians had built themselves mansions above Haight Street that the area had been nicknamed "politicians' row."

But in the intervening years the Haight-Ashbury had tumbled so far down the socioeconomic ladder that during World War II it had been considered an appropriate spot for worker housing. After the war refugees from Eastern Europe and a small population of Orientals had tried to resuscitate its former splendor, but when Blacks began moving into the district—encouraged by urban renewal, which was razing their traditional ghetto to the west—these homesteaders had packed up, leaving the Haight in the curious position of offering lavish living for dirt cheap prices. For a few hundred dollars it was possible to rent a whole house, complete with leaded windows and ballroom.

Now it happened that this abandonment coincided with the disintegration of the North Beach Beat scene, due to a combination of rising rents, police harassment, and obnoxious tourists who flocked to see the beatnik in his native habitat. The Haight was an obvious solution, and by the time the *Examiner* tumbled to what was happening, it supported a thriving bohemian community, of which the Unicorn was the heart and soul.

This, then, was the gist of what journalist Michael Fallon had to report to his readers: the Beat movement, far from being dead, was alive and flourishing in what had once been one of San Francisco's tonier neighborhoods. But if the Haight was where the Beat movement had fled to, then something had happened in the passage. Compared to the moody, nihilistic beatniks of old, those clichéd cave creatures in their black turtlenecks, the patrons of the Unicorn were like vivid butterflies in their pink striped pants and Edwardian greatcoats. They were sunny and cheery, and the word *love* punctuated their conversation with alarming frequency: all kinds of love, elevated ethereal love and plain old physical love. And on nights when LEMAR—the acronym for the legalize marijuana movement—wasn't meeting at the Unicorn, the Sexual Freedom League was.

Like any scientist fortunate enough to discover a new class of fauna, Fallon's first instinct was to give it a name, which he did by borrowing Norman Mailer's hipster and contracting it into hippie, a word that caught some of the Unicorn's buoyancy, but one the hippies themselves were never fond of. From their perspective, hippie was just another example of the subtle derogation practiced by the mainstream media whenever it was confronted by something outside its usual ken. Hadn't Fallon's fellow journalist, Herb Caen, done something similar when he tagged Ginsberg & Co. with the diminutive beatnik?

But whether they liked it or not, hippie it was and would be.

Oddly, Fallon's inventiveness later served to obscure the fact that in many respects the hippies were second-generation Beats. This was clearer in the early days, when it was still easy to trace the connection between the old Beat fantasy of creating an alternative culture—the word "counterculture" was still years off—and what was aborning in the Haight. "We have a private revolution going on," wrote Bob Stubbs, the owner of the Unicorn, in one of the policy statements he used to distribute to his customers. "A revolution of individuality and diversity that can only be private. Upon becoming a group movement, such a revolution ends up with imitators rather than participants."

A very private revolution: at the time of Fallon's article, there were probably only a dozen houses scattered throughout the Haight that could have been characterized as hippie. And yet the district pulsed with energy. "Even if you lived elsewhere, your forays to the neighborhood were always important," wrote one frequent visitor. "The Haight-Ashbury had four or five grapevines cooking at all times . . . and the two words that went down the wire most often in those days were *dope* and *revolution*. Our secret formula was grass, LSD, meditation, hot music, consolidation, and a joyous sexuality."

Had you lived in any of those houses in the autumn of 1965, it would have been immediately clear that the key ingredient in that formula, the reason why the Haight was not the North Beach six years later, was LSD. LSD was the Haight's secret weapon, with emphasis on secret. "Taking it was like being in a secret society," remembers one pioneer. "Hardly anything was being said about it publicly . . . [although] not an illegal drug, people acted as if it were; it seemed illegal."

It also seemed intensely serious. In the compelling phrase of one hippie, LSD was hard kicks: "hard kicks is a way of looking at your existence, not like mistreating your body or throwing your mind to the crows. It's a way of extending yourself [so that] something spectacular and beautiful can be available to you."

It was axiomatic, in the beginning, that hard kicks were dangerous. They were not a game for the timid or insecure. But insofar as they offered a way out of the white suburban world that so many of the early hippies had been born into, they were worth the risk. . . .

According to the hippies, LSD was "one of the best and healthiest tools available" for the examination of consciousness. "Acid opens your door, opens the windows, opens your senses. Opens your beam to the vast possibilities of life, to the glorious indescribable beauty of life." You could "drop down into your unconscious to see the pillars and the roots of the tree which is your personality. . . . You see what your hangups are; you might not even overcome them but you cope with them, and that's an amazing advance."

The Haight then, in its earliest incarnation, was a kind of sanitarium, an indigenous Baden Baden that offered a therapeutic regime of good vibes and drugs, rather than mountain air and mineral springs. . . .

By June 1966, an estimated fifteen thousand hippies were living in the Haight, an increase that baffled the hippies about as much as it did everyone else. "God has fingered that little block system between Baker and Stanyon Street," they told the curious. "And we spend all our time, verbally and nonverbally, trying to discover why." Helen Perry, one of the first of the social scientists to arrive on the scene, likened the Haight to "the delta of a river," where all the unrooted sediment of America was washing ashore. But even

Perry was unclear as to why the undercurrents of American life should be sweeping so many into this odd backwater . . . asked why they had chosen the Haight, the hippies murmured vague things like, "I fell in with some vibrational energies and ended up here.". . .

Although the Summer of Love officially began on June 21, the summer solstice, its actual beginning occurred the previous fall, specifically on October 6, 1966, the day the California law making possession of LSD a misdemeanor went into effect.

Declaring that the long arm of the State was reaching into their psyches, the hippies welcomed the new law with a sort of Boston tea party—plenty of drugs, free food, and music—which took place in a narrow strip of park paralleling Haight Street known as the Panhandle. The get-together had a name, the Love Pageant Rally, and to everyone's surprise and delight, several thousand extravagantly garbed hippies turned out, prompting one middle-aged tourist to remark to a local journalist: "Why, you don't see anything like this in Philadelphia."

Nor, discounting the Trips Festival, which already seemed ancient history, had anything like it been seen in San Francisco before. For the first time, surrounded by fellow freaks, it dawned on the hippies that their ruling fantasy might really be correct, that the evolutionary tides might really be flowing in their direction. Perhaps it was a consequence of all the LSD, but from the Love Pageant on, a naive optimism permeated the Haight, combined with a mystical faith that whatever was needed would be provided. Almost overnight the Haight found itself with its own newspaper, the San Francisco *Oracle*, its own police force, the Hells Angels, and its own radio station, KMPX, whose lobby usually included a hippie or two in full lotus; its own Chamber of Commerce in the HIP [Haight Independent Proprietors] merchants and its own social workers in the Diggers. And there was talk of a hip employment agency, a hip hotel, and a hip cafeteria that would serve food grown on communal farms run by hippies tired of the urban grind. . . .

The first Diggers—the name originally belonged to a group of seventeenth-century religious communists who made the mistake of demanding access to the uncultivated land in Cromwellian England, and were exterminated—were actors. They belonged to a theatrical enterprise known as the San Francisco Mime Troupe, which performed a kind of political *commedia dell'arte* wherever there was space for stage and audience. The Mime Troupe specialized in street theater, which was perhaps why a few of the company began to see the Haight as a wonderful context for a perpetual theater of the absurd.

The Diggers announced their presence in a series of anonymous broadsides that mocked the smell-the-flower fatuousness of so many of the hippies. Cosmic was fine, LSD was fine, they said, but when you came back down you still had to cope with outrageous rents and bad food and all the temptations of the established culture, particularly money. "Money lust is sickness," the broadsides said. "It kills perception . . . almost all of us were exposed to this disease in childhood, but dope and love are curing us." Not surprisingly, the HIP merchants were a frequent target of Digger critiques. "How long will you tolerate people [straight or hip] transforming your trip into cash?" And they even went so far as to picket one festival, the First Annual Love Circus, because admission was a steep $3.50.

From broadsides the Diggers progressed to street theater: the Birth and Death ritual, the New Year's Wail, the Invisible Circus, the Death of Money parade. This last, consisting of six pallbearers wearing enormous papier-mâché animal heads and carrying a black-draped coffin down Haight Street, was a spectacle worthy of the surrealists. Gradually, however, the Diggers began talking less and doing more. They set up shop in an old garage known as the Free Frame of Reference, which was a reference to the huge yellow frame that they lugged around, largely so they could make the pointed joke of inviting onlookers to "step into our frame of reference now." They opened a Free Store that was full of cast-off clothes and housewares scrounged in daily forays around San Francisco. And the goods really were free. More than one Samaritan watched in astonishment as the Diggers, after ceremoniously accepting a contribution, proceeded to light their cigarettes with it. And if anyone demanded to see the person in charge, the Diggers always replied, "You are!"

The Diggers made their most substantial contribution, however, with the food feeds. Every afternoon at 4 P.M. their Dodge truck arrived in the Panhandle loaded with big aluminum garbage cans of soup, the fruits of the sort of artful hustling that the Beats had perfected back in the Fifties. . . .

One reason this was happening was because the Haight-Ashbury was about to undergo an ambiguous fifteen minutes of fame as the most notorious streetcorner in the world. Every national magazine and major newspaper in the country would send a reporter to do a standard "I Was a Hippie for a Day" story. Some, like the *Chronicle*'s man, stayed undercover for a couple of weeks, and Washington *Post* reporter Nicholas Von Hoffman took in the whole three-act play that summer. But most donned blue jeans and a paisley shirt and spent a day or two standing around outside the Drugstore, trying not to sound like a narcotics agent, asking things like. "Why do you wear your hair so long?" *Because I think I'm beautiful.* "Why are your clothes so colorful?" *Because I have self-respect. Say, have you ever stopped to think that writing STOP on a sign is a pretty silly way to communicate that concept? It'd be much better if stop signs had God's eyes on them, don't you think. People would stop for God's eyes.* And so on, until you asked how he knew what God's eyes looked like, and he'd wink and say, "cause I looked into them, baby."

There was something about the psychedelic temperament that couldn't resist baiting the straights. They were so nervous about life; all you had to do was walk up to them on the street and hand them a flower and they'd freak, as though you'd just given them a joke flower that was about to spray them with *eau de deviant*. Perhaps the best put-on, the grandest, was the Great Banana Conspiracy, which first broke in the Berkeley *Barb* that March. A new psychedelic had been discovered, the *Barb* reported, one anyone could obtain, since the only ingredient was dried banana peel. Dry the peel, scrape off the inner portion, and smoke it. The high, according to cognoscenti quoted in the *Barb*, was comparable to opium, with some nice psilocybin shadings.

From the *Barb* the banana hoax bounced to the wire services and thence across the country. Students held banana smoke-ins and grocery stores experienced a repeat of the run on morning glory seeds a few years earlier, as scraggly young kids began appearing at the checkout counters with carts full of bananas. Was America going to have to ban the banana? Or require licenses before people could buy them? A congressman from New Jersey jokingly introduced two new acts to Congress: the Banana Labeling Act of 1967 and the Banana and Other Odd Fruit Disclosure and Reporting Act of 1967. But not everyone was laughing. United Fruit was more than a little alarmed. They asked Sidney Cohen to find out whether bananas really were hallucinogenic, a question that the FDA [Food and Drug Administration] also was taking very seriously. And after a lengthy and sober evaluation, it was announced that bananas were good sources of potassium and fiber, and definitely not hallucinogenic.

When it came to the hippies, the country alternated between "we are amused" and "we are not amused." A hippie is someone who "dresses like Tarzan, has hair like Jane, and smells like Cheetah," quipped the newly elected governor of California, Ronald Reagan, while in another speech he described the Bay Area as a hotbed of evil that he intended to stamp out. *Look* described the archetypical hippie pad as "a filthy litter strewn swarming dope fortress that was a great deal less savory and sanitary than a sewer," while *Time* praised its occupants as leading "considerably more virtuous lives than the great majority of their fellow citizens. This, despite their blatant disregard for most of society's accepted mores and many of its laws—most notably those prohibiting the use of drugs." But others detected, in their talk of pushing evolution and creating a new Man, the aroma of fascism. The hippies are a "fascistic reservoir" because "they are a rootless community that makes a fetish of having no leaders [and thus] may easily be mobilized by an unscrupulous leader.". . . Would they be rejected, or would the hippies, their internal compasses skewed by the drugs, follow like a slavish mob? Writing in the *Nation,* poet Karl Shapiro described the hippies as the "perfect cultural broth for fascism. The Beat people had a marginal politick and a sense of community; their drug was weed. The new generation has no need of politick or community or poetry. They have acid.". . .

There were the usual fulminations against LSD as a dry rot in the American soul and the usual symposiums of experts asking themselves why the kids of America were rejecting the time-honored stimulants of their parents. Sociologist Kenneth Kenniston attributed it to "psychological numbing." Part of the price of living in an advanced industrial society, he explained, was a deadening of the senses. "Our experiences lack vividness, three dimensionality and intensity. Above all, we feel trapped or shut in our own subjectivity." The hippies were using LSD as "a chemical sledgehammer for breaking out of [their] shell," Kenniston wrote, and while he deplored the means, he couldn't help but acknowledge the legitimacy of the search.

But that didn't console the San Francisco city fathers. Drug abuse was costing the city an estimated thirty-five thousand dollars a month; since the beginning of the year San Francisco General had been seeing an average of four bad LSD trips a day, many of them runaway adolescents barely out of puberty; and in two years the city-wide venereal disease rate had risen by a factor of six. The Haight was an open sore, and now these misguided deviants had the chutzpah to invite the youth of America to join them in a summer-long orgy of drugtaking and loitering. Mayor Shelley, in March, issued a statement that said, in effect, not in my city, you don't. "I am strongly opposed to any encouragement of a summer influx of indigent young people who are apparently being led to believe by a certain element of society that their vagrant presence will be tolerated in this city," said the mayor.

A few days later a platoon of health inspectors descended on the Haight, accompanied by a full complement of reporters. No doubt they were expecting a confirmation of filth and degradation thesis, since the adjective *dirty* had attached itself to the hippies like a birthmark. However, as public health director, Dr. Ellis D. ("LSD") Sox was forced to admit, "The situation is not as bad as we had thought." Of the fourteen hundred buildings examined, only sixty-four had violations, and only sixteen of those housed hippies.

But the raid presaged an increasingly active policy of official harassment. Police began daily raids in the Haight, sweeping the streets, demanding proof of age, arresting runaways, busting careless hippies for possession of pot and LSD, and in general wreaking havoc with the private revolution.

Paranoia, which was the shadow side of the kind of ecstatic energy that seemed to accompany prolonged LSD experimentation, began to build. A fascist putsch was being planned, went the whispers, every hippie in prison by July. "All spring the Haight shook with premonition," remembers Michael Rossman, "the airways of gossip were incessant with flashes of apocalypse . . . deep fear throbbed in the Haight."

As the Summer of Love approached, the Haight quivered in a contagion of first-night jitters.

Charles Perry, in his history of the Haight-Ashbury, describes the Haight in the summer of 1967 as "part old Calcutta with beggars squatting on the sidewalk, part football stadium crush, with people selling programs—the *Oracle,* the *Barb* and two new papers, the Haight-Ashbury *Tribune* and the Haight-

Ashbury *Maverick*." The street scene was a visual equivalent to the posters Bill Graham was commissioning to advertise the Fillmore, a swirling, colorful anarchy whose bizarre calligraphy, indecipherable at first, soon became second nature. So it was with the Haight. What to outsiders appeared demented madness was perfectly clear to anyone who was *attuned.*

Take clothes. An astute observer could date the various hippie fauna just by the cut of their clothes. The earliest residents were dandies, partial to cowboy outfits and Edwardian rigs, complete with bowlers and canes. Then came the Day-Glo superhero collages that the Pranksters had pioneered, followed by the ethnic borrowings, the serapes and desert robes, the peasant blouses, the Tibetan prayer costumes. Standing on Haight Street during the Summer of Love, an astute observer could pick out the older hippies, moving like peacocks through a monotonous sea of gray sludge: faded denim was the dominant hue that summer, blending into the fog that came rolling up Haight Street, mingling with the garbage smell and the dirt, accentuating the loneliness and despair—by midsummer it was clear that the yin had arrived to balance out the yang of the Be-In glow.

Haight Street, said the *Oracle,* had become the "abstract vortex for an indefinable pilgrimage . . . walking barefoot with hair askew, hand-made robes over torn blue jeans, the young people wander from noon until nearly two. Wandering aimlessly up Haight St., over to the free store at Carl and Cole, then back to Masonic for a cream pie and coke or to the Panhandle for Digger stew." And these wanderers weren't the true brothers of the post Be-In visions; rather they were the imitators that Bob Stubbs had warned about. They weren't beautiful, they had bad teeth and acne scars and it was easy to see they hadn't been voted homecoming king or queen back in Oshkosh or Biloxi, or wherever they'd come from. These kids were rejects; they'd come here because they were losers, and while that had a certain Christian appropriateness, it was not what the Council for the Summer of Love had expected. And along with the sheep came the usual complement of wolves, the hustlers and petty criminals. For the first time crimes other than shoplifting became a problem. One day Jerry Garcia was strolling down Haight Street when he came across a chilling bulletin:

> Pretty little 16-year-old-middle-class chick comes to the Haight to see what it's all about & gets picked up by a 17-year-old street dealer who spends all day shooting her full of speed again & again, then feeds her 3000 mikes & raffles off her temporarily unemployed body for the biggest Haight Street gang bang since the night before last.

Garcia was amazed. Why would anyone print such a depressing piece of news? "That was the point," he recalls, "where I thought, this scene cannot survive with that in there. It just goes all wrong."

Complicating the problem were the tourists, who crawled down Haight Street, bumper to bumper, windows shut, doors locked, as though passing through one of those zoos where the animals roam free and it is the humans who're encaged. In March the Gray Line, a bus company that had operated a similar tour during the heyday of the beatniks, began advertising the Hippie Hop: for six dollars it would take ordinary Americans beyond the "bearded curtain," on the "only foreign tour within the continental limits of the United States. . . . Among the favorite pasttimes of the hippies, besides taking drugs, are parading and demonstrating, seminars and group discussions about what's wrong with the status quo; malingering; plus the ever-present preoccupation with the soul. . . ."

The hippies devised various strategies to deflect this boorish scrutiny. At first they loped into the traffic and distributed mocking handbills which read, "Middle Class Brothers! Loosen Up, let God flow through you. Remember we are with you as you drive through the valley of the shadow of death." Then they discovered the mirror game. In one of their scrounges the Diggers came across a bin of broken mirrors. The next time the Gray Line buses arrived, the hippies ran alongside holding up mirrors to the windows so the tourists could take a good look at themselves. But then the Diggers thought up the walk-ins, which involved hundreds of people walking across the street in geometric patterns, snarling traffic for miles, and generally ending with the arrival of a vanload of police.

Then in early July a small riot broke out, as a group of frustrated hippies began jumping up and down on car bumpers, banging on hoods, terrifying the tourists. The police arrived, twenty carloads of them, and a fight broke out amid cries of "fascist bastards" and "police brutality." Although numerous bones were broken, the only fatality was a dog, clubbed to death by an overexcited policeman.

Malnutrition, overcrowding, a few bad apples, paranoia, bad drugs, big egos, the absence of any leaders who were willing to call themselves leaders, the constant police harassment—there were dozens of reasons why it was going bad. Meetings were called to try to puzzle out a strategy. . . . There was no dearth of suggestions, things like: "We have to say the Ommm sound. Every day there should be a procession down Haight Street to bring the good vibes back." Or: "I think it would be a good idea to open a cathouse because there's lots of straight guys on the street who're always asking where they can get laid. And when they can't get laid their energy gets very negative." Everyone knew the vibes were turning sour, could sense it with that awakened third eye. Whenever they took LSD it was all black apocalypse and visions of the bloody crucified Christ flying across the immense nothingness of the universe.

Bad trips became the most frequent trips (San Francisco General was treating an average of 750 panic reactions a month), and for the first time the LSD psychotic became something more than a media favorite. William Irwin

Thompson, a historian who was teaching at MIT, ran into the dark side of the hippie dream one night at Esalen: "His hair was very short, and it was clear from his looks that he had not been with the movement very long. Zen and the *I Ching* meant nothing to him, but the weeks of grass, speed and acid seemed to be taking him into a hell that increased his contempt and resentment for the hippies who surrounded him with talk of love." As Thompson watched, appalled, the kid began to chant to himself, "Blood, Blood, Blood, Hate, Hate, Hate." It was one thing, Thompson realized, to celebrate, à la Leary, the death of the mind. But it was something quite different "to stare unperturbed into the violent eyes of a person who has gone out of his mind."

Ralph Metzner, who had moved to California and was working up the coast from San Francisco at Mendocino State Hospital, had some equally grim visitations, as casualties from the Haight-Ashbury began arriving at the hospital. One told him, "It's coming so fast I can't function at that speed." Another said, "You, Leary and Alpert started this whole mess. That's why I took acid. Now I'm going straight to hell. I can't stop it."

Three days later he slit his wrists and bled to death.

Instead of coming together as one beautiful tribe, the Haight was getting zooier. Those who could, got out of town, like hosts abandoning their own party; others, like the Diggers, began carrying guns.

A miscalculation had been made, perhaps as far back as the gray November day when Leary, over hot milk, had rejected Huxley's elitist perspective in favor of Ginsberg's *pro bono publico* perspective. And this, with a generous nod to Kesey and the Pranksters, was the result: kids gobbling LSD wherever and whenever they could, completely ignorant of set and setting, without the least bit of interest in the Unspoken Thing. As Nicholas Von Hoffman, who was perhaps the most astute journalist to visit the Haight that summer, observed, "Their own genius for manipulating the mass media and dominating the youth culture undid them. The taste and demand for acid increased exponentially; the programming diminished. People didn't prepare themselves for dropping it; they didn't take it within the bounds of the little millennarian communities of the Haight . . . they just swallowed pills anywhere because they wanted to get stoned and see colors."

LSD wasn't a trip to the Other World for these kids: it was mind-blowing fun, better than a fast car or a quick orgasm. When there wasn't any acid around, they were equally willing to shoot up methedrine (which had the added byproduct of decreasing hunger) or heroin. The cliché that nobody who grokked (understood) the meaning of LSD could poison their body with speed or heroin turned out to be just that, a cliché. The older hippies ran around putting up signs saying "Speed Kills" but it didn't do any good. Instead of creating a taste for enlightenment, LSD was promoting a love of sensation, the more intense the better, and it began to dawn on the hippie leadership that there were a lot of kids in the Haight that summer who were going to keep sledgehammering at their shells until there was nothing left but the ubiquitous dust. . . .

It was rumored that the Mafia was moving in on the psychedelic trade, circulating bad acid so that the hippies would turn to more lucrative habits, like heroin and speed. Signs appeared saying "Boycott Syndicate Acid," but how could you tell?

It was a classic case of projection. The problems were not out there—they were at the heart of the Haight itself, and perhaps even at the heart of the psychedelic experience. There was a point, during every LSD user's career, when the trips to the Other World became negative. In a therapeutic sense, this was good. It meant that the subject was finally confronting the various repressions and neurotic clusters that were inhibiting the smooth evolution of the self. And provided the therapist or guide was skilled, the subject could usually pass through this personal Dark Wood and continue the journey. But what happened with individuals also happened with groups. There was a period when the group mind also passed through the shadow, as it were, and it was here, as the Pranksters learned during the Watts Acid Test, when the urge to erase all limits, to annihilate everything was overwhelming.

The Haight had reached this point in its collective journey, and one of the reasons it was unable to summon the wisdom to guide itself past this darkness was STP.

People took STP and went on three-day trips, many of them terrifying. "I saw myself on fire and then I began to feel the pain of fire . . . I was in hell." It was the ultimate macho trip and descriptions of it sounded like war stories, people exploding through the envelope and burning, or filled with a cold wind that wouldn't stop blowing through the hollows of their mind. STP didn't stay a secret for long. The authorities knew about the new superpsychedelic ("the next step," enthused the chemists, the first of many new combinations) almost immediately because as soon as STP hit the street the emergency rooms filled with nervous, flipped-out kids who quickly became screaming, sobbing kids when the thorazine (the traditional antidote for a bad LSD trip) took effect. Apparently thorazine acted as a booster to the STP, pushing the horror up a few more notches.

That wasn't the whole story, by any means, although it was the one that the average citizen received. What happened to most STP users was subtler, and perhaps even more profound. When Dick Alpert took it, he generally liked it and predicted a useful future. But he also made a curious remark: "I felt I had lost something human. I felt that I had lost my humanity." Alpert wasn't particularly bothered by this . . . but it really worried Ken Kesey. Kesey took STP and "forgot something. I lost a thing we take for granted, something that's been forged over I don't know how many thousands of years of human effort, and it's now in us. All I knew when this high was over was that I'd forgotten it, and it was the most important thing I'd ever known and I'd known it since I was a kid." Kesey had a hard time articulating exactly what this was ("a way of relating that, when it's gone, leaves you mighty bleak") but finally he settled for "the tiller." STP had burned away his tiller.

For the first time people were examining the fine print of the psychedelic contract, and one of the clauses they found most troubling was the possibility that besides burning away their "tillers," psychedelics were also altering their chromosomes. In March *Science* had reported that LSD, introduced to a test tube of chromosomes, caused significant breaks. And follow-up studies seemed to confirm that the white blood cells of people who had used LSD frequently showed a high percentage of breaks. The *New England Journal of Medicine* suggested that the effects of psychedelics might be similar to those of radiation, which was a sobering thought to the hippies, particularly since they were so fond of saying that God had given them LSD to counteract the Bomb. Although most scientists were quick to question the validity of the chromosome research (aspirin, thorazine, and the common cold affected chromosomes) and the underground newspapers published long (and ultimately valid) critiques of the work, it didn't diminish the anxiety that clutched at every hippie's heart: hadn't Leary always talked about LSD releasing cellular energies? What if it did? What if they really were becoming mutants? Or was it just another fusillade in the propaganda battle, an ingenious reply to Leary's thousand-orgasm gambit?

These were subtle psychological currents whose movements became clear only months later. At the time it was much simpler and much more satisfying to blame the government (the fascist putsch rumors had yet to abate) and the press. "This wasn't a Summer of Love" the hippie called Teddybear told one reporter. "This was a summer of bull and you, the press, did it. The so-called flower children came here to find something because you told 'em to, and there was nothing to find."

For the first time the next step was obvious. The Haight-Ashbury should die, so the rest of the country could be reborn. "I think it might be a good idea for us to get a pocketful of acid and go to Topeka, Kansas, and begin the work of turning people on," said Allen Cohen at one of the final strategy meetings. "There's a lot of turned-on people in New York and here, but in between is a tribal wasteland."

In a few days it would be a year since the California law criminalizing LSD had taken effect; a year since the Love Pageant Rally. It was a good time to say goodbye, so thousands of black-bordered notices were printed up:

> Hippie in the Haight-Ashbury District of this city
> Hippie, devoted son of Mass Media

> Friends are invited to attend services beginning at sunrise, October 6, 1967, at Buena Vista Park.

At noon on the sixth, a fifteen-foot coffin was solemnly paraded down Haight Street followed by some two hundred mourners in elaborate costumes shaking tambourines. Ten sweating pallbearers carried the giant box once around the entire Haight-Ashbury, ending in the Panhandle, where it was ceremoniously set alight. But someone had called the fire department and within minutes a couple of engines came screaming up. "The remains," someone yelled. "Don't let them put it out."

But they did, their giant hoses turning the coffin into a charred soggy mass. All that was left of hippie was a hissing cloud of steam that drifted off toward the center of the country.

REVIEW QUESTIONS

1. Stevens says that the sixties were characterized by a widespread "will to change." How was this desire for change manifested? Where did it come from? Since most aspects of American life in the sixties seemed pleasant on the surface, how do you explain the apparent discontent of so many people?

2. Many Americans deplored the hippies and what they stood for. What exactly did they find deplorable? Do you think their opinions were justified?

3. Describe the relationship between the hippies and the media. What was the impact of the media on the counterculture?

4. What role did drugs play in the counterculture? Why were they as important as they were? What effects did drugs have on the nature and development of the counterculture? How, if at all, was the use of drugs among the hippies different from the ways drugs are used today?

5. Most of those involved in the counterculture (and the other protest movements of the 1960s, too, for that matter) were relatively young, in their teens and twenties. Why do you suppose this was the case? What effects did the relative youth of its participants have on the counterculture?

FOR FURTHER READING

William O'Neill's *Coming Apart: An Informal History of America in the 1960s* (1971), is a very good place to start looking for understanding of that tumultuous decade. Morris Dickstein concentrates on its cultural history, including its popular culture, in *Gates of Eden: American Culture in the Sixties* (1977). Young people played a large role in giving the sixties a distinctive character. Landon Y. Jones, *Great Expectations: America and the Baby Boom Generation* (1980), details the impact they had. W. J. Rorabaugh, *Berkeley at War, the 1960s* (1989), tells the story of the Free Speech Movement. On the Beats, Bruce Cook, *The Beat Generation* (1971), gives a general treatment, but the writings of the Beats themselves are indispensable to understanding them. Jack Kerouac's novel *On the Road* (1957) is an autobiographical account of Beat life in which most of the prominent Beats appear as thinly disguised characters. Allen Ginsberg's poem *Howl* (1956) shows what the Beats found repellent about American civilization. On the counterculture itself, Theodore Roszak, *The Making of a Counter Culture* (1970), is a generally sympathetic scholarly account; Charles Perry, *The Haight-Ashbury* (1984), is a readable treatment of hippie life in its chief capital; and Tom Wolfe, *The Electric Kool-Aid Acid Test* (1969), paints a very vivid picture of one particular group, the Merry Pranksters, which gathered around the novelist Ken Kesey, and provides many insights into the nature of and the reasons behind the counterculture.

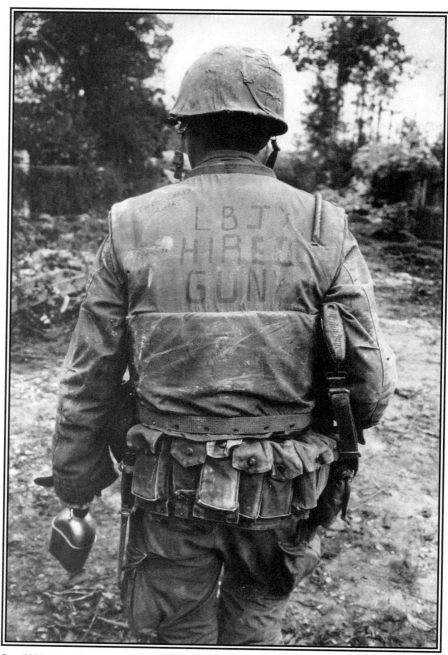

Donald McCullin/Magnum.

Many of the American troops in Vietnam were not happy about what they were doing there and made no attempt to hide their feelings.

20

Vietnam—and After

LOREN BARITZ

There is still widespread disagreement about the Vietnam War: what or who was responsible for our failure there, what we might have done to achieve better results, and what lessons we should learn from it. What seems abundantly clear is that the war traumatized the nation, both while it was going on and afterwards. We got into it without knowing precisely how, fought it for goals that were never entirely clear, argued among ourselves about it while it was in progress, and got out telling ourselves that we had won but knowing we really had not. As a consequence, when the war ended, most Americans seemed to want to forget the whole unpleasant experience as quickly as possible. That included, although no one said so in so many words, forgetting the men who had actually fought—the "grunts" as they called themselves.

However much the nation as a whole may have suffered from the war, certainly the ordinary soldiers suffered most. They risked, and 58,000 of them lost, their lives. Even more were wounded, and some of the wounds meant a lifetime in a wheelchair. Thousands suffered serious psychological wounds, and psychologists began to speak about a new kind of mental disturbance that some vets exhibited: Post-Traumatic Stress Disorder. In addition, some vets suffered long-term damage to their health as a result of exposure to Agent Orange, a chemical compound used in defoliants in Vietnam. And initially, all the veterans suffered from what seemed to them, and others, to be the indifference, ingratitude, or outright hostility of the general public.

An indication that things were changing was the dedication of the Vietnam Veterans' Memorial in Washington, D.C. in November, 1982, slightly less than ten years after the withdrawal of American troops from Vietnam. Although there were bitter debates about the Memorial's design when it was first made public, it has become a focal point for healing many of the psychological and social wounds left by the war and a force for helping to reconcile the still existing conflicts about it.

In the following selection, Loren Baritz describes the conditions that the ordinary "grunts" faced in Vietnam, how their experiences were rendered especially painful by the peculiar conditions surrounding the Vietnam War, and the problems with which they had to contend once they returned to the United States.

The drafted grunts who humped the boonies came from all over America. Street-smart ghetto kids, raised in the basketball wars, became battlefield buddies with dewy farm kids from Minnesota, patriotic, wide-eyed innocents who choked up a little when they sang "God Bless America." Hispanics, passionately ambivalent about Anglo culture, fought and drank alongside their closest war pals, the steelworkers, gas station attendants, and high school dropouts who never had a steady job. The entire nation went or was sent to war, except for the rich, the middle class, the vast majority of college students, and individuals who objected to war, or who objected to that war.

After LBJ decided to send combat troops, and after the draftees were moved into combat, the Vietnam War was fought by working-class teenagers. The draft was designed to produce that result. The average age of the American soldiers in Vietnam was just over nineteen. In World War II, the average age of the GIs who were in for the duration was about twenty-six. It was said that the military brass understood that Vietnam was a teenage war, that the kids were unruly, and that there was not much that could be done about actually imposing discipline on these post-adolescents, strong boymen who were juicers and drank too much, or were smokers on skag or pot, and were too irreverent to obey by instinct or tradition. . . .

As in Korea, the army, navy, and air force rotated individuals out in twelve months, and, until 1969, the marines in thirteen. They were almost always replaced one by one by new meat, or twinks, or cherries, or FNGs (fuckin' new

"The Warriors" from *Backfire: A History of How American Culture Led Us into Vietnam and Made Us Fight the Way We Did,* by Loren Baritz. Copyright © 1985 by Loren Baritz. Reprinted by permission.

guys) who were twelve or thirteen months younger than they were on their DEROS (date eligible for return from overseas).

When these kids enlisted or were drafted, at least after the American invasion in 1965, they knew that the so-called crazies were protesting the war, running away to Canada, hiding in colleges. Many of these soldiers had not thought much about the war, disliked the long hair of the hippies, and were offended by TV pictures of braless young women. Like most of the rest of the nation, they rejected the war protesters without thinking much about the war. Some men enlisted to get a better deal than the draft offered, or to get a new start in their young lives, or because a close friend signed up, or to escape the family, or to see the world, or to combat Communism. Some did not know why they enlisted. For some, it was an article of faith that the President knows best, and when he calls, you go.

George Ryan enlisted after he graduated from high school in Virginia. He had only read girlie magazines, sports magazines, and racing-car magazines. "If Vietnam was such a mistake," he asked, "how come the leaders of our country, the wisest men we have . . . how come they sent us in? None of the doves I ever met had any answers to *that*."

A student of the army collected more of these reactions:

I know one thing. Before I went in, my brother could kick my ass, but now he can't. . . . He ain't nothing no more.

The only thing I used to read was sports. . . . So I didn't have any feelings one way or the other. I figured it was more or less right, because why would I be going if it wasn't right?

I knew almost nothing about it. The war, I thought was like they taught us in high school, you know, you're fighting communism, you know, it was just the good guys against the bad guys.

A majority of the kids who were drafted thought of the draft as an event like measles, a graduation, the weather, something that happened to people. Young men got drafted as their fathers had in earlier wars. Sometimes brothers were already in. You had to do it because it had been done before, and probably would always be done, and you had to take your turn. It was usually more intimate and domestic than patriotism, although occasionally that too played a role. More often it was an unwillingness to let someone down, to hold up your end, and to do the right thing, as that was defined in the family and in the small circle of good friends. There is not much soul-searching required to honor so simple an obligation. Someday you have to earn a living, probably marry and have children, pay taxes, but first you get drafted.

There were more enlistees than conscripts, but the draftees were especially vulnerable. They were more likely than the enlistees to find themselves in the shooting war. The draftees made up 16 percent of the battle deaths in 1965; in 1969, they were 62 percent. Draftees represented 88 percent of infantry riflemen in 1970. The army apparently considered the draftees disposable—throw-away, nonreturnable men.

The Vietnam draft was an ideal model of discriminatory social policy. It kept the middle class from creating political pressure on the war administrations. So the draft was biased by level of income. The higher the income, the less chance of being drafted, importantly but not exclusively because of educational deferments. Poor young Americans, white as well as black and Hispanic, were twice as likely to be drafted and twice as likely to be assigned to combat as wealthier draft-aged youth. The draft rejected many blacks, but it was more likely to accept poor men than richer men with the same qualifications, or the same lack of qualifications. As a result, poor black Americans were swept into the fighting war in disproportionate numbers. Economic class, even more than race, except that people of color were more likely to be poor, was what determined who fought and who died. . . .

Education in this country is a badge of class. One study of Chicago neighborhoods found that kids from areas with low educational levels were four times as likely to be killed in Vietnam than those from more schooled neighborhoods. It was as if the war had been designed to digest America's victims, the men President Eisenhower called the "sitting ducks" for the draft. Class and education also shaped the experience of the young men who enlisted. Two staff officials of President Ford's clemency board showed that a college graduate who enlisted had about a 40 percent chance of being sent to Vietnam, while a high school graduate's chance was about 65 percent, and that of a high-school dropout was 70 percent. . . .

Survival was the strategy of the American GI, not different from soldiers in earlier wars. But, for the great majority of Vietnam grunts, there was no external purpose to the war—not defending national goals, not resisting an evil enemy, not defending motherhood and apple pie. As a result, there was no animating justification for combat or for risk. The best way to survive was to keep away from danger. This absence of external purpose made it difficult for some to develop a sense of shared enterprise with other GIs outside their own unit. Because the replacements were inserted into the war as individuals, not as members of a unit, these GIs were in fact movable parts, separate cogs in the war's machinery. Such separateness induced a sense of fragility, probably more intense and widespread than in other wars. The separate arrivals and departures, along with the absence of shared purpose, emphasized the individuality of the grunt, even while they formed the life-saving bonds of brotherhood in their small squads or platoons. It is touching and painful to hear how often the veterans felt alone.

The grunt was the instrument of General Westmoreland's "strategy" of attrition. For entirely different reasons, the grunts' war plan became identical with the general's. There was no real estate that had to be taken and held, there were no objectives to be seized. The plan was to kill the enemy, wherever and whoever he or she was. Because the body count was the scorecard,

killing supposedly proved progress. This made war sense from the grunt's perspective because it was simply based on the desire to live, not necessarily callousness or moral collapse, but war through the eyes of the walking conscripts.

That is why the "other war," the ideological war, meant nothing to most of
them. It did not seem, at least in the short run, the time that really mattered,
to protect their lives. So they mocked the entire effort to "win the hearts and
minds" of the Vietnamese by referring to it as WHAM and embroidering it
even further: "Grab 'em by the balls and their hearts and minds will follow."

Luis Martinez, a Puerto Rican marine, decided he would learn something
about the Vietnamese and treat them with respect because "if the Viet Cong is
going to do something, he remembers you and you have a better chance of
surviving." In this sense, winning hearts and minds might help him to return
home in one piece. It was like money in the bank that could produce interest
in the future. But in this war's twists, respect and friendship for the Vietnamese could backfire. For example, a sergeant became friends with a Vietnamese woman and her daughter. They were both killed by the NLF [Na-
tional Liberation Front: Viet Cong] because they had associated with him. He
decided that from then on he would leave them all alone. For most, the
"other war" would take too long, was out of focus, and was therefore not a
good shield for the vital or fatal 365 days they would be targets.

The grunts hated bloody fighting to take a fire base, perhaps losing buddies in the process, and then being ordered to abandon the base to fight or
patrol somewhere else, and then having to endure another fire fight to recap-
ture the first base. Some bases were retaken three or four or more times. One
GI put it this way: "We don't take any land. We don't give it back. We just mutilate bodies. What the fuck are we doing here?" It seemed senseless to risk
everything over and over for the same piece of turf. There was no achievement to show for the mutilations and deaths. Except the numbers. They had
to train themselves to think of achievement by the numbers. Many, probably
most, could not do it. They could not think of what they were doing only in
terms of the body count. Even in war, death was supposed to be for something, not a thing in itself.

They recognized that the body counts were being hyped to satisfy, or shut
up, corrupt officers who kept demanding higher numbers. The men could
deliver any number any REMF, "rear echelon mother fucker," wanted. Of
course that made the killing even more pointless. If the brass would accept
fake numbers, and if the whole point of the war was numbers, why risk your
life to get real kills? The war could have been fought over the radio, with a
squad or company reporting whatever number was wanted. That is what
sometimes happened. The grunts knew it was fraudulent and they became
contemptuous of their officers. For example, after one fire fight, Herb Mock,
a rifle-squad leader, said: "General Westmoreland flew in. All the news outfits
and everything. It was the most hilarious thing. As these son of a bitches came
out there, the GIs started lying. The newsmen would walk up to just anybody

and say, 'What did you do?' 'I singlehandedly killed three hundred thousand with my bowie knife.' " Lieutenant Robert Santos spoke for many when he said, "You come home with the high body count, high kill ratios. What a fucking way to live your life.". . .

Some grunts were stunned by the open hostility of some South Vietnamese, the people they had come to defend. When they had to run up chicken wire to block the objects, including grenades, that some South Vietnamese threw at them, there was no way they could avoid wondering what they were doing there. It was maddening to discover that the food or medicine they gave to friendlies would be handed to the guerrillas after dark. It was a shock to march past an aged mama-san selling Coca-Cola on the road and notice her head nodding as each grunt passed; she was counting them. What for? What could you make of the fact that the friendlies who washed your clothes or cut your hair were found dead in your ambush of the NLF during the night? And what about the mama-san who brought you things right into your fire base and hung around a little while so she could memorize where your bunkers were so the guerrillas that night could zero in with their mortars? What about the local whores telling you where you were going next, before your own officers had announced it? This war was not like others. You could never identify the enemy. That created constant danger, not merely at the front—there was no front—but everywhere, and not merely during a battle, but anytime. Any Vietnamese could be the one. A T-shirt worn by the grunts displayed the message: KILL THEM ALL! LET GOD SORT THEM OUT!

Having no larger external purpose, there were also often no external constraints. The line beyond which an action would become a transgression was a matter of individual conscience, a Protestant formula. This was as true for the officers as for the troops. The moral formlessness of the bureaucratic war necessarily emphasized technique and means, not goals or purpose. Bureaucracies typically do not do as well at expressing where they wish to go as they do at expressing how to get there. "If you're lost, drive faster; that way you'll get it over with sooner." This left the teenage warriors to their own moral devices, such as they were. Group pressures formed one code of conduct; a watchful officer might sometimes form another. Unlike earlier wars, the Vietnam rule was the moral independence of the foot soldier and his officers.

The rapid turnover of their immediate officers—usually every six months, often less—led to the conviction that the grunts knew better than anyone else, especially better than the six-month wonders, the shake-'n'-bake lieutenants, how to stay alive. These teenage warriors were therefore thrown back into themselves in a way unusual in war. They had to take care of each other if they were to make it. After a while they could wear earrings, write almost anything they liked on their helmets and flak jackets, shoot up on drugs, get drunk, and more often than not get away with it, especially when they were in the field, which everyone called Indian country. They enjoyed getting away with it, and hated "chicken shit officers" who worried about shined shoes; but getting away with it also taught some of them that the brass did not care, and that they were on their own both as a unit and as individuals. . . .

The grunts understood that they were endangered by the guerrillas, the regular army of North Vietnam, and their own temporary, rotating officers, in no particular order of threat. They knew that the home front did not support what they were doing. If no one cared about them, they could not care about the rules or established authority. Occasionally, around 1970, grunts would scribble UUUU on their helmets: the unwilling, led by the unqualified, doing the unnecessary, for the ungrateful. Other helmets proclaimed POWER TO THE PEOPLE, KILL A NONCOM FOR CHRIST, or NO GOOK EVER CALLED ME NIGGER. It was finally as if all they could believe and remember were pain and death. One young man from the Bronx, for example, was cited for heroism:

> They gave me a Bronze Star and they put me up for a Silver Star. But I said you can shove it up your ass. I threw all of the others away. The only thing I kept was the Purple Heart, because I still think I was wounded.

A wound is the most intimate souvenir.

It cannot be surprising that the grunts found ways to resist corrupt officers in a war that could not be understood. Desertions, excluding AWOLs, in the army alone rose from 27,000 in 1967 to 76,634 in 1970, a rate increase of 21 per thousand to 52 per thousand. The marines were even worse with 60 desertions per thousand. According to the Department of Defense, the rate of desertion in Vietnam was higher than in either Korea or World War II, and the rate increased as the intensity of the fighting declined and absurdity increased. As President Nixon began withdrawing troops, many of the grunts remaining on the ground lost even more conviction about why they should stay and fight. The desertion rate from 1965 to 1971 increased by 468 percent.

Fragging, defined as an attempt to murder by using a grenade, reached astonishing levels in Vietnam. It was usually a result of the fear and hatred felt by the workers toward their bosses. For example, marine Private Reginald Smith testified in a court-martial that his lieutenant was so slow in setting up a listening post that by the time he sent three marines out, the NLF was waiting and killed two of them. The troops were discussing the incompetence of this lieutenant just before he was killed by a fragmentation grenade. It was frequently said that combat squads raised a bounty to be awarded to anyone who would "waste" a particularly hated officer. The Criminal Investigating Department of the Third Marine Amphibious Force said there were more than 20 fraggings in eight months of 1969, according to the transcript of a court-martial. The Defense Department admits to 788 fraggings from 1969 to 1972. This figure does not include attempts to kill officers with weapons other than "explosive devices," such as rifles. Richard Gabriel calculated that "as many as 1,016 officers and NCOs may have been killed by their own men," but he points out that this figure includes only men who were caught and tried. There is no precedent in American military history for violence against officers on anything like this scale.

Another response of the "workers" was to "strike," that is, to disobey a combat order, that is, to commit mutiny. The Pentagon kept no records of mutinies, but Senator Stennis of the Senate Armed Forces Committee said that there were 68 mutinies in 1968 alone.

Yet another form of resistance by grunts was the pandemic use of hard drugs. In the spring of 1970, 96 percent pure white heroin appeared in Saigon; by the end of the year it was everywhere, sold in drugstores and by Vietnamese children on street corners. This junk was so pure and cheap that the troops smoked or sniffed, with only a minority reduced to injection. Its use was not remarkable in Vietnam because smoking was usually a group activity, accepted by almost everyone, and common for clean-cut midwestern boys as well as for city kids. Nothing in all of military history even nearly resembled this plague. About 28 percent of the troops used hard drugs, with more than half a million becoming addicted. This was approximately the same percentage of high school students in the States who were using drugs, but they were using softer stuff. In Vietnam, grass was smoked so much it is a wonder that a southerly wind did not levitate Hanoi's politburo.

The failure of senior officers is partly reflected in the fact that they knew what was going on and did nothing to stop it, and did not protest. Richard Gabriel and Paul Savage concluded that "the higher officer corps was so committed to expedience that the organized distribution of drugs was accepted as necessary to the support of the South Vietnamese government, which often purveyed the drugs that destroyed the Army that defended it." The CIA and the diplomatic corps in Vietnam prevented other governmental agencies from getting at the truth, while individuals with the CIA, if not the Agency itself, helped to fly drugs into Vietnam from Laos.

Despite an occasional attempt to do something—usually punishing the troops—about the blizzard of skag, neither the U.S. government nor the military ever accomplished anything worth mentioning. The much advertised urine testing (to be conducted in what the GIs called The Pee House of the August Moon) was ineffective because the tests were unreliable, the troops who were not hooked could flush their bodies before the tests, and no one was prepared actually to help the soldiers who were addicts. One scholar concluded that "in not rooting out the sources of heroin in Laos and Thailand, the government had simply made a calculation that the continued political and military support of those groups profiting from the drug traffic was worth the risk of hooking U.S. soldiers." General Westmoreland, as usual, blamed everyone but his own senior officers: "The misuse of drugs . . . had spread from civilian society into the Army and became a major problem. . . . A serious dilution over the war years in the caliber of junior leaders contributed to this. . . ."

Racial conflict was suffused throughout the war, from 1968 until the end. Every service, including the previously calm air force, had race riots of varying magnitude. As some of America's cities burned, or rather as the ghettos in some cities burned, the domestic rage found its counterpart in the military. Fraggings were sometimes racially motivated. One battalion commander said, "What defeats me is the attitude among the blacks that 'black is right' no matter who is right or wrong." One black soldier said, "I'd just as soon shoot whitey as the VC." In one incident that is what actually happened: Two white majors were shot trying to get some black GIs to turn down their tape recorder.

White officers were sometimes offended by expressions of black solidarity, including ritual handshakes, the closed fist, swearing, black jargon, and, especially, blacks arguing that they were being forced to fight "a white man's war." (The North Vietnamese and the NLF often tried to exploit that theme through various forms of psychological warfare.) The weight of the military justice system was lowered on black GIs far out of proportion to their numbers. The congressional Black Caucus did a study in 1971 that showed that half of all soldiers in jail were black. The next year, the Defense Department learned that blacks were treated more harshly than whites for identical offenses. The occasional race riots were invariably triggered by the increasing militance of American blacks in general, the peculiarly obtuse social attitudes of many older military officers, the frustrated hopes of the Great Society, the sense of an unfair draft, and an unfair shake in Vietnam.

Trying to make it to DEROS, that miraculous day one year after they had stepped foot onto Vietnam's red soil, the foot soldiers did what they could to survive the guerrillas or North Vietnam's army or their officers. For most of them, the point of the war was the clock ticking toward the shortening of their time, and, finally, the last day, the wake-up call, and home. Others, in a daze of battle, tried to put home out of mind. Many others, probably most, became increasingly cautious as their "sentence" wore down, and the ingenuity expended by the short-timers in avoiding combat, occasionally simply by threatening a hard-driving officer, was inspirational, almost enough to revive the American dream of self-reliant citizens. No one wanted to die with only hours, or days, or weeks, or months, left to serve. No one wanted to die in any case, but it was even more unbearable to think about with only a short time to go. The idea of home, the idea of making it, became increasingly real as the war became increasingly surreal.

They left Vietnam as they came, suddenly, by air, usually alone, and engulfed by impressions and anxieties that were too cascading to sort out. "We went to Vietnam as frightened, lonely young men. We came back, alone again, as immigrants to a new world," William Jayne, a marine rifleman, wrote. "For the culture we had known dissolved while we were in Vietnam, and the culture of combat we lived in so intensely for a year made us aliens when we returned." They were aliens for a great variety of reasons, some because they had grown up while their former buddies who had not gone to Nam seemed as if they had been frozen in time; they were still late adolescents whose lives revolved around six-packs, cars and chasing girls. Others because they were stunned by the nation's refusal to welcome them home as returning warriors. Others because of the continuing pain of flesh and memory. Yet others because the war had destroyed their earlier faith in "the World," in American institutions. . . .

. . . Thomas K. Bowen thought when he got home that the entire war had been a "mistake," and said, "I mean I have no—absolutely no—respect for my government." Still others could not get jobs, and some resented the women and the nonvets who were working. Joe Boxx finally decided that "bein' a Vietnam vet didn't mean shit." Skip Sommer had re-upped to survive, but finally could not endure the army and deserted; he eventually gave himself up and was later dishonorably discharged. He was a haunted, enraged man even twelve years later. But, he said, "I don't remember anything I really am ashamed of, besides the fact that I survived." Alberto Martinez was losing his mind and in despair killed himself. Edmund Lee became an expatriate in Australia. Frank Goins, back home in south Georgia, remembered the democracy of races in the foxholes, but discovered, "When we got home, they still didn't want us to go to Mr. Charlie's cafe by the front door. . . ." David Brown was not even given the usual four or five days off the line at the end of his tour; one day he was in combat and the next night the freedom bird landed him in San Francisco. He drank too much for a year or two. Charles Rupert said: "I risked my life for my country, and now nobody gives a shit. If I have a son, I won't let him go. I'll send him to Canada first." J. C. Wilson: "We were fools."

On the other side, Lieutenant Robert Kennish, a commander of Charlie Company: "I did pretty well. No problems at all, really, that are going to afflict me for the rest of my life. I think I gained more from my experience in the military and in Vietnam than I lost." What mattered to him most was that he grew in his own self-esteem as a man. An anonymous veteran grunt said that he simply grew up in the war. David Rioux, a devout Catholic who was blinded in the war, understood and approved the war as a struggle against Communism, one that he was proud to have fought. Michel, David's brother, fought in David's company and feels that David's faith prevented him from committing suicide. David said about himself and his brother: "We both knew why we were in Vietnam, and the men around us didn't, for the most part, or saw it only confusedly, but we saw why we were there and we were proud to be there, defending a people who were being oppressed by Marxist Communism. We were doing something that was commendable, in the eyes of God, our country and our family."

The stereotypes at loose in the nation when the troops began returning were largely shaped by the reports of My Lai as well as television reports of the heroin nightmare. Many Americans assumed the returning vets were junkies. Some vets were persistently asked how it felt to kill a human being. All the vets were subjected to an embarrassed national attitude about the war, and about their role in it. It got worse when the North overran Saigon, and television showed the pictures of the scramble to evacuate the remaining Americans. Then the question became even more insistent: What did we accomplish by fighting? For the veterans who had believed in the cause, Saigon's surrender was a terrible blow. Both the Rioux brothers, along with other traditionalists, believed that "giving up" was the mistake, not intervening in the first place. For the others, those who had decided the war was not worth fighting while they were fighting it, the fall of Saigon confirmed their opinion. In any case, the veterans faced an unprecedented social and political fact when they finally made it back: The nation did not know what to do with them, and would just as soon forget, or try to forget, the entire sorry "episode." None of the vets could forget.

They were not only not welcomed home, some of them were abused for their uniforms, their decorations, and their short hair. There was a revealing false rumor that antiwar critics were shooting vets as they climbed out of their planes. It is a mass delusion, of course, but thousands of vets claim that they were spat upon when they first arrived home. . . .

Most of the veterans returned home reasonably whole, as whole as returning veterans from earlier wars. The majority were not dopers, did not beat their wives or children, did not commit suicide, did not haunt the unemployment offices, and did not boozily sink into despair and futility. Yet, some prisons are still populated with black vets; the VA [Veterans Administration] hospitals still do their bureaucratic thing too often and fail to help. Some vets, more than a decade later, have not yet recovered, and some never will. The government has done less for these veterans than for those of other wars. The vets had to build their own monument. Now they are struggling to force the reluctant government to face up to the hideous question of the degree to which our war technology had poisoned our own men with Agent Orange. More than a decade after most of them had come home, the government in 1984 began to make small progress in admitting its responsibility in this issue.

Nonetheless, the majority returned home and found there was life after Vietnam. Tim O'Brien, a former grunt and prize-winning novelist, thought the adjustment was too good. He feared that the vets' experience was becoming too mellow, too nostalgic. He had hoped their recoil from war would have been more of a brake on national saber-rattling. He wished they could have retained the passion and convictions that sustained them while they were boonie-rats. He wrote, "We've all adjusted. The whole country. And I fear that we are back where we started. I wish we were more troubled."

When some grunts in Vietnam heard the news that the war was over, every-one began shouting. "They were ecstatic." One of them finally asked, "Who won?" They were told the NLF won. "They didn't care."

REVIEW QUESTIONS

1. How did the conditions the grunts faced in Vietnam differ from what Ameri-can soldiers had to deal with in previous wars? How did the reception they got at home differ?

2. Baritz's account implies that many in the Army itself, particularly those on the higher levels of command, were not as concerned as they should have been with the welfare of the troops under their command. Do you think this impli-cation is correct? If so, how do you explain it?

3. It has been suggested that the problems within the armed forces in Vietnam, drug use, racial tension, lack of respect for authority, and so forth, were sim-ply reflections of these problems within American society. Others argue, on the contrary, that these problems originated in the conditions in Vietnam it-self. Which explanation makes more sense to you? Why?

4. How are the conditions Baritz describes, both in Vietnam and the United States, related to the psychological problems some Vietnam veterans have experienced?

5. Does the information in Baritz's account give you any insights into why the United States was not able to achieve its objectives in Vietnam?

FOR FURTHER READING

The literature on the war in Vietnam is enormous and still growing. The following items represent only a tiny sample. One might begin by reading *The Pentagon Pa-pers,* published in many editions, including one in paperback (1971), edited by Neil Sheehan et al. of *The New York Times.* Volumes dealing with the war within the larger context of social and political developments within the United States in-clude Alexander Kendrick, *The Wound Within: America in the Vietnam Years, 1945–1974* (1974); David Halberstam, *The Best and the Brightest* (1972), a study of the false pride that Halberstam feels led to this and other national tragedies; William J. Lederer, *Our Own Worst Enemy* (1968), a look at the self-deception and igno-rance of the American people regarding the war in Vietnam; and Frances FitzGer-ald, *Fire in the Lake* (1972), an account of how cultural differences divided Ameri-cans from Vietnamese and led to mutual misunderstandings that contributed to the debacle. Stanley Karnow, *Vietnam, a History* (1983), is a general history of the war derived from a television series made for the Public Broadcasting System. Accounts of the war by those who experienced it firsthand are numerous. They include Alan Dawson, *55 Days: The Fall of South Vietnam* (1977), and Michael Herr, *Dispatches* (1977)—both by journalists—and Ron Kovic, *Born on the Fourth of July* (1976), and Tim O'Brien, *If I Die in a Combat Zone, Box Me Up and Ship Me Home* (1973)—which tell the story of the war from the soldiers' point of view. Al Santoli has collected soldiers' reminiscences in *Everything We Had: An Oral History of the Vietnam War by Thirty-Three American Soldiers Who Fought It* (1981). Christian G. Appy, *Working-Class War: American Combat Soldiers and Vietnam* (1993), is a recent historical work that summarizes much of the existing information about the experiences of soldiers in Vietnam. The commanding general, William C. Westmoreland, gives his view of the war in *A Soldier Reports* (1976). Robert Jay Lifton, *Home from the War* (1973), discusses the impact of the war on the veterans. Harrison E. Salisbury, ed., *Vietnam Reconsidered: Lessons from a War* (1984), contains the conflicting opinions of several people on the meaning and impact of the war and the lessons that we should draw from it.

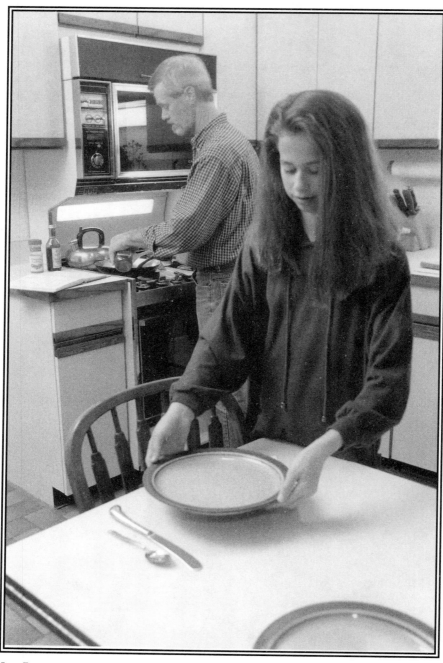

Scott Foresman

Single-parent families and changing ideas about proper gender roles are two features of modern American life.

21

Sexuality in Contemporary America

JOHN D'EMILIO AND
ESTELLE B. FREEDMAN

The sixties saw many challenges to prevailing notions concerning the way things should be and pleas—or demands—for change, often backed up by behavior that deliberately broke established rules. One of these challenges was the "sexual revolution." It was connected to the open flouting of conventions of all sorts that one found in the counterculture and to the search for alternative ways of living that members of the counterculture were conducting. It was connected to the questioning of gender roles and gender stereotypes that was a prominent feature of the women's liberation movement. It was also connected, although less obviously, to the political radicalism of the decade; to some, engaging in sexual activities that violated existing taboos was a revolutionary act, a way of affirming one's opposition to society and its norms. Perhaps most of all it was connected to the movement of the bulk of the baby boom generation into late adolescence and early adulthood, the period during which sexual interest is certainly at its peak and sexual activity probably at its highest level. The impact on the nation of the vast numbers of the baby boomers may well have been enough, all by itself, to have resulted in a challenge to prevailing sexual attitudes and modes of behavior.

Like the other movements for social and cultural change in the sixties and early seventies, the sexual revolution caused concern, consternation, fear, outrage, or some combination of those feelings, in those who did not share the desire for change. Despite this, again like the other movements for social change, the sexual revolution does seem to have left its mark. The furor, the tumult of that earlier period has died down, but some changes have endured, among them changes in the whole system of ideas and values regarding such matters as marriage, the family, gender, and sexual conduct. The following selection by John D'Emilio and Estelle B. Freedman details a few of those changes (and some of the things that have not changed). We may be too close to the recent past to assess the scope or significance of what has occurred with complete accuracy, but we can be sure that a great many people in the United States today have ideas that are different from those of their parents or grandparents and behave in ways that previous generations would find shocking.

As entrepreneurs were weaving sexuality into the fabric of public life, Americans were simultaneously experiencing dramatic demographic changes. Between the 1960s and the 1980s, the life cycle of many Americans became considerably more complex and unpredictable. The timing of marriage and childbearing, control over fertility, the instability of the traditional nuclear family, and innovations in living arrangements all encouraged a reorganization of sexual standards.

The unusual demographic patterns of the baby-boom era reversed themselves with startling rapidity in the 1970s. Between 1960 and 1980, the marriage rate declined by a quarter. By 1985, the median age of marriage for men had risen to 25.5 years, while for women it jumped to 23.2. Along with later marriage came an overall decline in fertility. Beginning in the mid-1970s, the fertility of American women hovered at the replacement level, far below the peaks reached in the late 1950s. The accessibility of legal abortions, the accelerating trend toward sterilization, and the availability of reliable contraceptives put absolute control of fertility within reach for the married. Especially within the middle class, childlessness emerged as a serious option to consider. As one couple noted, "we are the only people we know who have a child, or at least the only people we know well. . . . Some [of our friends] are married, a few might as well be, others aren't totally opposed to the idea—and they have all either ruled out families entirely or postponed them until the very distant

---

future." By the end of the 1970s more than a quarter of married women in their late twenties remained childless.

Not only were Americans marrying later and having fewer children, but families were much less likely to remain intact. Aided by the liberalization of state laws, the divorce rate began a steep climb in the mid-1960s. Between 1960 and 1980, the number of divorced men and women rose by almost two hundred percent; the divorce rate itself jumped ninety percent. For blacks, the impact of divorce was even more widely felt. In 1980, over a quarter of black men and women between the ages of twenty-five and fifty-four were divorced, in comparison to less than ten percent of whites. Many of the divorced remarried eventually, yet second marriages had even less chance of surviving. Although the rush to divorce had slowed somewhat by 1980, marriages of the late seventies had only a one-in-two chance of surviving.

All of these shifts affected the size and structure of American households, which tended to grow smaller and become more diversified in composition. During the 1970s, over half of the new households created were nonfamily ones. The traditional two-parent family with children accounted for only three-fifths of all living arrangements by 1980. Even that figure tended to overstate its predominance, since many of those families would experience dissolution, and most Americans could expect to spend a portion of their childhood and adult years in "nontraditional" situations.

One widely touted demographic innovation of the 1970s was the rise of cohabitation among men and women. Hardly noted by 1960 census-takers, it became a highly visible phenomenon in the 1970s, tripling in frequency. Although cohabiting couples constituted only three percent of American households, the chances of an individual participating in such an arrangement were much higher. One study found that almost one in five American men had lived for at least six months with a woman other than their spouse. The phenomenon was more common among blacks than whites, and a majority of the men had been previously married. Surveying the changing nature of American lifestyles, the sociologists Philip Blumstein and Pepper Schwartz confidently predicted that cohabitation "will probably become more visible and more common."

In the midst of this reorganization of household and family structure, one element of change elicited special comment—the rise of the working mother. White married women had been steadily entering the labor force since World War II, and for black wives work outside the home had always been a common experience. But the rapid movement of mothers into paid employment surprised most observers. By the early 1980s a majority of mothers, including those with children of preschool age, were working for wages. Some of this change owed its origin to feminism, which validated the choices of mothers who sought employment. Some of it was due to financial necessity. As inflation escalated in the 1970s, and the changing structure of economic and social life raised the consumption needs of many families, the pressure for mothers to work mounted. Among married couples in 1980, wives with family incomes between twenty-five thousand and fifty thousand dollars were most likely to be employed. The absence of female employment consigned many families to subsistence living. Moreover, as the divorce rate mounted and more women found themselves heading households, many mothers had no choice but to work.

Whatever the motives, the high proportion of women in the work force promised upheavals in the realm of personal life and heterosexual relations. Working women were both cause and effect of many demographic changes— the rising age of marriage, later childbearing, the decline in fertility, the spread of single-person households, and cohabitation. Unhappy marriages, in which spouses felt compelled out of duty or desperation to remain together, might more readily dissolve. As Paul Glick, a Census Bureau demographer who had studied marriage and divorce for a generation, commented, "women who enter the marketplace gain greater confidence, expand their social circles independent of their husbands' friends, taste independence and are less easy to satisfy, and more likely to divorce." Or, as one Indiana wife put it, "women don't have to put up with [men's] crap—they can support themselves." Working women brought greater confidence and more power to their relationships with men. Although conflict might ensue as couples readjusted their expectations, surveys indicated nevertheless that younger males in particular preferred the more egalitarian results that came with the modification of traditional sex roles.

These demographic shifts hit the black community with special force. Although black-white differentials in family structure actually narrowed in the 1970s, nontraditional living arrangements still appeared with much greater frequency among blacks. Overall incidence rates of divorce, female-headed households, and out-of-wedlock births remained higher. By 1980 almost half of black households were female-headed, a majority of black infants were born to unmarried women, and only a minority of black children were being raised in two-parent households. Approximately half of black adults were not married and living with their spouse. In assessing these statistics, one sociologist was moved to comment that "all is not well between black men and women." In contrast to the mid-1960s, when the Moynihan report provoked so much controversy within the civil rights movement, black leaders in the eighties felt freer to air their own concerns. By the early 1980s, many were rating the issue of family life equally with jobs and education as a critical concern of the community. Eleanor Holmes Norton, who served in the Carter administration, called it "the most serious long-term crisis in the black community."

When combined with the invasion of sexuality into so much of the public realm, these new demographic patterns among Americans presaged a major shift in sexual behavior and attitudes. The later age of marriage increased the likelihood that women as well as men would enter the institution sexually experienced. The rise in divorce meant that more and more Americans would be searching for new sexual partners as mature adults. Children and adolescents would know that their parents were having sex outside of marriage; the openness with which heterosexual cohabitation, lesbianism, and male homosexuality were discussed provided visible alternatives to marriage. Postponed childbearing and low fertility made obvious the distinction between sex for procreation and for pleasure. Women who worked and had more sexual experience were better placed to negotiate the terms of a sexual relationship with a partner. The new explicitness of so much popular literature about the erotic almost guaranteed that many Americans would have their sexual repertoires greatly enhanced. Perhaps most significantly, the growing complexity of the American life cycle substantially weakened the hegemony of marriage as the privileged site for sexual expression. As one longitudinal study of families in Detroit concluded, "the decision to marry or remain single is now considered a real and legitimate choice between acceptable alternatives, marking a distinct shift in attitude from that held by Americans in the past."

Survey data from a variety of sources confirm a striking shift in sexual values toward approval of nonmarital sexuality. As late as the 1950s, for instance, polls suggested that fewer than a quarter of Americans endorsed premarital sex for men and women. By the 1970s, these figures had been reversed. Especially among the young, substantial majorities registered their approval. Although males, blacks, the college-educated and higher-income families were more likely to accept premarital sexuality, the differences between groups were disappearing. Only older Americans and religiously devout whites tended to maintain a stance of moral disapproval. The generation gap was especially pronounced over some of the more radical departures from past orthodoxy. One study found that three-quarters of Americans over sixty-five opposed the practice of cohabitation, while the figures were reversed for the under-thirty population. Similarly, when confronted with the contemporary openness of the gay community, younger Americans proved more than three times as likely as their seniors to display tolerance for homosexuality. In their study of American couples, Blumstein and Schwartz found that among married couples, cohabiting heterosexuals, gay men, and lesbians, majorities of everyone except wives expressed approval for sexual relationships devoid of love.

One important ideological source for the revamping of sexual beliefs was feminism. Particularly among younger heterosexuals, traditional notions of male and female differences weakened in the 1970s. Most looked forward to marriages in which roles blurred. Many younger males abandoned the allegiance to a double standard of behavior for their female peers. For both men and women, expectations about sexuality and intimacy changed. As Sophie Freud Loewenstein, a Boston social worker, explained it,

Women who have taken it for granted that their sexual satisfaction was unimportant are now reading about women having multiple orgasms. Many men realize that they've been ripped off by being programmed to deny their expressive aspects. It becomes a possibility to throw out some of the old sex roles and change drastically. That change can be very frightening, but the atmosphere makes it more permissible.

As its critique of sex-role conditioning spread throughout the culture, feminism altered the attitudes of Americans about the proper behavior of men and women.

Demographic change, shifts in attitudes, and the eroticism that so much of the public realm displayed contributed to a major alteration in the sexual life of many Americans. Unmarried youth as well as conjugal pairs, urban male homosexuals as well as heterosexual couples, experienced important modifications in their patterns of sexual behavior. Among other things, sexual experience was beginning at a younger age, acts once considered deviant were more widely incorporated into heterosexual relations, and the gap between the sex lives of men and women was narrowing.

The behavior of the young and the unmarried dramatically illustrates the extent of change. From the mid-1960s onward the incidence of premarital intercourse among white females zoomed upward, narrowing substantially the disparity in experience between them and their male peers. Survey after survey of white college students in every part of the country confirmed this shift. By 1980 large majorities of female students were engaging in coitus, often in relationships that held no expectation of marriage. Among black women, too, there was evidence of change, though primarily in the age at which coitus began. Between 1971 and 1976, fifteen- and sixteen-year-olds were half again as likely to have engaged in intercourse. In the early 1970s, a much broader survey that included men and women of varying educational levels also documented the rise in premarital coitus among women. By then young women were as likely to have sex as were the men in Kinsey's study a generation earlier. Morton Hunt, the author, also confirmed a greater variety in practices. Where Kinsey had found few heterosexuals who had tried fellatio or cunnilingus, by the 1970s it was a commonplace experience among those in their twenties. The frequency of intercourse for young men and women was also substantially higher, while masturbation, especially among women, was starting earlier and had become more widespread.

Evidence of other sorts substantiates these survey findings. On college campuses, health services routinely distributed contraceptive information and devices to students. For those who began having intercourse earlier, or who did not attend college, Planned Parenthood clinics offered an alternative source of assistance. In Muncie, Indiana, for example, a third of teenage girls used the services of Planned Parenthood in 1979. The rise in births to unmarried teenagers, as well as the large number who sought abortions, also suggest that a growing proportion of the young were sexually active.

These changes in patterns of behavior took place in a social context different from that which had shaped the behavior of youth between the 1920s and the 1960s. For one, formal dating evinced a sharp decline. Teenage youth socialized casually in groups without pairing off; friendships between males and females were more common. As one high school boy described it, in drawing a contrast between himself and his father:

> Once he told me that he wasn't brought up to think about women the way guys like me do, and it was vice versa back then. 'We were scared of each other; we didn't really have *friends* of the opposite sex' is the way he said it to me. Now that's changed! I can talk with girls I'm not dating—I mean, be real friendly with them. There's one girl at school who's the person I feel easiest with there. We're pals, but I've never wanted to make out with her!

This ease of interaction had implications for the progress of sexual experience. When the young did pair off, it tended to signal an already serious relationship. They were less likely to move gradually through the stages of kissing, necking, and petting before deciding to have intercourse. In fact, one observer of the young concluded that petting, so important in the sexual initiation of midcentury adolescents, "seems destined to take its place as a historical curiosity."

The demographic patterns of the late 1960s and 1970s, as well as the less measurable effects of feminist ideology, also contributed to the shape of change. As women became sexually active earlier in life, as the age of marriage rose, and their participation in the labor force promised greater autonomy, more of them could approach sexual experience with different expectations. One twenty-eight-year-old blue-collar female, cohabiting with a male partner, firmly expressed her right to an erotic life. "I may have had an unusual upbringing, but it never occurred to me that a man wouldn't let me be sexy," she said. "I have the same needs and moods as a man, and I am not going to let some chauvinist pig stifle them." Another single woman, also in her twenties, justified nonmonogamy on the basis of her strong sexual desires. "I have a roving eye and sometimes I give in to it. . . . I consider myself a very sexual person and I need an adventure from time to time. And I think [my cohabiting partner] does too. But that's all it is—fun and a little bit of an ego thrill." Their comments suggest that at least some women had moved a long distance from the 1950s, when sexual intercourse had to be justified as a sign of an abiding romantic attachment. . . .

One reason, undoubtedly, for the shifts in heterosexual relationships was the availability of birth control. The dramatic move in the 1960s toward effective contraception continued into the 1970s. By mid-decade three out of four married couples relied on the pill, the IUD, or sterilization. Then, too, the legalization of first-trimester abortions provided a measure of last resort for wives whose contraceptive efforts failed. Though it is difficult to know how great an increase in the incidence of abortion took place in the seventies, the fact that it was medically safe and legal at least removed the dangers that formerly attached to it. The near universality of birth control practices had virtually eliminated the constraints that fears about pregnancy had imposed on the sex life of married women. It also highlighted the degree to which the erotic had been divorced from procreation.

The separation of sex from reproduction also emerged from another quarter. Not only could couples safely have sex without the expectation of conception, but technological innovations were making it possible to have babies without sex. Science was upsetting age-old certainties about the natural connection between sex and procreation. "Remember when there was only one way to make a baby?" an advertisement for a 1979 CBS special report asked. "That was yesterday. Today, nature's role is being challenged by science. Conception without sex. Egg fertilization outside the womb. 'Surrogate' mothers who can bear other couples' children. Frozen embryos stored in 'supermarkets' for future implantation." Among other things, scientific change was allowing lesbian couples to have children, without choosing marriage, through the cooperation of male sperm donors. Public policy added another dimension to technological change, as welfare agencies allowed single women and single men to adopt children, thus emphasizing the distinction between biological and social parenting. Though the new technology would raise some vexing problems of its own, as the controversy over Baby M revealed, people were nonetheless making choices that seemed to confirm that making love and making babies were not the same.

The new visibility that gay life achieved in the 1970s also emphasized the weakened link between procreation and the erotic. Although it is difficult to measure change in this area with any degree of precision, certainly the social life of gay men and lesbians had altered considerably. The many organizations that existed throughout the country allowed greater ease in making friends and acquaintances, and in embarking upon relationships. Less police harassment made it safer for bars to open and stay in operation. Regional music festivals brought thousands of lesbians together for several days of companionship; annual rituals such as the gay pride marches each June became celebrations of community cohesiveness even as they made a political statement. Church attendance, political club membership, and professional caucuses all contributed to a broadening of an identity in which the erotic played a prominent role. But the historic invisibility of gay male and lesbian life makes it impossible to compare the erotic dimension of gay experience from one generation to another. Even in the 1970s there were few studies that moved beyond the impressionism of journalistic observations.

A study that did, the work of Philip Blumstein and Pepper Schwartz, is interesting in part because of the comparison it allows between men and women, and between heterosexuals and homosexuals. The researchers found that a good sexual adjustment was as important to a successful relationship among gay male and lesbian respondents as among heterosexuals, and that the higher the frequency of sex the greater the sense of satisfaction. But lesbians seemed content to have sex less often, and after two years in a relationship, the lesbian couples tended to see a significant decline in the frequency of sex. Young lesbians were more likely to engage in oral sex than were older women, and among all the couples, gay men placed the greatest stock in variety in sexual technique. Lesbians proved very similar to heterosexual men and women in the extent of nonmonogamy—twenty-eight percent of lesbians, twenty-five percent of husbands, and twenty-one percent of wives—whereas for gay men, nonmonogamy was a way of life. Furthermore, among couples that did not practice monogamy male homosexuals tended to have sex with a far larger number of partners. One percent of the lesbians, seven percent of the husbands, but more than two-fifths of the gay men, had sex with more than twenty partners while living with a mate.

Even in the era that witnessed an expansion of erotic opportunities, the experience of some urban gay men appeared to stand outside the norm. When Kinsey undertook his study in the 1940s he found that although male homosexuals on average had sex less frequently than heterosexual men, some of them had far more partners in the course of a lifetime. In the 1970s, as the urban gay subculture became larger and more accessible, the chances for sexual encounters multiplied. Heterosexuals may have had their singles bars where they could meet a partner for an evening of sex, but in large cities, gay bathhouses, bars with back rooms, and stores showing pornographic films allowed gay male patrons to have sex with a series of men in rapid succession. For many, sexual promiscuity became part of the fabric of gay life, an essential element holding the community together. Yet the fact that such sex businesses could operate in the 1970s relatively free of police harassment and that the media could spotlight them in discussions of gay life says as much about heterosexual norms as about those of gay men. In the larger metropolitan areas, male homosexuals were no longer serving as symbols of sexual deviance; their eroticism no longer divided the good from the bad. Heterosexuals sustained a vigorous singles nightlife, and advertised in magazines for partners; suburban couples engaged in mate-swapping; sex clubs were featuring male strippers, with women in the role of voyeur. By the end of the decade, some "straight" men and women were even patronizing a heterosexual equivalent of the gay bathhouse, as the success of places like Plato's Retreat in New York demonstrated. The experience of the urban gay subculture stood as one point along a widened spectrum of sexual possibilities that modern America now offered.

Although it would be foolhardy to deny the depth and breadth of the changes that had occurred by the end of the 1970s, one must also acknowledge the continuities with the past. Blumstein and Schwartz, for instance, found that "there *are* new men and women, among both heterosexual and homosexual couples, who are dealing with sexual responsibilities in new ways and trying to modify the traditions that their maleness and femaleness bring to their relationships." But they were fewer in number than the pair of sociologists expected to find, and the persistence of tradition was particularly hard for some heterosexual women whose partners proved "less 'liberated' than she—or he—thought he was." Marriages were happier and more intimate than a generation earlier, but partly because so many unhappy ones ended in divorce. In a culture that was coming to identify frequent, pleasurable, varied, and ecstatically satisfying sex as a preeminent sign of personal happiness, the high rate of marital dissolution could easily mean that large numbers of Americans were failing to reach these standards. The differences in the patterns of behavior of gay men and lesbians also pointed to the continuing salience of gender in shaping sexual meanings. Moreover, while lesbians and male homosexuals had carved out some space for themselves in society, the frequency of physical assaults upon visibly gay men and women suggested that their form of nonprocreative sex still provoked outrage. Feminism, too, may have opened new realms of sexual expressiveness for women, but the extent of rape and other forms of male sexual violence still made sex an arena of danger for them. The much-vaunted "sexual revolution," though real in many ways, was hardly complete.

Two issues, in particular, were emerging by the end of the 1970s to suggest the contradictory emotions that still enshrouded sex. Since the advent of penicillin in the 1940s, the threat of venereal disease had, to a significant degree, faded as an inhibitor of nonmonogamous sexual expression. But, in the midst of Americans' recently acquired sexual "freedom," the media spotlighted a new venereal scourge. Herpes, which *Time* magazine labeled "today's scarlet letter" and the "new leprosy," was reaching epidemic proportions among young urban heterosexuals. Though the condition posed far less physical danger than syphilis, it provoked guilt and panic as well as a pulling back from erotic encounters for some. A medical professional reported that "we hear it over and over: I won't have sex again." Among victims, the disease elicited feelings of self-pollution—"you never think you're clean enough," said one. The *Soho Weekly News*, a New York paper popular among young professionals in the city, was moved to proclaim "current sexual practice" as "the real epidemic." For many, the spread of herpes came to symbolize the inherent flaws in an ethic of sexual permissiveness. Pleasure brought retribution; disease became a marker of weak moral character.

Another "epidemic," that of teenage pregnancy, also highlighted ambivalence about the erotic. Although most Americans tended to look benignly upon sex between unmarried adults, the spread of sexual experience among teenagers troubled them. To a large extent, adolescents were pursuing the erotic without the approval or the guidance of their elders. Despite the visibility of sex in the culture, the acquisition of knowledge by the young remained sporadic and haphazard, largely "a private, individually motivated and covert affair," in the opinion of one sex researcher. Some parents felt it was simply wrong, despite their own experience. As one middle-class mother in Muncie had phrased it, "just because it was right for me doesn't make it okay for my kids." A survey of high school youth in the early 1980s found that almost half had learned nothing about sex from their parents. Nor were schools rushing to fill the gap. By the late 1970s only half a dozen states mandated sex education; in most places, curriculum remained up to the local school districts, which generally displayed the same caution or disregard that occurred in the home. In one New York City suburb, a high school principal refused to let the editor of the school paper print an article about birth control methods. A California school district provided sex instruction in conjunction with drivers education, indicating how marginal it was to the academic curriculum. "In order to avoid controversy," according to the authors of *Sex and the American Teenager,* "schools embrace boredom."

The result of this abdication of responsibility by schools and parents was that the young were often left to drift into sexual activity without guidance and with little knowledge. Teenagers whose parents were unwilling to talk with them about sex, or who did not receive sex education in school, were more prone to engage in intercourse. Yet they were also likely to be ignorant of how conception occurred or how to prevent it. Even when schools did provide instruction, they often acted too late. One North Carolina fifteen-year-old learned about condoms in a junior high school class, after he had been having intercourse for two years. "And then I realized, man, I've been taking a lot of chances. Thirteen, fourteen, fifteen . . . Lord's been good to me," he said. Others were not so lucky, as the incidence of teenage pregnancy revealed. In 1976, among the premaritally sexually active, twenty-seven percent of white girls and forty-five percent of blacks had become pregnant by the age of eighteen. Ironically, in view of the laissez-faire stance that adults seemed to take, the young were looking for advice. As Robert Coles and Geoffrey Stokes concluded on the basis of their work with high school students,

> it seems clear from our interviews that some kids who are planning to enter sexual relationships *want* to be told to wait. But those who can't talk to their parents hear either nothing or a ritualized naysaying that has no bearing on their *immediate* situation—and those who can may find their parents unwilling to take the responsibility for saying anything more than "Be careful."

Meanwhile, for those who had made their choice to have sex, accurate information about reproduction, conception, and birth control might at least save them from the tragedy of unwanted pregnancies.

That so many teenage girls were becoming pregnant in an age when reliable contraception was available says much about the contradictions within the sexually permissive culture of the 1960s and 1970s. From everywhere sex beckoned, inciting desire, yet rarely did one find reasoned presentations of the most elementary consequences and responsibilities that sexual activity entailed. Youth had more autonomy from adult supervision than ever before, allowing them to explore the erotic at a time of profound physiological changes, but adults seemed to respond by implicitly drawing a boundary at sexual activity during adolescence. Perhaps one could not stop the young from experimenting, but neither would society endorse their behavior. The result was a social problem of tragic dimensions, one that placed in bold relief the ambivalence of American society toward sex. And, the fact that young girls were left to pay a higher price for sexual activity served as a poignant commentary on the persistence of gender in the structuring of sexuality in the postliberal era.

The reshaping of sexuality in the 1960s and 1970s was of major proportions. The marketing of sex, new demographic patterns, and the movements of women and homosexuals for equality all fostered a substantial revision in attitudes and behavior. In some ways, the process of sexualization represented pushing the logic of sexual liberalism to its extreme: once sex had been identified as a critical aspect of happiness, how could one justify containing it in marriage? Even before the 1960s, the behavior of youth and the commercial manipulation of the erotic had suggested the vulnerability of the liberal consensus. By the end of the 1970s, it was obvious that the consensus had dissolved. As Americans married later, postponed childbearing, and divorced more often, and as feminists and gay liberationists questioned heterosexual orthodoxy, nonmarital sexuality became commonplace and open. And all of this took place in a social environment in which erotic imagery was ubiquitous.

The collapse of sexual liberalism did not, however, lead to a new, stable consensus. By the end of the 1970s, conservative proponents of an older sexual order had appeared. Their efforts to stem the tide of change and, indeed, to restore sexuality to a reproductive marital context would demonstrate the continuing power of sex to generate controversy.

REVIEW QUESTIONS

1. The authors describe many things that have changed in Americans' sexual behavior and their attitudes toward it, but they also point out that some things have not changed. What are the most important changes? Are there any that the authors have not mentioned? What are the most important things that have remained more or less the same? Again, are there any you can think of that the authors have not mentioned?

2. Why have sexual behavior and attitudes about it changed as they have?

3. This selection describes conditions before people became fully aware of the extent and seriousness of AIDS. How has AIDS affected sexual behavior? What is its long-term impact likely to be, assuming no cure is found?

4. What is, what has been, what will be the impact on the subjects discussed in this selection of the recent upsurge of religious fundamentalism?

5. How, if at all, is the current controversy about abortion related to the changes the authors describe?

6. Does it seem likely to you that changes in traditional ideas about sex, marriage, and so forth are going to continue? Are they going to speed up? Slow down? Will there be a movement back toward traditional ideas? What makes you think so?

FOR FURTHER READING

Sidney Ditzion, *Marriage, Morals and Sex in America: A History of Ideas* (1953); Carl N. Degler, *At Odds: Women and Family in America from the Revolution to the Present* (1980); Christopher Lasch, *Haven in a Heartless World: The Family Besieged* (1977); Steven Mintz and Susan Kellogg, *Domestic Revolutions: A Social History of American Family Life* (1988); and E. Anthony Rotundo, *American Manhood: Transformations in American Masculinity from the Revolution to the Modern Era* (1993), provide historical background on some of the subjects covered in this selection. Past attitudes toward sex and sexuality are described in Beth L. Bailey, *From Front Porch to Back Seat: Courtship in Twentieth-Century America* (1988), and Karen Lystra, *Searching the Heart: Women, Men, and Romantic Love in Nineteenth-Century America* (1989). Alfred Kinsey et al., *Sexual Behavior in the Human Male* (1948) and *Sexual Behavior in the Human Female* (1953), are massive surveys of the subject, limited because of their nearly exclusive focus on middle-class men and women, but valuable nevertheless. Randy Shilts, *And the Band Played On: Politics, People, and the AIDS Epidemic* (1987), is not only the best single treatment of the whole issue of AIDS, it also has a great deal to say, directly and indirectly, about current attitudes concerning sex.

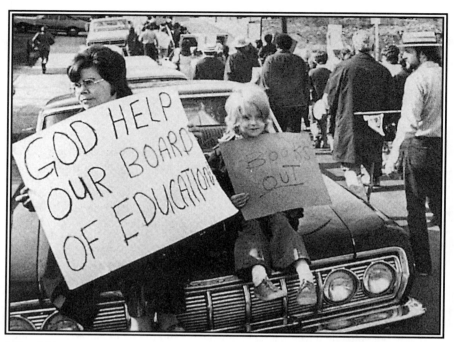

R. Ferrell Friend/Charleston Gazette

A rally protesting the introduction of new text books into the schools of Kanawha County,
West Virginia.

22

Culture War

WILLIAM MARTIN

The social movements of the 1960s had a number of long-term effects on the United States besides getting laws passed and policies adopted. One was to make new forms of protest and direct action seen feasible and desirable. Another was to awaken social groups that had previously been regarded—and possibly had regarded themselves—as marginal to the possibilities of social and political action on their own behalf. A final effect was to generate a series of conflicts and controversies that by the end of the decade had created a deeply polarized society and established the foundations for what are often referred to as the "culture wars" of contemporary society.

One specific manifestation of these effects has been the emergence in recent years of the religious right. Previously in the twentieth century, except for a brief flurry in the 1920s, there was little obvious connection between people's religious beliefs and their political preferences and actions. The effects of religion on politics were indirect, covert, or completely nonexistent. This situation began to change in the 1970s. Many people were deeply disturbed by what they saw as the excesses committed by the various social protest movements of the 60s and by the ways those movements had changed and were changing America. Some responded by reasserting their commitment to traditional values, including religious values, and the result was a powerful resurgence of political and cultural conservatism, culminating in the election of Ronald Reagan as president in 1980 and his re-election in 1984. In this process, a prominent role was played by ministers like Jerry Falwell and Pat Robertson who used television to spread views that combined religion and politics into a potent mixture. For many devout followers of these and other ministers, political activism became a way of bearing witness to their religious beliefs.

The following selection describes one particular conflict in one county in West Virginia, but it is representative of many others that became and have remained a significant feature of the nation's social and political landscape. It is also a clear example of how religious belief was wedded to political action in the emergence of the religious right.

Alice Moore read about the Battle of Anaheim [over a proposed sex-education program in the public schools] in the *Saturday Evening Post* in 1969, while sitting in a beauty shop in St. Albans, West Virginia. "I was shocked at some of the things I read," she recalled, "but I wasn't that concerned about it, because I knew this was West Virginia, not a radical state like California. I thought, 'It's not going to happen here.'" Not long afterward, however, she saw a newspaper story announcing that sex education was going to be introduced in Kanawha County schools. "That concerned me a little bit," she said, "but not all that much. And then I noticed that there was going to be a parents' meeting in a little restaurant in South Charleston, so I decided I'd go." That simple decision set Alice Moore on a course of action that erupted into a full blown "culture war," a violent and prolonged upheaval that laid bare deep fissures in the county's social structure.

In 1969, Kanawha County, West Virginia, was predominantly white, Anglo-Saxon, and Protestant—folks who, one would think, should find it easy to get along. But cutting across those broad categories were divisions of religion, class, and world-view that made real community for whites, much less for whites and blacks together, all but impossible. By its residents' own account, the county had at least two distinct populations of whites: the reasonably well-educated middle-class citizens of Charleston and the rural Appalachians who worked in the chemical plants and refineries of Nitro, St. Albans, and Dunbar, or carved a living out of the sometimes wild, coal-filled mountains gorged by hollows and creeks that drain into the Kanawha River. The social and cultural chasm between the capital city and the surrounding Upper and Lower Valleys is sufficiently wide that, at times, some have thought the county should be divided into two. Just about the only governmental jurisdiction that treated the area as a single unit was the Kanawha County school district, and in the 1970s that could serve more to divide than to unite. The closing of dozens of small schools during the 1950s and '60s has thrown more rural children into contact with urban culture, thereby undermining their own folkways. The changes wrought by the upheavals of the sixties also threatened the fragile peace that masked quite different ways of perceiving reality.

Alice Moore was a relatively new resident of the area, having moved there when her husband became minister of the fundamentalist Church of Christ in St. Albans, an industrial suburb south of Charleston. Though she had no deep roots in the county, she did have a great concern for children and strong convictions about how they should be reared. Nevertheless, while the leaders of the meeting in South Charleston were uneasy about the proposed sex-education program, Mrs. Moore tried to keep an open mind. "When I listened to some of the things they were saying," she remembered, "I still wasn't convinced that everything was necessarily true, because people get excited about things sometimes. So I decided I would go to the Board of Education and just ask to see the materials myself. Many of the pictures I had seen at the meeting simply weren't there. Many of the things they had said were in the materials, I didn't see." Later, she alleged, she learned that some of the more controversial materials had been withdrawn after the first flurry of objections. Even with those items removed, however, she still found the proposed curriculum disturbing. "What concerned me was that this wasn't just a sex-education course. It dealt with every aspect of a child's life. It dealt with their attitudes. In fact, the stated purpose of the course was to teach children how to think, to feel, and to act. And it covered everything, from their relationship with their parents, to their attitudes toward the use of drugs and social drinking, to their attitudes toward sexual conduct. So that concerned me."

The curriculum, a comprehensive health education program, had been prepared with the aid of a U.S. Office of Education grant and approved by the Kanawha County Board of Education and a Curriculum Advisory Committee of interested citizens—none of whom represented the county's more conservative rural population. To express her concern, Moore called Superintendent of Schools Walter Synder and explained her feeling that the proposed curriculum would intrude into "our relationship with our children, what we wanted to teach them, what we wanted them to believe, how we wanted them to behave." His reply, by her account, amounted to little more than, "I'm sorry, Mrs. Moore, but there's absolutely nothing you can do about it."

Alice Moore did not accept Synder's reading of the situation. Instead, she began speaking to various groups around the county and lobbying members of the state legislature to look into the matter. When her efforts seemed ineffectual, Moore and a few of her friends decided she should run for the single contested spot on the Board of Education. "We went down there with just minutes to spare and signed up to run," she recounted with a laugh. "It was really a spur-of-the-moment decision." A newspaper poll conducted a week before the election gave the incumbent nearly a third of the vote and Moore about eighteen percent, with the remainder split among seven or eight other candidates. Moore credits the newspaper poll, which indicated she had at least some chance, with rallying much of the anti-incumbent sentiment behind her. . . . [S]he took thirty-four percent to the incumbent's thirty-three, defeating him by approximately four hundred votes.

Within months of taking office in early 1970, Moore managed to overcome opposition to her view that the sex-ed curriculum was anti-Christian, anti-American, and indoctrinated students with an "atheistic and relativistic view of morality" that ran counter to her own firm conviction that "God's law is absolute." She acknowledged, "We pretty well won our case. Everything wasn't exactly to my liking, but we no longer had a program that was as disturbing to people as that one had been." In the course of this conflict, Superintendent Walter Snyder resigned and was replaced by Kenneth Underwood. These accomplishments made Alice Moore a champion in some circles. When she ran for re-election in 1976, she received 25,000 votes, two-and-a-half times her total in 1970 and 7,500 more than the nearest competitor. Moreover, she pointed out, most of the eight or nine people running against her shared her basic stand on most issues. Clearly, the rural "creekers" and factory workers, as well as a substantial number of white-collar city folk, felt they now had a voice on the Board of Education.

"Sweet Alice," as both friends and critics came to call her, though with different inflections, next made big news in 1974, when the school board sought to adopt 325 titles for its K–12 language-arts curriculum. In standard fashion, the books had been chosen by a school-system textbook committee. Under Superintendent Underwood, the Curriculum Advisory Committee had become dormant, so the textbook committee's recommendation reached the board in March and received rubber-stamp preliminary approval at a meeting Alice Moore missed. In keeping with the times, the books included substantial selections from black, Hispanic, and other minority writers, as well as a much greater than usual variety of other materials, all designed to help teachers create individualized programs of instruction that recognized differences in student interests, outlooks, and aptitude. The board followed established policy and put the books on display at the Kanawha County Library, to allow any citizen who wished to look them over to do so. They apparently drew almost no attention. When the time came to finalize adoption, however, Moore complained that not enough time had been allowed for inspection and persuaded her colleagues to extend the period of inspection until the June board meeting.

Mrs. Moore was particularly concerned about a growing toleration of "nonstandard English" and had read articles, she explained, "to the effect that it was as important for a child who spoke standard English to learn to speak ghetto English as it was for a child of the ghetto to learn to speak standard English. That was an outrageous idea. If that's the case, why do we hire English teachers? Why do we even bother?" She listened to English teachers tell the board about a broadening approach to teaching, and, she recalled, "The more they talked, the more I realized they were talking about teaching non-standard English. So I suggested we postpone the adoption."

Objection to "non-standard English" can be a coded way of registering dislike of blacks and other minorities. It can also be precisely what it purports to be: objection to non-standard English. Those to whom the substitution of "lay" for "lie" and the use of nominative pronouns after prepositions sound worse than fingernails on a blackboard need not be racist to hope their children will not "axe" such questions as "Do he have your grammar book?" Whatever Alice Moore's true motivation on that score, she soon found even more substantial problems with the new books. Indeed, moments after the April board meeting adjourned, her husband, who had been leafing through some of the books, said, "I want you to look at what you just adopted." The selection he handed her, she remembered, "was written by a man who said, 'Thank God' he had gotten out of the South, because if he hadn't, he'd 'still be a blankety-blank Christian.' ". . .

[C]omplaints about the textbooks fell into categories familiar to anyone who . . . was aware of similar struggles in other states. The objecting parents sought to shield their children from anything that smacked of a lack of patriotism or, in their oft-used phrase, "disregard for government authority." Mike Edds, an inner-city youth pastor who rallied to Moore's side early in the protest, explained that, "Those books challenged the sacredness of everything that we believe about America. I'm sure America's wrong at times, but we believe it's the best thing we've come across in this world. They never brought out what America did do that was good. They said the flag was just a piece of cloth. Well, that's not what we believe. We have a lot of relatives who died under that banner. To us, it's like a sacred symbol. You don't burn the flag; you don't challenge what our Founding Fathers have done, or the Constitution. If there're things that're wrong, you work to change [them] and make it better." Closely related to changes of a lack of patriotism were complaints that the books contained criticism of the free-enterprise system. Elmer Fike [a local businessman], regarded some of the readings as "obviously liberal, socialist, even communist-inspired." Alice Moore was less inclined to think actual communists were involved, but she did believe the books bore the marks of "people in our country who are maybe leftist leaning, who think socialism is a better system than we have. They were radical books."

In addition to these fears, Mrs. Moore voiced concern that the books might create "more race consciousness than they would otherwise have had." Numerous parents were disturbed by material written by such black writers as Nikki Giovanni, Alice Walker, James Baldwin, and Gwendolyn Brooks. Ruth

Davis, an English teacher who was also active in the local NAACP chapter, recalled her pleasure at seeing the work of black and Hispanic authors in the series: "I felt we had moved forward. We had faced integration and here we were now, teaching all students, and we were going to be able to have the black students see some of their culture within the textbooks for once in our career." Repeatedly, however, these writers were criticized for profane or negative language, for depressing content, and for exposing children to realities from which they should be shielded. Ms. Davis felt this was a transparent effort to hide the fact that many white parents did not want their children exposed to black influences, even in books.

Although selections by black authors contained some strong language and gritty scenes, racism could not account for all the discomfort over "realism" in the books. Board-member Matthew Kinsolving acknowledged that the books contained some "cuss words" and such terms as "tits" and "piss," which some parents found objectionable, but Alice Moore thought it more serious than that. "The books were filled with all kinds of profanity," she insisted. "It wasn't just an occasional thing." She felt the stories not only contained inappropriate vocabulary, but their content was often quite unsuitable for youngsters. "There was a play in a junior high book," she recalled, "to be acted out in a classroom, and it was a story of a fifteen-year-old boy's first visit to a prostitute. Now this was a book for junior high children! It was almost as if they were stretching the limits, to see how far they could go, to see what they could do."

Echoing a common . . . objection, Moore and her backers charged the books with being pervaded by a "morbid," "negative," "depressing" tone. "There's more to life than negative things," said Mike Edds. "The sun shines sometimes; it's not always rain and clouds and darkness and sadness. They said, 'We want to introduce you to real life.' Well, I thought I was living real life. Most of us were happy people. Maybe we were happy in our ignorance, but we were happy people. We were happy in our homes; we were happy with what we were teaching our children. I wasn't really concerned with what was taking place on the streets of New York City."

James Moffett, the editor-in-chief of a collection of books called *Interaction,* which comprised 172 of the 325 books on the adoption list, thought the matter more complicated. He noted that much literature and drama, including the ballads of Appalachian folk culture, has long dealt with dark subjects. He said, "We had a book called *Monologue and Dialogue* that had a lot of old chestnuts of English literature in there—Robert Browning, William Blake, Matthew Arnold, T. S. Eliot. But they said 'Trash, trash from beginning to end' about this book. They said it was 'morbid.' That criticism—that things were 'negative,' 'morbid,' 'depressed'—made me do a lot of thinking about what was in their mind. The psychological research on the authoritarian personality indicates that it's based on a very negative view of the world—'The world is a fearsome place and I'm not going to make it'—and on low self-esteem, low self-confidence, a view that mankind is evil, a feeling of being unable to cope. I think that comes out in their criticisms."

Since one aspect of a fearsome world is the absence of reliable road signs, the textbook critics assailed readings that smacked of moral relativity, that is, the belief that there are no definite right and wrong answers. Closely related was a distaste for symbolism, irony, satire, ambiguity, or role-playing, since all these invite interpretations that diverge from a literal reading of the text. In their view, schoolbooks—like the Bible—should have one meaning and one only, and it should be obvious to all. Cultivating a taste and talent for multiple interpretations can only increase the likelihood of thought and behavior that call into question the settled and dependable nature of one's community and religion. . . .

By the time of the June 27 school board meeting, Alice Moore had convinced most parent-teacher groups and numerous conservative white churches to line up against the textbooks. On the other side, the West Virginia Human Rights Commission and the chapters of the NAACP and YWCA endorsed the adoptions, as did the *Charleston Gazette*, the *Charleston Daily Mail*, WCHS television, and most black churches. A coalition of clergy representing the West Virginia Council of Churches, Roman Catholic churches, Jewish synagogues, most Episcopal, Presbyterian, and Methodist churches, and some Baptist congregations, issued a statement acknowledging that any wideranging set of books is likely to stir controversy but asserting that their own investigation had found the books "not nearly as bad as portrayed." The issues objected to, they said, must be discussed openly if students are to be prepared to face the challenges of living in a multifaceted world. "We know of no way to stimulate the growth of our youth if we insulate them from the real issues. We feel this program will help our students think intelligently about their lives and our society." In response, a conservative coalition organized by a Baptist pastor and members of the Dunbar Ministerial Association issued statements critical of the books. And in the most impressive show of opposition, the Magic Valley Mother's Club gathered twelve thousand signatures of Kanawha County citizens urging the board to rescind the adoption.

The June school-board meeting drew more than one thousand people. In the end, the five-member board voted three-to-two to approve the original list, with the exception of eight books from the *Interaction* series. Joining Alice Moore in casting a negative vote was Matthew Kinsolving, who admits he was less concerned about the content of the books than about peace in the county. "On the basis of what she had upstirred," he said, "I voted against adopting those books at that time." Kinsolving's apprehensions were to prove more than justified.

Some citizens expected the objectors to accept their defeat with resignation, if not with grace. The response, however, involved neither. During July and August, an organization called Christian-American Parents initiated a letter-writing campaign, bought newspaper ads, held a large public rally, picketed a board member's company, and held a demonstration in front of the governor's mansion. (Eventually, a different group of parents came together and called themselves Non-Christian American Parents, to make the point that people other than fundamentalists opposed the books.) Another new group, Concerned Citizens, picketed the Board of Education. And various parties . . . continued to circulate copies of material calculated to stir anger even further.

Some of the most inflammatory material, blatantly sexual in nature, was not even in the books that had been adopted, but few bothered to check; some of those who did check, and did not find the controversial passages, concluded that a deceitful administration was hiding the material until the furor died down. Because nearly all attacks on the books emphasized the profanity and sexual content, the entire collection soon came to be known as "the dirty books."

As summer wore on, Alice Moore began to urge parents to hold their children out of school in September if the board tried to force them to use the new books. On Labor Day, September 2, the day before schools were scheduled to open, Concerned Citizens sponsored a rally at which fundamentalist preacher Marvin Horan fervently urged the crowd of eight thousand to boycott the entire school system the next day. Tuesday morning, with national news media on hand to watch, approximately twenty percent of the district's forty-five thousand students stayed home. In the Upper Valley, where Horan and other fundamentalist preachers had been most vociferous in their objections to the books, some schools had absentee rates above eighty percent. Some parents doubtless kept their children home out of fear of what the protesters might do to those who violated the call for a boycott—this was, after all, strong union territory—but most observed the boycott because they believed it was a righteous cause.

The following day, the boycott received a tremendous boost when an estimated thirty-five hundred coal miners struck in a show of solidarity with the protesters, despite orders from United Mine Workers officials not to do so. Within a week, the number of striking miners in Kanawha County and seven surrounding counties ran as high as ten thousand. Meanwhile, protesters picketed schools, school-bus garages, businesses, and various other sites, sometimes erecting barricades to keep people and vehicles from passing through. Thousands of people mounted daily demonstrations at the school district's main administration building. On September 10, Charleston bus drivers honored the picket lines, leaving more than ten thousand regular riders without service.

On September 11, the school board caved in, announcing it would withdraw the disputed books from use and submit then to examination by a new Textbook Review Committee, to which each board member would be allowed to name three individuals of his or her choosing. . . .

Perhaps to Moore's surprise, the troops she had mobilized were not content with a partial victory. At a large rally on the evening of the board's concession, the crowd jeered when she called the agreement "the best we can expect." Marvin Horan, who had signed the agreement on behalf of Concerned Citizens, reversed himself and joined the crowd's call to continue the boycotts and pickets until the offending texts were permanently removed from the schools and the superintendent and school board members who approved them swept out of office.

The protests not only continued after the rally, but quickly turned to ugly violence over the next few weeks. While the Textbook Review Committee formed and began its work, one school was dynamited, two others were fire-bombed, and several were damaged by gunfire and vandalism. Two men were wounded by gunfire, one as he tried to cross a picket line and the other, a protester, shot through the heart by a pro-book demonstrator who said he thought he was being attacked. CBS News reporter Jed DuVall and his television crew were badly roughed up. School buses were fired upon while returning from their rounds, and at one point most of the buses in the upper part of the county were disabled by vandals. Protesters stoned the houses and broke car windows of parents who defied the boycott and sent their children to school. Teachers and administrators were repeatedly threatened. Shots were fired into a car belonging to the president of the Classroom Teachers Association. And someone set off fifteen sticks of dynamite under the gas meter at the school board building just minutes after Underwood and the board had left.

Supporters of the books were also guilty of violence. The car of one protester was destroyed by fire. Alice Moore was repeatedly threatened, guns were fired in front of her house, sugar was put in her gas tank, and police bodyguards stayed with her during times of greatest threat. At one point, concern for student safety moved Superintendent Underwood to cancel all classes and extracurricular activities for several days, during which he and several board members, including Mrs. Moore, left town for reasons of personal safety. All attacks on schools and school buses occurred when no children were present, but one man eventually convicted in the bombings testified that he and others had considered bombing carloads of children as a way to stop "people that was sending their kids to school, letting them learn out of books when they knew they were wrong.". . .

The renewal of hostilities triggered by the boycott drew new adversaries into the arena. Joining Marvin Horan were three other fundamentalist preachers—the Reverends Avis Hill, Ezra Graley, and Charles Quigley—who quickly assumed leading roles in court-defying mass protests at school headquarters, which resulted in their being arrested, jailed, fined, or released on bail, and accorded martyr status among their followers. Quigley gained early notoriety when he declared, "I am asking Christian people to pray that God will kill the giants [the three board members who voted for the books] who have mocked and made fun of dumb fundamentalists."

On the other side of the aisle, the Reverend James Lewis, rector of St. John's Episcopal Church in Charleston, emerged as a key leader of pro-textbook forces. Lewis was a newcomer to Charleston who had paid little attention to the textbook controversy before the boycott began. At the request of several student council leaders who objected when the new texts were withdrawn, Lewis, along with a rabbi and a Baptist minister, met with a group of students to see what might be done to get the books back into the classrooms. That meeting led to others and, soon, to the formation of the Kanawha County Coalition for Quality Education, which sought both to defend the new books and also to avoid further damage to the social fabric. One of the coalition's first steps was to hold meetings throughout the country to give citizens the opportunity to examine the books for themselves, to show that much of what they had been told about the books was simply not true. "Everyone was so frightened," Lewis said, "as though somehow the children would die if they read these books."

Lewis's meetings were reasonably effective in easing the minds of some parents, particularly those primarily concerned with the presence of graphic sexual material, but they did little to mollify those who disagreed with the overall multicultural thrust and innovative approach of the books. . . .

"What we saw in that struggle," he said, "was a real religious crusade. If you stepped in front of it and challenged it in any way, you were immediately demonized and seen as the enemy, as the Antichrist. When you move into that kind of demonization, you are just a hair away from killing the person or people associated with that view, because to kill something evil becomes something good. That was the aura and the mood of that whole struggle. A woman stepped up to me at a meeting one time and put her face up against mine, quoting Scripture in my face as though somehow I didn't read Scripture, and she said to me, 'We shouldn't cast our pearls before swine' as though I were swine. There's a sense in which this passion turned into a terrible crusade that got violent very quickly in a self-righteous way. That's the thing you could feel in that valley all the time: you could be killed 'for Christ's sake.' "

Following a telephoned death threat, Lewis's family and friends urged him to step away from the controversy, but he felt that was not an option. Comparing the struggle to an explosion outside the church door, he said, "You have to go to it. People were warring with one another. This was Bosnia. This was a deeply tribal struggle, and there was no way to stay out of it." Lewis consistently described the conflict as a clash between cultures. "It was a struggle," he said, "of people from lots of different persuasions. My concern was always, 'How can all of us in this valley study and work and live together and not kill one another, particularly over these textbooks?' It was crystal-clear to me from the very beginning that we were in a major struggle with folks who saw life from a different perspective. The seeds had been there for a long time, but something new was happening." In an article carried by newspapers across the country at the time, Lewis wrote, "The anti-textbook people of Kanawha County are confused and angry about everything from marijuana to Watergate. Feeling helpless and left out, they are looking for a scapegoat.

They are eager to exorcise all that is evil and foul, cleanse or burn all that is strange and foreign. In this religious war, spiced with overtones of race and class, the books are an accessible target."

Like James Lewis, evangelical youth pastor Mike Edds also felt he had no choice but to take a stand. "We'd been taught in the Bible Belt," he explained, "that there is a higher law, that if the civil law is contrary to biblical law, then we have to obey the higher law. I felt something great was at stake. That's where the majority of parents and many of the educators who grew up in West Virginia were. Our whole belief system was at stake, and we had to take a stand. That was the first time in my life I had ever known Christian people to march in a protest or resist something. Before that, Christians did nothing; whatever came down the pike—fine, good, bad, or in-between—it was 'Just don't bother me.' But this was striking at their very soul."

Edds agreed with Jim Lewis's assertion that the struggle over the books stemmed from cultural differences, but viewed it from a different angle. Recalling a report that Superintendent Underwood had remarked in exasperation, "These fundamentalists: How can we live with them?," Edds said, "That's where the split came. There was an elitism in the central office that saw the majority of the county's population as ignorant, uneducated folks. I'm sure some of the folks didn't use proper English; I speak with a little bit of hillbilly lingo and slang. Some of these folks maybe didn't finish high school, maybe some of them didn't go on to college, but that's not a mark of a person's intelligence. People in Kanawha County are very pro-American, very patriotic— it's apple pie, Mom, the flag, and the church. These textbooks struck at every area of that belief system, and parents felt like, 'We cannot just avoid this conflict; we have to face it; we have to do something about it.' It was a terrible time. It was almost like a civil war. The community was just split down the middle." . . .

Given the emotional climate, tensions ran high in anticipation of a public meeting the school board scheduled for November 8, at which time it planned to reach a final decision on the Textbook Advisory Committee's recommendations. Expecting a huge turnout, the board rented the Charleston Civic Center and had thousands of seats set up. To discourage violence, guards armed with metal detectors and guns were stationed at entrances; additional guards kept watch on the auditorium floor from positions in the rafters. These elaborate preparations proved to be superfluous. Alice Moore and a minister from the pro-book forces had both used radio and personal contact with various groups to urge citizens not to attend the meeting, lest trouble break out. As a result, the board conducted its deliberations in the huge hall before an audience of no more than fifty people. By a four-to-one margin, with Moore as the lone dissenter, it ruled that the books would be returned to the schools, but that no school or child would be forced to use them. Parents would have to provide written permission for their children to be assigned the books, and children whose parents objected would continue to use the old books or some acceptable alternative. Some books, including James Moffett's *Interaction* series, would be restricted to library use. Two weeks later, the board agreed that future texts would have to meet criteria set forth in a set of restrictive guidelines Alice Moore had prepared . . .

One might imagine that both sides would conclude they had done about as well as could be expected. Traditional parents could protect their children from the new books, and future books would be more to their liking. The children of more progressive parents could use the controversial books until they wore out and, if not too many of them turned into communists or criminals, a future board might relax some of the restrictions it had placed on itself. Ideological struggles, however, seldom end quite so peacefully, especially when they involve fundamentalists, for whom half-measures and partial victory are regarded as little better than defeat. . . .

On December 1, the Reverend Avis Hill led a demonstration in which two thousand people marched through the Charleston shopping district waving flags and carrying placards that read, "Trash Is for Burning," "No Peaceful Coexistence with Satanic Communism," and "Wish We Had More People Like Sweet Alice." A few days later, Hill and fellow fundamentalist preacher Ezra Graley went to Washington to discuss their concerns with conservative Indiana Congressman Roger Zion, who registered their complaints in the *Congressional Record*. On December 12, during a televised school-board meeting, protesters physically assaulted Superintendent Underwood and all the board members except Alice Moore. And on Christmas Eve, worshipers leaving a family service at St. John's Episcopal Church, which had backed the pro-book forces, found the church door decorated with stickers that announced, "You Have Been Paid a Visit by the Klan." On the other side, the National Educational Association held hearings and issued a report that criticized the board both for not being more sensitive to the concerns of a significant part of its constituency and also for caving in to most of the objectors' demands. . . .

On January 17, a grand jury indicted preacher Marvin Horan and five others for "conspiracy to blow up two elementary schools and other School Board property." The next day, nearly two hundred protesters, including Horan, welcomed several delegations of the Ku Klux Klan who gathered on the steps of the state capitol for a full-hood rally, followed by a larger gathering at the Civic Center, where Imperial Wizard James Venable darkly predicted that the "Communist, socialist, nigger race is going to dominate this nation," and other Klansmen declared their support of the protesters and invited them to join the Klan.

With the exception of some of the fundamentalist preachers, most leaders of the anti-textbook forces professed to be disturbed by such support. Elmer Fike . . . [said of] the Klan, "We didn't want anything to do with them. We wouldn't touch them with a ten-foot pole." Mike Edds was even more pointed: "We're not ignorant people. We felt like we were fully capable of representing ourselves. I was appalled when the Klan got involved. They just found a good thing going, that was getting some national attention, and they jumped on board. A lot of us dropped out toward the end. We were tired of other groups wanting to speak for us, trying to promote their organization's agenda, which wasn't the agenda that had us out on the streets. There is a religious right and a political right, and they're not one and the same."

The intrusion of uninvited outside forces and the arrest of Marvin Horan and his coconspirators, together with the increased presence of West Virginia State Police, soon brought an end to the boycotts and demonstrations and violence. After Horan was found guilty of conspiring to bomb the schools, the Reverend James Lewis appealed to the federal judge to give Horan a probated sentence, so he could remain in the community and use his influence to help try to heal fractures and restore peace to the valley. The judge sentenced Horan to three years in the federal penitentiary; his five accomplices received various lesser sentences.

By some accounts, the pro-textbook forces won the Kanawha County textbook wars; most of the offending books were restored to the classrooms and the most vociferous of their enemies went to jail or prison. The apparent victory, however, proved hollow. In schools where opposition ran high, the books were typically not used at all. When opinion was mixed, as was often the case, teachers found it difficult to devise comparable assignments and often abandoned attempts to use the new materials at all.

Because the Kanawha County conflict created such upheaval and was so widely publicized, its effects were felt throughout the country. To avoid similar problems in their own districts, many school boards and administrators refused even to consider adopting the controversial *Interaction* series, and competing publishers' salespeople quite happily spread the word that the books had been condemned as immoral in West Virginia. As a result, books languished and died before their time. Since then, publishers have been unwilling to produce books containing the range of subjects and ideas found in the books vilified and crippled in the Kanawha County struggle.

Though no battle has come close to the Kanawha County episode in intensity or scope, hundreds of school districts throughout the nation have experienced protests, usually initiated by small groups of conservative Christian parents, against textbooks and other books assigned in classes or available to students in school libraries. The protests are part of a general campaign. "They're the same old books all the time," James Moffett noted, referring to such titles as John Steinbeck's *Of Mice and Men*, J. D. Salinger's *The Catcher in the Rye*, Mark Twain's *Huckleberry Finn*, Shel Silverstein's *A Light in the Attic*, Judy Blume's *Forever*, Judith Guest's *Ordinary People*, Madeleine L'Engle's *A Wrinkle in Time*, and Maya Angelou's *I Know Why the Caged Bird Sings*. "I can think of much worse books to censor, but they're on a standard list that circulates throughout the censorship network. These parents just pick these books off the lists, look for them in their schools, and then complain."

As evidence of the growing power of the Religious Right, book banning efforts intensified after Ronald Reagan's election in 1980. A 1981 survey by the Association of American Publishers, the American Library Association and the Association for Supervision and Curriculum Development estimated that more than twenty percent of the nation's school districts and thirty percent of school libraries experienced challenges to literary works and textbooks. Four years later, in 1985, *USA Today* reported a thirty-seven percent increase in censorship efforts over the previous academic year, with incidents occurring in forty-six states.

The textbook controversy spurred another development that has had many counterparts throughout the country: the growth of private Christian day schools and an increase in home schooling. Kanawha County teacher Ruth Davis regarded this as an unfortunate turn for American education. "Students are segregated," she said; "We need to expose students to all types of literature and to people working together. They need to be able to see how people in different cultures can come together and work together and live together and go to school together." James Moffett agreed. While appreciating the desire to protect one's culture against a perceived invasion, he felt that establishing private schools tailored to subcultural preferences "sets a time bomb for the future" and "will seriously deepen community and national divisions. Children who grow up apart will probably fight as adults. Not having grown up learning to share resources despite personal differences, they will be unable to live, let live, and unite to solve common problems. Not speaking the same language, they will not talk together." . . .

REVIEW QUESTIONS

1. Detail the specific objections that Alice Moore and the other protesters had to the proposed new educational materials.

2. Many of the objections that the anti-book protesters had to the new materials were rooted in their religious views, yet many of those who supported the new materials were also religious. What, if anything, is different in the religious beliefs of the pro-book and anti-book forces?

3. Describe the methods used by the protesters in their campaign against the proposed books. How are those methods similar to and different from the methods used by civil rights protesters in the 1960s?

4. One of the defenders of the books said that the protesters' objections were a result of their feelings of "low self-esteem, low self-confidence, a view that mankind is evil, a feeling of being unable to cope." What do you think of this argument? Do you agree with it? Why or why not?

5. The protesters believed that school textbooks have the power to shape the minds of children and thus determine the nation's future. Do you think that the influence of schoolbooks is that great?

6. What connections do you see between the growth of protests like that described in the selection, the rise of the so-called religious right, and the upsurge of political conservatism in the 1970s and 1980s?

7. Relate the conflict described in the selection to contemporary "culture wars" over issues such as abortion, school prayer, flag burning, gay rights, and so forth. What similarities do you see in the lineup of contending forces and in the arguments advanced by each of the two sides?

FOR FURTHER READING

Leo Ribuffo, *The Old Christian Right: The Protestant Far Right from the Great Depression to the Cold War* (1983) is a critical look at the religious right in the period before it became politically powerful. The book from which this selection was taken, William Martin, *With God on Our Side: The Rise of the Religious Right in America* (1996) takes the story from the 1950s into the 1990s. James Moffett, *Storm in the Mountains* (1982) is a detailed account of the Kanawha County book controversy by one of those on the pro-book side. Jeffrey K. Hadden and Anson Shupe, *Televangelism: Power and Politics on God's Frontier* (1988) shows how some evangelical ministers have learned to use television as a way of spreading their religious and sometimes their political views. Jerry Falwell, *Listen America!* (1980) is by a leading televangelist, the founder of the Moral Majority, one of the more powerful organizations on the religious right. James Davision Hunter, *Culture Wars: The Struggle to Define America* (1991) details and analyzes the ideas of those involved in current controversies over such issues as abortion, gay rights, and prayer in schools.

To the student:

We as publishers, realize that one way to improve education is to improve textbooks. We also realize that you, the student, have a large role in the success or failure of textbooks. Although teachers choose books to be used in the classroom, if the students do not buy and use books, those books are failures.

Usually only teachers are asked about the quality of texts; their opinions alone are considered as revisions are written or as new books are planned. Now, Addison Wesley Longman would like to ask you about this book: how you liked or disliked it; why it was successful or dull; if it taught you anything. Please fill in this form and return it to us at Addison Wesley Longman, Inc., 1185 Avenue of the Americas, New York, NY, 10036. It is your chance to affect directly the publication of future textbooks.

Book title: _____ School: _____

Course title: _____ Course enrollment: _____

Instructor's name: _____

1. Did you like the book? _____

2. Was it too easy? _____

   Did you read all the selections? _____

   Which did you like most? _____

   Which did you like least? _____

3. Did you like the cover? _____

   Did you like the size? _____

   Did you like the illustrations? _____

   Did you like the type size? _____

4. Were the study questions and bibliographies useful? ———————

   How should they be changed? ————————————

   ——————————————————————

5. Are the introductions useful? ——————————————

   How might they be improved? ————————————

   ——————————————————————

6. Do you feel the instructor should continue to assign this book next year?

   ——————————————————————

7. Will you keep this book for your library? ————————

8. Please add any comments or suggestions on how we might improve this
   book, either in content or in format.

   ——————————————————————

   ——————————————————————

   ——————————————————————

   ——————————————————————

   ——————————————————————

9. May we quote you, either in promotion for this book or in future publishing
   ventures? ——— yes ——— no

   ————————————   ————————————————

   Date   Signature